THE FOLKLORE OF BOMBAY

THE
FOLKLORE OF BOMBAY

BY

R. E. ENTHOVEN, C.I.E.
Late of the Indian Civil Service
Author of Tribes and Castes of Bombay

GYAN

Published by

Gyan Publishing House
5, Ansari Road
Daryaganj, New Delhi-110002
Phone: 011-47034999, 9811692060
E-mail: books@gyanbooks.com

Distribution Network
gyanbooks.com
India, USA, Canada, UK, Australia, France

ISBN : 978-81-212-3389-7 (PB)
First Published, 1923

2nd Impression 2020

Printed at: Gyan Press, Delhi.

The Folklore of Bombay
Author: R. E. Enthoven

THE
Folklore of
BOMBAY

BY

R. E. ENTHOVEN, C.I.E.
Late of the Indian Civil Service
Author of *Tribes and Castes of Bombay*

OXFORD
AT THE CLARENDON PRESS
1923

CONTENTS

PREFATORY NOTE

The funds for the preparation of the materials on which this work is based were provided by the Bombay Branch, Royal Asiatic Society.

LIST OF ABBREVIATIONS

H. H. & C.	*Hindu Holidays and Ceremonials.* B. A. Gupte.
J. R. A. S.	*Journal of the Royal Asiatic Society.*
S. B. B. C.	*Notes on the Spirit Basis of Belief and Custom.* Sir James Campbell, K.C.I.E.
S. B. E.	*Sacred Books of the East.*
T. & C. B.	*Tribes and Castes of Bombay.* R. E. Enthoven, C.I.E.

INTRODUCTION

Some thirty years ago the present writer, then a Junior Magistrate in the Dharwar District of the Bombay Presidency, was called upon to investigate a case against a Muhammadan, Jemal Din, and two Hindus, Mudewala and Adevi, who were charged with causing the death of a girl, Giddawa, in the following circumstances:

The deceased left her husband on Christmas Day to visit her parents, and while with them she complained to her father of a pain in her back. At her suggestion, Jemal Din, an exorcist of repute locally, was called upon to treat the ailment. Jemal Din, having summoned the assistance of another exorcist, Mudewala, caused the deceased to lie flat on the ground, and commenced to tread and jump on her body, calling on the evil spirit Uzzi to come forth and leave the patient. These comparatively mild measures failing to take effect, Jemal Din seized a stick hanging in his house, and administered a vigorous blow on the back to the girl Giddawa. Smarting under the injury, she fled from the house, hotly pursued by Jemal Din and Mudewala, who both professed to be possessed by powerful spirits. The unfortunate girl, fearful of further blows, cried out, 'Uzzi, Uzzi', and 'I am going now', suggesting to her pursuers that the disease spirit possessing her was named Uzzi and was departing under pressure of the beating which they administered.

The girl, thus crying out, fled to the Hindu burial-ground, the home of evil spirits, where the exorcists overtook her and again beat her severely. The girl's father actively assisted the spirit-scaring rite by making offerings of water, fruit, cow-dung, and other articles to the spirit Uzzi, during the beating of his daughter, whom he fed with cow-dung, under the impression that he was thus feeding the spirit which possessed her. The third accused, Adevi, also an exorcist, here joined in the beating of Giddawa, assisting the other two in their work by throwing a lemon at the patient to attract the disease spirit in her. As the result of the severe beating administered by these three men, the unfortunate girl became unconscious and died on the spot where she was being beaten.

It was clear from the evidence that the three men, assisted up to a certain point by connivance of the victim, honestly believed that they were curing the pain in the girl's back by driving out the disease spirit which possessed her. They were committed to the higher court, and subsequently transported for life.

The facts of this unfortunate case, which were brought to light on account of the unhappy victim's death, are typical of the attitude adopted towards disease by the mass of the population of the Bombay Presidency. Many similar practices will be found described in Chapter IX of the present work,[1] which deals with the beliefs prevailing in regard to disease and epidemics, and the methods adopted for prevention and cure of illness. Thus, for instance, in the Konkan, in cases of illness, after incense has been burnt and drums beaten before an exorcist, the latter waves a burning wick, strikes the ground with a broom of peacock's feathers, and proceeds to draw out the disease spirit from the sick person. The spirit is then put into a bottle, which is either carried out of the village and buried under a big tree, or thrown into the sea. Equally prevalent in the case of epidemics is the worship of the disease goddess (*Mata*), who is placed on a small hand-cart and conducted with special ceremonies to the village boundary, whence she is passed from village to village and finally thrown into the sea. The two principal causes of disease are either the anger of the gods or godlings, who must be propitiated by offerings and sacrifices in the case of epidemics and sickness, or the entry into the patient of some evil spirit, who can be driven out by an almost endless variety of rites, resembling those adopted in the case of the murdered Giddawa.

Similarly, far more than disease is held to be the work of evil spirits. As Sir James Campbell has well remarked, to these people ' the unwilled is the spirit-caused ' ; [2] and accordingly we find widespread throughout the Presidency a mass of

[1] See also *S. B. B. C.*, p. 244 et seq., for similar spirit-scaring rites adopted in the case of individual ailments.

[2] *S. B. B. C.*, p. 158.

superstition regarding the causes of natural phenomena and the methods of propitiating the hordes of evil spirits that are held to be responsible for them.

Sir James Campbell has recorded a series of very valuable notes on this subject in papers contributed by him to the *Indian Antiquary* under the heading of the 'Spirit Basis of Belief and Custom'. One of his fellow-workers, the late A. M. T. Jackson, an Oriental scholar, whose promising career was cut short at Nasik in the year 1909 by the hand of a political assassin, evolved a scheme for collecting further information on the folk-lore of the Presidency by circulating to all masters of Primary schools a list of questions drawn up by well-known folk-lore experts.[1] At the time of his death some interesting materials had been secured in this way.

At the request of the Bombay Branch of the Royal Asiatic Society, I undertook to supervise the translation from the vernacular of the replies, and to issue the results in two volumes, *Folk-lore Notes of Gujarat* and *Folk-lore Notes of the Konkan.* These were published in 1914 and 1915.

The two volumes, hurriedly compiled in the scanty leisure available while I was Secretary to the Government of India, contained much that needed revision. It was the desire of the Society that they should be completed by adding the results of similar inquiries in the remaining portions of the Presidency, i.e. the Deccan and the Kanarese country. Returning to India in 1920, after four years' absence, I was able, with the valuable assistance of the Educational Authorities, to complete the notes by collecting fresh materials from these hitherto untapped sources. These, though in many ways inferior in interest to the original notes, contained much new matter. The present work is a compilation of the whole of the materials thus collected. In effect, it is an attempt to carry out Jackson's design of a work dealing with the folk-lore of Bombay.

The present writer is fully conscious of the extent to which such a work in the hands of an Oriental scholar of Jackson's standing would have surpassed in value and interest the present volume.

The distinguished author of *The People of India*, the late

[1] *Vide* Appendix.

Sir Herbert Risley, on numerous occasions, drew attention to the fact that writers on primitive belief and custom have made comparatively little use of the vast store of materials to be found in India, though few other portions of the globe have escaped their attention. This omission is specially noticeable in Sir James Frazer's and Dr. Westermarck's comprehensive works. Probably the reason is to be found in the fact that, with the exception of Dr. Crooke's well-known work,[1] such materials are not easily accessible to students. The provincial Gazetteers, especially Campbell's *Gazetteer of Bombay*, contain much valuable information hidden in their pages. Campbell's papers on the spirit basis of belief and custom, to which reference has already been made, though printed in one volume, have never been published in collected form. They deserve far more notice than they have as yet received.[2] Unfortunately the author died a few years after his retirement from active service, without finding an opportunity to record in their maturity the fruits of his many years' research, and these raw materials still await a competent editor.

Campbell's examination of the beliefs and practices of the people of the Bombay Presidency seems to have led him to the conclusion that spirits were in origin ancestors, and that the scaring or housing of these spirits formed the basis, not only of most of the beliefs and practices of the wild tribes and low castes forming the primitive elements of the population, but, to a much larger extent than has been recognized, of the elaborate ritual of the twice-born. He writes:

> Much happens to a man without his will or against the wish of himself and those around him. Thus, he sneezes, he itches, he sickens, he wearies, he mopes, he raves, body and mind are vexed by spasms, cramps and fits. These unwilled results, reasons primitive man, are the work of some outside power, and that outside power is: the spirits of the dead.

Examining from this point of view the elaborate rites practised by Hindus at the time of pregnancy, birth, adolescence, marriage, and death, Campbell aims at proving that the basis

[1] *Popular Religion and Folklore of Northern India*, 2 vols., Constable, 1896.

[2] Some use of these materials has been made by Dr. Crooke in the work above referred to.

of these practices is spirit scaring. It will be found that the materials contained in the present volume lend a considerable measure of support to Campbell's theory.

Quoting Herbert Spencer's dictum that ancestor worship is the rudimentary form of religion, Campbell draws attention to the facts that 'among high-class Hindus ancestor worship is one of the most universal faiths, and among the lower classes and ruder tribes of Hindus the family dead hold the place of the house or village god'. These spirits of the dead, at first held to be themselves mortal, were feared as the cause of sickness or misfortune. Thence proceeded the search for articles which would drive away such spirits. Campbell thus passes on to a lengthy survey of the articles which are valued as spirit scarers, such as fire, water, and metals.

Hunger, which comes upon a man without his willing it, is spirit-caused. Food removes hunger and thus food takes a place among spirit scarers. Similarly, noise—the beating of drums, the rattling of gourds, the clashing of metal plates, restores to consciousness or life one who is in a swoon. Swoons are due to the attacks of evil spirits. Therefore, reasons the primitive mind, spirits are afraid of noise and music. Noise and music are thus spirit scarers. Campbell then deals with spirit haunts such as funeral places, borders, cross-roads, stones, and trees. A study of spirit entries, spirit seasons, the effects of spirit possession, and finally of witchcraft and the evil eye completes the notes.

Of particular interest among his long list of spirit scarers and spirit homes are the following:

1. Kissing.
2. Drinking of alcohol.
3. Music.
4. The wearing of jewellery.
5. Circumambulation.

No doubt other reasons than the warding off or housing of evil spirits will occur to the reader as sufficient to account for the popular use of certain of these scarers. Campbell, however, presents a mass of evidence in support of the assumption that these practices, so far as they are resorted to on the ceremonial occasions to which he refers, such as thread-girding, adolescence, marriage, and funerals, were originally adopted with the object of warding off or housing evil influences.

Ancestor worship, according to Campbell, led in very early times to the worship of trees and animals in which the spirits of ancestors resided. The tree and animal so possessed came to be regarded as an ancestor, and hence developed into the totem, regulating the marriage of its descendants. For this reason Campbell calls the totem trees and animals of the Presidency 'marriage guardians'. Further reference to the widespread prevalence of totemism in the Presidency is made below.

Campbell discriminates between spirit scaring and spirit housing as being earlier and later forms of primitive practice. In the earlier and more savage stage, influences were held to be so fiercely hostile to man that no treatment but scaring could save him from their attacks. In the later and milder stage, the housing or squaring of spirits developed into the guardian idea, the earliest guardian being the squared fiend. Spirits were then held to be not so much hostile to man as uneasily in search of a new body or a material home, and therefore ready to turn into guardians if a suitable lodging were provided for them. The process is pithily described by Campbell as the change from spirit scaring to spirit squaring.

Granting that many primitive practices are based on the belief of spirit possession and spirit scaring, as, for instance, the attempt to cure the sick girl already described, there would clearly be risk of error in any attempt to attribute to one origin the whole mass of early beliefs and practices recorded in the following pages. The present writer once showed how, with a little ingenuity, the Governor's levee in Bombay could be proved to be a sun myth, the worship of the corn spirit, or a spirit-scaring rite, according to the point of view from which the various features of this ceremony were approached by an observer.[1]

The origin of primitive beliefs and practices must clearly be sought in more than one direction; and it is probable that Campbell would have been prepared to admit this if he had developed his researches into a fuller treatise on folk-lore.

[1] Presidential Address to the Bombay Anthropological Society, 1911.

One source of primitive beliefs underlying protective rites is obviously to be found in the hasty inductions which result in two events being classed as cause and effect; and thus give rise to beliefs in good and bad omens, the significance of dreams, &c. Evils following on inauspicious omens and dreams are not attributable to spirit influences, and cannot be held to be spirit-caused. There is also a widespread tendency in all classes in India to worship and propitiate possible sources of good and evil. Thus the gods, saints, ancestors, those wielding authority of any kind, objects of a striking or unusual form, and implements or tools yielding a livelihood are all common objects of worship. This worship of sources and manifestations of power, as well as the propitiation of tools and implements, though akin to spirit scaring, is clearly distinct, and must be treated as belonging to a different category of primitive ideas.

In the writer's first years of service passed in the Kanarese districts of the Presidency, it was part of his duty to visit the villages in his charge, while on tour in the fair season. The cultivators of these areas always addressed him by the title of *devarappa* or *devaru*. *Deva* means god, and *appa* father, in Kanarese. *Devaru* is god in the plural, being an honorific plural. This local practice of styling the magistrate god and father, if carefully considered, affords an illustration of the feelings underlying much of the primitive ritual described in the following pages. The ruling factor in worship and propitiation would appear to be fear, fear of power, all power being a form of god (*deva*) which must be propitiated by offerings if it cannot be rendered harmless by some special rite. The Assistant Collector and Magistrate thus becomes a god (*deva*). The sun, moon, earth, stars, rivers, mountains, trees, stones, diseases, are all gods or spirits, with power to work good or evil, and therefore requiring worship, offerings, and propitiation in various ways.

The earth, being godlike, must be propitiated by any one who happens to place a foot on the ground when rising in the morning, for gods must not be touched by the human foot. An offering must be made to the giant mounds of earth forming the white-ants' nests, lest an evil influence emanate therefrom.

A certain kind of stone found in the Narbada river, of peculiar shape, is worshipped and subsequently identified with the god Vishnu, an obvious Hindu gloss on a primitive custom. Tools and implements must not be touched with the foot, lest they take offence, and fail to act as bread-winners.

The difference between the great gods of the Hindu sacred books, Brahma, Vishnu, Shiva, and the village god Maruti, or the disease goddess Shitala, who causes small-pox, seems to be chiefly one of degree. All have power to injure. All are therefore feared and require to be kept satisfied by ritual, sacrifice, and offerings of food, &c.

The apparently almost endless elaboration of special rites and ceremonies declared to be suitable for the propitiation of all these manifestations of power are the natural product of Indian mentality, which delights in subtle distinctions and is prepared for, and patient of, almost any extravagance. Those who believe in the influence of climate and physical surroundings on the development of character will be disposed to assume that people residing in a country of vast plains, great rivers, and mountains nearly 30,000 feet high, which has a climate first wet and then dry for several months in succession, passing from extreme heat to great cold, will reproduce in the character of their thought this tendency to extreme variations. The oceans of milk and the divine monsters that drove Macaulay to reject Oriental culture as a basis for education in India may be held to be the natural product of people living in such a *milieu*.

It is evident that fear of the numerous hostile powers by which the Hindu of the Presidency feels himself to be surrounded, a fear fostered by natural timidity due to poor physique, lies at the root of many of the practices described in the following pages.

It must also be remembered that, to the Hindu of all ranks, life is neither limited to the animal kingdom, nor is it interrupted or ended by the change we call death. A stone or a tree has life differing only in degree from that of a tiger. A human soul passing from its temporary habitation in the body may become the life of a snake or of an insect, if it has not sufficient merit to resume its career in human form. Misers after death become snakes guarding the hoarded treasures which they accumulated during their lifetime. Infants, when born, are examined to see whether they bear certain marks indicating that they are the re-incarnation of a deceased ancestor. If identified, this reborn ancestor is renamed with his original name. Those who fall victims to beasts of prey, tigers, panthers, &c., are believed to be reborn in the form of the beasts that slew them. Evil-doers find themselves re-incarnated in loathsome forms.[1] A poetic fancy describes the falling stars as the souls of good men who, having exhausted the merit acquired in their previous existence, return to the earth in this form on their way to another birth. This rebirth is said to occur immediately in the house near which a meteor is seen to fall.

It is clear, from many indications, that ceaseless anxiety arises in the minds of simple people owing to the proximity, after a death has occurred, of the disembodied spirit of the deceased with power to work harm to the survivors. An interesting example of the results of this concern is to be found in the practice of tree-marriages. When a bachelor desires to marry a widow, it is usual to marry him first to a tree, usually the *Rui* (*Calotropis gigantea*) or *Shami* (*Prosopis spicigera*), both, it may be noted, frequently regarded as totems. After the tree wedding, the tree-bride is cut down and destroyed. The marriage with the widow may then safely take place. From the special precautions adopted at the time of performing these tree-marriages, it appears that the spirit of the widow's husband is the chief source of anxiety. To prevent this spirit making himself disagreeable to his successor, the bachelor is required to provide a spirit wife, i. e. the spirit of the tree-bride, in the hope that the two widowed spirits may console each other and desist from plaguing their living partners.[2]

Persons dying with wishes unfulfilled are specially likely to become troublesome spirits. Thus, one of the most formidable members of the spirit world is the ghost of a woman who dies in child-birth.

[1] Compare *S. B. E.* xxv, *The Laws of Manu*, Chapter XII.

[2] For numerous instances of such marriages, see my *Tribes and Castes of Bombay*, 1920–2. See also vol. i, p. 101, and vol. ii, p. 412, for certain rites in use among the lower castes for preventing the spirit of a widow's late husband becoming troublesome in the event of her remarriage.

In Chapters I and II will be found the beliefs generally current among the people regarding the great natural objects that are familiar to all, the sun, moon, stars, earth, rivers, &c., and the rites adopted to propitiate these divine beings, which rank as gods in the Hindu mind. The procedure to be followed in the event of an eclipse of the sun is also described. In many cases the explanations offered of such natural phenomena as eclipses and earthquakes are those to be found in the Hindu sacred books. Indeed, a comparison of the present materials with works dealing with the rites of high-caste Hindus, e. g. Mrs. Stevenson's *Rites of the Twice-born*, will show that there is much common ground between the orthodox beliefs and ceremonies and local superstition; in fact, the two are to a great extent inseparable. Where the Hindu priestly caste, the Brahmans, are accustomed to direct the worship and conduct of ceremonies of the people, the orthodox practices of the Hindu law books are naturally followed. But the minor gods are usually worshipped by men of low caste, who apply a ritual unknown to the Brahmans.

It is usual to consult and to be guided by exorcists (*Bhagats*)[1] when epidemics are feared, illness is to be cured, the Evil Eye guarded against, or when precautions are required against witchcrafts and spells. The Brahman serves to propitiate the great gods of the Hindu pantheon, Brahma, Vishnu, Shiva, &c.; lower castes, such as Guravs, Atits, Kunbis, act as ministrants to the minor godlings; and, when spirit scaring is necessary, the lowest castes, such as Kumbhars, Chamars, Mahars, and Dheds, furnish the exorcists who prescribe effective measures for propitiating the evil spirits. In Chapter V will be found examples of the minor godlings and the names of the castes which supply their attendant priests or worshippers. Aryan culture introduced by the Brahmans into the areas dealt with in these pages has absorbed many of the local beliefs that prevailed before their advent; and it is a reasonable inference that the gods who can be propitiated only by priests from low castes were known and worshipped in the country-side before the Aryan-speaking tribes entered India.

The most interesting feature of the primitive religion in the

[1] For a description of the method of training exorcists, see *S. B. B. C.*, p. 244.

Presidency is to be found in the widespread survival of totemism, which is dealt with very briefly in Chapter VI. Neither the Vedas nor subsequent orthodox Hindu writings contain any mention of the worship of trees, animals, and other objects in connexion with a belief that they are in the position of ancestors, and that all who worship the same object should refrain from intermarrying. It may be assumed that the survival in full vigour of the worship of totems in the south of the Presidency, as well as the unmistakable traces of a former totemistic organization found throughout the Deccan and Konkan, are indications of a culture that is not Aryan in origin. Recent research has brought to light a number of totem divisions among the Marathas and the occupational castes of the Deccan allied to the Marathas by common descent.[1] In full vigour, the totemism of Bombay means the worship of a tree, animal, &c., on important occasions such as marriage, the first occupation of a new house, or the setting up of a threshing-floor at the commencement of harvest. The totem must not be injured by its adherents, they must not use its products, e. g. the fruit or wood of a totem tree, or the ivory from the tusk of an elephant totem. The ban on intermarriage between those worshipping the same totem is complete in the Kanarese districts, where the system is still in full vigour. Over eighty totems have been identified. The totem is there known as a *bali*. In the Deccan and Konkan the totem organization that formerly prevailed has been overlaid by a system of family stocks, but the totem object, known as a *devak*, is still worshipped. In many instances it still acts as a barrier against intermarriage, though this is by no means invariably the case. Campbell, who drew attention to the existence of these totems among Marathas of the Deccan, in his Kolhapur volume of the *Bombay Gazetteer* described them as 'marriage guardians'. Subsequent research has discovered over 80 *devaks* in the Deccan and Konkan, and leaves little doubt that they possess, or once possessed, all the essential attributes of a real totem.

It has been already remarked that totemism is not, so far as we are aware, a social organization known to the Aryans

[1] See *T. & C. B.*, Article on Marathas.

when they entered India. On the other hand, Risley and Russell, writing of the tribes and castes of Bengal and the Central Provinces, show that the primitive tribes in those areas possess numerous totems that are not only similar to those discovered in Bombay, but in some instances are identical with them.[1] We have therefore in the totem trees and animals the undoubted remains of an early form of primitive religion, unknown to the Aryan invaders. Investigations of the subject in Bombay have so far only touched the surface. Further study offers the promise of interesting developments.

In Chapter VIII will be found information regarding the meaning attached to dreams and beliefs regarding good and bad omens. The active imagination of the Oriental mind has furnished a very full list of auspicious and inauspicious events. To dream of a god, a horse, a king, an ancestor, a cobra, one's own death, a bird flying, an elephant, muddy water, fire, a cart, clarified butter, and a funeral procession, for instance, are all auspicious. When starting on a journey, to hear the braying of an ass on the right-hand side, to meet a labourer carrying a load on his head, a potter carrying earth on a donkey, a woman carrying molasses, are all good omens. Experts in folk-lore may be prepared to offer reasons for some of these strange beliefs. Viewing them as a whole, it seems at first sight probable that the objects or incidents which are classed respectively as auspicious and inauspicious have on some occasion coincided with lucky or unlucky events, and thus by an uncritical assumption, *post hoc ergo propter hoc*, have been taken by the masses to be the cause of these events. To attribute a closely logical process of reasoning to the ignorant among whom such beliefs are common would be unsafe. It is clear that the life of the individual who is obsessed by the fear

[1] Compare the following lists:

	Bombay	*Bengal*	*Central Provinces*
Animals	Tiger	Tiger	Tiger
	Snake	Snake	Snake
	Tortoise	Tortoise	Tortoise
	Horse	Horse	Horse
Trees	*Zizyphus jujuba*		*Zizyphus jujuba*
	Eugenia jambolana		*Eugenia jambolana*

See also Crooke's *Popular Religion and Folklore of Northern India*, vol. ii, p. 150 et seq., for totems among the Dravidian tribes and castes of the United Provinces.

of these endless inauspicious signs must necessarily be full of anxiety.

This anxiety is not lessened by the widespread belief in witchcraft and the Evil Eye (*vide* Chapter VII). Women who resort naked to a burning ground at midnight, holding fire in their hands, to dig up the bones of the dead, acquire mysterious powers over their neighbours. By the practice of imitative magic or the services of a familiar spirit, they are able to secure the milk of their neighbours' cows, the grain of their threshing-floors, and other desirable possessions. In the Kanarese districts, the story is still told of a female who was turned into a tigress by a witch, and when restored to human form, retained both the tail and the carnivorous habits of the tiger, much to the inconvenience of her friends and relations.

If an individual suffers from loss of appetite or sudden sickness, if a cow fails to give milk, or food turns bad, the influence of the Evil Eye is suspected. Domestic animals and beautiful objects are particularly susceptible to its effects. Children require special protection from the baneful Evil Eye. The danger can be averted by giving them opprobrious names, such as 'dung-heap', 'dirt', 'stone'. A newly born child is occasionally thrown away on a dung-heap, temporarily, in order that it may thus escape evil glances or the attention of evil spirits.

All Hindus desire a son to perform their funeral ceremonies, and their wives are therefore filled with a longing for a male child. The cure of barrenness thus becomes a special preoccupation of women. Chapter X, dealing with women's rites and festivals, gives particulars of the numerous devices adopted to secure the birth of a son. To steal a portion of the robe of a woman who has given birth to a child may procure a similar favour for another woman. To beat a woman during an eclipse is a sovereign remedy for barrenness. If on a new-moon night a woman is bathed in water brought from seven wells, and she then circumambulates a temple of the monkey god Maruti from left to right twenty-one times, in a state of nudity and in complete silence, she will be blessed with male progeny.

Sympathetic magic may explain the belief that to touch

a woman who is pregnant will cure barrenness, and the practice of causing a woman to keep her eyes fixed on grains of barley and grain in order to ensure the birth of a male child is clearly imitative magic; but it is hard to find the origin of the practice, which prevails in some localities, of giving bread to a black dog in order to secure the gift of a son.

Less than twenty per cent. of the population of the Bombay Presidency are resident in towns. The people for the most part live in villages, and are dependent on agriculture for their livelihood. Special importance, therefore, attaches to the rites connected with the founding of a village site, the cultivation and harvesting of crops, and the protection of village cattle (Chapter XI). Being assured that the omens are favourable, and having worshipped and anointed the plough and the bullocks, the cultivator proceeds to his field, where he takes the advice of an exorcist regarding the corner at which sowing should commence. In some places it is usual to dress up the seed drill in woman's clothes and to fill the lap with offerings. This fertility rite is believed to ensure a bountiful crop. Before the crop is reaped, milk and clarified butter are poured over it as an offering.

At the time of harvesting, a portion of the crop is offered to the local gods. The gods are worshipped when the threshing-floor is prepared. In the Konkan, before threshing commences, there is a curious practice of first threshing a coco-nut. In order to scare noxious animals from the growing crops, a figure of a tiger made of dry leaves of sugar-cane is posted in the field. One of the cultivators then impersonates a tiger, and is made to run beating his mouth with the palm of his hand. The other cultivators pursue him and beat him with sticks. Water brought by a man in a state of nudity from a sacred well is held to be efficacious in protecting fruit and vegetables from insect pests.

Numerous ceremonies are performed to cure diseases affecting the village cattle. They resemble those in vogue for treating human beings, and are clearly of the nature of spirit-scaring rites. It is clear that disease in cattle is held to be caused by spirit possession in the same way as spirits enter human beings. In the Kanarese districts cattle disease is said to be cured by killing a wild boar and burying it feet upwards beyond the village boundary. Generally, the use of amulets is favoured ; and offerings are made to the local deities when cattle are attacked by disease.

Rites for bringing or averting rain are of an elaborate description. Perhaps one of the most curious is that in vogue in the Kanarese districts when it is desired to check a storm of hail. The shepherds seize a black sheep by the hind legs, and, after dragging it thus from left to right, hurl it in the direction that they desire the storm to pass. Immoderate rainfall may be made to cease, in some places, if a naked person turns a spinning wheel made of human bones in the reverse direction to the usual one. Again, rain can be made to fall, it is reported from some areas, by disinterring the corpse of a man who has died of white leprosy, and throwing it into a river. Rain can be brought by immersing in water the symbol of the god Shiva. This is obviously an instance of imitative magic. Of the same nature is the ceremony known as *Dhondiljagya*. A member of a low caste, having stripped, takes a small image of black earth on his head. Carrying this image, he visits each house in the village, where water is sprinkled over it by a woman while the bearer of the image dances. Pouring water over stones taken from a sacred pool is similarly held to be efficacious in causing a fall of rain. Rain can also be brought by climbing certain hills, by heating slabs of marble, or by eating special cakes known by the name of ' clouds '.

It must be recognized that, although many of the beliefs and practices described in the following pages are purely local in origin, the earliest Hindu scriptures contain mention of some of them. Water spirits (*apsaras*) are known to the *Rigveda*. Totemism is not traceable to the Vedas, but the worship of trees and plants is mentioned. Snake worship as later developed is unknown ; but the worship of implements and tools was enjoined at the time of the *Rigveda*. The *Rakshasas* and *Asuras* which are described in Chapter IV were known in Vedic times as evilly disposed spirits. The *Rigveda* contains mention of spells against disease and dangerous animals.[1] The *Atharvaveda* also refers at length to spells and

[1] *Cambridge History of India*, i. 107.

sympathetic magic for the cure of numerous diseases, fevers, rheumatism, abscesses, &c.[1] Later, in the Sutras, spirit possession is described.[2]

Students of the following pages may usefully compare the practices now in vogue for the cure of disease with the passage in the *Grihya Sutra* describing the treatment of a child attacked by epilepsy. The evil spirit Kumara is there held to have entered the boy very similarly to the way in which the spirit, Uzzi, entered the girl, in the incident described at the commencement of this introduction. The father of the patient covers him with a net, and appeals to the possessing spirit to release the child.[2] Nearchus, describing India in the time of Alexander, refers to the exorcists who were called in to cure snake-bites, just as they are called upon to-day in many a village.[3]

Similarly, the use of amulets, of which many instances will be found in Chapter IX, is recognized in the Sutras. They are described as made of lac or herbs, probably from the *Darbha* grass (*Eragrostis cynosuroides*) used for similar amulets at the present time.[4] We read also how spirits issue from a person in a yawn or a sneeze, the belief that underlies the modern practices described in Chapter XII relative to yawning and sneezing.[5] A parallel to the agricultural rites described in Chapter XI will be recognized in the sacrifice enjoined to the thunderbolt at the time of ploughing, as well as in the offerings and sacrifices made on the occasion of driving the first furrow, sowing, reaping, and harvesting.[6] In the time of the Sutras, mole-heaps appear to have been worshipped just as the white-ant heap is worshipped at the present day. It is certain that the Aryan invasion of North-west India brought with it the worship of the sun, the sky, the winds, and other phenomena of nature, and it is probable that to this simple cult residence in India, previous to the date of the compilation of the Sutras, added the spirit-scaring rites and the belief in omens which were in vogue among the indigenous population. Hinduism, as is well known, is plastic and receptive to a high degree,

[1] Vide *Cambridge History of India*, i. 138.
[2] *Ibid.*, 231.
[3] *Ibid.*, 406.
[4] *Ibid.*, 239.
[5] *Ibid.*, 237.
[6] *Ibid.*

and thus in the earliest records which have come down to us we find the traces of popular folk-lore such as the instances quoted above.

A description of the people residing in the Bombay Presidency, divided into the numerous tribes and castes that indicate social cleavage based either on occupation, religion, race, or residence, will be found in my *Tribes and Castes of Bombay*.[1] For the present purpose, it is not necessary to touch on their social organization, which presents certain special features in each of the four divisions of the Presidency. So far as their religious rites and primitive beliefs are concerned, we find a certain measure of similarity between all Hindus, extending to certain of the Musalman castes which represent converts from Hinduism during the days of Musalman power. It is not possible to draw a hard and fast line between those who worship Brahma, Vishnu, and Shiva, with other gods and heroes of the Hindu orthodox tradition, and those who address themselves to the monkey-faced Maruti, Shitala, and the mother goddesses controlling disease, scarcity, and other evils. The lower we go in the social scale the less respect and consideration is paid to the higher gods compared with the minor godlings and the more numerous tree, field, and forest spirits. For these latter, the most fruitful field of research is to be found among the Bhils, Kolis, and similar wild tribes, who practise their primitive rites in the forest tracts of Khandesh and the less accessible regions of the Western Sahyadris. Aryan culture has never completely displaced in Bombay the previously prevailing spirit worship. It has frequently attempted to absorb it by placing an interpretation based on the Brahmanic tradition upon practices that are presumable pre-Aryan in origin. In this fashion the totem worship of a certain tree will be explained as due to the fact that one of the heroes of the Indian epics, the *Mahabharata* or the *Ramayana*, hung his weapons on this tree, or that the tree was the abode of Vishnu, one of the persons of the Hindu trinity, on a certain classic occasion.

The Puranic rule that a Hindu who has lost two wives must,

[1] *Tribes and Castes of Bombay*, 3 vols., Government Central Press, Bombay, 1920–2.

before marrying a third, be married to the *Rui* (*Arkha*) tree (*Calotropis gigantca*) is clearly an adaptation, in a form modified to meet the orthodox objection to widow remarriage, of the widely prevailing practice of tree marriage to which reference has been made above.

These introductory remarks may conclude with a brief description of the area from which the information has been collected, i. e. the Bombay Presidency with the exception of Sind. The latter province, which is under the administration of the Bombay Government, differs so markedly from the rest of the Presidency in its history, population, and physical features, that it could not conveniently be included in the following folk-lore survey. The natural divisions of the Presidency, excluding Sind, are four, namely, Gujarat (including the peninsula of Kathiawar), the Konkan, the Deccan, and the Kanarese districts known as the Karnatak. The plains of Gujarat are remarkable for richness of soil and density of population. Watered by many rivers, these plains support a prosperous population, cultivating the fertile valleys and trading at numerous large towns and seaports. Broach, the ancient Barugaza, received and sent fleets to Egypt in the dawn of history, and is known to have entertained merchants from Imperial Rome. It may be assumed that the markets of Gujarat were known to the early kingdoms at the head of the Persian Gulf, Sumer and Akkad. It was from Mesopotamia, according to Jackson,[1] that India received the Brahmi alphabet, the art of brick-making, and possibly the knowledge of the lunar mansions (*nakshatras*). The *padmasana*, a curiously intricate design which, as is the case also with the *swastik*, is in common use in the Presidency to-day for the installation of the goddesses (*matrikas*), has been found engraved on Sumerian seals in 2850 B.C.,[2] affording an indication of the connexion existing between early India and the civilization that developed at the head of the Persian Gulf in the third millenium B.C.

As Gujarat passes into the Konkan, its continuation southward along the coast, the formidable barrier of the Western Sahyadris, rising to heights of 3,000 and 4,000 feet, running

[1] *Imperial Gazetteer of India*, vol. i (Bombay), p. 15.
[2] *J. R. A. S.*, Oct. 1922, p. 533.

parallel to the coast-line, divides the coast tract from the uplands known as the Deccan. The Konkan, with its hills and numerous tidal creeks, is a difficult country to travel in. It has received at different periods many foreign elements into its population by sea, such as Arabs, Jews, Abyssinians, Portuguese, &c. Owing to the barrenness of the soil, the population largely seeks support by temporary migration to the labour markets of Bombay. The Deccan is for the most part a vast plain, fertile in the valleys of the rivers flowing eastwards to the sea, but mainly rocky and arid. It breeds a sturdy race of husbandmen, and possesses a population more homogeneous in race and culture than the other portions of the Presidency. The Kanarese-speaking districts in the south, known as the Karnatak, form an area of more certain rainfall and therefore more fertile than the Deccan plains. The western portion is heavily afforested, and scantily inhabited by a decreasing population. The east, under numerous irrigation tanks, produces rich crops of wheat, cotton, and millets. The coast-line from the north of the Konkan to the Madras Presidency is one of great picturesqueness. A succession of creeks and curving bays, where rollers break on white sands beneath palm and casuarina, support a hardy race of fisher-folk, who ply their craft in roughly hewn vessels during the fair season. Inland, the bare hills of red laterite yield scanty crops to supplement the rice grown in the valleys between. Farther south these are replaced by the well-clad hills bearing the evergreen forests of North Kanara, famous for its spice gardens and yielding good supplies of timber.

The population inhabiting these areas is divided into castes and tribes with very numerous subdivisions, the main groups being over three hundred in number.

In all four divisions the Brahman, the Hindu priestly caste, though not necessarily engaged in priestly functions, supplies, with the other twice-born castes, the doctrine of Hindu orthodox teaching, and the rites that have been in use with no very important alterations since the early centuries of the Christian Era. The wild tribes, Bhils, Kolis, Varlis, Naikdas, Berads, &c., inhabiting the remote areas of each division, either the fastnesses of the hills or the jungle-clad areas lying beneath them, as well as the unsettled areas in Gujarat and Kathiawar, have, by the nature of their manner of living, a closer contact with the sights and sounds of these wild regions than the more civilized Hindus. Not a few spirits must be traceable in origin to some awesome experience of those who encounter in their daily tasks wild animals, poisonous snakes, and mysterious sounds from the forest depths. The thick evergreen groves are sacred as the abode of some forest godling. Natural phenomena in such surroundings give rise to beliefs that are based on the fear they inspire. The ignorant, unclean classes, dwelling in the larger centres of population, share the superstitions of the remoter areas, as will be gathered from the contents of the following pages.

I desire in conclusion to acknowledge my indebtedness to the Director of Public Instruction and the Primary Schoolmasters who have rendered valuable assistance by furnishing the raw materials from which these notes and the previous two volumes have been compiled. I have also received much voluntary help from Rao Bahadur P. B. Joshi and Mr. G. M. Kalelkar in the arduous work of translation of the materials received from the schoolmasters.

1st SEPTEMBER 1923.

I

WORSHIP OF NATURAL OBJECTS

THE SUN

THE sun, the beneficent night-dispelling, light-bestowing great luminary, is believed to be the visible manifestation of Almighty God, and inspires the human mind with a feeling of grateful reverence which finds expression in titles like *Savita*, Life-Producer, the nourisher and generator of all life and activity.[1] It is the sun that gives food and drink, health and wealth, and affords protection from evil spirits.

He is the chief rain-sender. There is a couplet used in Gujarat illustrative of this belief. It runs: 'Oblations are cast into the Fire; the smoke carries the prayers to the sun; the Divine Luminary, propitiated, responds in sending down gentle showers.' 'The sacred smoke, rising from the sacrificial offerings, ascends through the ethereal regions to the sun. He transforms it into the rain-giving clouds, the rain produces food, and food produces the powers of generation, multiplication, and plenty.' Thus, the sun, as the propagator of animal life, is believed to be the highest deity.

It is generally believed that vows in honour of the sun are highly efficacious in curing eye-diseases and strengthening the eyesight. It is customary to quote from the *Bhagavadgita* the saying of Krishna: 'I am the very light of the sun and the moon.' Being the embodiment or the fountain of light, the sun imparts his lustre either to the bodies or to the eyes of his devotees. From Kathiawar it is reported that a Rajput woman of Gomata in Gondal and a Brahman of Rajkot were cured of white leprosy by vows in honour of the sun. Similar vows are

[1] The sun has eight names in the Hindu scriptures. These are used in Gujarat, the Deccan, and Konkan, and are: Ravi, Bhanu, Vivasvan, Bhaskar, Savita, Arka, Sahasrakirana, and Sarvatma. In the Karnatak the names are as follows: Tapashi, Tapastri, Dhume, Marichi, Shushamne, Bhogadi, Vishvabodini, Dharini, Kshami-Prabhe.

made to this day for the cure of the same disease. Persons in Kathiawar suffering from ophthalmic disorders, venereal affections, leucoderma, and white leprosy are known to observe vows in honour of the sun.

The Parmar Rajputs believe in the efficacy of vows in honour of the sun deity of Mandavraj, in Muli State in Kathiawar, in curing hydrophobia.

Women believe that a vow made to the sun is the sure means of attaining their desires. Their vows are made chiefly with the object of securing a son. On the fulfilment of this desire, in gratitude to the Great Luminary, the child is often called after him, and given such a name as Suraj-Ram, Bhanu-Shankar, Ravi-Shankar, Adit-Ram.

Many cradles are received as presents at this temple of Mandavraj, indicating that the barren women who had made vows to the deity have been satisfied in their desire for a son, the vows being fulfilled by the presents of such toy-cradles to the sun. In the case of rich donors, these cradles are made of precious metal. In this temple the Parmar Rajputs, as well as the Kathis, bow to the image of the sun, on their marriage-day, in company with their newly married brides. After the birth of a son to the wife of a Rajput, the hair on the boy's head is shaved for the first time in the presence of the Mandavraj deity, and a suit of rich clothes is presented to the image by the maternal uncle of the child.

The sun is *Survasakshi*, i. e. the observer of all things, and *Jagatchakshu*, i. e. the Eye of the World. Nothing can escape his notice. His eye is believed to possess the lustre of the three Vedic lores, viz. *Rigveda*, *Yajurveda*, and *Samveda*, and is therefore known by the name of *Vedatrayi*. The attestation of a document in his name as Surya-Narayana-Sakshi is believed to be ample security for the sincerity and good faith of the parties. Oaths in the name of the sun are considered so binding that persons swearing in his name are held to be pledged to the strictest truth.

Unmarried girls observe a vow, called the *tili-vrat* in the sun's honour, for attaining eternal exemption from widowhood. In making this vow, the votary, having bathed and worshipped the sun, sprinkles wet red-lac drops before him. In the

Karnatak a woman, as soon as she attains puberty, takes a bath and is made to stand in the sun in order to beget children. A barren woman is treated by exposure to the sun's rays.

According to Forbes's *Ras Mala*, the sun revealed to the Kathis the plan of regaining their lost kingdom, and thus commanded their devout worship and reverence. The temple named Suraj-deval, near Than in Kathiawar, was set up by the Kathis in recognition of this favour. In it both the visible resplendent disk of the sun and his image are adored.

People whose horoscopes declare them to have been born under the solar influence have from time to time to observe vows prescribed by Hindu astrology.

Cultivators observe vows in honour of the sun for the safety of their cattle.

It is customary among Hindus to cleanse their teeth every morning with a wooden stick, and then to offer salutations to the sun in the form of a verse which means: 'O God, the tooth-sticks are torn asunder and the sins disappear. O the penetrator of the innermost parts, forgive us our sins. Do good unto the benevolent and unto our neighbours.' This prayer is common in the mouths of the laity.

Better educated people recite a verse which runs: 'Bow unto Savita, the sun, the observer of this world and its quarters, the eye of the universe, the inspirer of all energy, the holder of a threefold personality (being an embodiment of the forms of the three gods of the Hindu Trinity, Brahma, Vishnu, and Shiva)—the embodiment of the three Vedas, the giver of happiness and the abode of God.'

After his toilet a high-caste Hindu should take a bath and offer morning prayers and *arghyas* [1] to the sun. Every Brahman should perform the *Sandhya* thrice during the day: in the morning, at midday, and in the evening. The *Sandhya* is the prayer a Brahman offers, sitting in divine meditation, when he offers three *arghyas* to the sun and recites the *Gayatri* verse 108 times.

[1] An *arghya* is an offering which consists of water and some of the following: rice, sandal oil, sesamum seed, white flowers, and *Durva* grass (*Cynodon Dactylon*).

In offering the *arghyas* the right foot is folded back below the left, the spoon is lifted to the forehead and is emptied towards the sun after reciting the *Gayatri* verse. If water is not available for offering the *arghyas*, sand may serve the purpose. But the sun must not be deprived of his *arghyas*.

The *Gayatri* is the most sacred verse in honour of the sun, containing, as it does, the highest laudations of him. It runs as follows: 'Let us adore the light of the divine sun (Savita). May it enlighten our minds.' A Brahman ought to recite this verse 324 times every day. Otherwise he incurs a sin as great as the slaughter of a cow. Accordingly a rosary of 108 Rudraksh (*Elaeocarpus Ganitrus*) beads is used in connecting the number of *Gayatris* recited. It is exclusively the right of the twice-born to recite the *Gayatri*. None else is authorized to recite or even to hear a word of it. Neither females nor Shudras ought to catch an echo of even a single syllable of the *Gayatri*.

A ceremony, called *Survopasthan*, in which a man has to stand facing the sun with his hands stretched upwards at an angle towards the sun, is performed as a part of the *Sandhya*.

Of the days of the week, Sunday is naturally the most suitable for sun-worship. Persons wishing to secure wealth, good health, and a happy progeny, especially people suffering from disorders caused by heat and from diseases of the eyes, barren women, and men anxious for victory on the battle-field, weekly observe vows in honour of the sun, and the day on which the vow is to be kept is Sunday. It is left to the devotee to fix the number of Sundays on which he will observe the vow, and he may choose to observe all the Sundays of the year. On such days the devotees undergo ceremonial purifications by means of baths and the putting on of clean garments, occupy a reserved clean seat, light a *ghi*-lamp, and recite the prescribed verses for sun-worship. Then follows a recitation, during which the devotee has to make certain gestures and movements. First the tips of all the four fingers are made to touch the thumb as is done in counting. Then the tips of the fingers are made to touch the palm of the other hand. Then one hand is laid over the other. Then the fingers are made to touch the heart, the head, the eyes, and the hair in regular order. The right hand is then put round the head and made to smite the left. An *ashtadal* or eight-cornered figure is drawn in red powder, and frankincense, red ointment, and red flowers are offered to the sun. *Durva* grass (*Cynodon Dactylon*) is also commonly used in the process of sun-worship.

Sometimes a hexangular figure is drawn instead of the *ashtadal*, a copper disk is placed over it, and the sun is worshipped by a fivefold ceremony known as *Panchopachar.* Of all ceremonials a deep bow is especially dear to the sun. It is said : 'A bow is dear to the sun : a stream of water (pouring water in a small stream over Shiva's idol) is dear to Shiva : benevolence to Vishnu, and a good dinner to a Brahman.'

In observing vows in the sun's honour on Sundays, the following special foods are prescribed in particular months :

(1) In Kartik (October–November), the first month, the devotee is to take only three leaves of the *Tulsi* (holy Basil) plant.

(2) In Margashirsh (November–December) the devotee may only lick a few pieces of candied sugar.

(3) In Paush (December–January) the devotee may chew three stalks of green dub grass (*Eragrostis cynosuroides*).

(4) In Magh (January–February) a few seeds of sesamum and sugar mixed together may be swallowed.

(5) In Phalgun (February–March) a consecrated draught of curds and sugar may be drunk.

(6) In Chaitra (March–April) people should break their fasts with a little *ghi* and molasses.

(7) In Vaishakh (April–May) the only satisfaction allowed to those observing the vow is to lick their own palms three times.

(8) In Jyeshth (May–June) the fast is observed simply on three palmfuls of pure water.

(9) In Ashadh (June–July) three chillies may be eaten.

(10) In Shravan (July–August) only cow-urine and molasses are tasted.

(11) In Bhadrapad (August–September) cow-dung and sugar are partaken of.

(12) In Ashvin (September–October) the application of sandalwood either in the form of an ointment or of powder should be made.

Only a few very pious and enthusiastic devotees observe all Sundays in the above manner. In average cases, the devotee allows himself rice, *ghi*, sugar, milk, i.e. white food, the restriction being only as to colour.

People observing vows in honour of the sun take food only once during the day, and that too in dishes made of *Palas* (*Butea frondosa*) leaves. This is considered one of the conditions of worship, there being some mysterious relation between the sun and the *Palas* tree.

Of the days of the month, the seventh day of both the bright and the dark halves of each month and the no-moon day are set apart for sun-worship. The ceremonies of the worship are the same as those on Sundays. In fact, in almost all the observances in connexion with the sun the same ceremonials are to be gone through. Very often a Brahman recites the sacred verses directing his hosts or hostesses to perform certain ceremonial gestures. On the last of the number of days which the devotee has decided to observe, the vow is celebrated and Brahmans are feasted.

The special occasions for sun-worship are the *Sankranti* [1] days and the solar eclipses.

Sun-worship is performed on all *Sankrants*; but the *Makar-Sankrant*, which falls on the 12th or 13th of January, is considered the most important. The sun now crosses to his northern course from his southern, and the time is considered so holy that a person dying then directly attains salvation. On this day, many Hindus go on a pilgrimage to holy places, offer prayers and sacrifices to the sun, and give alms to Brahmans in the shape of sesamum seeds, gold, garments, and cows. Much secret, as well as open, charity is dispensed, grass and cotton-seeds are given to cows and wheat flour fried in *ghi* with sugar and loaves to dogs. Sweet balls of sesamum seeds and molasses are eaten as a sacred food and given to Brahmans, and dainties such as wheat flour fried in *ghi* with sugar are

[1] *Sankrant* is the passage of the sun from one sign of the zodiac to another.

partaken of by Hindu households, in company with a Brahman or two, who are given money offerings after the meal.[1]

The four monsoon months vow known as the *Chaturmas* vow, very common in Kathiawar, is a favourite one with Hindus. The devotee, in performing this vow, abstains from food on those days during the monsoons on which, owing to cloudy weather, the sun is not visible. Even if the sun is concealed by the clouds for days together, the devout votary keeps fasting till he sees the deity again.

Barren women, women whose children die, and especially those who lose their male children, women whose husbands suffer from diseases caused by heat, lepers, and persons suffering from ophthalmic ailments observe the vow of the sun in the following manner. The vows are kept on Sundays and no-moon days, and the number of such days is determined by the devotee in accordance with the behests of a learned Brahman. The woman observes a fast on such days, bathes herself at noon when the sun reaches the zenith, and dresses herself in clean garments. Facing the sun, she dips twelve red *Karan* (*Mimusops hexandra*) flowers in red or white sandal ointment and recites the twelve names of the sun as she presents one flower after another to the sun with a bow. On each day of the observance she takes food only once, in the shape of wheat flour fried in *ghi* with sugar, in dishes of *Palas* (*Butea frondosa*) leaves; white food in the form of rice or rice cooked in milk is sometimes allowed. She keeps a *ghi*-lamp burning day and night, offers frankincense, and sleeps at night on a bed made on the floor.

People who are declared by the Brahmans to be under the evil influence of the sun observe vows in the sun's honour and go through the prescribed rites on Sundays. Such persons take special kinds of food and engage the services of priests to recite holy texts in honour of the sun. If all goes well on Sunday, Brahmans, Sadhus, and other pious persons are entertained at a feast.[2] Some persons have the sun's image in the form of an eight-cornered figure or *ashtadal* (see p. 33,

[1] On the occasion of *Makar-Sankrant* it is usual to send small packets of sugared sesamum to friends, with words of greeting.

[2] This ceremony is commonly known as *vrat-ujavavun*.

supra) engraved on a copper or a golden plate for daily or weekly worship.

On the twelfth day after the delivery of a child, the sun is worshipped and the worship of the sacred fire sacrifice is performed.

If at a wedding the sun happens to be in an unfavourable position according to the bridegroom's horoscope, an image of the sun is drawn on gold-leaf and given away in charity. Charity in any other form is also common on such an occasion.

A Nagar Brahman bride performs sun-worship for the seven days preceding her wedding.

In Hindu funeral ceremonies three *arghyas* [1] are offered to the sun, and the following verse is chanted:

'One should ever recite the six names of the sun, Aditya, Bhaskar, Bhanu, Ravi, Surya, Divakar, which destroy sin.'

The sun is also worshipped on the thirteenth day after the death of a person, when *arghyas* are offered, and two earthen pots, containing a handful of raw rice and pulse and covered with yellow pieces of cotton, are placed outside the house.[2]

Rulers who are of the solar race always worship the rising sun.[3] They also keep a golden image of the sun in their palaces and engage learned Brahmans to recite verses in his honour. On Sundays they take only one meal, and that of simple rice, for white food is most acceptable to the sun.

As all seeds and vegetation receive their nourishment from solar and lunar rays, the latter are believed in the same way to help embryonic development.

The heat of the sun causes the trees and plants to give forth new sprouts, and therefore he is called *Savita* or Producer. Solar and lunar rays are also believed to facilitate and expedite delivery. The medical science of the Hindu declares the *Amavasya* (new-moon day) and *Purnima* (full-moon day) —on both of which days the influence of the sun and the moon is most powerful—to be days so critical for child-bearing women as to cause, at times, premature delivery. Hence, before delivery, women are made to take turns in the sunlight

[1] See p. 31, *supra*. [2] This ceremony is known as *Gadaso bharvo*.

[3] Rajputs, Marathas, and other warlike races are fond of tracing their descent from the sun and the moon. The respective descendants are known as the sun-family (*Suryavanshi*) and the moon-family (*Somavanshi*).

and also in moonlight, in order to invigorate the foetus, thus securing that their delivery may be easy. The assistance rendered by solar rays in facilitating the delivery is said to impart a hot temperament to the child so born, and that by the lunar rays a cool one. After delivery, a woman should glance at the sun with her hands clasped, and should offer rice and red flowers to him. Sitting in the sun after delivery is considered beneficial to women enfeebled by the effort. It is a cure for the paleness due to exhaustion and infuses new vigour.

The Bhils believe that the exposure of a new-born child to the sun confers upon the child immunity from injury by cold and heat.

In the Deccan it is more commonly held that the sun's rays have an injurious effect on a pregnant woman, and she is made to take meals in the dark or in the moonlight to preserve the offspring.

The practice of making recently delivered women sit in the sun does not seem to be widespread, nor does it prevail in Kathiawar. In this locality, on the contrary, women are kept secluded from sunlight in a dark room at the time of child-birth, and are warmed by artificial means. On the other hand, it is customary in many places to bring a woman into the sunlight after a certain period has elapsed since her delivery. The duration of this period varies from four days to a month and a quarter. Sometimes a woman is not allowed to see sunlight after child-birth until she presents the child to the sun with certain ceremonies, either on the fourth or the sixth day from the date of her delivery.

A ceremony called the *Shashthi-Karma* is performed on the sixth day after the birth of a child, and the *Namkaran* ceremony—ceremony of giving a name—on the twelfth day. The mother of the child is sometimes not allowed to see the sun before the completion of these ceremonies. Occasionally on the eleventh day after child-birth, the mother is made to take a bath in the sun.

Exactly a month and a quarter from the date of delivery a woman is taken to a neighbouring stream to offer prayers to the sun and to fetch water thence in an earthen vessel.

This ceremony is known as *Zarmazaryan*. Seven small betel-nuts are used in the ceremony. They are carried by the mother and distributed by her to barren women, who believe that by eating the nuts from her hand they are likely to conceive.

In difficult labour cases, *chakrava* water is sometimes given to women. The *chakrava* is a figure of seven cross-lines drawn on a bell-metal dish, over which the finest white dust has been spread. This figure is shown to the woman in labour: water is then poured into the dish and offered her to drink. The figure is said to be a representation of Chitrangad. It is also believed to be connected with a story in the *Mahabharata*. Subhadra, the sister of the god Krishna and the wife of Arjuna, one of the five Pandavas, conceived a demon, an enemy of Krishna. The demon would not leave the womb of Subhadra even twelve months after the date of her conception, and began to harass the mother. Krishna, the incarnation of God, knowing of the demon's presence and the cause of his delay, took pity on the afflicted condition of his sister and read *Chakrava* (*Chakravyaha*), a book consisting of seven chapters and explaining the method of conquering a labyrinthine fort with seven cross-lined forts. Krishna completed six chapters, and promised to teach the demon the seventh, provided he came out. The demon ceased troubling Subhadra and emerged from the womb. He was called Abhimanyu. Krishna never read the seventh chapter, for then Abhimanyu would have been invincible and able to take his life. This ignorance of the seventh chapter cost Abhimanyu his life on the field of Kurukshetra in conquering the seven cross-lined labyrinthine forts. As the art of conquering a labyrinthine fort when taught to a demon in the womb facilitated the delivery of Subhadra, a belief spread that drinking in the figure of the seven cross-lined labyrinthine fort would facilitate the delivery of all women who had difficulties in child-birth.

The sun-face or *surya-mukh* is one of the chief guardians against evil in India, being carved on temples or carried in procession worked on banners.[1]

In the Konkan, Deccan, and Karnatak it is considered by

[1] *S. B. B. C.*, p. 291.

the Hindus very meritorious and holy to worship the sun; and by Brahmans the sun is considered to be their chief deity. Those who want health, wealth, and prosperity propitiate the Sun-god by prayers and ceremonies. In the Deccan, on every Sunday in *Shravan* (July–August), a picture of the sun represented by twelve concentric circles, and of his mother Ranubai with a *Swastik*[1] and mace, is drawn on a low wooden stool in quartz powder and worshipped. *Ratha saptami*, the 7th day of *Magh* (January–February), is considered to be the principal day for special worship and festivities in honour of the Sun-god. In the Deccan the sun's chariot is held to be drawn by a deer until *Ratha saptami*, and after that by horses. Thus the days become longer from *Rathi saptami* onwards. On this day, on a low wooden stool, is drawn, in red sandal paste, a figure of the sun in human shape seated in a chariot drawn by seven horses, or by a horse with seven faces. This figure is then placed in the sunshine, and it is then worshipped by offering it spoonfuls of water, red powder, red flowers mixed with red sandal paste, camphor, incense, and fruits. Some people kneel down while offering to the sun. These offerings are either three or twelve in number. Some persons make a vow not to eat anything unless they have worshipped the sun and performed the twelve salutations by falling prostrate and bowing with folded hands twelve times, and at each time repeating one of the twelve names of the sun.

In the Konkan some people worship the sun on the Sundays of the month of *Shravan* (July–August). In the Deccan Monday is sometimes favoured by the women for the worship of the sun in this month. Low castes favour Monday for sun-worship.

At *Ratha saptami*, after the ceremony already described, milk is boiled on a fire made of cow-dung cakes in front of the household *Tulsi* (holy Basil) plant. If the milk overflows to the east, it is believed that there will be abundance of crops, but if it flows to the west it is taken as a sign of the near approach of famine. In the Deccan the direction of the flow is occasionally held to be inauspicious. More commonly a flow of milk to the east is held auspicious and in any other

[1] See below, p. 42.

direction inauspicious. The Sun-god is also worshipped on such special occasions as the *Vyatipat*,[1] *Trikal, Ardhodaya, Mahoduya,* the *Sankrants,* and the solar eclipse. On these occasions corn is not ground, the hair is not combed, and cotton-seed must not be ginned. Though there are few temples dedicated to the sun, the village of Parule, in Ratnagiri District, has the honour of having one called 'the temple of *Adi-Narayan*'. A vow named *Dhanurmas,* common to all districts in the Konkan, requires a person to complete his daily rites before sunrise, and to offer a preparation of rice and pulse to the Sun-god. The observer of this vow then partakes of the food, regarding it as a gift from that god. This is either done for one day or repeated for a month till the *Dhanu-Sankrant.* On the *Somavati-Amavasya* day (the 15th day of the dark half of a month falling on Monday), and the *Kapila-shashthi* day,[2] the sun is held in especial reverence. A curious story is narrated regarding the offering of *arghya* to the sun. It is said that the sun rejoices at the birth of a Brahman, and gives 1,000,000 cows in charity, believing that the *arghya* which the Brahman will offer later on will devour his foes, one drop of the *arghya* killing 1,000 of them. The repetition of the *Gayatri* verse 108 times a day is supposed to release a Brahman from the debt of 1,000,000 cows owed in this way to the sun. The Yoga-Sutras of Patanjali, however, prohibit a man from looking at the setting sun, though the sin thus incurred is made amends for by the offering of *arghya* to that god.

Women bow down to the sun on the 11th, 12th, 30th, or 40th day after their delivery; but Kunbi women generally worship that god on the 7th day. On this occasion some women show a churning handle to the Sun-god and offer him some grains of rice.

The Swastik

Campbell, in referring to the cross generally as a protection against spirits, offers an interesting comment on the generally accepted belief that the gammadion, fylfot, or *Swastik* is an

[1] See Gupte, *H. H. & C.*, p. 97.

[2] *Ibid.*

emblem of the sun. He suggests that the worship of crossed lines passes back into beliefs earlier and coarser than the refinements of sun-symbolism. In particular, he instances the fact that the cross is in places a symbol of the moon and of other guardians, and has thus been supposed to be a general sign of divinity.[1]

A simple design such as a cross or a circle may clearly have been in use as a symbol from the earliest times in which graphic expression of ideas was possible. It seems, however, that the gammadion, or *Swastik* as it is called in India, has always been closely connected with the sun.

In the Bombay Presidency Hindus make special drawings of designs in powder, red or white, as seats for the deities when they are to be installed and invoked, a triangle for one, a square for another, a circle, a pentagon, a *padmasana*,[2] or a *Swastik* for others. Of these the *Swastik* is the seat for the sun deity to repose on. Hence the general belief that the *Swastik* represents the sun.[3]

The figure *Swastik* (literally auspicious) drawn as shown in Fig. 1 of the table on p. 42 is an auspicious sign, and is believed to be a mark of good luck and a source of blessings. It is one of the sixteen line-marks on the sole of the lotus-like feet of the god Shiva, the Creator of the Universe. The fame of the good effects of the *Swastik* figure is said to have been first diffused throughout society by the sage Narad, as instructed by the god Brahma.

Various conjectures have been made concerning the origin of this figure. The following explanation is found in a work named *Siddhantsar*: The Eternal *Sat* or Essence, that has neither beginning nor end nor any maker, exhibits all the religious principles in wheel-form. This round shape has no circumference; but any point in it is a centre; which being

[1] *S. B. B. C.*, p. 55.

[2] An elaborate geometrical design used as the seat of Lakshmi. It has been discovered on Sumerian seals as early as 2850 B.C. Vide *J. R. A. S.* 1922, p. 533.

[3] The *Swastik* is found at Pompeii and in the Greek 'key' pattern. It is also found on Persian and Assyrian coins and in the Catacombs at Rome. It is to be seen on the tomb of the Duke of Clarence who was drowned in a butt of malmsey wine at Tewkesbury, and occurs in Winchester Cathedral, where it is described as the fylfot.

(1) Deasil or common

right-handed Swastik.[1]

(2) Widdershins or common

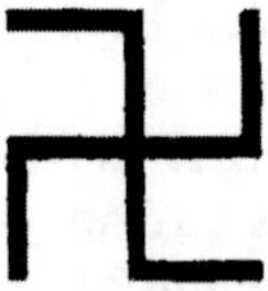

left-handed Swastik.

(3)

(5)

(4)

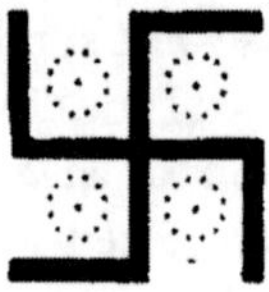

(6) Pisa University 1888.

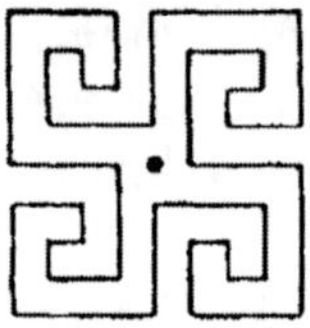

(7) Jain Swastik.

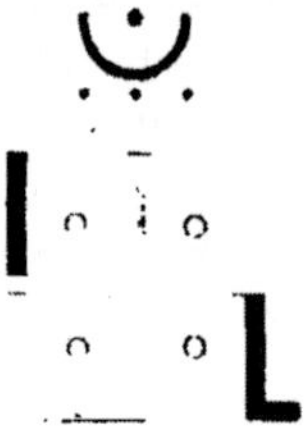

(8) Greek shield in the Louvre.

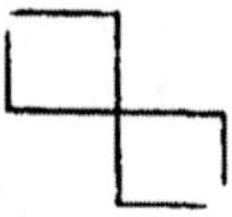

(9) Ditto.

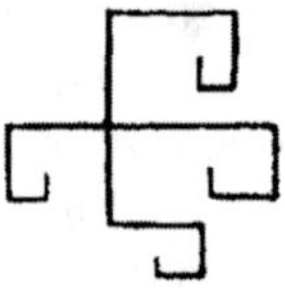

(10) Chasse de Calydon Vase in Louvre.

(11) Hercules and Cerberus Vase in Louvre.

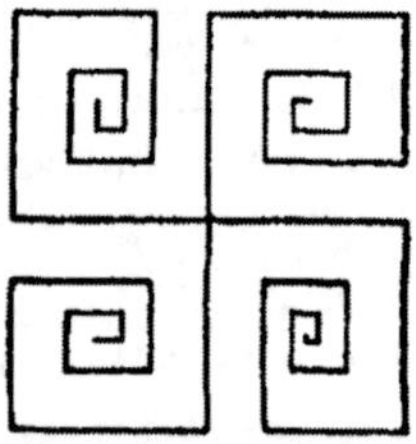

[1] When the *Swastik* faces towards the right, i. e. in the direction followed by the sun in its course through the heavens, it is lucky. When it faces towards the left it is unlucky. In Tibet it has been found on the same temple in both forms.

specified, the explanation of the whole universe in a circle is easy. Thus the figure ⊙ indicates the creation of the universe from *Sat* or Essence. The centre with the circumference is the womb, the place of creation of the universe. The centre then expanding into a line, the diameter thus formed represents the male principle, *linga-rup*, that is, the producer, through the medium of activity in the great womb or *maha-yoni*. When the line assumes the form of a cross, it explains the creation of the universe by an unprecedented combination of the two distinct natures, animate and inanimate. The circumference being removed, the remaining cross represents the creation of the world. The *Swastik*, or *Sathia*, as it is sometimes called, in its winged form (卐) suggests the possession of creative powers by the opposite natures, animate and inanimate.

Another theory is that an image of the eight-leaved lotus, springing from the navel of Vishnu, was formerly drawn on auspicious occasions as a sign of good luck. The exact imitation of the original being difficult, the latter assumed a variety of forms, one of which is the *Swastik*.

Some people see an image of the god Ganpati in the figure. That god, being the master and protector of all auspicious ceremonies, has to be invoked on all such occasions. The incapacity of the devotees to draw a faithful picture of Ganpati gave rise to a number of forms which came to be known by the name of *Swastik*.

There are more ways than one of drawing the *Swastik*, as shown in the illustration opposite, but the original form is thought by some to have been in the shape of a simple cross. The first consonant of the Gujarati alphabet, *ka*, now drawn thus ક, was also originally drawn in the form of a cross (+). Some persons therefore suppose that the *Swastik* may be nothing more than the letter ક (*ka*), written in the old style and standing for the work *kalyan*, i. e. welfare.

Though the *Swastik* is widely regarded as the symbol of the sun, some people in Gujarat ascribe the figure to different deities, viz. to Agni, to Ganpati, to Lakshmi, to Shiva, besides the sun. It is also said to represent *Swasti*, the daughter of Brahma, who received the boon from her father of being worshipped on all auspicious occasions. Most persons, however, regard the *Swastik* as the symbol of the sun.

A number of other ideas are prevalent concerning the significance of the *Swastik.* Some persons believe that it indicates the four directions; some think that it represents the four courses or objects of human desires—viz. (1) Dharma, religion; (2) Artha, wealth; (3) Kam, love; (4) Moksha, salvation. Some again take it to be an image of the ladder leading to the heavens. Others suppose it to be a representation of the terrestrial globe, and the four piles of corn placed in the figure, as shown in Fig. 4 on p. 42, represent the four mountains, Udayachala, Astachal, Meru, and Mandarachala. The *Swastik* is also believed in Gujarat to be the foundation-stone of the universe.

The *Swastik* is much in favour with the gods as a seat or couch, and as soon as it is drawn it is immediately occupied by some deity. It is customary therefore to draw the *Swastik* on most auspicious and festive occasions, such as marriage and thread ceremonies, the first pregnancy ceremonies, and the Divali holidays. In the Konkan the *Swastik* is always drawn on the piece of cloth which is held between the bride and the bridegroom at the time of a Hindu wedding. And at the time of the *Punyaha-vachan,* a ceremony which precedes a Hindu wedding, the figure is drawn in rice and is worshipped. Throughout the four monsoon months, some persons paint the auspicious *Swastik,* either on their thresholds or at their doors, every morning.

On the sixth day from the date of a child's birth, a piece of cloth is marked with a *Swastik* in red lac, the cloth is stretched on a bedstead, and the child is placed upon it.

Before joining the village school, little boys in Gujarat are made to worship Saraswati, the goddess of learning, after having installed her on a *Swastik,* in order that the acquisition of learning may be facilitated.

A Brahman host, inviting a party of brother-Brahmans to dinner, marks the figure 1 against the names of those who are eligible for gifts of money, and a *Swastik* against the names of those who are not eligible. These latter are the patrons of the inviting Brahman, who is himself their *pujya,* i.e. deserving of being worshipped by them. A dot, in place of the *Swastik*, is considered inauspicious.

The *Swastik* is used in calculating the number of days taken in pilgrimage by one's relations, one figure being painted on the wall each day from the date of separation.

It is said that the *Swastik* when drawn on a wall is the representation of Jogmaya. Jogmaya is a Nature Power, bringing about the union of two separated beings.

The Jains paint the *Swastik* in the way shown in Fig. 7 on p. 42, and explain the figure in the following manner: The four projectors indicate four kinds of souls: viz. (1) Manushya or human, (2) Tiryach or of lower animals, (3) Deva or divine, (4) Naraki or hellish. The three small dots denote the three Ratnas or jewels, viz. (1) Jnan or knowledge, (2) Darshana or faith, (3) Charita or good conduct; and the semicircular curve, at the top of the three dots, indicates salvation.

Every Jain devotee, while visiting the images of his gods, draws a *Swastik* before them and places a valuable object over it. The sign is held so sacred that a Jain woman has it embroidered on the reticule in which she carries rice to holy places.

In the Konkan it is believed that the *Swastik* is the central point of the helmet of the sun, and a vow known as the *Swastik* vow is taken in its honour. A woman observing this vow draws a figure of the *Swastik* and worships it daily during the four months of the rainy season, at the end of which she gives to a Brahman a gold or silver plate bearing the sign of the *Swastik* graven upon it.

By some persons in the Konkan the *Swastik* is regarded as the foundation-stone of the universe, or is held to be the symbol of the god Shiva, and not of the sun. Generally, throughout the Presidency, the *Swastik* is considered to be an emblem of peace and prosperity. It is for this reason that Brahman women draw a figure of the *Swastik* in front of their houses.[1]

[1] See also Gupte, *H. H. & C.*, pp. 53 and 78.

The Moon

'I am the very light of the sun and the moon,' observes Krishna in his dialogue with Arjuna; and the moon also receives divine honours like the sun. Moon-worship secures wealth, augments progeny, cures diseases, and betters the condition of milch-cattle. The suitable days for such worship are the second and the fourth days of the bright half of every month and every full-moon day. On any of these days the devotees of the moon fast for the whole of the day and take their food only after the moon has risen and after they have seen and worshipped him. Some dainty dish, such as sweetened wheat flour or plantains and wheaten cakes, is specially cooked for the occasion.

A sight of the moon on the second day of the bright half of every month is considered auspicious. After seeing the moon on this day, some people also look at silver and gold coins for luck. The belief in the value of this practice is so strong that, immediately after seeing the moon, people refrain from beholding any other object. Their idea is that silver, which looks as bright as the moon, will be obtained in abundance if they look at a silver piece immediately after seeing the moon. Moon-worship on this day is also supposed to guarantee the safety of persons at sea. In the south, milk and sugar is offered to the moon after the usual worship, and learned Brahmans are invited to partake of it. What remains after satisfying the Brahmans is divided among the community. On this day, those who keep cattle do not churn whey nor curd milk nor sell it, but consume the whole supply in feasts to friends and neighbours. The shepherd castes of Gujarat, known as Ahirs and Rabaris, especially are very particular about the use of milk in feasts only: for they believe that their cattle are thereby preserved in good condition.

In the Deccan and Konkan, on the second day of the bright half of each month, a bow is made to the moon and an old rag or thread from an old garment offered to him with the words, 'Take old and give new'. In the Karnatak it is the custom to offer white cloth and white flowers to the moon, and to draw an image of him in white grain.

The fourth day of the dark half of every month is the day for the observance of the fourth-day vow. This vow is observed in honour of the god Ganpati and by men only. The devotees fast on this day, bathe at night after seeing the moon, light a *ghi*-lamp, and offer prayers to the moon. They also recite verses in honour of Ganpati, and, after worshipping that god, take their food consisting of some specially prepared dish. This vow is said to bring fulfilment of the dreams of the devotees.

The day for the fourth-day vow in the month of *Bhadrapad* (August–September) is the fourth day of the bright half instead of the fourth day of the dark half, and on this day (*Ganesh Chaturthi*) [1] the moon is not worshipped. The very sight of him is regarded as ominous, and is purposely avoided. The story is that once upon a time the gods went out for a ride in their respective conveyances. It so happened that the god Ganpati fell off his usual charger, the rat, and this awkward mishap drew a smile from Chandra (the moon). Ganpati, not relishing the joke, became angry and cursed Chandra, saying that no mortal would care to see his face on that day, which happened to be the fourth day of the bright half of *Bhadrapad* (August–September). If any one happens to see the moon even unwittingly on this day, he may expect trouble very soon, such as being falsely accused of some theft or other offence. There is one way, however, out of the difficulty, and that is to throw stones on the houses of neighbours. When the neighbours utter abuse in return, the abuse atones for the sin of having looked at the moon on the forbidden night. The day is therefore called the Fourth day of Stones.[2]

On the fourth day of the dark half of *Phalgun* (February–March) some villagers fast for the whole of the day and remain standing from sunset till the moon rises. They break their fast after seeing the moon. The day is, therefore, called Standing-fourth.[3]

Virgins sometimes observe a vow on the full-moon day of *Paush* (December-January). On this day a virgin prepares her evening meal with her own hands on the upper terrace of her house. She then bores a hole through the centre of a loaf,

[1] See *Gujarat Notes*, p. 18. [2] i.e. *Dagad choth*. [3] i.e. *Ubhi choth*.

and observes the moon through it, repeating while doing so a verse which runs : 'O Poshi-Punemadi, rice and pulse mixed together is cooked on the terrace, and the sister of the brother takes her meal.'[1] The meal usually consists either of rice and milk, or of rice cooked in milk and sweetened with sugar, or of sweetened wheat flour. She has to ask the permission of her brother or brothers before she may take her food ; and if the brother refuses his permission, she has to fast for the whole of the day. The whole ceremony is believed to prolong the lives of her brothers and her future husband. The moon is also worshipped at the time of the ceremonies performed before inhabiting a newly built house.

In the Thana District the rays of the moon are held to influence conception.

If the moon is unfavourable to a man born under a particular constellation, on account of his occupying either the 6th, the 8th, or the 12th square in a *kundali*[2] (see opposite page), prayers are offered to the moon ; and if the occasion is a marriage, a bell-metal dish, full of rice, is presented to Brahmans.

The appearance of the moon and the position of the horns of his crescent at particular times are carefully watched as omens of future events. Cultivators believe that if the moon is visible on the second day of the bright half of *Ashadh* (June–July), the sesamum crops of that season will be abundant ; but if the moon be hidden from sight on that day, the weather will be cloudy during the whole of *Ashadh* (June–July) and will prove unfavourable to vegetable growth. If the moon appears reddish on the second day of the bright half of a month, and if the northern horn of the crescent be high up, prices in the market are believed to rise ; if, on the other hand, it is low, it prognosticates a fall in prices. If the two horns are on a level, current prices will continue.

Similarly, the northern horn of the crescent, if it is high up on this day, augurs abundant rainfall ; if it is low, it foreshadows a season of drought.

If the moon presents a greenish aspect on the full-moon day

[1] The original is: Poshi Poshi Punemadi, Āgāshe rāndhi khichadi, jame bhāini benādi.

[2] See *Gujarat Notes*, p. 18 (see also under Planets, *infra*).

of *Ashadh* (June–July) excessive rains may be expected in a few days; if on that day he rises quite clear and reddish, there is very little hope of good rains; if he is partly covered by clouds when he rises and then gets clear of the clouds, and then again disappears in the clouds in three *ghadis* (24 minutes), three *pohors* (three hours), or three days, rain is sure to fall.

If on the fifth day of the bright half of *Chaitra* (March–April) the moon appears to the west of the Rohini constellation, the prices of cotton are believed to rise; if to the east, they are said to fall; and if in the same line, the current rates are believed to be likely to continue.

The second day and the ninth day of *Ashadh* (June–July) falling on a Sunday is a combination that foretells excessive heat. If they fall on Wednesday, intense cold is said to be the result. Their occurring on a Tuesday threatens absence of rains, and on a Monday, a Thursday, or a Friday, foreshadows excessive rainfall.

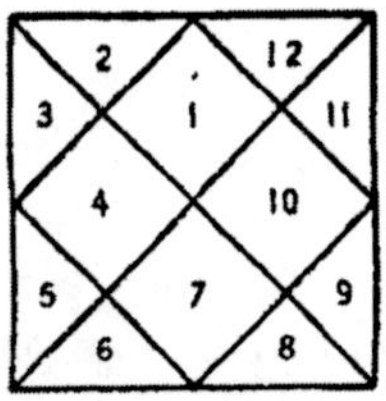

The spots on the moon have given rise to numerous beliefs, mythological as well as fanciful. One of them is that they are the result of a curse, pronounced by the sage Gautama on Chandra. Indra, the god of rain, was infatuated with the charms of Ahalya, the wife of Gautama, and with the help of Chandra laid a cunning plot to gain his ignoble object. Accordingly, one night, Chandra set earlier than usual, when Indra assumed the form of a cock and crowed at midnight in order to deceive Gautama into the belief that it was dawn and therefore his time for going to the Ganges to perform his religious services. The trick was successful; and the holy sage being thus got rid of, Indra assumed the form of Gautama himself and approached Ahalya, who was surprised to see her husband (as she thought) so quickly returned. The wily god allayed her suspicions by explaining that it was not yet time for the morning ceremonies, and thus enjoyed the favours due to her husband. Gautama, in the meanwhile, finding the water of the Ganges cool and placid, and discovering that it was not yet dawn, returned to his hermitage. On reaching home he detected the treachery of Indra, who tried to escape in the disguise of a tom-cat. The exasperated sage then cursed Indra, Chandra, and his wife: Indra to have a thousand sores on his person, Ahalya to turn into a stone, and Chandra to have a stain on his fair face.

Another mythological story is that Daksha Prajapati, the son of Brahma, gave all his twenty-seven daughters in marriage to Chandra, who was inspired with love for one of them only, named Rohini, the most beautiful of them all. The slighted twenty-six sisters complained to their father, Daksha, of Chandra's preference for Rohini. Daksha in anger cursed Chandra, causing him to be attacked by consumption (which is supposed to be the reason of the waning of the moon) and his face to be marred by a stain.

The curse of Gautama and the curse of Daksha are also supposed to be reasons of the waxing and the waning of the moon.

Another belief regarding the moon-spots is that when the head of Ganpati was severed by Shiva's trident, it flew off and fell into the chariot of the moon. The spots are either the head itself or are due to drops of blood fallen from the flying severed head.

The spots are also said to be explained by the fact of the image of the god Krishna or Vishnu residing in the heart of the moon, who, as a devotee of Vishnu, holds this image dear to his heart.

The moon is often called *mriganka* (lit. deer-marked) and *mriga-lanchhana* (lit. deer-stained): and a further explanation of the spots in this connexion is that the moon-god took into his lap a strayed deer, out of compassion, and thus his lap became stained. Jains believe that, in the nether parts of the moon's vehicle, there is an image of a deer whose shadow is seen in the spots.

In Gujarat some persons declare the spots to be a *Shami* tree (*Prosopis spicigera*). In the Deccan they are held to be a Banyan or a *Nim* tree (*Melia Azadirachta*). The belief of the masses in Gujarat is said to be that the spot on the moon's disk is the seat of an old woman, who sits spinning her wheel with a goat tethered near her. If the droppings of the goat were to fall to earth, departed souls would return to life.

The spots on the surface of the moon are believed by some to be the chariot of the god. Others think that they are lunar mountains; but many believe that the spots are visible signs of the stain on the character of the moon-god due to his having outraged the modesty of the wife of the god Brahaspati or Jupiter. In the Puranas it is stated that on one occasion a dispute arose between the moon and Brahaspati or Jupiter about the wife of Brahaspati, each of them claiming to be the cause of her conception. Subsequently a son was born who was named Budha (Mercury). Brahaspati's wife, on being asked who was the father of the child, named the moon. Thereupon Brahaspati cursed the moon for his adultery. The spots on the surface of the moon are said to be the effect of this curse. Being unable to bear the pain of the spots the moon, it is said, propitiated his preceptor, who directed him to bathe in the Bhima river. The pain was assuaged, and the portion of the Bhima where the moon bathed thus came to be called *Chandra-bhaga*.

In the Ratnagiri District several conflicting theories are held regarding the spots on the surface of the moon. Some believe that the spot observed on the moon is a Tamarind tree in which that god has stationed himself; others hold that the spot is the reflection of a deer which is yoked to the chariot of the moon; while many more believe that it has been occasioned by the hoof of the horse of King Nala. Some say that the spot on the surface of the moon represents a *Pipal* tree (*Ficus religiosa*) and a cow or two deer fastened to the roots of the tree; others, on the authority of Hindu mythology, suppose that God created *Madan* (Cupid) from the essence taken from the body of the moon, and hence the moon-god has spots on his body. In the *Mahabharata* it is stated that on the surface of the moon is reflected the island of Sudarshan on this earth, together with some trees and a great hare, the bright part being nothing but water. Some believe that Yashoda, the mother of Krishna, after waving an earthen dish round the face of Krishna, threw it at the sky. It struck the moon and thereby the spots on the surface of the moon were caused. Nectar is supposed to have been derived from the rays of the moon; and in some sacred books it is stated that the

Chakora bird (Bartavelle partridge) drinks the rays of the moon.

The people of the Thana District hold similar notions regarding the spots on the surface of the moon. It has been said by some that the portion in question represents mud. Others hold that the spots on the surface of the moon are due to his having been kicked by a deer which, when pursued by a hunter, was refused shelter.

The moon-god is believed to distribute nectar through his rays, and therefore this deity is said to have the power of removing diseases and restoring human beings to health. The moon is the king of herbs, and all trees, plants, &c., thrive owing to the influence of the moon. Sometimes people place, at night, figs, plantains, sugar-cane, and other eatables in the moonlight and eat them early in the morning; and it is said that those who do so improve in health.

In the Deccan on the full-moon day Devi and Khandoba are worshipped.

On a full-moon day people perform the special worship of their chosen deity. On the full moon of the month of *Kartik* (October–November) temples are illuminated, and on the full-moon day of *Magh* (January–February) grain such as wheat, millet, &c., is cooked and offered to the household and other deities. On this day also are performed the special rites and ceremonies that are required in connexion with the family gods or goddesses. On the full-moon day of *Phalgun* (February–March), the *Holi* fire is kindled and worshipped. In certain families the full moon of *Chaitra* (March–April) is considered auspicious for making offerings to family deities.

It is said that a child and a tree are never seen to grow except during the night. Such growth is therefore held to be due to lunar rays. As all trees, plants, &c., thrive owing to the influence of the moon, the moon-god is called the lord of herbs. The moon is also a reservoir of nectar and is called *Sudhakar*, i.e. one having nectarine rays. As the lord of herbs, the moon-god is supposed to have the power of removing all diseases that are curable by drugs, and of restoring men to health.

Persons suffering from white leprosy, black leprosy, consumption, and diseases of the eyes are believed to be cured by the observance of the second-day and full-moon-day vows. Consumption in its incipient and latter stages is also said to be cured by exposure to the rays of the moon. Constant glimpses of the moon add to the lustre of the eyes. On the fifteenth day of the bright half of *Ashvin* (September–October), tailors pass a thread through their needles in the belief that they will thereby gain keener eyesight. On this day also a cotton-wick is exposed to the moon and is afterwards lighted in oil poured over the image of Hanuman. The soot which is thus produced, if used on the fourteenth day of the dark half of *Ashvin* (September–October), is said to possess much efficacy in strengthening the eyesight and also in preserving the eyes from any disease during the ensuing year.

Sweetened milk or water is exposed to moonlight during the whole of the night of the full-moon day of *Ashvin* (September–October) in order to absorb the nectarine rays of the moon, and is drunk next morning. Drinking in the rays of the moon in this manner is believed to cure diseases caused by heat as well as eye-diseases, and it similarly strengthens the eyesight and improves the complexion. In the Konkan men look at the moon steadily for a while every moonlit night to strengthen their vision. Sugar-candy thus exposed and preserved in an air-tight jar is partaken of in small quantities every morning to gain strength and to improve the complexion. The absorption of the lunar rays through the open mouth or eyes is also believed to be of great effect in achieving these objects. In the Karnatak it is believed that by lying down and looking up at the moon a person suffering from eye affections is cured.

In the Deccan on the new-moon days water is poured over Maruti's image, and oil, grain, salt, and chillies are given to Mangs. On the new-moon day the *Pitras* or *Manes* are worshipped. Lighted lamps are worshipped on the new-moon day of *Ashadh* (June–July). In the Kolhapur State this is called *Tadali* new-moon day, and in the Konkan it is called *Divali* new-moon day. On the new-moon day of *Ashvin* (September–October) Lakshmi, the goddess of wealth, is worshipped. All special ceremonies for the propitiation of evil spirits are usually performed on the new-moon day.

On the fifteenth day of the bright half of the month of *Ashvin* (September–October) people put milk in the rays of the moon for some time, and then, after offering it to the moon, they drink it. Drinking milk in this way is called drinking the rays of the moon. On the *Sankasti-Chaturthi* day and on that *Chaturthi* which immediately follows the *Dasara* holiday, people draw an image of the moon and worship it.

In the month of *Magh* (January–February), from the eighth or tenth day of the bright fortnight up to the full-moon day, a figure of the moon is drawn with lime daily in the courtyard of the house and duly worshipped in the Karnatak. This is done mostly by unmarried girls.

If the no-moon day falls on Monday, Brahman women of the Thana District walk round a *Tulsi* plant (holy Basil) or a *Pipal* tree (*Ficus religiosa*), and make a vow to a Brahman.

In the Kolaba District a special ceremony is held in honour of minor goddesses on the eighth day of a month. The following things are avoided, one in each of the fifteen lunar days respectively :

Kohala (pumpkin), *dorli* (*Solanum indicum*), salt, sesamum, sour things, oil, *avale* (*Emblic Myrobalan*), coco-nuts, *bhopala* (gourd), *padval* (snake-gourd), *pavte* (*Dolichos Lablab*), *masur* (*Lens esculenta*), *brinjal*, honey, gambling.

The people observe a fast on the thirteenth (*Pradosha*) and the fourteenth (*Shivaratra*) of the dark half of every month. On the fifteenth day of the bright half of *Chaitra* (March–April) a fair is held in honour of the guardian deity of a village, and hens, goats, &c., are offered as a sacrifice.

The following are days of special importance in the lunar months :

Gudhi-padva, i.e. the first day of the bright half of *Chaitra* (March–April). This being the first day of the year in the Deccan, flags (*gudhis*) and garlands (*toranas*) are hoisted in front of every house and are worshipped.

Bhau-bij. On the second day of the bright half of *Kartik* (October–November) every sister waves round the face of her brother a lamp, and makes him a present.

The ceremony on the *Bhau-bij* day has come into vogue on account of Subhadra having given a very pleasant bath to her brother Krishna on that day. The Court of Yama, the king of the infernal regions, is also said to be closed on that day, since he goes to his sister; and consequently persons who die on that day, however sinful they may be, are not supposed to go to *Yamaloka*, i. e. hell.

Akshya-Tritiya. On the third day of the bright half of *Vaishakh* (April–May) cold water and winnowing fans are distributed as tokens for appeasing the *manes* of ancestors. On this day is also celebrated the birth of the god Parashuram.

Ganesh Chaturthi. On the fourth day of the bright half of *Bhadrapad* (August–September) an earthen image of Ganpati is worshipped and a great ceremony is held in his honour. The fourth day of the bright half of every month is called *Vinayak-Chaturthi*; while that of the dark half is called *Sankasti-Chaturthi.* On the *Vinayak-Chaturthi* day people fast the whole day and dine the next day; while on the *Sankasti-Chaturthi* day they fast during the day-time and dine after moonrise. That *Sankasti-Chaturthi* which falls on Tuesday is considered the best.

Nagpanchami. On the fifth day of the bright half of *Shravan* (July–August) pictures of serpents and snake holes are worshipped.

Champa-Shashti. On the sixth day of the bright half of *Margashirsh* (November–December) some ceremony relating to the family deity is performed

Ratha-Saptami. On the seventh day of the bright half of *Magh* (January–February) the sun is worshipped and milk is boiled until it overflows.

Gokul-Ashtami. On the eighth day of the dark half of *Shravan* (July–August) the birth of the god Krishna is celebrated.

Ram-Navami. On the ninth day of the bright half of *Chaitra* (March–April) the birth of the god Rama is celebrated.

Vijayadashmi. On the tenth day of the bright half of *Ashvin* (September–October) people cross the boundary of their village and distribute *sone* (leaves of the *Shami* (*Prosopis spicigera*) and *Apta* (*Bauhinia racemosa*) trees). It is a popular belief that a work commenced on this day is sure to end well. Weapons are also worshipped on this day.

Ekadashi. On the eleventh day of *Ashadh* (June–July) and *Kartik* a special fast is observed. People also fast on the eleventh day of each month. A man who dies on this auspicious day is supposed to go to heaven. Sometimes the *Ekadashi* falls on two consecutive days; in which case the Smartas, i. e. worshippers of Shiva, observe the first, while the Bhagvats, i. e. worshippers of Vishnu, observe the second.

Waman-Dwadashi. On the twelfth day of the bright half of *Bhadrapad* (August–September) Waman is worshipped and one or twelve boys are adored, being held to represent Waman. The marriage of the *Tulsi* (holy Basil) plant is sometimes celebrated on this day.

Dhana-Trayodashi. On the thirteenth day of the dark half of *Ashvin* (September–October) Lakshmi, the goddess of wealth, is worshipped.

Narak-Chaturdashi. On the fourteenth day of the dark half of *Ashvin* (September–October) the demon Narakasur was killed. In consequence, on this day people take their bath before sunrise, break the gourd *Karinta* (*Cucumis trigonus*), regarding it as a demon, and apply its seeds to their heads.

Naral Paurnima. On the fifteenth day of the bright half of *Shravan* (July–August), people worship the sea and throw into it a coco-nut.

Wata Paurnima. On the fifteenth day of the bright half of *Jyeshth* (May–June) women whose husbands are alive fast the whole day, and worship the Banyan.

Tripuri Paurnima. On the fifteenth day of the bright half of *Ashvin* (September–October) people keep themselves awake the whole night and amuse themselves in a variety of ways. On the fifteenth day of the bright half of *Kartik* (October–November) houses are illuminated. On this night people illuminate with earthen lamps all temples in the village, but particularly the temple of Shiva. This is done in commemoration of the triumph of the god Shiva over the demon Tripurasura. The full-moon day of the month of *Magh* (January–February) is called *Chudi Paurnima.* On this night people light torches and with them slightly burn certain flowers, trees, and plants. The full-moon day of the month of *Phalgun* (February–March) is called the *Holi* or *Holi Paurnima* and is the biggest holiday of the lower-class Hindus. On this night the Hindus kindle the *Holi* fire and worship it. On the fifteenth day of the bright half of *Ashvin* (September–October) people eat grain of the new harvest. On the full-moon day of *Shravan* (July–August) they perform the *Shravani* ceremony and give a lamp in charity. On the full-moon day of the months of *Chaitra* (March–April), *Vaishakh* (April–May), and *Margashirsh* (November–December), the births of Maruti, Narasimha, and Dattatraya respectively are celebrated. The Kunbis of the Ratnagiri District believe that on the fifteenth or full-moon day of *Paush* (December–January) the Hindu gods go out hunting, and that they return from their hunting expedition on the full-moon day of the month of *Magh* (January–February). During this period the Kunbis abstain from worshipping their gods.

Amavasya. On the fifteenth day of the dark half of every month oblations are given to the *manes* of the dead. The commencement of a good deed, journey to a distant place, and the ploughing of land are postponed on the no-moon day of a month. *Sanyasis* are enjoined to get their beards shaved on the *Paurnima* and *Amavasya* days only.

People do not set out on a journey on the following *tithis*, regarding them as *rikta* (unfruitful or inauspicious) :

Chaturthi, *Navami*, and *Chaturdashi*.

The *Chandrayana Vrata.* Widows fast on the no-moon day of a month. They are required to regulate their diet in such an increasing proportion that on the next full-moon day they should have a full meal. The reverse process follows for a fortnight after, so that they observe an absolute fast on the following no-moon day.[1]

The following story is current in the Deccan in connexion with the worship of the moon at midnight :

Three *Nag* (snake) girls of the Kaliya stock, with the object of obtaining wealth, worshipped the moon at 12 o'clock at night on the full moon of *Ashvin* (September–October), and after drinking coco-nut milk, commenced to play the game of *Saripal* with a Brahman as the fourth player. In three succes-

[1] Further details of these festivals and celebrations will be found by the reader in *Hindu Holidays*, by B. A. Gupte.

sive games the *Nag* girls defeated the Brahman and won all he had, including his waist-cloth and even his sacred thread. In the next game also the Brahman was defeated, but having nothing to give to the *Nag* girls he devoutly prayed to Lakshmi, the goddess of wealth, who being pleased with his devotion endowed him with wealth and made his body as beautiful as that of Cupid. The *Nag* girls, being enamoured of him, married him by the *Gandharva* form of marriage, and thus the Brahman was made happy. Since then it has been the custom to worship the moon at midnight under the belief that it brings wealth. After worship, milk is offered to the moon and drunk by all present.

Eclipses of the Sun

The traditional story of the eclipse is as follows:

Once upon a time the gods and demons, by their united efforts, churned the ocean and obtained therefrom fourteen jewels (*ratna*) or precious things. These were distributed among them. Lakshmi, the *kaustubha* jewel, the Sharnga bow, and the conch shell fell to the share of Vishnu, and the poison *Halahal visha* was disposed of to Shiva. Only two things remained, *sudha* or nectar, and *sura* or liquor. To both gods and demons the nectar was the most important of all the prizes. A hard contest ensuing between them for the possession of it, the demons, by force, snatched the bowl of nectar from the gods. In this disaster to the gods, Vishnu came to their help in the form of Mohini—a fascinating woman—and proposed to the demons that the distribution of the immortalizing fluid should be entrusted to her. On their consent, Vishnu, or Mohini, made the gods and the demons sit in opposite rows and began first to serve the nectar to the gods. The demon Rahu, the son of Sinhika, fearing lest the whole of the nectar might be exhausted before the turn of the demons came, took the shape of a god and placed himself amongst them between Chandra (the moon) and Surya (the sun). The nectar was served to him in turn, but on Chandra and Surya detecting the trick, the demon's head was cut off by Vishnu's discus. Rahu, however, did not die: for he had tasted the nectar, which had reached his throat. The head and trunk lived and became immortal, the former being named Rahu, and the latter Ketu. Both swore revenge on Chandra and Surya. At times, therefore, they pounce upon Chandra and Surya with the intention of devouring them. In the fight that ensues, Chandra and Surya are successful only after a long contest, with the assistance of the gods, and by the merit of the prayers that men offer.

The reason of the eclipse is thus popularly said to be either that Chandra and Surya bleed in the fight with Rahu and their forms get blackened; or that the demons Rahu and Ketu, who are members of the Mang caste, come between the two luminaries and this earth, or attempt to touch or devour the sun and moon; or because Rahu obstructs the sun and the moon in their daily course, and this intervention causes an eclipse; or because Rahu swallows the sun and the moon, but his throat being open, they escape, their short disappearance causing an eclipse.

Besides the mythological story, there is a belief in Gujarat that a Bhangi creditor of the sun and the moon goes to recover his debts due from them, and that his shadow falling against either of them causes an eclipse. It is also said that Rahu and Ketu go to collect debts from the sun and the moon.

Another explanation of the eclipse is that the sun and the moon revolve round the mountain known as Meru, and the shadow of the mountain falling upon either of them causes an eclipse.

It is believed amongst Hindus of the Presidency that eclipses occur when too much sin accumulates in this world. They regard an eclipse as ominous, and consider the eclipse period to be unholy and inauspicious. The contact of the demon Rahu with the rays of the sun and the moon pollutes everything on earth. Great precautions therefore become necessary to avoid pollution. A period of nine hours in the case of the moon, and of twelve in the case of the sun, before the actual commencement of an eclipse, is known as *vedha*, i.e. the time when the luminaries are already under the influence of the demon. During this period and during the time of an eclipse people observe a strict fast. Any one taking food within the prohibited period is considered ceremonially impure, as if a death had happened in his family. An exception is, however, made in the case of children, pregnant women, and suckling mothers who cannot bear the privation of a strict fast. From the beginning of an eclipse to its end, everything in the house is believed to be polluted, if touched. Water found in a house during an eclipse is not used. Food which has been cooked is purified with *Tulsi* (holy Basil) leaves or thrown away.

At the commencement of the eclipse, as well as at its close, people bathe. Some sit on a low wooden stool with a rosary in their hands, repeating the names of the gods, or the hymn to the sun, &c., in a low tone (*jap*). But those who want to acquire the art of magic or witchcraft, or the power of removing the evil effects of snake-poison or scorpion sting, go to a lonely place on the river-side, and there standing in water repeat incantations taught to them by their teacher. People give alms to Mahars and Mangs on this occasion, and therefore persons of this class go about the streets saying loudly, 'Give us alms and the eclipse will be over.'

The eclipse time is so inauspicious that children and animals born at that time are considered unlucky. If a pregnant woman does household work, such as washing clothes or preparing vegetables during an eclipse, the child born of her is said to be deformed. Mangs, Mahars, &c., are supposed to be the descendants of Rahu and Ketu; and for this reason gifts are made to them in charity on an eclipse day.

As the sun and the moon are believed to be in trouble during an eclipse, people offer prayers to God for their release from the time of commencement of the *vedha*. It is the custom to visit some holy place on an eclipse day, to take a bath there, and to read holy passages from the Shastras. Some people, especially Brahmans, sit devoutly on river-banks and offer prayers to the sun. Brahmans put on new sacred threads on this occasion. Much secret as well as open charity is given at the time of an eclipse. But the receivers of charity during the actual period of an eclipse are the lowest classes only, such as Bhangis, Mahars, and Mangs. When an eclipse is at its full these people go about the streets giving vent to such cries as 'Give alms for the relief of the moon'.

Among the gifts such people receive are cotton clothes, cash, grain such as sesamum seeds, black gram, pulses, and salt. The gift of a pair of shoes is much recommended. Sometimes a figure of the eclipsed sun or moon is drawn in *juvari* (*Sorghum vulgare*) seeds and given away to a Bhangi.

Although the period of an eclipse is considered inauspicious, it is valued by those who profess the black art. All incantations, applications, or experiments, which ordinarily require a long time to take effect, produce the wished-for result without delay if performed during the process of an eclipse. Thus the iron of a horseshoe, five kinds of metal, or ships' nails, are made into rings, wristlets, and amulets during an eclipse and possess special efficacy.

If a man's wife is pregnant, he may not smoke during the period of an eclipse lest his child become deformed. Ploughing a farm on a lunar eclipse day is supposed to cause the birth of Chandra-children, i.e. children afflicted by the moon.

After an eclipse Hindus bathe, perform ablution ceremonies, and dress themselves in clean garments. The houses are cleansed by cow-dunging the floors, vessels are rubbed and cleansed, and clothes are washed, in order to get rid of the pollution caused by the eclipse. Unwashed clothes of cotton, wool, silk, or hemp, according to popular belief, do not become polluted. The placing of *Darbha* (*Eragrostis cynosuroides*) grass on things which are otherwise liable to pollution is also sufficient to keep them unpolluted.

Brahmans cannot accept anything during the impious time of an eclipse; but after it is over alms are freely given to them in the shape of such costly articles as fine clothes, gold, cattle, and the like.

After an eclipse Hindus may not break their fast till they have again seen the full disk of the released sun or the moon. It sometimes happens that the sun or the moon sets while still eclipsed, and people have then to fast for the whole of the night or the day after, until the sun or the moon is again fully visible.

There is a verse in the *Jyotish Shastra* to the effect that Rahu would surely devour Chandra if the constellation of the second day of the dark half of a preceding month were to recur on the full-moon day of the succeeding month. Similarly, in solar eclipses, a similar catastrophe would occur if the constellation of the second day of the bright half of a month were to recur on the last day of that month. The year in which many eclipses occur is believed to prove a bad year for epidemic diseases.

In the Deccan and Konkan, at the time of an eclipse, a rice-pounder is held erect in a vessel filled with water. If it stands by itself, the eclipse is thought to be still in progress; if it falls, the eclipse is held to be over. This is in cloudy weather when the eclipse cannot be seen.

In the Deccan, if a cow is calving on eclipse day and a person moves round her, he is held to obtain the merit of moving round the earth.

The Jains do not believe in the Hindu theory of the eclipse. Musalmans do not perform the special ceremonies beyond the recital of special prayers; and even these are held to be supererogatory.

The people of the Thana District believe that corn grows abundantly in a year that witnesses many eclipses. During an eclipse the images of the gods are kept immersed in water in the houses.

The popular cause of an eclipse in the Kolaba District is the *Girha,* a minor deity which is said to wander through the sky and swallow the sun and the moon when they cross his path. The people of the Ratnagiri District also believe that the *Girha* throws his shadow on the sun and the moon, when he comes to demand his dues from them. In the Deccan it is said that a worm-eaten tree is made sound if cut with an axe during an eclipse. The Konkan villagers, on an eclipse day, strike barren trees with a pestle, in order that they may bear fruit and flowers. A barren woman is also beaten with the same motive. Similarly, many other superstitious beliefs are connected with an eclipse. Pregnant women are not allowed to see the eclipse of the sun or the moon, nor are they to engage in cutting, sewing, &c., as such acts are believed to be injurious to the child in the womb. The eclipse time is supposed to be the most suitable to learn incantations. The exorcists also mutter incantations in a naked condition during an eclipse. The people who believe that eclipses are caused by the influence of the planets *Rahu* and *Ketu* offer prayers to *Rahu* on the lunar eclipse day and to *Ketu* on the solar eclipse day.

STARS AND PLANETS

With the exception that some people believe that the stars are the shades of the gods, the popular belief about the heavenly bodies seems to be that they are the souls of virtuous and saintly persons, translated to the heavens for their good deeds and endowed with a lustre proportionate to their merits. This idea is illustrated in the traditions that are current about some of the stars. The seven bright stars of the Great Bear are said to be the seven sages, Kashyapa, Atri, Bharadwaj, Vishwamitra, Gautama, Jamadagni, and Vasishtha, who, having mastered several parts of the Vedas were considered specialists in the branches studied by each, and were invested with divine honours in reward for their proficiency. The Great Bear is therefore known as the (Seven Saints) *Saptarishi*. Another story relates how a certain hunter and his family, who had unconsciously achieved great religious merit, were installed as the constellation the Great Bear. A hunter, it is narrated in the *Shivaratri-mahatmya*, was arrested for debt on a *Shivaratri* [1] day, and while in jail heard by chance the words 'Shiva, Shiva' repeated by some devotees. Without understanding their meaning, he also began to repeat the same words, even after he was released in the evening. He had received no food during the day, and had thus observed a compulsory fast. In order to obtain food for himself and his family, he stationed himself behind a *Bel* (*Aegle Marmelos*) tree, hoping to shoot a deer or some other animal that might come to quench its thirst at a neighbouring tank. While adjusting an arrow to his bow-strings, he plucked some leaves out of the thick foliage of the tree and threw them down. The leaves, however, chanced to fall on a *phallus* of Shiva which happened to stand below, and secured for him the merit of having worshipped the god Shiva with *Bel* leaves on a Shivaratri day. He was also

[1] The *Shivaratri*, i.e. Shiva's night, is a fast in honour of the god Shiva. It falls on the thirteenth day of each half of the lunar month and is a full twenty-four hours' fast. (*Vide* Gupte, *H. H. & C.*, p. 214.)

all the while repeating the god's name and had undergone a fast. The result was that not only were his past sins forgiven, but he was placed with his family in heaven.

Similarly, Dhruva, the son of King Uttanapad, attained divine favour by unflagging devotion, and was given a constant place in the heavens as the immovable pole-star.

According to Hindu astrology, there are nine planets, twelve signs of the zodiac, and twenty-seven constellations. Books on astrology explain the forms of the constellations. For instance, the Ashvini constellation consists of two stars and presents the appearance of a horse. It ascends the zenith at midnight on the full-moon day of *Ashvin* (September–October). The constellation of Mrig consists of seven stars, four like the legs of a cot and three others under them in a line. All these twenty-seven groups of stars reach the zenith at midnight on particular days in particular months; and the months of the Hindu calendar are named after them. The seven stars of the Great Bear are sometimes known as *Khatale* and *Bagale*. Four are thought to be a cot with a man asleep thereon, and the other three are thieves.

All planets influence the life of a person, one way or the other, according to their position in the heavens at the time of his birth. At puberty, marriage, and other auspicious occasions in the Deccan the nine planets are worshipped. A *kundali*, i.e. a figure like the one shown here, is drawn by astrologers to illustrate the respective positions of the planets. The twelve squares of the diagram represent the twelve signs of the zodiac, and the positions of the planets in different squares influence persons in different ways. Ravi (the Sun), Budha (Mercury), and Shukra (Venus) occupy one sign for one month; Chandra (the Moon) occupies a sign for two days and a quarter; Mangal (Mars) for one month and a half; Guru (Jupiter) for thirteen months; Shani (Saturn) for two years and a half, and Rahu for a year and a half. This is their normal and ordinary motion. But if they take an abnormal course and move either too fast or too slow, they finish their revolution through a sign within a shorter or a longer period.

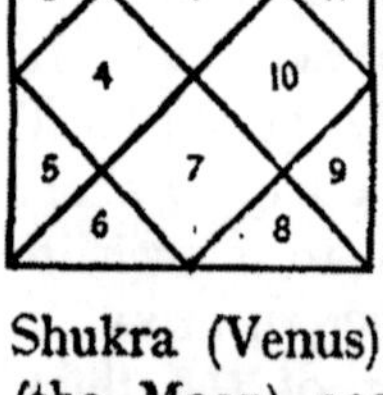

If the planet Guru (Jupiter) occupies either the 1st, 3rd, 4th, 6th, 8th, 10th, or 12th square of a *kundali*, it is said to bring about a rupture with friends, pecuniary want, and an increase in the number of enemies.

If Shaṇi (Saturn) occupies the 1st, 2nd, 4th, 5th, 7th, 8th, 9th, or the 12th square in a man's *kundali*, it causes despondency of mind, family quarrels, imminent injuries from foes and pecuniary wants.

The presence of Mangal (Mars) in the 3rd, the 6th, or the 11th square is auspicious.

Of the nine planets, Budha, Guru, and Chandra are benevolent; Mangal and Ravi are neither benevolent nor baneful; and Shani, Rahu, and Ketu are downright malevolent. This is the belief in Gujarat; but in the Deccan Mangal and Shani are considered dangerous, and Shukra favourable. Each planet has a story connected with it concerning its benevolence or malevolence, and showing also the way to secure its propitiation. For instance, the malevolence of Shani drove King Vikrama to unknown countries, and subjected him to grave calamities. On the advice of a wise man, however, he observed the Saturday-vows and thus overcame his difficulties.

When a planet is unfavourable to a person, it has to be propitiated by vows, and the person who is under its evil influence often lays upon himself the obligation of abstaining from particular articles of food or from wearing certain articles of clothing for a certain number of days. Offerings of oil, marking nuts, black gram, nails, and blankets are made to planets. Particular days of the week are set apart as appropriate for the worship of particular planets, and on such days the person keeping the vow observes a fast and worships the planet through the medium of a Brahman. For instance, vows are observed on Tuesdays in honour of Mangal (Mars), when an image of the planet, engraved on a golden dish, is worshipped, and the person observing the vow takes food consisting of wheat only, and that too, only once during the day. This mode of fasting is followed for a number of consecutive Tuesdays prescribed by an astrologer; and on the last Tuesday, when rice, *ghi*, and coco-nuts are offered, Brahmans are feasted and a present is given to them. A piece of red cloth and some corn are used in the installation of the planet; these and the golden engravings are carried away by the priest.

Similarly, in propitiating Rahu and Ketu the same ceremonies are gone through; only, instead of wheat, *mug* (*Phaseolus Mungo*) is eaten by the devotee. In the same way Shani (Saturn) is said to favour a diet of black gram, Guru (Jupiter) inclines to gram (*Cicer arietinum*), while Shukra (Venus) favours *chola* (*Dolichos sinensis*).

Certain forms or figures, called *mandals*, are favoured by particular planets, and are drawn in their honour in worshipping them. Different things, too, are given in charity in honour of different planets.

All the nine planets and the twenty-seven constellations are worshipped on the occasion of the *Griha-Shanti*, i.e. planet-soothing ceremony, which is performed before occupying a newly erected building.

It is considered inauspicious to hold a marriage ceremony while Shukra (Venus) is invisible. In such a case, however, the ceremony may be performed after setting up and worshipping a small golden image of the planet.

Of the stars, the constellation of the Great Bear is perhaps the one most often worshipped. Its worship forms a part of the ceremonies performed on the occasion of investing boys with the sacred thread, and also of the ceremonies of marriage. The worship of the Great Bear on marriage occasions is believed to be an attestation of the marriage, and to secure the benign care of the Great Bear for the couple. The form of worship is sometimes as follows: a red and white piece of cloth is stretched on the ground, bearing an image of the Great Bear over it; wheat and rice are scattered over the cloth, a *ghi*-lamp is lighted, and red lac and flowers are offered to the image. Another form of worship is to mark seven red-lac dots on a wooden stool, and to place seven pice and seven betel-nuts thereon. After worshipping the seven pice, the bridal pair are made to take four turns round the stool, touching the stool with their great toes at every turn. A proverb runs to the effect that, whatever may happen to the couple, still the seven pice of *satpati* (i.e. the ceremony described) are secure. A third process is to form seven small piles of rice on each of which, successively, the bride places her right foot while the bridegroom removes each pile one by one. On the full-moon day of *Kartik* (October–November) 27 lamps are lit in honour of 27 stars, and waved before them, for success in enterprises about to be undertaken.

The fifth day of the bright half of *Bhadrapad* (August–September) is observed as a day of worship in honour of the Great Bear group. People observe a fast on that day. Brahmans set up seven twisted braids of *Darbha* grass (*Eragrostis cynosuroides*) in honour of the seven sages, adding an eighth in honour of Arundhati, the wife of Vasishtha, and worship them by a sixteen-fold ceremonial. The worship is said to secure felicity for departed souls.

The Great Bear is also annually worshipped by Brahmans on coco-nut day (the 15th day of the bright half of *Shravan* (July–August) on the occasion of changing their sacred threads. Women worship it on the fifth day of the bright half of *Bhadrapad* (August–September) thus securing purification. Hindu seamen also worship the constellation on the same day.

In the performance of the *Nil-parvan* ceremony, which is held to propitiate the spirits of departed ancestors, and which requires a calf and a heifer to be married, an entertainment being simultaneously given to one hundred and eight Brahmans, and on the occasion of *Vastu* or the ceremonies performed before or at the time of occupying a newly built house, burnt offerings and worship are offered to the Great Bear.

Every Brahman must offer *arghyas*[1] to, and worship, the *Agastya* constellation, in a hut of *Darbha* (*Eragrostis cynosuroides*) and *Kasada* (*Cassia occidentalis*) within seven days from the date of its appearance. Failure to make this offering brings pollution on him for seven months, and disqualifies him from performing any of the rites or ceremonies prescribed by the Shastras.

In the Bijapur District the bride and bridegroom are made to look at *Arundhati*, one of the stars of the Great Bear. This is said to be a lesson in chastity to the bride.

Married couples are made to look at the pole-star immediately after the marriage knot is tied by the priest, in the hope

[1] See p. 31, *supra*.

that they may be as long-lived or as inflexible or unmoved by the ups and downs of life.

The twelfth day after the death of a person, the Star-twelfth,[1] is kept as the day of star-worship by the relatives of the deceased, when one member of the family observes a fast on that day in honour of the deceased, and takes food only after worshipping the stars at night. It is customary on this day to give up the use of bronze vessels and to give them away in charity.

In the Deccan it is the practice of a man who has been away from home for nine days to look at the stars before re-entering his house. Women after their periods look at the stars.

Just as persons carrying or accompanying a corpse to the cemetery are considered under ceremonial impurity, so those who witness this rite are also considered unclean: but they are purified by a sight of the stars.

Young girls watching the starry sky at night recite a verse as follows: 'I worshipped the star-spangled firmament first and then my lover. Ye stars! blind the prowling thief and seize him if he tries to steal away, and your blessings on my lord confer!'

The *Rohini* and *Krittika* constellations, popularly known as *Gadli*, are supposed to indicate the rise and fall in the cotton-market.

On the authority of the *Mahakala Nirvan Tantra*, some people in the Konkan believe that a person who cannot get a view of the pole-star will die within six months; while others substitute the *Arundhati* star for the pole-star and determine the duration of life of a diseased person by the same process.

The dimmest star of the Great Bear group foretells the death of a person within six months from the date on which it becomes invisible to him. Again, if a man cannot perceive the Great Bear or the galaxy in the sky, it is considered such a bad omen that his end is believed to be near at hand.

From the movements of the planets past and future events of one's career are foretold by Brahman and other astrologers. And as it is believed that man's good and bad luck are dependent upon the influence of the planets, offerings of various

[1] This is known as *Tara-baras*.

kinds are made and sacrifices performed for securing the favour of the nine planets. In order to avert the effect of the evil influence of certain planets people sometimes wear rings of those precious stones which are supposed to be the favourites of the planets.

The worship of stars and planets is in vogue among Konkan and Deccan Hindu families of the higher castes. A very interesting story is connected with the pole-star. By the great power of his penance the sage Vishvamitra dispatched King Trishanku to heaven, but the gods hurled him down. Thereupon Vishvamitra became enraged and began to create a new heaven. Hindu mythological books say that he thus created the sages Vashishta, Angiras, Pulah, Pulastya, Rutu, Atri, and Marichi, and stationed Trishamku in the sky. The nine planets are worshipped before the commencement of all important ceremonies. The seven Wise Men, i. e. *Saptarishi*, are said to have been created by the god Brahma from his own body: and teaching them the four Vedas, he handed them over to them and asked them to regulate the affairs of the world.

Some people of the Kolaba District believe that holy persons such as Kashyapa, Arundhati, and other sages, who lived on this earth in ancient times, are seen shining in the sky by the sacred lustre of their powers. Hindu women worship the planets Budha and Guru (Mercury and Jupiter) in the month of *Shravan* (July–August).

METEORS

There are two goals which a pious Hindu tries to attain by leading a life of purity and virtue, viz. (1) *moksha* or final emancipation, merging into the Eternal Spirit, and (2) *swarga* (heaven or paradise), where meritorious persons enjoy pure pleasures unalloyed by earthly cares. The stars are the spirits of so many righteous persons who are translated to *swarga* for their good actions, and are endowed with a lustre proportionate to their individual merits. But every moment of enjoyment in *swarga* diminishes the store of merit (*punya*): and those whose whole merit is thus exhausted, on receiving their proportionate share of pleasures, must resume their worldly existence. The *Bhagavadgita* says: 'They enter the mortal world when their merit is expended.' Meteors are believed to be spirits of this description who fall from their position as stars, to live again on this earth.

Another explanation of meteors is that they are the sparks produced when the vehicles of the gods clash against each other.

Meteors are also held to be the excreta dropped either by a curious water-bird, by Garud, the favourite eagle and vehicle of Vishnu, or by a fabulous bird Anal. The latter is said to fly at an immeasurable height from the surface of the earth, and to take food only once a day. It is almost impossible to catch the droppings when they fall to earth: but if ever they can be secured, the application of them to the eyes of a blind man will restore his eyesight. They also furnish an effective remedy for leprosy, and give a golden lustre to the body of a person suffering from that disease.

Some declare that meteors are stars which fall owing to the curse of Indra, and subsequently assume the highest human form on earth.

Whenever a great person or a very holy man is about to be born, it is believed that he alights on the earth in the shape of a shooting star. Sometimes a big star falls on the earth, and thereby a noise like that of thunder is produced. When this happens, people believe that a great king or a holy saint whose merit has been exhausted is going to be born on earth.

The sight of a shooting star should be kept a secret. To report the fact is unlucky. In the Deccan it is held to indicate the death of a chaste woman or a good man.

It is also said that the stars descend to earth in human form when sins accumulate in the celestial world.

The influence of meteors on human affairs is treated at length in the *Varahasanhita*. The phenomenon is popularly regarded as an evil omen: it is supposed to portend devastation by fire, an earthquake, a famine, an epidemic, danger from thieves, and storms at sea. The appearance of a bright shooting star is supposed to foretell the death of some great man; and on beholding one, it is customary to repeat the words 'Ram, Ram' several times. A shower of meteors is believed to presage some civil commotion or a change in the ruling dynasties.

Some persons, however, regard the appearance of meteors as auspicious or baneful, according to the group of stars from which they are seen to fall. Meteors from the *Vayu-mandal* (or the groups of stars known by the name of Vayu), portend the breaking out of an epidemic: those from *Varuna-mandal* are believed to be favourable to human happiness: if they fall from *Indra-mandal,* they forebode danger to all kings; those from *Agni-mandal* threaten war between nations.

During the monsoons, rain is believed to fall in that direction in which a meteor is seen to shoot. A meteor in the west is ominous to kings, and if it falls into the sea, it forebodes evil to the dwellers on earth. In the Kanara District the fall of a meteor into the sea is held to promise a fall of rain.

Comets

The appearance of a comet is believed to portend some dire calamity to the king and the nation. It is said that if a heavenly body is seen, great and celebrated kings are in danger of their lives. A comet is also believed to threaten all tailed animals with destruction.

The appearance of a comet is regarded by the Hindus as symptomatic of a coming evil, e.g. a big war, a great famine, or a terrible contagious disease spreading itself throughout the length and breadth of a country.

Children born when a comet appears are supposed to turn out bad characters.

The following verse from the *Mrichhakatiha Natak* supports the view in accordance with which orthodox people in the Konkan avoid looking at shooting stars:

'The following four things, viz. the rainbow, the fall of shooting stars, the delivery of a cow, and the death-struggle of saints or holy men, should not be looked at.'

It is generally believed by Hindus that a child will immediately be born in the house towards which shooting stars are directed.

The Milky Way

The Milky Way is known as the *Akashganga, Vastupurush,* and *Kavadgantak.* According to the Puranas, it is the celestial River Ganga which was brought down by Bhagirath to the earth. King Sagar once performed the horse-sacrifice, when, according to custom, he let loose a horse, and sent his sixty thousand sons with it. Indra, jealous of the growing power of Sagar, stole the horse and concealed it in the hermitage of Kapila, when the sage was deeply absorbed in religious meditation. The sixty thousand sons of Sagar followed it to this asylum, where they taunted and insulted the sage, believing him to be the thief. Kapila, who was ignorant of the theft, opened his long-closed eyes in anger, emitting sparks of flame from them, and destroyed the sons of Sagar together with the whole of their army. Bhagirath, the grandson of Sagar, propitiated the sage, and on his advice practised religious austerities in honour of Shiva for the purpose of bringing down the River Ganga from heaven. Through the kindness of the god Shiva, Bhagirath was at last successful in bringing the celestial river down to this world ; and with the water of the river he revived the sons of Sagar. The River Ganga (i.e. the Ganges) in this world is therefore also known by the name of Bhagirathi. It is this heavenly river which we see as the Milky Way. Like the sacred Ganges on the earth, the River Ganga in the celestial regions is held in great respect by the gods and purifies the heavenly bodies, just as the earthly Ganges washes away the worst sins of mortals.

It is related in the Karnatak that the Milky Way is the path along which the Sun-god travels in his one-wheeled chariot. Some people, however, believe the Milky Way to be the track by which the holy Ganges descended from heaven to earth.

Another belief is that the god Vishnu, at the time of his dwarf incarnation, touched the *ina* (i.e. the Egg) in his third footstep and thus caused a flow of waters, which is known as *Akashganga.*

Well-known tradition relates how Waman (the fifth or dwarf incarnation of Vishnu) went to Bali, the king of the lower regions, and asked him to give him land measuring three feet only. The king consented, whereupon the god Waman enlarged his body to such an extent that by his one footstep he occupied the whole earth and by the second he occupied heaven. Upon this the god Brahma worshipped the foot of the god Vishnu which was in heaven, and from that foot sprang the heavenly Ganges which flows in heaven and is called Dudha Ganga or the milky Ganges.

Some suppose the Milky Way to be a ladder leading to the heavens. In the Deccan the dead are thought to ascend to heaven by the *Akashganga*. Astrologers call it *Vatsu*, a fictitious creature with numerous horns, mouths, and tails. According to another belief, the Milky Way consists of two lines, one of sin and the other of good and meritorious actions. The length of one line compared to the other betokens the predominance of good or evil as the case may be. The Milky Way is also supposed to be the track left by the car of Ramchandra.

The Milky Way is said to consist of 18,000,000 stars. If a man cannot perceive the Milky Way in the sky, his end is believed to be near at hand.

Musalmans declare the Milky Way to be the track formed by the footstep of the horse of the Prophet on the occasion of his night-journey to heaven.

By some Hindus in the Presidency, it is believed that the Milky Way is a heavenly river which is a favourite bathing-place of the gods. Some persons, however, believe that, since the great sage Agastya is said to reside at Rameshwar in the south of India, the heavenly Ganges (the Milky Way) runs through the sky to the south in order to bathe him.

II

WORSHIP OF NATURAL OBJECTS

(Continued)

THE RAINBOW

THE rainbow is believed to be the bow of Indra, the god of rains, and is therefore called *Indra-dhanushya.* We see it when Indra draws his bow to release the rains from demons; or when, successful in bringing down rain, Indra manifests his glory by drawing a bow; or when, in the struggle for supremacy between the hot weather and the rainy season, Indra draws his bow to defeat the hot weather. In the Deccan, incense, a lamp, and cooked rice are offered to Indra on the appearance of a rainbow.

It is also believed that when Ramchandra, the hero of the *Ramayana,* adjusted an arrow to the bow of Shiva, to compete for the hand of Sita in the *swayamvara* (maiden's-choice marriage) celebrated by her, the bow was split into three pieces, which ever since present themselves as rainbows in the sky. Rama and Lakshman are held to revisit the earth as the larger and smaller rainbows.

The rainbow is popularly regarded as an indication of good or bad rainfall according as it appears at particular hours and in particular directions. If a rainbow appears in the east a speedy rainfall is expected; if, on the other hand, it is seen in the west, rainfall is apprehended to be distant. Some people, however, believe the contrary, i. e. they regard the appearance of a rainbow in the west as an indication of good rains, and in the east as a sign of scarce rainfall. In the Deccan and Konkan, if a rainbow appears on a hill, it is thought that rain will cease; if on a river, that rain will fall. In the Deccan a rainbow in the west in the morning is held to bring rain within three days.

If a rainbow is seen at sunset or sunrise just before the

commencement of rain, the fall of rain will be excessive ; but if it appears after rainfall, the rain will probably cease. According to some persons, the appearance of a rainbow in the morning portends a drought. There is, however, a popular saying to the effect that, were the rainbow to be seen at sunrise in the west, it foretells great floods before nightfall. In the Deccan generally the appearance of the rainbow is held to herald the cessation of rainfall. But again in many places it is held to promise rain. The direction in which the rainbow appears is held to be auspicious.

The sight of a rainbow in some places is regarded as a bad omen. Some believe that it shortens a man's life and brings misfortunes to him. Others believe that it is calamitous to a man's relations by marriage, especially to the mother-in-law, who is sure to lose her powers of hearing. People sometimes clash earthen vessels against one another to avert the evils which are to be feared from a rainbow. It is also said that the sight of the whole of the rainbow is a good omen, but the sight of a part, however large, is inauspicious.

In the Konkan the appearance of a rainbow in the east is regarded as symptomatic of the approach of rain, while its appearance in the west is equivalent to the departure of rain.

The people of the Thana District believe that the rainbow is caused by the accumulation of moisture in the air. The rainbow is said to consecrate the region over which it appears. The appearance of the rainbow in the morning is supposed to forebode the approach of rain. The rainbow is said to foretell good if it appears either at the beginning or end of the rainy season, while its appearance at any other time is supposed to forebode evil. The short duration of the rainbow is held to indicate an excessive fall of rain, while its long duration forebodes a scarcity of rain.

The rainbow to be seen in the spray of the Gersoppa Falls in North Kanara District is believed to be caused by a certain king having cast a crown set with diamonds into the Shiravati river as an offering to the Ganges.

THUNDER AND LIGHTNING

Indra has twelve clouds under his control, and he directs each of them to pour out their waters wherever he likes. When in the least irritated in the execution of his orders, Indra's voice is heard in this world in thunder-claps which rise to a terrible pitch if the deity becomes downright angry. Thunder is also said to be the loud laughter of Indra when in a happy mood. Another belief is that during the rainy season Indra plays a game resembling tip-cat, and the strokes given in the course of the game produce what we call thunder; or, that the clouds are the god's footballs, and thunder is produced by his foot striking them while at play during the rainy season. Some believe thunder to be due to the loud sounds produced by various musical instruments which are played upon the occasion of the marriage-ceremony of Indra. According to others, thunder is produced by the cannon of Indra; or, as some again say, by the trumpetings of *Airavat*, the elephant of Indra; or, we hear thunder when Indra draws his bow and adjusts an arrow to the bow-string, in order to bring about a fall of rain.

A further belief attributes thunder to the very rapid pace of the chariot of Bhagwan. Some people, however, say that it is produced when Bhima (one of the five Pandavas) wields his prodigious club or bludgeon; or that when Indra beats the clouds with his whip, i.e. lightning, the clouds roar and this is thunder. In the opinion of others, Vidyut or Tanyatun, the offspring of Lamba, the daughter of Daksha, and the wife of Dharmaraja, thunders in the rainy season. It is also suggested that the god of rains shakes the heavens and thus produces thunder. The Shastras, it is said, declare that thunder is caused by the sounds of the kettledrums beaten by the gods in delight at the sight of rain. There is also a popular belief in the Surat District that an old hag causes thunder either when she grinds corn or when she rolls stones in the clouds. In the Deccan thunder is thought to be the noise made by Parvati grinding corn.

According to Campbell[1] the spirit of lightning is much

[1] See *S. B. B. C.*, p. 198.

afraid of the *Apta* tree (*Bauhinia racemosa*). Hence in the Konkan people carry leaves of this tree in the rainy season.

The prevalent belief about lightning seems to be that it is the girl whom Kansa tried to dash against a stone, but who escaped and went up to the sky. Kansa, the tyrant king of Mathura, was informed by a heavenly voice, by way of prophecy, that a son would be born to his sister who would cause his destruction. Kansa thereupon confined his sister Devaki and her husband Vasudeva in prison, loaded them with fetters, and kept the strictest watch over them. He took from Devaki, and slew, every child of hers as soon as it was born. In this way he disposed of her first six children. On the seventh occasion, however, on which Devaki gave birth to a son named Krishna, a girl was born at the same hour to Nanda in Mathura; and Vasudeva secretly interchanged the two children in spite of the vigilance of Kansa. When Kansa knew of his sister having been delivered, he seized the infant girl and tried to dash her against a stone. The little one immediately flew away to the skies, where she still dwells in the form of lightning.

The Shastras describe *Vijli* (lightning) as the distinctive weapon of Indra, just as *Pashupataka* is peculiar to Shiva and the *Gandiva* bow to Arjuna.

Other beliefs about lightning are that it is the sister of Megharaja, the god of rains, and appears to announce his approach; that it is a goddess who rests upon winds, fire, and rains; that it is but the thunderbolt of Indra; that lightnings are the flashes of the bright weapon of Indra; that lightning is the lustre of the fireworks and the lamps lighted by the gods in honour of the nuptials of Indra; that lightning is produced by the sparks caused by the friction of Indra when playing tip-cat. Lightning is also known as Saudamini, i. e. one residing on Mount Sudama.

The occurrence of thunder and the appearance of lightning on particular days and in particular directions are regarded as signs of the abundance or scarcity of rain during the season.

In the Deccan it is held that, on hearing thunder, a man should bathe to remove the evil likely to beset the hearing.

A ball of cooked rice or wheat flour should also be offered when lightning is seen.

Thunder during the Rohini *nakshatra*[1] is a bad omen: it foreshadows either a famine, or a *Boterun*, i. e. complete cessation of rains for seventy-two days, after the thunder-claps are heard. According to another view, if the Rohini *nakshatra* lasts for a fortnight and if the sky is clear during the period and yet lightning and thunder occur, a *Boterun* will be the consequence; but if lightning and thunder were to accompany the clouds in the same *nakshatra*, heavy and plentiful rains may be confidently expected. Lightning without clouds in the same *nakshatra* is believed to be the cause of what is popularly called Rohini-*dazi*, i. e. the burning heat of Rohini.

Some persons expect a *Boterun* after crashing thunder. Others apprehend a famine if they hear thunder on the second day of the bright half of *Jyeshth* (May–June).

Thunder or lightning in the Hasta *nakshatra* foretells good harvests and a prosperous year. Thunder in the same *nakshatra* is believed to muzzle the jaws of serpents and other noxious creatures; and to achieve this object, also, a log of wood is struck against a hollow stone used for threshing corn. If thunder is not heard during this *nakshatra*, mosquitoes and other insects and vermin are believed to be likely to multiply.

If thunder is heard during the Ardra *nakshatra*, the rainfall will be delayed for a month.

Lightning is commonly seen on the second and the fifth day of the bright half of *Ashadh* (June–July), and is considered a sign of good rainfall, while its absence indicates a probable scarcity of rain. Its appearance on the fifth day of *Ashadh* (June–July) is believed by some to foretell an early fall of rain. Since the rainfall and therefore the state of the crops during the ensuing year are suggested by lightning on this day, corn-dealers settle a rise or fall in the price of corn according as lightning is or is not seen on that occasion.

Thunder in the east predicts a speedy fall of rain. If flashes of lightning are seen in the north-east or the north, rain will fall within three days. Lightning in the south-east or the south foretells extreme heat.

[1] *Nakshatras* are the lunar mansions or constellations.

Long-continued thunder shows that the rainfall is distant. Similarly, continued flashes of lightning intimate danger to the lives and property of people. Sudden thunder portends an immediate cessation of rain. Thunder or lightning out of season threatens calamity to the country.

Lightning is said to be fettered on the fifth day of the bright half of *Ashadh* (June–July)—or, as some say, on the second day of *Shravan* (July–August)—after which date no apprehensions of its destructive powers need be entertained. Till then, however, it is free, and is likely to injure those persons who have not cut or shaved their hair from their birth.[1]

The occurrence of lightning is believed to cause the delivery and sometimes even the death of pregnant women. In Bankapur in the Dharwar District, it is believed that thunder has a serious effect on pregnant women, and also that it brings on diseases of the stomach.

Any period marked by the occurrence of lightning is considered inauspicious.

Various conflicting motions are entertained in the Konkan regarding thunder and lightning. The people of the Ratnagiri District believe that the clouds are animals that roar. When these animals emit water it bursts forth on account of the circular motion of the winds called Chanda and Munda. This bursting is supposed to produce thunder and lightning. Somewhere thunder and lightning are said to be the signals given by the god Indra, to birds, beasts, &c., of the setting in of the rainy season. Some people believe that the god Indra sends rain through his elephants, who, being excited, make a noise like thunder.

Others regard the thunder as the roaring of the elephant of the gods while sucking sea-water. The thunder is also believed to be the roaring of the god Varuna, the king of the clouds. The boys of the Ratnagiri District believe that thunder is a sign of the wedding ceremonies performed in the heavenly houses of the gods.

[1] Among Hindus it is customary for those who have lost children to keep subsequent infants unshaved for a number of years. They are then taken to a holy place and there shaved for the first time with special ceremonies.

EARTHQUAKES

The Puranas speak of fourteen worlds—the seven celestial regions and the seven nether regions. Underneath the seventh nether region lies Shesha (the divine cobra), who supports all the fourteen worlds on one of his thousand hoods. On account of the heavy burden, the serpent-god sometimes gets tired, and tries to change his position. The result of the movement is an earthquake. According to another version, an earthquake occurs when Shesha changes his posture in sleep, or is the result of a hair falling from the body of Shesha, or of the shaking of one of the thousand hoods. Some people say that ordinarily Shesha does not feel the weight of the fourteen worlds on his head: he bears the load as if it were only a single sesamum seed. But when too much sin accumulates in any of the regions, the earth becomes heavy and the burden becomes unbearable for him; he begins to shake under it, and an earthquake occurs.

Some believe that there is a tortoise under the divine cobra who supports the world; others go farther, and add a frog below the tortoise; and it is said that the slightest motion on the part of either the tortoise or the cobra is the cause of an earthquake.

Another belief is that earthquakes occur whenever there is tyranny or injustice on the part of a king, or whenever immorality spreads in society, because the earth is unable to bear the sin, and trembles at the sight of it.

According to another opinion, the earth is supported by the favourite bull of Shiva, on one of his horns. An earthquake is caused whenever he transfers the earth from one horn to another in order to relieve the former from the constant pressure of the burden.

There is also a belief that deities of some strange species reside in the nether regions, and the earth is shaken whenever these beings fight among themselves.

According to the *Varahasanhita*, an earthquake is always the precursor of some unprecedented calamity. The prevalent belief in the popular mind seems to be that an earthquake is the result of immorality and sin, and further that it forebodes some dire calamity, such as famine, pestilence, an outbreak of fire, a revolution, or a great war. In the Deccan the occurrence of an earthquake is held to portend evil to the king or some other great personage. The phenomenon is, therefore, regarded with great fear; and when it occurs, people endeavour to avoid the contingent evils by such meritorious acts as the giving of alms, by worshipping the earth, and generally by leading a virtuous life.

In the Konkan it is said that at one time a demon named Gayasur became very troublesome, and all the gods held him down by standing on his body. Thereupon the demon requested all the gods to remain on his body for ever. Occasionally this Gayasur shakes his body and this causes an earthquake. Some people believe that the earth trembles of its own accord when sins accumulate upon it. Others hold that the earthquake takes place in the hollow parts of the earth. Some people, however, believe that since the earth floats upon water, it naturally quakes at times.

The Earth

Hindus regard the earth as one of the important deities and worship it on numerous occasions, especially when anything is to be built upon its surface. In the Deccan, Hindus on rising in the morning ask pardon of the earth before stepping on the floor. At the time of setting up the first pillar of a marriage-bower, or a bower for a thread ceremony, before commencing the construction of wells, reservoirs, and tanks, and in laying the foundation-stone of, or first entering, a house, or founding a temple, a sacrificial pit, a street, a fortress, a city, a village, or any constructive work raised upon or made in the ground, certain ceremonies, called *khat-muhurt* or *khat-puja*, are performed. The earth-mother is then worshipped in the manner prescribed in the Shastras, to propitiate her and thus to avoid interruptions in the course of the work undertaken. The owner or the person interested in the new construction pours a little water on the earth where the foundation-pit is to be dug, sprinkles red lac and red powder, places a betel-nut and a few precious coins, and digs out the first clod of earth himself. Some of the things offered to the earth at the time of *khat-puja* are *panchamrit*, betel-nuts, betel-leaves, *pancharatna* (or the five kinds of precious things, namely, gold, silver, copper, coral, and pearls), a bowl, and green garments. Sandal-leaves, flowers, and rice are offered to the earth in the Deccan. In the Deccan, if flowers or leaves to be offered to the gods fall on the ground, they are held to be polluted.

Under the influence of particular signs of the zodiac, particular corners of the building under construction are required to be dug in the *khat-muhurt* ceremonies. For instance, a little digging in the north-west corner is believed to be favourable to the constructor who happens to be under the influence of *Sinha* (Leo), *Kanya* (Virgo), and *Tula* (Libra); in the north-east corner, if under the influence of *Vrishchika* (Scorpio), *Dhanu* (Sagittarius), and *Makar* (Capricornus); in the south-east corner, if under the sway of *Kumbha* (Aquarius), *Min* (Pisces), and *Mesha* (Aries); in the south-west corner in the case of *Vrishabh* (Taurus), *Mithun* (Gemini), and *Karak* (Cancer). After the worship of the earth-mother, sugar or molasses is distributed among neighbours, bystanders, and relatives, in token of the auspiciousness of the occasion. An image of Ganpati is worshipped in a copper dish, which is buried underground, and a brick is laid on it when starting the work of construction. In setting up the first pillar of a marriage-bower on marriage occasions, a small earthen bowl is filled with milk, curds, turmeric, *durva*-sprouts (*Cynodon Dactylon*), and *mug* seeds (*Phaseolus Mungo*), and buried in the ground after being sprinkled over with red lac and rice.

Sacred books, cooked food, and the feet of holy men or kings must not touch the earth. Similarly a conch shell or blade of a sword should not touch the earth, nor should charmed amulets, or they lose their power.

The ceremonies appertaining to *khat-muhurt* are treated of at length in a book called *Dharma-sindhu*. They are believed to secure durability of construction.

On the *Dasara* day, i.e. the tenth day of the bright half of *Ashvin* (September–October), Hindu kings go out in state with their ministers and subjects to worship the earth-mother and the holy *Shami* tree (*Prosopis spicigera*). A wetted plot of ground is first dug over with pikes, tender wheat-plants and *Shami* leaves are then mixed with the muddy earth, and small balls of the mixture are made. A pice and betel-nut are placed in each ball, and they are presented to the worshipper as a mark of good luck. Travellers carry such balls with them on their journeys, for luck. Kings carry the same to obtain success on the battle-field. The Pandavas had such balls with them on the field of Kurukshetra when they obtained a victory over the Kauravas. The balls are also used as a *pastana*.[1] The wheat-plants in the balls are taken out and allowed to grow in an earthen vessel filled with clay and manure till they reach a span in height, when they are taken up and used.

In the Deccan the fall of a burning wick to the earth is held to portend calamity, and propitiatory ceremonies must be performed to avert the same.

Earth-worship is performed before burying treasure underground, and also when a marriage procession, at the time of returning, reaches the limits of the bridegroom's village.

In some places, virgins worship the plot of ground on which the *Holi* fire is lighted, for about ten or twelve days after the *Holi* holiday.

Another occasion for earth-worship is the third day of the bright half of *Chaitra* (March–April), on which day Vishnu saved the earth, in his Boar incarnation, when it was being carried to the nether regions by the demon Shankhasur.

On the eighth day of the bright half of *Magh* (January–February), and also of *Ashvin* (September–October), an oblation of food is offered to the earth-mother, and is then used as her *prasad* (gift). No cooked food is allowed to fall on the ground on this day; even the leavings after meals are given away to cows.

When any ceremony is to be performed on the earth's surface, as much of the spot as is required for the ceremony is cleansed by watering it and plastering it with cow-dung. A betel-nut and a pice are then placed on it as the rent of the spot.

[1] Some Hindus, when intending to go on a journey, consult an astrologer as to the auspicious hour for setting out. If they do not happen to leave at the prescribed moment, they put a *pastana*—some of the articles to be carried by them on their journey, such as a suit of clothes or a box—in a neighbour's house as a token of their having set out at the stated time.

On these occasions when presents are given to Brahmans outside the village limits, worship of the earth-mother is performed by pouring milk on the ground, and by placing seven betel-nuts and seven single copper pieces thereon.

Some ambitious Brahmans dig earth from near the roots of a Banyan tree after offering prayer to the earth, and out of it make an image of *Parthishwar*—Lord of the Earth—hoping thereby to obtain wealth. The same ceremony, if observed near the roots of a *Pipal* tree (*Ficus religiosa*), is believed to confer wealth and male issue.

When Vishnu killed the demons Madhu and Kaitabha, the earth was strewn with their flesh and marrow (vern. *meda*). Therefore the earth is called *medini*, and for the same reason is unclean, and no holy objects are allowed to touch it. Another explanation is that the earth was rendered unclean because blood was shed on its surface in the combat of the demon Vritrasur with the god Indra.

The things polluted by a contact with the earth are either objects which are to be dedicated to gods, such as sandalwood ointment, *panchamrit*, the leaves of the *Bel* tree (*Aegle Marmelos*), *Tulsi* leaves (leaves of the holy or sweet Basil plant), betel-leaves and flowers; or objects which are sacred because of their having been dedicated to the gods, including water used in bathing the images of gods; or things which are by nature so holy that it is improper to place them on the bare earth; for instance, images of deities, water of the sacred Ganges or the Jumna, any holy writ, a conch shell, and even gold. Cooked food also deserves respect, as it supports the lives of men, and it is sinful in a Hindu to let it lie on the bare ground. Any irregular conduct in this respect arouses the wrath of the food deity. In the Karnatak the following articles must not be placed on the bare earth: mercury, silk, peacocks' feathers, *Rudraksha* seeds (*Elaeocarpus Ganitrus*), the *Shaligram*, the images of gods, *vibhuti* (sacred ashes), and a woman's breasts. The *Linga* of the Lingayats is not allowed to touch the earth.

It is, however, maintained by some that the reason why certain things, such as materials of worship, are not allowed to touch the earth, is that the earth itself being a deity, such things would be dedicated to this deity by a contact with the earth and would thus become incapable of any further use, as things that are dedicated to one deity cannot again be offered to another.

During the course of the recitation of hymns in honour of Vishnu and Mahadeva ; on the occasion of offering prayers to the planets for their propitiation ; and on occasions like *Vishnuyaga, Maharudra, Shatachandi,*[1] *Gayatripurashchara,*[2] and *Brahmana-varana,*[3] the devotee or the sacrificer and the priest sleep on *Darbha* (*Eragrostis cynosuroides*) grass or on clean woollen blankets spread on the bare ground.

Other occasions for sleeping on the floor are the days of the observance of certain *vrats* (vows) ; such as the *Divasa* or the fifteenth day of the dark half of *Ashadh* (June–July), the *Janmashtami* or the eighth day of the dark half of *Shravan* (July–August), the days of *Goatrad*, a *vrat* lasting from the eleventh day to the fifteenth day of the bright half of *Bhadrapad* (August–September), *Mahashivaratri* or the fourteenth day of the dark half of *Magh* (January–February), the *Ekadashi* day or the eleventh day of both the bright and dark halves of a month, the *Navratra* days or the first nine days of *Ashvin* (September–October), eclipse days, and the day of *Jagran* or the fifteenth day of the bright half of *Ashadh* (June–July), besides, sometimes, the whole of the months of *Shravan* (July–August), the Purushottam or intercalary month, and the four months of the rainy season.

A Brahman in his *brahmacharya* (the period of his life which, according to the Shastras, should be devoted to the acquirement of learning, and which commences from the date of his being invested with the sacred thread and terminates at the age of twenty-three) and a widow are not allowed by the Shastras to sleep elsewhere than on beds made on the ground.

Pregnant women worship the earthen slope of a draw-well. Women, while in menstruation, sleep on the floor for four days. Some women, when they are separated from their husbands, also sleep in this fashion.

[1] Sacrifices in honour of Vishnu, Shiva, and Chandi respectively.

[2] A form of worship involving the repetition of the *Gayatri* verse, see p. 32, one hundred thousand times.

[3] The appointment of Brahmans to perform religious ceremonies.

In the Deccan, Brahman women draw in quartz powder the earth, sun, moon, cow's foot, the conch shell, &c., and worship the earth.

A dying person, two or three minutes before his death, is placed on the ground, which is first purified with cow-dung plaster. For ten days after a death, the members of the deceased's household and his relatives sleep on beds spread on the bare ground. If the loss be very affecting, the nearest relatives sleep on the floor for periods which may extend to three months, six months, or even for a year, and sometimes the penance lasts for their whole lives.

It is customary, among some sects, not to allow the spot lately occupied by a corpse in the house to be unoccupied for a single night. Some one must sleep on the spot for twelve consecutive days from the date of demise.

Pilgrims, after pilgrimage, abandon sensual pleasures, take their meals only once every day, and sleep on the floor. It is customary to sleep always on the ground while in holy places. Devotees, ascetics, *Sadhus*, and their disciples sleep on the ground.

Since it is held unholy in the Konkan to sleep on the bare ground, those whose parents die sleep on a woollen cloth on the ground till their parents' anniversary is over. Holy men, such as Wanprastas, Sanyasis, and Brahmans, are required to sleep on the ground. Some pious men sleep on the bare ground during the four months of the rainy season, at the expiry of which they present a bed to a Brahman. It is enjoined upon a prince to sleep on the bare ground on the eve of the coronation day.

Widows and women are required to sleep on the ground during their monthly courses. Women whose husbands are away are also to do the same. In the Ratnagiri District *Katkaris*,[1] on the day on which they wish to be possessed by a particular deity or spirit, are required to sleep on the earth. When people are on the point of death, they are made to lie on blades of *Darbha* grass (*Eragrostis cynosuroides*) placed on the earth. The performer of a sacrifice as well as one who has observed a vow are to sleep on the ground. The following

[1] A hill tribe in the Konkan Districts; see *T. & C. B.*, vol. ii, p. 170.

articles should not be allowed to touch the earth, viz. pearls, the *Shaligram* stone, an image of the god Vishnu, the *phallus* of Shiva, a conch shell, the sacred thread of a Brahman, flowers intended for worship, Basil leaves, and Govardan. The involuntary slaughter of a cow in the Deccan is expiated by sleeping on the earth.

The following lines are repeated in the morning before setting foot to the ground :

'O Goddess ! who is clothed (surrounded) by the sea, whose breasts are mountains, and who is the wife of Vishnu, I bow down to thee ; please forgive the touch of my feet. O Goddess Earth ! who art born by the power of Vishnu, whose surface is of the colour of a conch shell and who art the storehouse of innumerable jewels, I bow down to thee.'

Some women of the Thana District worship the earth daily during the four months of the rainy season, at the end of which they give a Brahman a piece of land or the money equivalent of it. Persons who perform a particular rite, i. e. the Sixteen-Mondays vow, are required to sleep on the bare ground. At sowing and harvest time, farmers appease the earth by offering it coco-nuts, fowls, rice mixed with curd, &c. The blood of a king and the balls of rice given to the *manes* of the dead are not allowed to touch the ground. People convey to a distant place the water of the Ganges, without placing it on the ground.

The earth is required to be worshipped before taking a portion of it for sacrificial purposes. A vessel containing water over which incantations have been repeated or water from a holy well or river is not allowed to touch the ground. On the fifteenth day of the bright half of *Ashvin* (September–October) every farmer prepares some sweetmeats in his house, and takes them to his farm. There he gathers five stones, worships them, and offers the sweetmeats to the earth. Afterwards he takes a portion of the food and scatters it over the farm. His family then gather there and take a hearty meal. In the evening the person who carried the food to the farm picks up some grains of barley and puts them into a basket. On return home the grains are thrown over the house.

In the Deccan, when new grain is heaped on the threshing-floor, Mother Earth is worshipped by offering to her cooked food or some animal. At the time of putting in the bullock stake in the middle of the threshing-floor, a coco-nut is offered to the earth. At the time of ploughing, red powder is offered to the earth. A small earthen jar containing a lamp, food, betel-leaves and nuts, is buried in the ground at the new moon of *Margashirsh* (November–December). This is dug up at harvest, filled with new grain, and brought home with the grain.

Musalmans sleep on the earth on the fortnight of the Muharram.

At the time of installing the godlings Kanubai and Ranubai, people visit a black-soil field, worship the earth, and take a little to place on the installation site.

Mountains and Hills

Mountains are held to be sacred in a variety of circumstances ; thus, some are valued for possessing medicinal drugs ; some are revered as the birthplaces of the gods, or as the residences of saints ; some for possessing many holy spots ; some because they were visited by Rama or the Pandavas ; some serve as guardians of the four quarters ; and some contain the sources of holy rivers.

Both the important ranges of the Presidency, the Sahyadri and the Satpura, are subjects of veneration in the popular mind. The Himalayas, the Vindhya Mountains, and the Nilgiris command special respect. Other sacred mountains are Girnar and Shetrunja in Kathiawar, Mount Abu, Pavagad near Baroda, Brahmagiri Arasur, Trymbak near Nasik, Koyalo, Govardhan near Mathura, Revatachal near Dwarka, and Hinglaj in Sind.

It is said that in ancient times there were deep miry ditches where Girnar and Abu stand at present. One day a cow belonging to the sage Vasishtha fell into one of them and was found by Kacha, the son of Brihaspati, after a long search. When the incident was brought to the notice of Vasishtha, he requested Meru (a mythical mountain) to send his two sons Girnar and Abu to occupy and fill the ditches. Girnar required sixty-eight holy places to accompany him ; and the boon was granted by the gods.

Girnar is one of the seven great mountains which once possessed wings. It is also known as the place where the sage Dattatraya performed religious austerities. The place is so holy that any person dying within a radius of sixteen miles from it is believed to attain salvation. A visit to the temples on Girnar absolves one from all sins ; and taking a turn round Girnar and Shetrunja is said to bring good fortune. Bhagwan manifests himself to those who ascend the Bhairavajaya summit on Girnar. There is a rock on this mountain of which it is said that those who cast themselves from it directly attain heaven.

Pavagad is known for the temple of Mahakali Mata. It is said that King Patai once propitiated her by austerities, and on being desired to demand a boon, asked the goddess to accompany him to his palace. The goddess was highly incensed at this request, and promptly destroyed him.

Hanuman, the monkey-god, once promised to take the mountain Govardhan to meet Rama. It is well known how the monkey allies of Rama constructed a bridge of rocks across the sea to Lanka, and how Hanuman supplied the requisite material by fetching huge mountains. Whilst engaged on this work, he was one day carrying the Govardhan mountain to the site of the bridge, when Rama issued an order that all monkeys who were fetching mountains should deposit their burdens at the spot where they stood at the moment of the order. Hanuman could not disobey the order of his lord, and he had accordingly to drop the Govardhan mountain near Mathura. In order to fulfil Hanuman's promise, however, Vishnu held the mountain over his head for seven days, at the time of his Krishna incarnation.

It is said that the inhabitants of the districts round Govardhan formerly revered and adored Indra. But Krishna condemned this custom, and introduced the worship of Govardhan. Indra was exasperated at this conduct, and poured tremendous rains on Gokal in order to drown Krishna and his followers. But Krishna held up the Govardhan mountain on his little finger and sheltered all his people under its cover. The mountain was supported in this manner for seven days, by the end of which the rains subsided and Indra confessed himself vanquished. Even now Vaishnavas form an image of Govardhan out of mud and worship it on the *Janmashtami* day, i.e. the eighth day of the dark half of *Shravan* (July–August).

The Oshama Hill near Patanvav (in the jurisdiction of Gondal) is noted for the beautiful temples of Tapakeshwar Mahadev and Matari Mata. It is said that Bhima, the second of the five Pandavas, first met the giantess Hidimba on this hill. The charcoal-like stones which are dug out in numbers from this hill are believed by the people to have been blackened by the blood of the giant Hidimb, the brother of Hidimba who was killed by Bhima.

Mount Shetrunja (or Shatrunjaya) possesses numerous Jain shrines and attracts thousands of pilgrims every year. The hearts of all pilgrims are believed to be purified from the moment they come within six miles of the mountain.

Mount Abu possesses the temple of Amba Mata, where Krishna's hair was clipped for the first time. Trymbak in Nasik is known for the temple of Trymbakeshwar and the source of the holy Godavari. About Revatachal, it is said that the mountain was golden in ancient times. In the Vindhya Mountains is situated the famous temple of Omkar Mandhata. The hermitage of Kakbhushundi in the Nilgiris was visited by Rama when he listened to the religious stories read out by that sage. The sage Agastya also is said to have resided in these mountains.

The temple of Hinglaj [1] stands on a hill, which is situated at a distance of eighteen days' journey by road from Karachi. The Mata is ministered to by a Musalman, and the place is mostly visited by *Atits, Bavas, Khatris, Chhipas, Mochis,* and other low-caste Hindus. On occasions the doors of the temple spontaneously open, and after the devotees have visited the goddess they again shut in the same mysterious manner.

As the abode of Shiva and as containing the sources of the holiest of rivers, the Himalayas are the most sacred of all mountains, and possess many holy places of pilgrimage, such as Badrinarayan, Kedarnath, Hardwar, &c. Badrinarayan is the favourite resort of those who have relinquished the world and who only wish to meditate on the Divine Being.

[1] The Babylonian Nanna, according to some authorities.

The sages Nara and Narayan are said to have performed religious austerities in this place, and eighty-eight thousand sages are believed to be similarly occupied there to-day. Owing to the excessive cold, the place is extremely difficult to reach. Pilgrims carry burning hearths with them to protect themselves against cold. Besides it is necessary to cross the Pathar-nadi (or stony river), of which the water, if touched, turns one into stone. The method of crossing this river is to suspend slings above it and to swing from one sling to another.

A hill called Swargarohan is believed to be twenty miles to the north of Badrikedarnath, and is said to lead to heaven. In ancient times the Pandavas had repaired to this place in order to do penance for the sin of having killed their kinsmen in the Great War. But when they tried to ascend to heaven by the Swargarohan Hill, only Yudhishthir and his faithful dog were able to reach their goal; the rest were frozen in the snow.

Mount Kailasa, the abode of Shiva, is supposed to be situated in the northern part of the Himalayas. The mountain is described as always covered with verdure and full of beautiful gardens and of palaces made of jewels, with roads paved with golden dust and crystal stone. It is said that Ravan, the king of Lanka, once uprooted this mountain and held it on the palm of his hand, in order to display his prowess. The demon Bhasmasur, who was enamoured of the goddess Parvati, is said to have performed the same feat in order to frighten Shiva.

Another mythical mountain is Meru, which is supposed to occupy the centre of the earth. The sun, the moon, and all the planets revolve round this mountain, and it therefore plays an important part in the causation of day and night. For night falls on one side of the earth when the sun goes to the other side of Meru; and the day begins when the sun emerges from that side of the mountain. Meru is five hundred thousand miles in height, and penetrates the earth to the depth of one hundred and twenty thousand miles. Its eastern side appears white, the southern is yellow, the western is black, and the northern red. The mountain is also believed to consist of gold and gems. The Ganges, in her fall from the heavens, is said to have descended first on the top of this mountain and then to have flowed in four streams in four directions. The southern stream is known as the Ganges; the northern, in Tartary, is called Bhadrasoma; the eastern is the same as the Sita; and the western is named Chax or the Oxus. The top of this mountain is believed to be inhabited by gods, celestial musicians, and sages. According to the *Yogavasishtha*, there is a magic tree (*kalpa-vriksha*) on the Lalmani summit of Meru, where a sage named Bhushundkak is engaged in devotional prayers since time immemorial. The Puranas declare that Vaivasvat Manu, the first man, resided near Meru, and that his descendants migrated to Ayodhya to found there a kingdom which was afterwards ruled over by Rama.

It is believed by some people that mountain-tops are inhabited by a class of recluses, called Aghori-bavas, who devour human beings. The Kalika hill near Girnar is believed to be frequented by *Joganis* (female harpies) who take the lives of visitors to the hill, and it is said that none who visits the place is ever known to return. Persons who visit the temple of Kalikamata on Mount Girnar always lose one of their party, who falls a victim to the goddess.

A mountain near the village Pule, in the District of Ratnagiri, is held sacred on account of the residence of the god Ganpati in that place. For this reason people walk round the mountain and worship it. Tradition says that Ganpati was at first at Gule in the Ratnagiri District, but on account of the sanctity of the place being violated by some wicked persons the god transferred his residence to Pule. At Gule there is still a very beautiful temple of Ganpati, though it is now in a dilapidated condition. The cave of the sage Much-kund near Machal on the Sahyadri mountains is considered sacred. In the Konkan it is not held sinful to ascend a mountain or a hill, though to sit upon its summit is considered sinful. The hill of Mirya near Ratnagiri is considered sacred. This hill is believed to be a particle (*miri*) of the mythological mountain Dronagiri.

A hill near Dharavi in the Thana District is consecrated by the temple of a goddess upon the top. This goddess is said to preserve ships at sea, and people are occasionally possessed by her. It is said that a Roman Catholic priest met instantaneous death on having insulted her.

The hill of Mahalakshmi in the same District is held sacred.

The villagers consider it dangerous to ascend this hill. On the hill of the same name is a temple of the goddess Jivadhani, who is said to preserve children from small-pox. The following story is told in connexion with the goddess: A person in need of money used to place before her image as large a heap of flowers as he wanted gold, stating that he would return the gold when he had done with it. He used then to go home and return on an appointed day for the gold, which was sure to be found where he had placed the heap of flowers. Once a man failed to return the gold, and thenceforth the goddess withheld her bounty. There is no door to the temple of this goddess. It is only through a hole in a big stone that one can have a view of her image. Sweet scent is said to be continually emitted from this hole. The goddess is said to have fastened the door of her temple for the following reason: One day the goddess was walking at the foot of the hill at night. A cowherd who happened to be there was bewitched by her matchless beauty and fell a prey to evil desire. He pursued her to the top of the hill, when the goddess, divining his motive, fastened the door of her temple with a prodigious stone. On the same hill is a cattle shed in which fresh cow-dung is said to be always found. This place being inaccessible to cows and other quadrupeds, the people believe that the goddess keeps a cow of her own.

The hill of Tungar is consecrated by the temple of a certain goddess upon it. There is also a very famous hill near Arnala, called the hill of Buddha. This hill was once the seat of a king belonging to the weaver caste. Recently a pond was discovered upon it, in which was found a stone-box containing a begging-pot and a diamond. A great fair is held annually on the hill of Motmavali near Bandra in the Thana District. The devotees of the deity are Hindus, Parsis, and Christians. It is said this goddess was once worshipped by Hindus only. A Brahman is the priest of the *Pir* on the hill of Baba Malang near Kalyan. It is said that the *Pir* has declared that no Moslem priest should worship him. The Hindus and Moslems worship him alike.

Brahmans do not cross the top of a mountain without stopping for a short time before ascending the summit.

At a short distance from Chaul in the Kolaba District is a hill dedicated to the god Dattatraya, in whose honour a great fair is held annually. The following story is told in connexion with this hill: In ancient times a Brahman used to practise austerities on this hill near a *Tulsi* or holy Basil plant (the place on which the present temple stands). He used to spend the whole day there, but returned home at nightfall. On his way home fearful scenes were often presented to him, and in his dreams he was asked not to go there any more. But the Brahman was obdurate. He persisted in his resolution to practise austerities for a number of years, and at last succeeded in obtaining a personal interview with the god Dattatraya, who commanded him to bow down to his feet. From that time pious men live on this hill and offer their prayers to the god Dattatraya. Nearly four hundred steps have been constructed for the ascent of this hill, and additional steps are being built every year. Here also are some springs of pure water. It is worth while to note that the priest of this god is a Shudra by caste. On the north-east side of the hill dedicated to the god Dattatraya stands the temple of the goddess Hinglaj. To the north of this temple are four caves, while to the west is a deep den resembling a well, through which a lane appears to have been dug. This is said to be the road excavated by the Pandavas to enable them to go to Benares. At a distance of two miles from Akola in the Kolaba District is a hill called Mallikarjun. This is said to be a small stone fallen from the mythological mountain Dronagiri. This hill is said to contain many medical herbs. The hill at Kankeshwar near Alibag is held sacred, and tradition says that in ancient times it had golden dust upon it. A cave at Ambivali near Karjat in the Kolaba District consists of seven rooms, one of which is spacious enough to accommodate five hundred persons. In the same District there is another cave at Kondhavane.

The mountains having caves and temples of deities are generally worshipped by the Hindus. The Abucha Pahad, the Girnar, the Panchmadhi, the Brahmagiri, the Sahyadri, the Tungar, the Jivadancha hill, the Munja hill at Junnar, the Tugabaicha hill, the Ganesh Lene, and the Shivabai are the principal holy mountains in the Bombay Presidency.

Mount Abu, known as the Abucha Pahad, is believed to be very sacred, and many Hindus go on a pilgrimage to that mountain.

Hills are worshipped at Ganpati Pule and Chaul. At Pule there is a temple of the god Ganpati, the son of Shiva, and at Chaul in the Kolaba District there is a temple of the god Dattatraya.

The place which produces sound when water is poured over it is considered to be holy, and is worshipped by the people.

In the Deccan, hills are worshipped by the people on the *Narak chaturdashi* day in *Dipawali*, the fourteenth day of the dark half of *Ashvin* (September–October). The legend of this worship is that the god Shri Krishna lifted the Govardhan mountain on this day, and protected the people of this world. A hill made of cow-dung is worshipped at every house on the *Narak chaturdashi* day.

Rivers and Ponds

The most popular of the holy rivers are the Ganges, the Jumna (or Jamuna), the Narbada, the Saraswati (near Sidhpur), the Kaveri, the Godavari, the Gandaki, the Sarayu, the Damodari, the Sindhu (or Indus), the Mahanadi, the Gomati (near Dwarka), the Brahmaputra, the Sabarmati, the Ghels (near Gaddheda), the Tungabhadra, the Suvarnabhadra, the Bhadrashita, the Jambuvati, the Phalaku (or Phalgu), the Kaushiki, the Tamraparni, the Sita, and the Alakananda. Any point where three rivers meet is also a sacred place. Most of the holy rivers are the subject of many traditions, and books have been written to celebrate their merits.

The Ganges, the Jumna, and the Godavari are said to be the holiest of all rivers. There are a number of beliefs about the origin of the Ganges. One of them is that the Ganges is the stream caused by King Bali washing the feet of Vaman (the dwarf incarnation of Vishnu). Another story relates that the god Brahma was exhausted by overwork at the time of the marriage of Shiva and Parvati. The gods, therefore, created water from their own lustres, and gave it to Brahma in a gourd, to be used in a similar contingency. When Vishnu in his dwarf incarnation bestrode the heavens with a single step, Brahma washed his toe in the water from this gourd. A stream was thus created called Swarga-ganga and brought down to the earth by Bhagirath, the grandson of Sagar. When the Ganges fell from the heavens, it was supported and held fast by Shiva, in his matted hair. It was released by his loosening the hair, and in its course inundated the sacrificial ground of King Jahnu. The latter, being angry, drank up its waters. On the entreaties of Bhagirath, he released the stream by tearing off his thigh. The river then flowed to the spot where the sixty thousand sons of Sagar were burnt to ashes; and it is said by some that one of the sixty thousand was saved at the end of each year up to the year 1955 of the Samvat era (corresponding to A.D. 1899), by the end of which period all the sixty thousand had attained salvation. From the earth the Ganges went to the nether regions. Thus flowing in the heavens, on the earth, and in the lower regions, the Ganges is called *Tripathaga* (i.e. flowing in three courses). In its divine form the Ganges is the wife of Shiva. Owing to the curse of Brahma, she was born in human form in this world and was married to Shantanu, by whom she became the mother of Bhishma, the heroic uncle of the Kauravas and the Pandavas.

It is customary among Hindu pilgrims when they visit Benares to take away with them copper vessels filled with water of the Ganges, and to worship the Ganga when they reach their homes after the pilgrimage. A figure is drawn in seven different kinds of corn; the bowl is placed on it; red powder, frankincense, and an oblation of food are offered; a *ghi*-lamp is lighted; a Brahman woman is dressed as Uma, the wife of Shiva, and Brahmans are entertained at a feast, presents being given to them.

The water of the Ganges, as well as that of the Jumna, is believed to be so pure that it cannot be affected by microbes, even if kept for years in the house. This quality is believed to be a manifestation of its divine nature. It is further called 'purifier of the fallen' and exculpates the sinful from their sins, either by a single draught or by bathing in it. Ganges water is kept in most Hindu families, a draught of it taken by a dying person being believed to secure eternal salvation for the soul.

A vow is observed by women, in honour of the Ganges, for the first ten days of the month of *Jyeshth* (May–June). On these days they rise early in the morning and bathe in the holy waters of the Ganges.

Sometimes *ghi*-lamps are placed upon the waters of the Ganges or the Jumna, and vessels of metal, pice, and coco-nuts are cast into the stream. At such a time, when many people are standing on the banks offering prayers with folded hands, or engaged in the waving of lights, the river presents a very picturesque scene, the numerous lights being reflected in the water.

The Jumna or Yamuna is the daughter of the Sun, and the sister of Yama, the god of death. The banks of the Jumna are well known as the scene of the amorous sports of the god Krishna. The story of the defeat of the demon Kaliya Nag, who was ejected from the Jumna by Krishna, is well known.

It is said that those who have bathed in the Jumna or have once tasted its water need not be afraid of Yama, the god of Death. It is considered meritorious among the Hindus to bathe the image of Shiva in water from the holy Jumna or the Ganges or the Godavari. There is a popular verse in honour of the Jumna which runs: 'Victory to thee, O Yamuna, flowing through the Madhu-vana (the Madhu woods), the bearer of shining waters, the companion of Jahnavi, the daughter of Sindhu, the ornament of the enemy of Madhu (viz. Krishna), the appeaser of Madhava, the dispeller of the danger of Gokal, the destroyer of the sins of the world, the giver of intellect, the scene of the amorous sports of Keshava. Victory to thee! O remover of difficulties, purify me.'

The banks of the Godavari are known as the site of the hermitage of Gautama. When the planet Grihaspati (Jupiter) enters the *Sinha-rashi* (the constellation Leo) the holy Ganges goes to the Godavari, and remains there for one year. During that year, all the gods are believed to bathe in this river. Thousands of pilgrims visit Nasik to offer prayers to the Godavari, and after bathing in the river, give alms to Brahmans. Similarly, on the *Kapilashashthi* day, on which six conjunctive incidents occur simultaneously, the virtue of all holy places is believed to be concentrated in the Godavari at Nasik

The mere sight of the Narbada has the same effect as a bath in the Ganges or the Jumna. It is said that the Narbada is the image of Shiva, and that fragments of the stony bow of Shiva are to be found in its bed. The stones in the bed of this river have the same sanctity as the images of the god Shiva. *Shaligram* stones, which are worshipped as the images of Vishnu, are found in this river. It is an act of high merit among Hindus to take a turn round the Narbada, i.e. to travel along the banks of the river, inhabited as the region is by many *Sadhus* and other holy persons. Ashvatthama, the immortal son of Drona, is believed to reside on the banks of this river and to pay occasional visits to the Bhils in the neighbourhood. The *Shukla-tirtha*, situated on the Narbada, is visited by numerous pilgrims, and a fair is held there in every sixtieth year.

The sage Kapila instructed his mother Devahuti with divine knowledge on the banks of the Saraswati. Since then, the river is held sacred and funeral ceremonies—*Shraddhas*—are performed on its banks in honour of departed female ancestors. Similarly *Shraddhas* in honour of male ancestors are performed at the confluence of the Ganges, the Jumna, and the Saraswati at Allahabad.

Of the Gandaki it is said that it contains as many images of Shiva as there are stones. The *Shaligram* stone is found in this river also. The Sarayu is sacred as the scene of the childish sports of Ramchandra, the hero of the *Ramayana*. On the banks of the Phalaku or Phalgu, Ramchandra performed *Shraddha* ceremonies in honour of his father Dasharath.

If a river source issues from an opening in the shape of a cow's mouth, the stream is called *dhodh*, and is considered as sacred as the holy Ganges. A bath in such a *dhodh* has the same efficacy as the Ganges for absolving persons from their sins.

The River Savitri in the Kolaba District takes its rise near Mahableshwar and is considered very sacred. The following traditionary account is given of its origin: The god Brahma had two wives, Savitri and Gayatri. A dispute having arisen between them, they both jumped over a precipice. Savitri assumed the form of a river and fell into the sea near Bankot.

Gayatri, on the other hand, concealed herself in the River Savitri and manifested herself as a spring near Harihareshwar in the Janjira State.

Women anxious for sons throw into the Godavari plantains, flowers, coco-nuts and winnowing fans as offerings. A bath in the waters of a holy river washes away the sins of the bather. It is also meritorious to repeat the names of the several holy rivers. The performance of *Shraddha* ceremonies on the banks of a holy river secures the felicity of deceased ancestors in heaven. At the time of performing *Shraddhas* at a holy place, Hindus shave their moustaches, bathe in the sacred waters, and then go through the necessary ceremonies, in the course of which rice-balls (*pindas*) are offered to the spirits of dead ancestors. Brahmans are feasted after the ceremonies, and a money offering is given to them. *Tarpan* (an offering of water with flowers, ointment, red lac, coco-nuts, and betel) is frequently made to the river on the banks of which the ceremonies are performed. The bones of a deceased person, left unburnt after cremation of the body, are gathered together and thrown into holy rivers such as the Ganges, the Jumna, and the Godavari, for the purification of his soul.

When heavy floods threaten a village or a city with serious injury, the king or the headman should go in procession to propitiate the river with flowers, coco-nuts, and other offerings in order that the floods may subside. A story is related of the occurrence of heavy floods in a village in the Jatalpur subdivision, when a certain lady placed an earthen vessel (ordinarily used for curdling milk), containing a *ghi*-lamp, afloat on the floods, whereupon the waters were at once seen to recede.

Besides the holy rivers, there are numerous *kunds*, i.e. sacred pools, which are regarded with equal reverence, and in which a bath has the same efficacy for destroying sin. Similarly, they are equally suitable places for the performance of *Shraddha* ceremonies. These *kunds* are the subject of numerous beliefs, and each of them has a certain peculiar merit of its own. Six miles to the east of Dwarka, near the sea-coast, there is a *kund* called Pind-tarak, where many persons go to perform the *Shraddha* and the Narayan-bali ceremonies. They first bathe

G 2

in the *kund*: then, with its water, they prepare *pindas*, and place them in a metal dish; red lac is applied to the *pindas*, and a piece of cotton thread wound round them, the metal dish being then dipped in the *kund*, when the *pindas*, instead of sinking, are said to remain floating on the water. The process is believed to earn a good status for the spirits of departed ancestors in heaven. It is further said that physical ailments brought on by the degradation or fallen condition of ancestors in the other world are remedied by the performance of *Shraddha* on this *kund*.

The Damodar *kund* is situated near Junagadh. It is said that if the bones of a deceased person which remain unburnt after his cremation are dipped in this *kund*, the soul of that person obtains final emancipation.

There is a reservoir on Mount Girnar, known as Rasakupi-kavav. It is believed that the body of a person bathing in it becomes as hard as marble, and that if a piece of stone or iron is dipped in the water, it is instantly transformed into gold. But the reservoir is only visible to saints and sages who are gifted with a supernatural vision.

Benares contains a *vav* (well) called Gyan-vav, in which there is an image of Vishweshwar (the Lord of the universe, i.e. Shiva). A bath in the water from this *vav* is believed to confer upon a person the gift of divine knowledge.

In the village of Chunval, a few miles to the north of Viramgam, there is a *kund* known as Loteshwar, near which stands a *Pipal* tree. Persons possessed by ghosts or devils are freed from possession by pouring water at the foot of the tree and taking turns round it, remaining silent the while.

A bath in the Man-sarovar pool near Bahucharaji is said to cause the wishes of the bather to be fulfilled. There is a local tradition that a Rajput woman was turned into a male Rajput of the Solanki class by a bath in its waters.

There is a *kund* called Zilaka near Zinzuwada with a temple of Naleshwar Mahadev near it. The *kund* is said to have been built at the time of King Nala. It is believed locally that every year, on the fifteenth day of the bright half of *Bhadrapad* (August–September), the holy Ganges visits the *kund* by an underground route. A great fair is held there on that day, when people bathe in the *kund* and give alms to the poor. There is also another *kund* close by, known as Bholava, where the River Saraswati is believed to have halted and manifested herself on her way to the sea.

There is a *kund* in Baladana near Wadhwan, dedicated to Hol, the favourite goddess of the *Charans.* In this *kund,* black or red pieces of cotton thread are sometimes seen floating in the water. They appear only for a moment, and sink if any one endeavours to seize them. The appearance of black pieces forebodes famine : but the red one foretells prosperity.

In Bhadakon near Chuda there is a *kund* called Garigavo. The place is celebrated as the spot of the hermitage of the sage Bhrigu, and a fair is held there annually on the last day of *Bhadrapad* (August–September).

Persons anxious to attain heaven bathe in the Mrigi *kund* on Mount Girnar ; and a bath in the Revati *kund,* which is in the same place, confers male issue on the bather. There is also a *kund* of the shape of an elephant's footprint, *Pagahein,* on Mount Girnar. It never empties and is held most sacred by pilgrims. People bathe in the Gomati *kund* near Dwarka, and take a little of the earth from its bed, for the purification of their souls. In the village of Babara, Babhruvahan, the son of Arjun, is said to have constructed several *kunds,* all of which are believed to be holy.

The Lasundra *kund* near Lasundra in the Kaira District and the Tulsi-shyama *kund* on Mount Girnar contain hot waters. There is also a hot *kund* called *Devki-unai,* about thirty miles to the south of Surat. There the waters remain hot throughout the whole of the year, except on the fifteenth day of the bright half of *Chaitra* (March–April). On this day the waters cool, and people can bathe in the *kund.* Many pilgrims visit the place on this occasion, to offer money, coconuts, and red lac to the Unai deity whose temple stands near the *kund.* It is said that King Rama built this *kund* while performing a local sacrifice, and brought water up from the nether regions by shooting an arrow into the earth.

Other holy *kunds* are : the Bhim *kund,* the Gomukhi-ganga, and the Kamandalu *kund* on Mount Girnar near the temple of Bhimnath Mahadev ; the Radha *kund,* the Lalita *kund,* and the Krishna-sarovar in Dwarka; the Rama-sarovar, the Sita *kund*, and the Devki-unai *kund* in Oudh; and the Suraj *kund* and the Hanumandhara *kund* on Mount Girnar.

A man is said to be released from rebirth if he takes a bath in the pond named Katkale-tirtha near Nasik. Bows are said to be reduced to powder if thrown into a certain *kund* at Uddhar-Rameshwar in the same District. *Kupotsarga* is defined to be the digging of a well for the benefit of the public and abandoning one's right of ownership over it.

A pond near Khopoli in the Kolaba District is held very sacred. The following story is related in connexion with it: The villagers say that the water-nymphs in the pool used to provide pots for marriage festivities if a written application were made to them a day previous to the wedding. The pots were, however, required to be returned within a limited time. But one man having failed to comply with this condition, they have ceased to lend pots. Another interesting story is associated with the same pond. It is as follows: A man had fallen into the pond and was taken to the abode of the nymphs. He was, however, returned by them after a few days on the understanding that he would be recalled if he spoke of what he had seen there. One day he communicated to the people the good things that he enjoyed there, and to the surprise of all he was found dead immediately after. Water-nymphs are said to reside in a pond at Varsai in the Kolaba District. Consequently persons that are held unclean, e.g. women in their monthly courses, &c., are not allowed to touch it. The nymphs of the same lake were once said to lend pots on festive occasions. It is said that the water-nymphs used to provide ornaments for marriage and other ceremonies, if returned within a prescribed period. But some people having failed to return them, they ceased to lend them.

In the Ratnagiri District the spring at Rajapur, called the *Rajapurchi Ganga*, is considered very sacred. It flows from the roots of a Banyan tree. There are fifteen *kunds* or ponds, and the principal *kund* always remains filled with water. On occasions a big fair is held and people from distant places come to bathe and worship at the spring. Some people believe that many of the lakes, springs, &c., situated in the Kolhapur

State are sacred. A spring or rivulet that flows to the east is considered specially sacred. It is called a *Surya-Vansi* spring, and it is considered meritorious to bathe in it. In the village of Kunkauli in the Ratnagiri District if a person is bitten by a snake or other poisonous reptile, no medicine is administered to him, but holy water brought from the temple of the village goddess is given to him to drink, and it is said that the patient is thus cured. The waterfall at Maral near Devarkuha, where the River Ban takes its rise, is held sacred. At Shivam in the Ratnagiri District the people use the *tirths* of a deity as medicine for diseases due to poison. They say that it is the sole remedy they apply in such cases. There are ponds at Manora in Goa territory, and Vetore in the Savantwadi State, the water of which is used as medicine for the cure of persons suffering from the poison of snakes, mice, spiders, and scorpions. There are seven *kunds* at Nirmal in the Thana District, forming a large lake. This lake is said to have been formed from the blood of the demon Vimalasur. At Shahapur there is a holy spring of hot water under a *Pipal* tree. It is called *Ganga*. There are *kunds* of hot water in the *Vaitarna* river in the Thana District, in which people bathe on the thirteenth day of the dark half of *Chaitra* (March–April). There are also springs of hot water on the bank of the Surya river at Vajreshvari and at Koknere, in the Thana District. A handful of corn, if thrown into the hot-water *kunds* at Tungar, is said to be boiled at once. It is held holy to bathe in the *kunds* of hot water that are situated in the Rivers Tansa and Banganga in the Thana District. The water of a well which is drawn without touching the earth or without being placed upon the ground is given as medicine for indigestion. Similarly, the water of seven tanks, or at least of one pond, in which lotuses grow is said to check the virulence of measles, small-pox, &c. A bath in a certain tank in the Thana District is said to cure persons suffering from the itch, and water purified by repeating incantations over it is also said to be a good remedy for the same disease.

The water of a tank or a well is supposed to be wholesome to a person of indifferent health, if given to him to drink without placing it upon the ground. Some people believe that the water of the Ganges is so holy and powerful that if bows are thrown into it they are instantly reduced to powder. The repair of lakes, caravansaries, temples, &c., is held more meritorious than their actual erection. It is enjoined upon a man to perform a certain rite if he wishes to relinquish his right of ownership over a well or tank, and after this rite is performed it can be utilized for public purposes. But no ceremony is required to be performed if a well is dug for the benefit of the public.

The most famous of the sacred lakes are Pampa, Bindu, Pushkar and Sambhar near Ajmere, Man-sarovar near Bahucharaji, Narayan-sarovar in Cutch, Ravanrhad in the Himalayas, and Ramarhad. The following popular myth is related about Man-sarovar:

Two kings once agreed that the two children that should first be born to them should marry each other. But it happened that both the kings had daughters. One of them, however, concealed the fact, and gave out that the child born to him was a son. So that when the children attained a marriageable age, they were married to each other according to the agreement. But the wife found out the secret when she went to stay with her supposed husband, and disclosed it to her parents, who invited the counterfeit son-in-law to their house with the object of ascertaining the truth. The alleged son, however, suspected the design and fled, with a mare and a bitch. On arriving near Man-sarovar, the animals went into the lake in order to refresh themselves, when there was an immediate transformation; and the bitch and the mare came out a dog and a horse. On observing this miracle, their mistress followed their example and was also turned into a male. The story is still sung by girls in a song during the *Navaratra* holidays.

There is a belief that the ancient golden city of Dwarka, the capital of the god Krishna, still exists in the sea, although it is invisible to the eyes of mortals. A story is told of a man named Pipo Bhagat who, once perceiving a golden bowl floating in the sea, plunged into the water and saw the golden palaces of Dwarka and the god Krishna resting therein. It is said that he returned with the tide and related his experience to several people.

WELLS

When a well is to be dug, an expert is first called to select a likely spot on which to dig. A Brahman is then consulted as to the auspicious hour on which the work of digging should be commenced. For this purpose, Tuesdays and those days on which the earth sleeps are to be avoided. The earth is supposed to be asleep on the following six days in every month, namely, the 1st, the 7th, the 9th, the 10th, the 14th, and the 24th days following the day on which the sun crosses from one constellation to another. Excluding these days, a date is generally fixed on which the moon is favourable to the constructor of the well.

On the appointed day, the expert, the constructor of the well, the Brahman priest, and the labourers go to the place where the well is to be dug, and an image of the god Ganpati—the protector of all auspicious ceremonies—is first installed on the spot and worshipped with five kinds of offerings, milk, curds, *ghi*, honey, and sugar. A piece of green silk cloth, about two feet long, is then spread on the spot, and a pound and a quarter of wheat, a coco-nut, betels, dates, and copper coin are placed on it. A copper bowl, containing some silver or gold coins and filled with water, is also placed there; the mouth of the bowl is covered with the leaves of the Asoka tree (*Polyalthea longifolia*) and a coco-nut is placed over the leaves. After this, the priest recites sacred hymns and asks his host to perform the earth-worshipping ceremonies. Among favourite offerings to Ganpati and the earth in the course of worship and in the performance of these ceremonies are: curds, milk, honey, molasses, coco-nuts, *dhana* (a kind of spice), leaves of *nagvel* (*Piper Betel*), and red lac. The expert who is called to choose a proper site for the well offers frankincense and a coco-nut to the spot, and lights a lamp thereon. After the earth-worshipping ceremonies are over, the host distributes sugar or molasses among the bystanders, and offers a sum of money to the expert, who usually refuses it, asking the host to spend it in charity. Those who accept money give away a part of it in alms to the poor.

Sometimes, to secure the unobstructed completion of the

work, the god Ganpati and the goddess Jaladevi are installed and worshipped daily, till water appears in the well. Some people, however, install the goddess Jaladevi after the appearance of water, when a stone is taken out from the bottom of the well and is plastered with red lead to represent the goddess, and is ceremoniously worshipped. When the construction of the well is complete, the ceremony in vogue after the completion of a new building [1] or the water-festival [2] is celebrated, Brahmans being entertained at a feast, and presents given.

In the Karnatak (Dharwar) the site selected for a well is worshipped with red powder, limes, and coco-nuts, and a square is drawn in quartz powder. When water is found, it is worshipped in a silver cup and offered to the priests.

It is a belief among Hindus that to give alms in secret confers a great merit on the donor. Some orthodox people, therefore, throw pice into wells, considering it to be a kind of secret charity.

A golden cow is often thrown into a newly built well as an offering to the water deities. There is a well at Mandangad in Kathiawar, the water of which serves as medicine to cure the poison of snakes and other reptiles.

The water of the Krukalas well in the island of Shankhodwar is believed to cure fever and diseases caused by morbid heat. A draught of the water of the Gomukhi-ganga near Girnar makes one proof against an attack of cholera.

The water of a well which is polluted on account of a person being drowned in it cures children of bronchitis and cough.

There is a well near Ramdorana, of which the water is effective against cough, and the water of the Bhamaria well near Vasawad possesses the same virtue.

The water of the Mrigi pool near Junagadh remedies leprosy.

The Pipli well near Zalawad and the Detroja well near Kolki are well known for the stimulative effect of their waters on the digestion.

If a dark stone is found in the course of digging a well, the water of that well is believed to have medicinal properties.

The birth of a child under the *mul nakshatra* endangers the life of its father; but the misfortune is averted if the child

[1] *Vastu.* [2] *Jalotsava.*

and its parents bathe in water drawn from one hundred and eight wells. Such water, if swallowed, is said to cure delirium.

In the island of Shial there is a well where mothers who cannot suckle their children for want of milk wash their bodices. When they afterwards wear these bodices, these are believed to be able to cause the due secretion of milk.

Rags are never offered to wells, but it is common to offer them copper coins and betel-nuts. Sometimes flags are hoisted near holy wells in honour of the water-goddess Jaladevi. Travellers hoist flags on certain wells and throw copper coins into them in the course of their journey. The origin of this offering is said to be in the desire of travellers to prevent people from committing a nuisance near wells.

Some wells are noted as being the abode of spirits who have the power of effecting certain cures. It is customary to throw a pice into such wells. When a person is bitten by a rabid dog, he goes to a well inhabited by a *vachharo*, the spirit who cures hydrophobia, with two earthen cups filled with milk, with a pice in each, and empties the contents into the water. One such well, known as *Kutri-bavadi* or dog's-well, is found near Sholapur in the Deccan.

In Kanara it is believed that the water of a well if drawn out early in the morning, in a pot which does not touch the sides, cures disease.

Water-nymphs

It is believed that there is a class of wicked water-nymphs called *Asara* or *Mavaliya* who generally dwell in wells, ponds, or rivers, far from the habitation of men. Other names for these nymphs are *Khais, Zoting, Yakshini, Vilashi, Lav, Varuna, Jala matrika*. Campbell for the Konkan gives also *Bapdev, Hadal*, or *Hedali*.[1] Whenever these nymphs come across a lonely man or woman entering a well, pond, &c., they drag that person under water. The village of Mithbav in the Ratnagiri District is a well-known resort of these *Asaras*, and many instances are given by the villagers of persons being drowned and carried off in the river by these wicked nymphs.

[1] *S. B. B. C.*, p. 203.

A tank in the village of Hindalem in the same district has a similar reputation. The people of the Konkan believe that water-nymphs are sometimes seen in the form of women near wells, rivers, and ponds. Some say that the water-nymphs and water-spirits confer objects desired by worshippers if they are propitiated by prayers. At Sangamner in Ahmednagar District, the water-spirits are believed to claim a yearly victim. It is usual in the Deccan to feed seven unwidowed women in the name of water-spirits to ensure their favour.

A spirit called Girha is supposed to reside in water. It is said to make mischief with man in a variety of ways by enticing him into deep water. The Jakin is said to be a deity residing in water. Persons drowned in water are believed to become water-spirits, and to trouble innocent passers-by.

When a person dies an accidental death and before the fulfilment of his worldly desires, his soul passes into a degraded or fallen condition, and it is not released from this state till *Shraddhas* have been duly performed in its name, and the objects of its desire dedicated to it with proper ritual. The same fate befalls those souls which do not receive the funeral rice-balls with the proper obsequies. Such fallen souls become ghosts and goblins, and are to be found where water is, i.e. near a well, a tank, or a river.

Those who meet death by drowning or who commit suicide by drowning become spirits, residing near the scene of their death, and are a source of danger to all who approach the water; for instance, in Monapuri and Sasai, there are two mysterious watery pits haunted by spirits which take the lives of one or two buffaloes every year. *Matas* and *Shenkhinis* also haunt wells, springs, and tanks, and either drown or enter the persons of those who go near their resorts. There is a widespread belief in the Deccan that a drowning person is being claimed by water-spirits and that any one attempting to rescue him would also become a victim.

The people of the Thana District believe that water-nymphs reside in every reservoir of water. Some people, however, believe that the water-nymphs dwell in those lakes in which lotuses grow. These nymphs are said to do harm to children and young women, especially when they set out for a walk accompanied by their brother Gavala. They are usually dangerous on the no-moon day. The people worship the images of the following seven water-nymphs, viz. Machhi, Kurmi, Karkati, Darduri, Jatupi, Somapa, and Makari.

Persons who are possessed in this manner can be freed by sorcerers, who give them a magic thread to wear. In the Deccan men are thought to be possessed at times by water-spirits. Eggs, fowls, &c., are waved round them and left on the bank of the river where the nymph is thought to have possessed them.

There is a well near Movaiya in which a Pinjari (a female cotton-carder) is said to have been drowned, and to have been turned into a ghost, in which form she occasionally presents herself to the people.

Another water-spirit haunts an old well, called Madha, in Wadhwan and drowns one human being every third year as a victim. But a male spirit named *Kshetrapal* resides in the entrance to the well and saves those who fall near the entrance. A person is, however, sure to be drowned if he falls into any other part of the well. A ghost also resides in the well at Hampar near Dhrangadhra and terrifies the people at times.

The goddess Rainadevi resides in water, and is worshipped by virgins on the fifteenth day of the bright half of *Ashadh* (June–July), when they grow tender wheat-plants in an earthen vessel and present them to her, remaining awake for the whole of the night to sing songs in her honour.

Darya-Pir, the patron of Luhanas and Kharvas, resides in the sea; and vows are observed in his honour by these people on the second day of the bright half of every month, when they pass a little water through his sieve.

It is well known that a drowning person clings fast to any one who tries to save him, and endangers the lives of both himself and his saviour. There is also a widespread belief in the Konkan and Karnatak that it is unlucky to rescue a drowning person, as the water-spirit, deprived of its victim, will bring some evil on the rescuer. It is also believed by some people that the messengers of Varuna (the lord of all waters) seize those persons who bathe in a river earlier than the usual hour in the morning; and the act of saving a drowning person thus deprives Varuna of his victim and brings down the wrath of that deity.

Sometimes, for the sake of salvation, a person drowns himself in a holy river, such as the Ganges or the Jumna. In such a case the relatives and other persons refrain from interference, and do not try to rescue the person.

The following places are said to be inhabited by water-spirits: The channel of Kalamba, the tanks of Sopara and Utaratal, and the lake called Tambra-tirtha at Bassein. Water-nymphs are supposed to drown a person who tries to save another fallen into water. A species of small men named *Uda*, otherwise called water-spirits, are said to dwell in water and subsist on fishes.

Similarly, the golden Lanka of Ravan is still believed to exist under the sea, ruled over by Bibhishan, the brother of Ravan, and visible only to the eyes of saints and holy persons. It is a common belief that the nether regions are inhabited by a species of semi-divine beings, half men and half serpents, called Nags, who possess magnificent palaces under the water. The story of Kaliya Nag, who resided at the bottom of the Jumna and was driven from that place by Krishna, is well known. There are a number of mythological traditions in the Puranas of kings and princes having visited these palaces in watery regions, and of their having brought back beautiful daughters of Nags therefrom. For instance, Arjuna married one named Ulupi when he was living in exile with his brothers. He also stayed for some time with the Nags.

Ghosts and demons sometimes inhabit palaces under the water. Deep waters, unfrequented by men, are the favourite resorts of such beings.

The god Varuna, who resides in the waters, is said to have once carried off Nand (the adoptive father of Krishna) to his watery abode, for having bathed in the Jumna before dawn.

Kalindi, the daughter of the king of the Kalingas, practised religious austerities in a palace under the waters of the Jumna with the object of securing a suitable husband. Krishna, on being informed of this by Arjuna, went to the place and married her.

There is a story in the Puranas that a king, named Nandraj, used to bury his treasures in the sea with the assistance of a jewel which furnished a safe passage through the water. The jewel was in the end burnt by the queen of Nandraj and the treasure still lies hidden in the waters of the sea.

It is narrated in the fourth chapter of *Bhagvat-puran* that the ten thousand sons of Prachetas used to reside in palaces built under water.

Stones

Stones of certain kinds are first considered as one of the deities, or as one of the chief heroes in the family, and then worshipped by the people. Many such stones are found worshipped in the vicinity of any temple.

A stone coming out of the earth with a *phallus* of Shiva is worshipped by the Hindus. If such a stone lies in a deep jungle, it is worshipped by them at least once a year, and daily, if practicable, in the intercalary month which comes every third year.

The red stones found in the Narbada river represent the god Ganpati, and are worshipped by the people.

A big stone at Phutaka Tembha near Murud in the Ratnagiri District is worshipped by the people, who believe it to be the monkey-god Hanuman. All the stone images of gods that are called *Swayambhu*, or self-existent, are nothing but rough stones of peculiar shapes. There are such *Swayambhu*—natural images—at Kelshi and Kolthare in the Ratnagiri District.

There is a big stone at Palshet in the Ratnagiri District which is worshipped as *Kalikadevi.*

The stones Shaligram, Chakramjit, Harmada, Ganpati, Ban, and Tandale are worshipped in the Deccan. The round red stones found in the Narbada are called Ganpati. White egg-shaped stones with lines on them found in sacred rivers are called *Bans* of Shiva. Black stones flat and perforated found in the Gandaki are called *Shaligram.*

In the Deccan in *Vaishakh* (April–May) and *Ashadh* (June–July) women go to the jungle and worship stones.

Stones are sometimes worshipped by the people in the belief that they are tenanted by evil spirits. We have, for example, a stone called *Mora Dhonda* lying by the seashore at Malwan in the Ratnagiri District. It is supposed to be haunted by one of the class of spirits known as *devachar.*

The stones which are once consecrated and worshipped as deities have to be continually worshipped, even when perforated. The small, round, white stone slab known as *Vishnupada*, which is naturally perforated, is considered to be holy, and is worshipped daily by the Hindus along with the other images of gods. The holes in this slab do not extend right through.

It is considered inauspicious to worship the fractured images of gods, but the perforated black stone called *Shaligram*, taken from the Gandaki river, is considered very holy, and worshipped by the people as representing Vishnu. It is smooth on one side and perforated on the other, and is believed to have been perforated from its very beginning. Every *Shaligram* has a hole in it, even when it is in the river. It is kept among the household gods and worshipped daily.

Broken stones are not worshipped by the people. But the household gods of the Brahmans and other higher classes which are called the *Panchayatan*—a collection of five gods—generally consist of five stones with holes in them.

In the Konkan districts, stones are generally worshipped for the purpose of averting evil and curing diseases. In every village stones are found sacred to spirit deities like Bahiroba, Chedoba, Khandoba, Mhasoba, Zoting, Vetal, Jakhai, Kokai, Kalkai, and others. The low-class people, such as Mahars, Mangs, &c., apply red lead and oil to stones, and call them by one of the above names, and ignorant people are very much afraid of such deities. They believe that such deities have control over all the evil spirits or ghosts. It is said that the spirit Vetal starts to take a round in a village on the night of the no-moon day of every month, accompanied by all the ghosts. When an epidemic prevails in a village, people offer to these stones eatables such as coco-nuts, fowls, and goats.

There is a stone deity named Bhavai at Kokisare in the Bavada State, to whom vows are made by the people in order that they may be cured of diseases. As the deity is in the burning ground, it is naturally believed that this is the abode of spirits.

At Achare, in the Ratnagiri District, the round stones known as *Kshetrapal* are supposed to possess the power of curing diseases, and are also believed to be the abode of spirits.

At Adivare in the Ratnagiri District there is a stone named *Mahar Purukha* which is worshipped by the people when cattle disease prevails, especially the disease of a large tick or the cattle- or dog-louse.

At Ubhadanda in the Ratnagiri District there are some stones which are believed to be haunted by Vetal, Bhutnath, Rawalnath, and such other servants of the god Shiva, and it is supposed that they have the power of curing epidemic diseases. People make vows to these stones when any disease prevails in the locality.

There are a few stones which are supposed to have the power of curing certain diseases. One of such stones is known as *Ratvano Paro.* It is found at a distance of about two miles from Kolki. It is marked with red lines. It is bored and worn round the neck by persons suffering from a disease in which red spots or pimples, known as *ratawa,* are seen on the skin.

There is another stone called *Suleimani Paro* which is supposed to have the power of curing many diseases.

There is a kind of white semicircular stone which is supposed to cure eye diseases when rubbed on the eyes, and fever when rubbed on the body.

It is believed among the Hindus that the deity *Satwai* protects children for the first three months from their birth. The deity is worshipped on the fifth day from the birth of a child, and if there occurs any omission or error in the worship of that deity, the child begins to cry, or does not keep good health. On such occasions the parents of the child make certain vows to the deity, and if the child recovers, the parents go to a jungle, and collect seven small stones. They then besmear the stones with red lead and oil, and worship them along with a she-goat in the manner in which the vow was promised to be fulfilled.

All the gods, goddesses, and spirits mentioned in the preceding pages are represented by idols made of stone, metal, or wood. In addition to stone idols of gods, there are certain stones which are considered to represent gods and worshipped as such. Some of these stones are described below.

All the stones found in the river Narbada are believed to represent the god Shiva and are worshipped.

There is another kind of hard, white, porous stone found near Dwarka. It is also worshipped along with the idol of Vishnu.

Sometimes tridents are drawn with red lead on stone to represent goddesses.

There is a pond near the Pir in Kutiana in which bored stones are found floating on the surface of the water. These stones are considered sacred.

Certain stones are considered sacred on account of their supposed curative properties. One of such stones is called *Paro*. It is believed to be efficacious in curing rheumatism.

There is also a kind of red stone which is supposed to cure skin diseases.

Each of the nine planets is supposed to be in touch with a stone of a particular colour. For instance, the stone in touch with *Shani* or Saturn is black, and that with *Mangal* or Mars is red. These stones are bored, and set in rings which are worn by persons suffering from the influence of these planets.

A kind of stone called *Akik*, found in abundance in Cambay, is considered sacred by the Muhammadan saints, who wear garlands made of beads carved out of these stones.

Fire-worship

Fire is considered to be holy among high-class Hindus. It is considered as an angel that conveys the sacrificial offerings from this earth to the gods in heaven. It is considered as one of the Hindu deities, and worshipped daily by high-class Hindus. A Brahman has to worship the fire every day in connexion with the ceremony *Vaishwadeva*—oblations of boiled rice and *ghi* given to the fire. It is also worshipped by the Hindus on special religious occasions.

Fire is worshipped at the time of sacrifices. Sacrifices are of five kinds. They are :

Devayadna, *Bhutayadna* or *Brahmayadna*, *Rishiyadna* or *Atithiyadna*, *Pitruyadna*, and *Manushyayadna*. Offerings of rice, *ghi*, firewood, sesamum, barley, &c., are made in these sacrifices. Fire is also worshipped at the time of the ceremony of renewing the sacred thread annually in the month of *Shravan* (July–August).

Among the lower classes fire is worshipped on the *Mahalaya* or *Shraddha* day. They throw oblations of food into the fire on that day.

The fire produced by rubbing sticks of the *Pipal* (*Ficus religiosa*) or *Shevari* (*Sesbania aegyptiaca*) tree is considered sacred, and it is essentially necessary that the sacred fire required for the *Agnihotra* rites should be produced in the manner described above.

Agnihotra is a perpetual sacred fire preserved in the *Agni-kunda*—a hole in the ground for receiving and preserving consecrated fire. A Brahman who has to accept the *Agnihotra* has to preserve in his house the sacred fire day and night after his thread ceremony, and to worship it three times a day after taking his bath. When an *Agnihotri* dies, his body is burnt by the people, who prepare fire by rubbing sticks of *Pipal* wood together.

There are some Brahmans who keep the fire continuously burning in their houses only for four months of the rainy season of the year. The fire which is preserved and worshipped for four months is called *Smarta Agni*.

The Parsis consider fire so sacred that they do not smoke. Neither do they cross fire. In their temples a fire of sandal-wood is kept constantly burning. It is considered a great mishap if this fire is extinguished.

Fire is specially worshipped on the *Holi* day, that is, the full-moon day of the month of *Phalgun* (February–March).

Other special occasions on which it is worshipped are the thread ceremony, the ceremony of installing a new idol in a temple, the first pregnancy ceremony, and the ceremony performed at the time of entering a new house.

Fire is also worshipped in *Maharudra*, *Vishnuyag*, *Gayatri-puraschara*, *Nilotsarga*, *Vastupujan*, *Shatachandi*, *Laksha-chandi*, and the sacrifices performed during the *Navaratra* and on the *Dasara* day.

Fire is considered to be the mouth of God, through which He is supposed to receive all offerings.

The offerings made to fire generally consist of clarified

butter, coco-nuts, sesamum seed, barley, chips of the wood of the *Pipal* (*Ficus religiosa*) and the *Shami* (*Prosopis spicigera*), curdled milk, and frankincense.

The fire to be used for sacrifices and *Agnihotras* is produced by the friction of two pieces of the wood of the *Arani* (*Premna integrifolia*), the *Pipal*, the *Shami* (*Prosopis spicigera*), or the bamboo while incantations are being recited by Brahmans.

III

TREE AND SNAKE WORSHIP

TREE-WORSHIP

APART from the totem trees,[1] certain trees are considered sacred, and they are neither cut nor is their wood used as fuel.

The *Pipal* (*Ficus religiosa*) is the chief of such trees. It is considered to be the incarnation of a Brahman, and to cut it is considered to be as great a sin as murdering a Brahman. It is believed that the family of one who cuts it becomes extinct.

Some people believe that the spirits of the deceased do not get water to drink in the next world. The water poured at the root of the *Pipal* on the 13th, 14th and 15th day of the dark half of *Kartik* (October–November) and *Shravan* (July–August) and on the 14th day of the bright half of *Chaitra* (March–April) is believed to reach these spirits and quench their thirst.

Although to cut the *Pipal* is supposed to be a great sin, it is believed that if a corpse is burnt with its wood, the soul of the deceased attains salvation.

There is a belief that the sanctity attached to the *Pipal* tree was conferred on it by the god Krishna. According to tradition, Krishna breathed his last under a *Pipal* tree. This tree is invested with a sacred thread.

It is related in parts of Gujarat that once blood gushed forth from a *Pipal* tree when it was cut. Thenceforward it came to be regarded as a Brahman and it is no longer cut.

There is a *Pipal* tree in the village of Prachi near Prabhas Patan in Kathiawar, vows in honour of which are believed to favour childless persons with children.

In the Konkan it is held inauspicious to cut the *Banyan* and *Pipal* trees of which the thread ceremonies have been

[1] See *infra*, Chapter VI.

performed. After the thread ceremony of these trees is over, a stone platform is raised around them.[1]

In the Deccan and Konkan the *Pipal* tree is considered very sacred because it is believed that the god Brahma resides in the roots, the god Vishnu in the trunk, and the god Shiva on the top of this tree. Persons who make a particular vow or have any objects to be fulfilled worship the *Pipal* tree, and walk round it several times every day. The evil spirits *Sambandh, Devachar, Munja,* and *Vetal* haunt the *Pipal* tree.[2] These spirits are considered to be the servants of the god Shiva. It is also believed that persons who worship and walk round this tree daily are not affected by those spirits. The *Pipal* tree is specially worshipped at dawn on Saturday, as it is considered that the gods Brahma, Vishnu, and Shiva happen to be there at that time. In other parts it is held that Vishnu and Munja live in the *Pipal*, Brahma in the *Banyan*, Datta in the *Umbar* (*Ficus glomerata*) Lakshmi Koli in the *Nim* (*Melia Azadirachta*), and Shiva in the *Bel* (*Aegle Marmelos*).

In the Ratnagiri District red flags are hoisted on *Banyan, Pipal,* and *Umbar* trees, and on certain occasions offerings of coins and coco-nuts are made. It is believed that when the three kinds of trees happen to grow together, i.e. close to each other, near a well or on the bank of a river, the god Datta resides there, but such cases are very rare. These trees are supposed to be the haunts of the *Munja* spirit, and therefore copper coins waved round the persons suffering from evil spirits are thrown underneath them. At Achare in the Ratnagiri District a spirit, known as *Mahapurush*, of a Brahman well versed in the Vedas is believed to haunt the *Pipal* and *Umbar* trees. The *Banyan* is worshipped by women on the full-moon day of the month of *Jyeshth* (May–June) and on the no-moon day when it falls on Monday. On these occasions a cotton thread is tied round the tree, and offerings of glass beads, coco-nuts, fruits, &c., are made. These trees are also worshipped with offerings of copper coins, &c. At Ibhrampur in the Ratnagiri District offerings of cotton thread, copper coins, and

[1] It is a common practice, in villages of the Bombay Presidency, to build a platform round some holy tree, on which the villagers sit and discuss village matters after the day's work is done.

[2] See p. 199, *infra*.

fruit are made to *Banyan* and *Pipal* trees on the full-moon day of the month of *Jyeshth* (May–June) and on every Saturday in the month of *Shravan* (July–August).

At Vavanje in the Kolaba District offerings of coins, &c., to sacred trees are made on holy days. For instance, when the no-moon day falls on Monday, the women worship the *Pipal* tree, and on the full-moon day of *Jyeshth* (May–June) they worship the *Banyan* tree. At Varsai in the Kolaba District offerings of cotton cloth, copper coins, coco-nuts, betel-nuts, and plantains are made to the *Banyan*, *Pipal*, and *Umbar* trees and also to holy wells. The *Pipal*, *Tulsi*, and *Umbar* trees are worshipped daily by women in this district, while the *Banyan* is worshipped on the full-moon day of *Jyeshth* (May–June). The materials of worship are: rice, fruits, water, sandal-paste, flowers, mangoes, and jack fruits.

At Malad in the Thana District the *Banyan* tree is worshipped by women of the twice-born castes on the full-moon day of the month of *Jyeshth* (May–June). Copper or silver coins and fruit are offered to the tree. These offerings are taken by the Brahman priest, who explains to them the modes of worship. The Brahman priest is also given some money as a gift. This vow is observed by women by fasting for three successive days, from the 13th to the 15th day of the bright half of *Jyeshth* (May–June). The *Pipal* tree is worshipped daily by men and women of the Brahman caste. Women walk round this tree for a hundred and eight times or more daily. Some persons hold a thread ceremony for the *Pipal* tree in order to obtain a son, and worship the tree for a certain period. It is worshipped with fruit and copper coins. Wooden cradles are also offered to the tree. Wells are worshipped on auspicious days by women of the upper castes. At Padghe in the Thana District the *Banyan* tree is worshipped on the full-moon day of *Jyeshth* (May–June), and the *Pipal* is worshipped every Saturday in the month of *Shravan* (July–August). The *Pipal* tree is not worshipped before the performance of its thread ceremony, and its thread ceremony is not performed till the tree bears at least one thousand leaves.

At Kolhapur the *Banyan* and *Pipal* trees are considered very holy, and offerings of rags, coins, &c., are made to them.

It is a custom among the Hindu women to worship the *Banyan* tree on the full-moon day of *Jyeshth* (May–June). Offerings of cloth and fruit are made to this tree, and copper or silver coins are given. Some women make a small model in gold, silver, or copper of the *Banyan* tree or of its leaf, and present it to the Brahman priest along with a present of money. All these rites are required to be strictly performed as enjoined in the Shastras.

The *Vad* or *Banyan* tree (*Ficus indica*) is believed to be a representation of the god Shiva. There is a proverb to the effect that one who cuts this tree is punished with the extirpation of his family. According to another belief, the god Vishnu once slept on this tree.

It is related in the Puranas that a prince named Satyawan died of snake-bite under the *Vad* tree. His wife, named Savitri, daughter of King Ashupati, who was very chaste and dutiful, petitioned Yama, the god of death, and succeeded in securing from him the life of her husband Satyawan. As the prince Satyawan returned from the jaws of death under the *Vad* tree, this tree was specially worshipped by her, and it is therefore believed that Savitri has ever since then been responsible for the practice of worshipping the *Vad* tree by women for the purpose of securing a long life to their husbands. Since then women perform a vow called *Vat Savitri* vow on the 13th, 14th, and 15th days of the bright half of *Jyeshth* (May–June) by observing a fast and worshipping and circumambulating the *Banyan* tree. It is also believed that the god Vishnu takes shelter under the *Vad* at the time of the general destruction of the world. The worship of this tree is similar to that of the other deities, and women take turns around it at the close of the worship.

The *Banyan* known as Habib's *Banyan* on the road leading from Mavaiya to Gondal in Kathiawar is a favourite haunt of spirits, who frighten persons passing by, scaring them out of their senses. In Rajkot in Kathiawar there is a *Banyan* tree which is said to be the abode of a spirit known as *Hunthia*.

In the village of Vadal near Bhiyal in the Junagadh State there is a *Banyan* tree called *Lal Vad* said to have sprung from the sticks of a *Vad* used as tooth-brushes by Lal Bava, a preceptor of the Vaishnav school. A silver staff and silver umbrella belonging to Lal Bava are kept near this tree, which is visited and worshipped by the followers of the preceptor. It is related that in this *Lal Vad* there is an opening through which the virtuous can pass to the other side, but not the sinful.

There are two *Banyan* trees near Anandpur in Kathiawar, one of which is called *Bhut-vad* or the *Banyan* tree of the evil spirits, as it is supposed to be inhabited by ghosts. The other is called *Visal-vad*, because a devotee named Visaman Bhagat lived under this tree.

Near the religious house of the Lingayat saint Kadappa, close to Kolhapur, there is a famous *Banyan* which is regularly worshipped by people from the neighbouring villages.

The *Tulsi* plant, i. e. Sweet Basil (*Ocimum sanctum*), is worshipped daily by the Hindus in general, and women in particular, by keeping the plant near their houses. The god Vishnu is worshipped particularly in offering the leaf of this plant. The *Tulsi* plant is considered by the people to represent the goddess Lakshmi, the wife of Vishnu. Hindu women will not take their meals before worshipping the *Tulsi* plant daily in the morning.

It is related that when Krishna desired to kill the demon Jalandhar, he could not be killed on account of the merit of the chastity of his wife, Vrinda. Krishna, therefore, assumed the form of Jalandhar, violated the chastity of Vrinda, and was thus enabled to kill the demon. Krishna next expressed a desire to marry Vrinda, when she transformed herself into the *Tulsi* plant. As Krishna loved Vrinda very dearly, he began to love this plant also, and hence the image of Bal Krishna, or the god Vishnu, is married to this plant every year on the twelfth day of the bright half of *Kartik* (October–November), known as *Dev Divali*. As it is also believed that the god Vishnu resides in the *Tulsi* plant, the worship of this plant is equivalent to the worship of the god Vishnu.

It is considered a great sin to uproot this plant, though no sin attaches to the plucking of its leaves during the day-time. The leaves of the *Tulsi* are considered holy and are offered to the image of the god Vishnu, and are required in all religious ceremonies.

The *Shami, Saundad,* or *Khijada* (*Prosopis spicigera*) tree is held sacred. When the Pandavas lost their kingdom in gambling with the Kauravas, the latter promised the former that they would give them back their kingdom if they lived in the forest for twelve years and unknown for one year. After having completed their stay in the forest, the Pandavas remained unknown for one year in the city of Virat. During this year they concealed their weapons on a *Shami* tree. Before taking these weapons they worshipped the tree. Next took place the great battle of Kurukshetra, in which the Pandavas won a splendid victory. This has given rise to the custom of worshipping the tree on the tenth day of the bright half of *Ashvin* (September–October) or the *Dasara* day.

It is a common belief that a tree haunted by ghosts should not be cut. So the *Shami* is not cut, because it is the favourite residence of ghosts.

There is a branch of the followers of Kabir called the *Khijada* sect. They worship the *Khijada* or *Shami* in their temples.

It is said that Rama, the seventh incarnation of Vishnu, when he marched to Ceylon to kill Rawan, the demon king, bowed to the *Shami* tree, and as he was successful in his undertaking, the Marathas used similarly to start for a campaign on the *Dasara* day after worshipping the *Shami* tree, and distributing its leaves among their friends, calling it *Suwarn*, i.e. gold. This is said to be the origin of the festival of the *Dasara.*

It is related that at the gate of the village of Surel in Kathiawar a spirit lived in a *Shami* tree. For ten years he showed himself dressed in white garments, and scared travellers out of their senses. When offerings of wheaten bread were made to the tree, the victims recovered their senses.

A species of the *Tamarind* tree called *Gorakh Chinch* is said to be connected with the Hindu saint Gorakhnath. For this reason this tree is worshipped by the people. A great fair is held every year at Battis Shirale in the Satara District, which is situated at a distance of about ten miles from Kolhapur.

From Limbdi in Kathiawar, it is reported that a *Tamarind* tree is haunted by a spirit which refuses to allow the recitation of songs in honour of Kali. No woman has succeeded in completing such a song, in consequence of the tree's opposition.

Groves of *Mango* trees are considered to be sacred, as they have a pleasing appearance, and afford grateful shelter against the heat of the day. It is a general belief among Hindus that trees from which such pleasure and protection are derived must naturally be the abode of the gods. There are many such groves in Satara. During the spring season people go to these groves and worship the trees.

Umbar (*Ficus glomerata*). When the god Vishnu in his fourth incarnation, called Narsinh, i. e. half man and half lion, tore into pieces the body of the demon named Hiranyakashipu with his claws, he felt a burning sensation of the poison from the body of that demon, which was assuaged by thrusting his hands into the trunk of the *Umbar* or *Audumbar* tree.

In order that they may obtain the auspicious sight of a deity early in the morning, Hindus generally plant the *Umbar* and *Tulsi* trees in front of their houses, and worship them daily. The juice of the root of the *Umbar* has a cooling effect, and hence it is freely used in cases of measles or itch. Its sap is also used as medicine for swellings. It is very pleasant to sit under the shade of this tree, and as it is believed that the god Dattatraya resides beneath this tree, it is held very sacred by the Hindus. At Bhillawadi and Ganagapur in the Kolhapur State there are *Umbar* trees known and worshipped as 'Dattatraya's *Umbar*'.

The *Apta* tree is worshipped by Hindus on the *Dasara* day, and its leaves are distributed under the name of *sone*, or gold, among their friends and relatives.

At Medhe in the Kolaba District there is a tree *Vehala* (*Beleric Myrobalan*) which is believed to be connected with the local deity Mhasoba. It is considered to be a sacred tree, and nobody dares to cut it or to touch it with their feet.

At Shirgaon in the Thana District there is a *Ranjani* (*Mimusops hexandra*) tree on the bank of a pond called Khambale which is said to be connected with the deity Brahma; and therefore no branch of that tree is cut by the people. This tree, also known as the *Karan*, is believed to represent Shiva and to be the abode of the mother goddesses. To cut it is said to be a sure way to disaster.

The *Avali* (*Phyllanthus emblica*) is worshipped on *vaikuntha*-

chaturdashi, i.e. the twelfth to fourteenth day of bright half of *Kartik* (October–November), in the belief that the Hindu Trinity are to be found in the tree on that day. This tree is also propitiated in the Konkan in the belief that it is possessed by the ghost of a widow.

Besides the above-mentioned trees, the *Palas* (*Butea frondosa*) and the *Bel* (*Aegle Marmelos*), a tree sacred to the god Shiva, are considered to be holy by the Hindus.

The *Kadamb* (*Anthocephalus Cadamba*) is considered sacred because it is believed that Krishna rested under this tree when he took cattle to graze.

The *Nim, Nimb*, or *Limbdo* (*Melia Azadirachta*) is also considered sacred, as it represents the god Brahma. Some believe that it represents Jagannathji.

The *Rudraksha* (*Elaeocarpus Ganitrus*) is believed to be a representation of the god Shiva. It is therefore considered a sin to cut it. Garlands of *Rudraksha* beads are worn round the neck by the devotees of Shiva.

The leaves of the *Bel* (*Aegle Marmelos*) are offered to the god Shiva, as they are supposed to be liked by him. It is also considered a sin to cut this tree.

The *Marjoram* (*Origanum vulgare*) is considered sacred by Musalmans. They dip its leaves into oil and rub them against the face of a corpse.

A *Babul* (*Acacia arabica*) near Kolki in Kathiawar is haunted by a spirit which frightens persons passing under it.

There is a temple of Bhimnath Mahadev near Baravala in the shade of an ancient *Babul* tree. The worshipper at the temple, a wealthy man, once thought of erecting a grand temple over the image, but he was prevented from doing so by the god appearing in his dream and telling him that he preferred to live under the tree.

Under a *Babul* tree near Dhandhuka there is a shrine of Bhimnath Shankar, who is known as Bhimnath Jalvalo after the tree *Jal = Babul*.

There is a *Sakhotia* tree near Kutiana, which is supposed to be the abode of a snake deity. In Kathiawar, near Rajkot, there is a tree called *Gandu* or mad, vows in honour of which are said to cure children of bronchitis. Similarly, near Jasdan there are two tall trees known as 'mad trees'. The fruit of these trees is said to resemble the face of a saint, and they are therefore worshipped with offerings of red lead, oil, and coco-nuts.

At Phonda in the Ratnagiri District it is considered inauspicious to cut the trees and the groves that surround the temple of a village deity, for they are believed to belong to that deity.

At Padghe in the Thana District the trees which are supposed to have been haunted by evil spirits such as *Sambandh, Munja, Devachar,* &c., are not generally cut by the people through fear of these spirits. When any tree is cut down, the custom is to keep a stone at the root of the tree in order that the place may no longer be affected or haunted by the spirit in the tree. There are certain families who do not burn *Pipal* (*Ficus religiosa*), *Khair* (*Acacia catechu*) or *Shiwani* (*Gmelina arborea*) wood. They believe that the burning of these trees causes harm to their families. It is said that the burning of the *Apta* (*Bauhinia racemosa*) tree causes the breeding of the cattle- or dog-louse.

The *Plantain* tree is considered to be sacred. While gathering a bunch of plantains, the tree is first cut before the bunch. It is considered inauspicious to gather the bunch without so doing.

There are certain groves at Ubhadanda in the Ratnagiri District which are supposed to be haunted by *Devachars*, and are therefore not cut by the people.

Alwant, the ghost of a woman dying at child-birth or during her menses, lives in the *Nagchampa* (*Mesua ferrea*), *Surang* (*Ochrocarpus longifolius*) and the *Kajra* (*Strychnos Nux-vomica*) trees. Devachar, Sambandh, Munja, Zoting, Khavis, and Khapra reside in trees and plants.

The people of Kolhapur believe that the spirits known as Bramhasambandh, Brahma-Rakshasa, and Khavis reside in trees.

The deities of the forest reside in groves of trees or near the *Piludi* tree (*Salvadora persica*), to which their devotees must go in order to fulfil their vows. These deities do not receive any formal worship. But they are noted for the cure of certain diseases, and the groves which they haunt are frequently visited by afflicted persons. These deities are installed in those places where they have manifested their powers.[1]

TREE-MARRIAGE

A common custom among Hindus, for which authority is found in the Puranas, is for a person who has lost his two wives and wishes to marry a third, to be first married to a *Rui* (*Calotropis gigantea*) plant, and then to the actual bride. His marriage with the *Rui* plant is considered as a third marriage, and is known as *ark-vivaha*. After the marriage, the *Rui* plant is cut down and buried, and thus the marriage with the third bride is considered to be a fourth marriage. The marriage with the *Rui* plant has been adopted in the belief that the third wife is sure to die unless the spirit of the deceased is made to enter the *Rui* plant. In some places the *Shami* (*Prosopis spicigera*) or the *Bor* (*Zizyphus Jujuba*) takes the place of the *Rui*. The *ark-vivaha* seems to be founded on the widow marriage rite of the Shudras referred to below.

When a girl is born under the influence of inauspicious planets which may be harmful to her husband, she is first married to a tree or an earthen pot, and then to the bridegroom. The marriage with the earthen pot is called the pot-wedding. It is believed that by observing this practice the danger to her husband is avoided. The danger passes to the tree to which she is first married.

Among the lower classes in the Thana District a poor man unable to marry owing to his poverty is first married to a *Rui* (*Calotropis gigantea*) plant and then to a widow. This marriage with a widow is called *pat lavane*. This remarriage of a widow among the lower classes is generally performed at night, and under an old *Mango* tree. It is never performed in the house. A widow who has remarried cannot take part in any auspicious ceremony such as a marriage, &c.

If the betrothed husband of a girl dies before the celebration of the marriage, she is married to a *Pipal* or *Ankdi* (*Alangium*

[1] For a list of trees sacred to Hindu deities, trees mentioned in Hindu scriptures and used for sanctified purposes, see Birdwood's *Industrial Arts of India*, p. 35 et seq.

Lamarckii), in the belief that the danger of death will fall on the tree, and that the next husband of the girl will survive.

In some places, if a man's wives do not live, his next wife is married to an *Ankdi* (*Alangium Lamarckii*) plant before her marriage with him.

If a girl attains puberty before marriage, she is married to a *Pipal* tree. A girl with congenital deformities is also married to a *Pipal* tree.

In the Deccan it is held in some places that the corpse of a married man only may be burnt. Thus if a man die unmarried, his body is wedded to a *Rui* (*Calotropis gigantea*) before the pyre is lit. This belief also prevails in the Karnatak.

Bachelors desiring to marry widows among Shudras must first marry a *Rui* (*Calotropis gigantea*) plant: Bhils marry them to an *Apta* (*Bauhinia racemosa*).[1] Among Bhils, Pavaras, and Mawchis, if a girl bears children before marriage, she and her seducer are both married to the *Rui* before their marriage may take place. Their marriage is then performed as a widow remarries. In the Karnatak it is held that by marrying a *Rui* tree first, a man may ensure long life for his wife by a subsequent marriage.

Snake-worship

All Hindus in the Presidency worship the snake. The day especially devoted to its worship is the fifth day of the bright half of *Shravan* (July–August), which is called *Nag panchami*, i.e. the Cobra-Fifth. In some places *Nagpanchami* is observed on the fifth day of the dark half of *Shravan* (July–August). On this day an image of a snake is made of cow-dung or earth, or its picture is drawn on the wall. In the Deccan the snake image, made of *Darbha* (*Eragrostis cynosuroides*) grass, is worshipped on the fourteenth day of *Bhadrapad* (August–September), i.e. *Anantchaturdashi*, in a copper pot.

The image is worshipped as a deity, and a mixture of wheat, oat, or rice flour, clarified butter, and sugar or molasses is offered to it. After worship, the members of the household

[1] Many instances of these tree-marriages will be found in the sections dealing with widow remarriage under each tribe or caste in *Tribes and Castes of Bombay*. See, for example, articles on Bhoi, Katkari, Kolhati, Od, Tamboli, Sudir.

take their meal and eat the offerings with coco-nuts and cucumbers. Only one meal is taken on this day by men and women. No fruit or vegetables are picked on this day, nor are fried dishes prepared from them. It is usual also to worship ant-hills as the abode of snakes. Women sing songs and move round the ant-hills in a circle.

The *Nagpanchami* is observed as a vow, generally by women. They do not take any meal on this day, but live only on the food offered to the snake. On this day the Maharani of Baroda, mounted on an elephant, goes in procession to the woods to worship an ant-hill. The pipers who accompany the procession blow their pipes, and, allured by the sound, the snakes come out of their holes, when they are worshipped and fed with milk. Women do not pound, grind, or sift corn, or cow-dung the floors on the *Nagpanchami* day, and all try to see a snake.

It is obligatory in some families to offer a coco-nut to the snake-god on the *Nagpanchami* day. Other days for snake worship are the *Nagchaturth* and *Satnarayan Chathi*.

In some places the likeness of the snake is engraved on a stone or copper plate and worshipped. In others, it is drawn on a piece of paper which is affixed to the wall.

In many places in Gujarat and Kathiawar there are temples dedicated to snake-gods. These gods are known by various names. Some of the temples with the names of the gods installed in them are given below:

1. The temple of Ragatio Nag, midway between Kanaza and Vanthali in the Junagadh State.

2. The temple of Charmalio Nag at Chokdi near Chuda. Vows to offer sweets are made to this Nag by persons bitten by snakes, who visit the temple, hold the sweets before the image of the god, distribute them among the visitors, and are in return presented with cotton thread, which they wear round the neck. This god is also reputed to have the power of blessing childless persons with offspring. The offerings concerned consist of cradles, which are presented to the god after the wished-for object has been obtained.

3. The temple of Vasuki Nag near Thangadh. This Nag is supposed to be a servant of the god Shiva. An old snake with grey moustaches is said to live in this temple. He drinks milk

at the hands of visitors. Many vows are made in honour of this snake-god.

4. The temple of Khambhadio Nag at Khambhada.

5. The temple of Nag Mandal at Dadvi.

6. The temple of Bhujia Nag at Bhuj.

7. The temple of Shimalia Nag near Jadeshvar in the neighbourhood of Jetpur.

8. The temple of Fulia Nag near Jopanath.

9. The temple of Malodaro Nag at Malod.

10. The temple of Charmalio Nag at Chudia.

11. The temple of Chhatrasia Nag in Chhatrasa.

12. The temple of Monapario Nag at Monpar near Chitral.

13. The temple of Ashapal at Nanadiya in the Bantya State.

14. The temple of Khodial Nagini at Khokharda in the Junagadh State.

15. The temple of Gondalia Nag at Gondal.

It is related that there were once divine snakes in the royal fort of Jodia in Kathiawar. When a pair (male and female) of these snakes were found killed, the heinous act was atoned for by the bodies of the snakes being buried and a temple erected over the grave. The male snake of this pair is known as Nag Nath or the Lord of Snakes. According to others, Nag Nath was a big white snake with grey moustaches. He once waylaid a milkman of the royal household, forced him to put down the milkpot he was carrying, drank the milk, and went away. This snake is believed to be divine.

The god Shiva is supposed to wear a snake round his neck like a garland of flowers. So in all temples of Shiva, an image of a snake is installed behind the idol of the god with his hood spread over the idol.

In ancient times dead snakes were buried and temples and altars were erected over their graves. An image of the dead snake was engraved on the altar.

There is a shrine dedicated to Chandalia Nag on the bank of the river Palavo on the road from Mota Devalia to Tramboda in Kathiawar. It is visited by a sect of beggars called Nag-magas. The Nag-magas beg wealth of the snake-god, and it is said that he bestows it on them. They are never seen begging from anybody else.

In the Puranas the Shesh Nag, the Takshak Nag, Pundarik, Kali Nag, and Karkotak Nag are described as gods. In modern times, Sarmalio, Bhujo, and Gadhio are believed to be as powerful as gods, and vows are observed in their honour. Dhananjaya, Pushkar, and Vasuki are also considered to be very powerful. Takshak is believed to have drunk the nectar of immortality.

A tradition is current that Vishnu sleeps on the Shesha Nag in the Milky Ocean. This snake is believed to have a thousand mouths and to support the earth on its hood.

It is described in the Puranas how King Parikshit was bitten by Takshak Nag and King Nala by Karkotak Nag. King Nala became deformed owing to the bite, but he could assume his original form by wearing a special dress, through the favour of Karkotak.

Vasuki Nag was wrapped round the Mandar mountain, which was used as a churning handle by the gods and demons to churn the ocean for the recovery of the fourteen jewels from the water.

It is a common belief that treasures buried underground are guarded by snakes.

Generally a miser dying without an heir is supposed to be born as a snake after his death, to guard his hoarded money.

It is believed by some people that on the establishment of a new dynasty of kings after a revolution, a snake makes its appearance to guard the accumulated wealth of the fallen dynasty.

It is also believed that a rich man dying with his mind fixed on his wealth, or who has hidden his treasure, is born as a snake, to guard the treasure.

There is a further belief that one who makes money by foul means and does not spend it, is born as a snake in his next life to guard his buried treasure.

The beliefs mentioned above have given rise to the impression that places where big snakes are found have treasure trove concealed in them.

It is believed that the snake guarding the treasure acquired during his existence as a human being does not allow anybody to remove it, and bites any one who attempts to do so. If, in spite of this, a man succeeds in seizing the treasure by force, or by the power of incantations, it is believed that he leaves no heirs to use it. A belief is also current that such guardian snakes allow those persons to take away the treasures guarded by them if they are destined to possess them.

To the south of Kolki in Kathiawar, there is a site of a deserted village. It is believed to contain a buried treasure which is guarded by a snake with white moustaches. This snake is seen roaming about the place.

It is related that a Brahman once read in an old paper that there was a treasure buried under a *Shami* (*Prosopis spicigera*) tree in Deola. He communicated the information to the Thakor of Dhrol, who secured the treasure by excavating the place. The Brahman went to worship the spot, but was buried alive. The Thakor buried the treasure in his castle, but the Brahman, becoming a snake, guarded the treasure and allowed none to touch it. All attempts to dig it up were frustrated by attacks of bees and the appearance of the snake.

A Kshatriya named Dev Karan, while the foundation of his house was being dug, found a treasure guarded by a snake. He killed the snake by pouring boiling oil over it and secured the treasure.

A Kunbi of Malia, while digging a pit for storing corn, found a large vessel filled with costly coins guarded by a snake. He killed the snake and secured the vessel.

A belief prevails that there is a precious stone in the head of the snake. Such stones are called *mohors*. They are occasionally shown to the people by snake-charmers, who declare that it is very difficult to procure them.

It is stated that on dark nights snakes take these *mohors* out of their head and place them on prominent spots in order to be able to move about in the dark by their light. It is believed that snakes give these *mohors* to those who please them. If one tries to take a *mohor* by force, the snake swallows it and dissolves it into water. The *mohor* has the property of absorbing the poison from snake-bites. It is because a snake is believed to hold a precious stone in its head that it is called *manidhar*, that is, holder of a jewel. It is believed by some people that the *mohor* shines most when a rainbow appears in the sky.

According to the Puranas the nether world is as beautiful as heaven. It is inhabited by *Nags* or snakes in human form. The *Nag* girls are reputed to be so handsome that an extraordinarily beautiful girl is commonly likened to a *Nag* girl. It is believed that in ancient times intermarriages between *Nags* and human beings were common.

It is a common belief that Kshetrapal, the guardian snake of fields, married human brides. So, to propitiate him, his image is installed on the marriage altar, and the bride takes three turns round it when walking round the sacrificial fire with the bridegroom.

According to the Puranas, King Dasharath married a *Nag* girl Sumitra. Similarly Indrajit, the son of Ravan, the Lord of Lanka or Ceylon, married a *Nag* girl.

At times snakes are seen in houses. They are believed to be the guardians of the houses, and worshipped with offerings of lamps fed with *ghi*. After worship, the members of the family pray to the snake, 'O snake! thou art our guardian. Protect our health and wealth. We are thy children and live in thy garden!'

In a family at Junnar in the Poona District, a woman is believed to have given birth to a snake, which grew up and lived peacefully with the members of the household

Some people in Gujarat believe that the spirits of deceased ancestors, on account of the anxiety for the welfare of their progeny, become snakes and guard the house.

In the Deccan and Konkan, snakes are believed to be the stepbrothers of the gods. They reside under the earth and are very powerful. The snake is considered to be very beautiful among creeping animals, and is one of the ornaments of Shiva. An image of a snake made of brass is kept in the temple of Shiva, and worshipped daily along with the god.

It is said that at Battisa Shirale in the Belgaum District the real *Nag* comes out of its abode below the earth on the *Nagpanchami* day, and is worshipped by the people. Milk and parched rice are put outside the house at night on this day with the intention that they may be consumed by a snake. Hindus do not dig or plough the earth on the *Nagpanchami* day. Earthen images of snakes are worshipped by some people in the Konkan districts on the *Nagpanchami* day. The *Nag* is considered to be a Brahman by caste, and it is believed that the family of the person who kills a snake becomes extinct. The cobra being considered a Brahman, its dead body is adorned with the sacred thread, and then burnt as that of a human being. A copper coin is also thrown into its funeral pile.

A snake is said to appear on every *Shravan* (July–August) Monday in the temple of Shankar at Karanje Bhimthadi, Poona. This snake has a cut on its head owing to a blow of an axe from a cowherd (*Gaoli*). The form which it takes each year is an indication of a plentiful harvest or a scarcity.

At certain villages in the Deccan a big earthen image of a snake is consecrated in a public place on the *Nagpanchami* day, and worshipped by Hindus in general. Women sing their songs in circles before this image, while men perform ceremonies by its side. In fact, the day is enjoyed by the people as a holiday. The snake is removed next day, and an idol in the form of a man made of mud is seated in its place. This idol is called Shiralshet, who is said once to have been a king and to have ruled over this earth for half an hour only. This day is observed as a day of rejoicing by the people.

The names of the snake deities in common use in the Deccan and Konkan are Takshak, Vasuki, and Shesha. Their shrines are at Kolhapur, Nagothane, Prayaga, Nagadevachi Wadi, and Subramhanya. A great fair is held every year at Battisa Shirale in the Satara District on the *Nagpanchami* day.

There is a shrine of a snake deity at Savantwadi, the capital of the state of that name in the Konkan. The management of the shrine is in the hands of the state officials. It is believed that a real snake resides therein.

There is a shrine of a snake deity at Awas in the Kolaba District, where a great fair is held every year on the fourteenth day of the bright half of *Kartik* (October–November). It is said that persons suffering from snake-bite recover when taken in time to this temple.

It is said that a covetous person who acquires great wealth during his lifetime and dies without enjoying it, or without issue, becomes a snake after death, and guards his buried treasures. At Kolhapur there was a money-lender named

Kodulkar who is said to have become a snake and to guard his treasures. In the village of Kailava in the Kolhapur District there is a snake in the house of a village accountant, who scares away those who try to enter the storehouse.

At Kapadne in West Khandesh the headman (*patil*) left his house and took another from fear of a snake guarding a treasure. At Mehergaon in the same district a snake is said to guard the treasure of a Lad Vani. From numerous other places in the Deccan the existence of such treasure-guarding snakes is reported. In the Deccan snakes are made of wheat flour and put to guard buried treasure. It is said that there are certain places guarded by snakes in Goa territory. Persons who were compelled to abandon Portuguese territory owing to religious persecutions at the hands of the Portuguese buried their treasures beneath the ground. Those who died during exile are said to have become ghosts, and it is believed that they guard their buried treasures in the form of snakes.

The Hindus generally believe that the snakes who guard buried treasures do not allow any one to go near them. The snake frightens those who try to approach, but when he wishes to hand over the treasure to anybody he goes to that person at night, and tells him in a dream that the treasure buried at such and such a place belongs to him, and requests him to take it over. After the person has taken possession of the treasure as requested, the snake disappears from the spot.

It is said that a snake which guards treasure is generally very old, white in complexion, and has long hair on its body.

It is reported that a snake has been seen by many persons guarding seven jars of buried treasure at Belapur in the Deccan, near Maruti's temple.

A snake festival is observed in the Nageshwar temple at Awas in the Kolaba District on the night of the fourteenth day of the bright half of *Kartik* (October–November). Nearly four hundred devotees of the god Shankar assemble in the temple, holding in their hands long cane sticks with snake images at their ends.[1] They advance dancing and repeating certain words, and take turns round the temple till midnight. After getting the permission of the chief devotee, they scatter

[1] These sticks are known as *vetra-sarpa*.

throughout the neighbouring villages with small axes in their hands, and cut down and bring from the gardens coco-nuts, plantains, and other edible things that are seen on their way. They return to the temple after two hours, the last man being the chief devotee called *Kuwarkandya.* The fruits are then distributed among the people assembled at the temple. Nobody interferes with them on this day in taking away coco-nuts and other fruits from the village gardens. On the next day they go dancing in the same manner to the Kanakeshwar hill with the snake sticks in their hands.

In the Deccan, in the temples devoted to snake deities on the full-moon day of *Kartik* (October–November), which is sacred to the snake deity, the deity is worshipped with special pomp, and the crests of the temples are illuminated on that night.

In the Deccan it is believed that if a big snake is seen several times in a house, it is the owner of the house who has assumed the form of a snake.

A snake is believed to have a white jewel in its head, and it loses its life when this jewel is removed. This jewel has the power of drawing out the poison of snake-bite. When it is applied to the wound, it becomes green, but when kept in milk for some time it loses its greenness and reverts to its usual white colour. It gives out to the milk all the poison that has been absorbed from the wound, and the milk becomes green. This jewel can be used several times as an absorbent of the poison of snake-bite. The green milk must be buried underground, so that it may not be used again by any one else.

It is believed that an old snake having long hair on its body has a jewel in its head. This jewel is compared with the colours of a rainbow. The snake can take this jewel from its head at night, and search for food in its lustre. Such snakes never come near the habitation of human beings, but always reside in the depth of the jungle. This species of snake is called *Deva Sarpa*, i.e. a snake belonging to a deity. It is related that a snake was born of a woman in the Kinkar's house at Tardal in the Sangli State, and another one in the Gabale's house at Kolhapur in the Karnatak.

There are many practices in vogue to render the poisonous bite of a snake ineffective.

(1) If the man bitten by a snake be bold, he cuts off the bitten part.

(2) Some have the bitten part branded with fire or a red-hot coin.

(3) Those who have no ulcer in the mouth suck the poison and spit it out.

(4) The powder of the fruit of the *Nol Vel* (*Brassica oleracea*) is administered with water.

(5) A fly-whisk made of peacock's feathers is waved round the patient's body.

(6) Emetics and purgative medicines, such as soap-nut juice or water in which copper coins have been boiled by the patient, are given.

(7) A mixture of pepper and clarified butter is also believed to be efficacious.

(8) Charmed water is applied to the wound, or a sorcerer is called to use incantations.

(9) In the Dharwar District a man bringing news of a person being bitten by a snake is given a box on the ear. This is held to cure the patient.

(10) The patient is made to wear a cotton thread in the name of Charmalia Nag, Sharmalia Nag, or Vasangi Nag, and certain observances, as stated above, are promised to the snake deity.

(11) The ends of peacock's feathers are pounded and smoked in a clay pipe by the patient.

(12) A *mohor* (stone found in the head of a snake) is applied to the wound caused by the bite. It absorbs the poison, and, on being dipped into milk, transfers the poison to the milk. Thus it can be used any number of times.

There is a Girasia in Lakhtar in Kathiawar who is believed to cure patients suffering from snake poison. As soon as a person is bitten by a snake, one of the garments worn by him is taken to the Girasia, who ties it into a knot and this cures the patient.

There is a *Bava* or exorcist in Rajpara, a village near Anandpur. He and all the members of his family are reputed to be able to cure snake-bites. When a person is bitten by a snake he or a friend goes to the *Bava's* house and informs him or any member of his family of the occurrence. The *Bava*, or the person who receives the intimation, folds into a knot a garment of the informant, which he afterwards unfolds. As soon as this is done, the patient is in great pain, loses his senses, is seized with convulsions, and tells why the snake bit him. Thereupon the relatives of the patient implore the pardon of the snake, which is granted on condition that the patient should give alms to the poor.

In some places in Gujarat *Bhagats* or devotees of the goddess Mataji are invited to dinner along with a number of exorcists, who in Gujarat are generally Rabaris. After they have assembled at the house of the patient, they start out in a procession headed by one who holds in his hand a bunch of peacock's feathers, to bathe in a river. On their way to and back from the river they sing songs in praise of the goddess to the accompaniment of drums and other musical instruments. After their return from the river, the whole party are treated to a feast, which is supposed to cure the patient of the effects of the snake-bite.

Some people believe that snakes, like evil spirits, can enter the bodies of human beings. Such persons, when possessed, are supposed to have the power of curing snake-bites.

Every village has an exorcist who is a specialist in curing the effects of snake-bites. When a person is bitten by a snake the exorcist is at once sent for. He gives the patient *Nim* (*Melia Azadirachta*) leaves and pepper to chew, to determine the extent of the effect of the bite. When the leaves begin to taste sweet he is held to be recovering. Next he asks one of those present to bathe and bring water in an unused earthen jar. He then recites incantations, and sprinkles water from the jar over the body of the patient. If this does not counteract the effects of the poison, he throws red-hot pieces of charcoal at the patient, when the snake speaks through the patient and states that he bit the patient because he committed a certain offence, and that he will leave him if certain offerings are made. After he has ceased speaking, the patient begins to shake and to crawl about like a snake, and is then cured. If the man be doomed to death, the snake would say, 'I have bitten him by the order of the god of death, and I will not leave him without taking his life'. In the Deccan the patient is occasionally bathed in cow's urine.

Sometimes the exorcist fans the patient with branches of the *Nim* (*Melia Azadirachta*) tree, reciting incantations, and thereupon the patient becomes possessed by the snake and declares the cause of his offence. In the Deccan he is given *Nim* leaves to eat and made to circumambulate the god of the village temple. If he vomits he is held to be cured.

Some exorcists present a magic epistle or charm asking the snake that bit the patient to be present. The snake obeys the call, and appears before the exorcist. The latter then asks the snake to suck the poison from the wound of the patient, which is done by the snake, and the patient is then cured.

In some places the exorcist ties up the patient, when the snake tells the cause of the bite. Next the exorcist calls on the snake to leave the body of the patient, who then begins to crawl about like a snake and is cured.

On some occasions, the exorcist slaps the cheek or beats the mouth of the person who calls him to attend the patient. It is said that the poison disappears as soon as the slap is given on the mouth, and this cures him.

Some exorcists take a stick having seven joints and break them one by one. As the stick is broken, the patient recovers, his recovery being complete when the seventh joint is broken.

It is believed that the Dhedas are the oldest worshippers of snakes. When a person is bitten by a snake, he is seated near a Dheda, who prays the snake to leave the body of the patient. It is said that in some cases this method proves efficacious in curing the patient.

It is stated that exorcists who know the incantation for the cure of snake-bites must lead a strictly moral life. If they touch a woman in child-bed or during her periods the incantation loses its power. This can be regained through purification, bathing, and by reciting the incantation while inhaling the smoke of burning frankincense. Some exorcists abstain from certain kinds of vegetables and sweets, e.g. the *Mogri* (rat-tailed radish), *Julebi* (a kind of sweet), &c. They have also to abstain from articles of a colour like that of a snake.

A patient suffering from snake-bite must not touch a woman

wearing a black garment, or hear the sound of a bangle. To test whether a man is really suffering from snake-bite he is given chillies to eat. If he finds them sweet it is held that he is suffering from snake-bite. If in chewing betel-nut his mouth does not redden the same cause is suspected.

In the Deccan the exorcist called to cure snake-bite makes the patient crawl about with an old shoe in his mouth, and this cures him.

In the Deccan a person suffering from snake-bite is taken to a village temple, and the ministrant is requested to give him holy water. The deity is also invoked. Thus keeping the person for one night in the temple, he is carried to his house the following day, if cured. The vows made to the deity for the recovery of the person are then fulfilled. There is a tomb of *Avalia*, a Muhammadan saint, at Panhala in the Deccan, where persons suffering from snake-bite are made to sit near the tomb, and it is said that they are cured. In some villages there are enchanted trees of the *Nim* (*Melia Azadirachta*) where persons placed under the shade of such trees are cured of snake-bite. In the Deccan the patient is covered with leaves from this tree and taken to the temple of Kal-bhairav or Shiva. Some people tie a stone round the neck of the sufferer as soon as he is better, repeating the words *Adi Gudi Imam*, the name of a Muhammadan saint. After recovery from snake-bite the person is taken to the mosque of the *Adi Gudi Imam Saheb*, where the stone is untied before the tomb, and molasses equal to the weight of the stone are offered. A feast is also given to the ministrant of the mosque. There is a famous enchanter at Satara who cures persons suffering from snake-bite. It is said that he throws charmed water on the body of the sufferer, and in a few minutes the snake begins to speak through the victim. The sorcerer inquires what the snake wants. The snake gives reasons for biting the person. When anything thus asked for by the snake is offered, the victim comes to his senses, and is cured. There are many witnesses to the above fact.

In Kanara a ruby is applied to a snake-bite as a cure, or a mixture of *Rui* (*Calotropis gigantea*) and Mango juice is used, some of the potion being given to the patient to drink.

In Dharwar the root of the *Amratbali* (*Tinospora cordifolia*) is gathered on a Sunday new-moon day. A little of this root is mixed with cow's urine and applied to the patient's eye and to his wound, as a cure for snake-bite.

At Mitbav in the Ratnagiri District chickens numbering from twenty to twenty-five are applied to the wound caused by the snake-bite. A chicken has the power of drawing out the poison from the body through the wound, but this causes the death of the chicken. The remedy above described is sure to be successful if it is tried within three hours of the person being bitten. There are some men in this village who give charmed water for snake or any other bites. Many persons suffering from snake-bite have been cured by the use of incantations and charmed water.

In the Konkan, water from the tanks of Vetavare in the Savantwadi State and Manjare in Goa Territory is generally used as medicine for snake-bite. It is believed that by the power of incantations a snake can be prevented from entering or leaving a particular area. This process is called ' tying the snake '. There are some sorcerers who can draw snakes out of their holes by the use of incantations, and carry them away without touching them with their hands.

At Adivare in the Ratnagiri District roots of certain herbs are mixed with water and applied to the wound caused by the snake-bite, and given to the sufferer to drink.

At Naringre in the Ratnagiri District persons suffering from snake-bite are given the juice of *Nim* (*Melia Azadirachta*) leaves, and are kept in the temple of Hanuman. The feet of the deity are washed with holy water, and the water is given to the victim to drink.

IV

WORSHIP OF ANCESTORS, HOLY MEN, AND SAINTS

SIR JAMES CAMPBELL, in commencing his notes on the spirit basis of belief and custom, draws attention to the widespread custom of the worship of ancestors, from which arises the worship of, and belief in, spirits, leading to the installation of godlings, the practice of spirit-scaring rites, and all the ritual of primitive religion.[1]

Throughout the Presidency the spirits of a deceased father, grandfather, great-grandfather, and of a mother, grandmother, and great-grandmother, i.e. all the male and female ascendants up to the third degree, receive systematic worship when the funeral ceremonies (*Shraddha*) are performed either on the anniversary of the death of any of them or on the day when the *Narayan bali* is performed in such holy places as Gaya, Sidhapur, or Prabhas Patan. The spirits of those who meet heroic deaths on fields of battle are called *Suropuros* in Gujarat, and pillars are erected in their memory on the spot where they breathed their last. They receive only occasional worship.

The spirits of the deceased (*purvajas*) receive worship on the thirteenth or fourteenth day of the dark half of *Shravan* (July–August), on the fourteenth of the dark half of *Ashvin* (September–October), on the death anniversaries, and on days on which the *Shraddhas* and similar funeral ceremonies are performed. On these occasions the deceased ancestors are represented by twisted braids of *Durva* grass (*Cynodon Dactylon*).

Ancestral spirits descend to the level of ghosts when they are strongly attached to worldly objects. Such spirits often possess the bodies of their descendants, in spite of the necessary *Shraddhas* having been performed for their release. The thirteenth, fourteenth, and fifteenth days of the bright half of the months of *Kartik* (October–November) and *Chaitra* (March–April) are the special days for propitiation of departed spirits

[1] Vide *S.B.B.C.*, p. 1 et seq.

by their relatives, either at home or in holy places, while the whole of the dark half of the month of *Bhadrapad* (August–September) is devoted to this purpose. During this fortnight the *Shraddha* is performed in honour of the deceased on the day corresponding to the day of his death,[1] when Brahmans are feasted. Thus, a person dying on the fifth day of *Kartik* (October–November) has his *Shraddha* performed on the fifth day of this fortnight. On this occasion, water is poured at the root of the *Pipal* (*Ficus religiosa*), offerings of water are made, and balls of rice are offered to the deceased.

Of the days of the *Shraddha* fortnight, the thirteenth, fourteenth, and fifteenth are considered to be of special importance.

The ancestors are also worshipped on auspicious occasions, such as marriages, by the performance of a *Shraddha* called *nandi*, when balls of molasses are offered instead of rice. It is considered an act of merit to perform a *Shraddha* in honour of ancestors on the banks of a river or pond at midday on the eighth day of the dark half of a month.

From the thirteenth to the fifteenth day of the bright half of *Chaitra* (March–April), or of the dark half of *Kartik* (October–November) and *Shravan* (July–August), after their morning ablutions, orthodox people pour water over the *Pipal* (*Ficus religiosa*), the *Babul* (*Acacia arabica*), the *Bor* (*Zizyphus Jujube*) the Banyan, the *Tulsi* (holy Basil) and *Durva* grass (*Cynodon Dactylon*), and on those places where cows are known to congregate, in the belief that by so doing the thirst of the spirits of the deceased is quenched. It is also believed that if feasts are given to the relatives of the deceased and to Brahmans, the ancestral spirits are satisfied.

The *Shraddhas* of those who die on the full-moon day of a month are performed on the full-moon day of *Bhadrapad* (August–September), and similar rites of those who die on the no-moon day of a month are celebrated on the no-moon day of *Bhadrapad* (August–September). The thirteenth day of the dark half of *Bhadrapad* (August–September) is called the Children's Thirteenth. This day is specially devoted to the propitiation of the spirits of children.

[1] The death anniversary of an ancestor is called *samvatsari samachari* or *chhamachhari*.

On the fourteenth of the dark half of *Ashvin* (September-October) it is customary to apply red lead to the pillars erected in honour of men who die heroic deaths on fields of battle, to break coco-nuts before them, to light lamps fed with *ghi*, and to offer cooked food to their spirits.

The spirits of those who die with strong attachment to the objects of this world are said to enter the path of demons. In this condition the spirit of the deceased possesses the person of one of his relatives and torments the family in which he lived. The members of the family, when worried by his persecutions, engage the services of an exorcist, who sets up a wooden image of the tormenting spirit in a niche in a wall of the house. A lamp fed with *ghi* is lighted daily before this image, and in times of trouble a coco-nut is offered to it in the belief that the spirit can protect the offerers from injuries.

On the third day of the bright half of *Vaishakh* (April–May), which is called *Akha Trij*, women offer to Brahmans two earthen jars filled with water and covered with an earthen cup containing a betel-nut, a pice, and a betel-leaf, for the propitiation of the spirits of their deceased ancestors.

For the propitiation of a male spirit a party of Brahmans is feasted, and for the propitiation of a female spirit three unwidowed married women (*suvasinis*).

In Gujarat the shepherd tribes, such as Bharvads, Ahirs, and Kolis, set up either a pile of stones or a single stone on the boundary of their village in honour of those among them who die on battle-fields. These piles or stones are called *Palios*. On the *Palios* are placed engraved images to represent the deceased in whose memory the *Palios* are erected. Small pillars are also raised in the localities where such persons met their death. On the fourteenth day of the dark half of *Ashvin* (September-October) the *Palios* are daubed with red lead and worshipped with offerings of coco-nuts. Women who have become *sati* receive worship and offerings on the Hindu new year's day.

In the Konkan, especially among the lower classes, a strong belief prevails regarding the mortality of the spirits of the dead and of their reappearance or rebirth in their children. Persons dying with wishes unfulfilled are specially liable to rebirth in their descendants; and for this reason, as well as for protection against evil, ancestors are worshipped.

In the Deccan it is believed that if a dark spot can be found on the thigh, back, or stomach of a new-born child, it is an ancestor returned to life. Ashes are applied to its forehead in the name of the ancestor. A similar belief exists regarding infants that refuse to be fed, and wail incessantly. The application of ashes and the ancestor's name are said to act as an immediate cure.[1]

The custom regarding the worship of ancestors prevailing in the Konkan is as follows: It is performed on the no-moon day of every month, on the date of the death of the person every year, and also on the same date of the dark half of the month of *Bhadrapad* (August–September). Among Brahmans, Brahman priests are invited, worshipped, and are given a feast, after worshipping balls of boiled rice as representing the dead ancestors. The special materials used for worship are sesamum and barley grain. The same custom prevails among non-Brahmans, with the exception that the balls are made of rice flour and not of boiled rice. To partake of the food on such occasions, the lower classes invite married persons of their own caste. The anniversary day of holy men and ascetics is called the day of merit (*Punya tithi*).

It is believed that evil spirits undergo a transformation after a lapse of twelve years. The practice of giving the names of ancestors to children is common, and is due to the belief that the spirits of the dead are reborn in children in the same family.

At Pendur in the Ratnagiri District ancestors are worshipped on the last day of every Hindu calendar month. This monthly worship is called *Darsha Shraddha*. If any ancestor has died after becoming a recluse (*Sanyasi*) his body is buried, and a tomb (*samadhi*) is erected over it; and his descendants, instead of performing the annual *Shraddha*, worship the tomb of the recluse every day. It is believed that the spirits take a different form after the lapse of seven generations. The

[1] In some places numerous names of ancestors are uttered in such cases. The name which causes the crying to cease is held to be the ancestor who has returned.

belief that the spirits of the dead are reborn in the same family prevails among the people of this district. The following measures are adopted for the purpose of identification: When a person dies in a family, a *Tulsi* (holy Basil) or *Bel* (*Aegle Marmelos*) leaf is placed on a certain part of the body, or some familiar sign is made in sandal paste; and when a child is born in the family, its body is carefully examined to ascertain whether there are any signs on the body of the child such as were made on the dead body of the ancestor. If the same sign appears to the satisfaction of the members of the family, it is believed that the dead person has been reborn in the same family.

Throughout the Konkan the anniversary day of saints is observed by the performance of a *Bhajan*, which consists in singing the good deeds of saints, raising their banners, and in offering prayers. It is believed that spirits are mortal, but that they do not die like ordinary human beings. They cease to exist as spirits as soon as the period of their release is over. The spirits obtain absolution by visiting certain holy places.

At Shirvade in the Ratnagiri District ancestors are worshipped every year by performing rites (*tarpan*) which consist in offering oblations of holy water, sesamum, barley, and repeating prayers. The *tarpan* is observed on the very date of the month in which the person died. Owing to the belief that the spirits of the dead are reborn in children in the same family, the name of the grandfather is frequently given to the grandson.

At Naringre in the Ratnagiri District ancestors are worshipped by inviting Brahman priests, and worshipping them with sandal paste and flowers. These Brahmans are supposed to represent the father, grandfather, and great-grandfather of the worshipper.

At Bandivade in the Ratnagiri District leaves of mint (a good medicine for worms), sesamum, and *Darbha* grass (*Eragrostis cynosurides*) are required for the worship of ancestors. The man who worships the ancestors has to turn his sacred thread from the right hand to the left.

At Phonda in the Ratnagiri District ancestors are worshipped by making balls of boiled rice on their anniversary day. The balls are supposed to take the place of the dead parents, and they are worshipped with sandal paste and flowers, and by burning incense and lighting a lamp of clarified butter. Betel-nuts and leaves, coco-nuts, and presents of money are given to them. People also bow before them. Holy men and religious ascetics are worshipped by washing their feet, sandal paste is applied to their body, and they are garlanded with flowers. Coco-nuts, a piece of cloth, and a gift in coins are given to them according to the means of the giver. It is said that spirits can remain as spirits for about a thousand years.

In the Konkan a person whose father is alive, but who has lost his mother's father, has to perform the *Shraddha* of that grandfather on the first day of the bright half of *Ashvin* (September–October). This *Shraddha* is called *Duhitra.* A person who has lost his wife has to perform the *Shraddha* for that wife on the ninth day of the dark half of the month of *Bhadrapad* (August–September). This day is called *Ahev Navami.* These different sorts of *Shraddhas* are observed only by high-class Hindus. The lower classes worship their ancestors on the last day of the month of *Bhadrapad* (August–September) by preparing a ball of boiled rice or flour, and putting it out for the crows to eat. It is believed that spirits are mortal. The ceremony called *Narayan Nagabali* is performed when it is believed that the spirit of an ancestor is giving trouble to the family. When this rite is performed, the spirit is saved and the ailment ceases. It is believed that the spirits of the dead are sometimes reborn in children in the same family, and in such cases the names of the ancestors are given to their children by the people.

At Khopoli in the Kolaba District the form of worship of ancestors is similar to that of the ordinary Hindu deities. In the case of the worship of the deities the person performing the worship has to sit with his face towards the east, while at the worship of the ancestors he has to sit with his face towards the south.

The people of Chidhran in the Kolaba District believe that the period for which the soul has to remain in the spirit state depends upon the sins of the person, or the wishes which remained unfulfilled during his lifetime. It is not that all spirits of the dead are reborn in children. The rebirth depends upon the good or bad deeds of the deceased. However, if the nature of any child suggests the nature of any dead person in the family, it is assumed that the spirit of the deceased has returned to the family.

At Nagothane in the Kolaba District some of the communities worship small images called *tanks* on the anniversary of their ancestors' death: among *Shudras* food is given to the crows on the last day of *Bhadrapad* (August–September). The custom of giving a grandfather's name to the grandson prevails largely, and is due to the belief that the spirits of the dead are sometimes reborn in the same family. It is also said that in some of the Hindu communities, if a child cries continuously, ashes are applied to its forehead in the name of one of the ancestors in the family; and if the child sleeps quietly or stops crying, the name of that ancestor is given to it.

At Malad in the Thana District the worship of ancestors is performed on the day of the father's death every month till the completion of one year by inviting Brahmans and giving them a feast. This is done among Brahmans only. The other communities worship their ancestors by performing the rite called *Chata Shraddha* and by giving rice, pulse, vegetables, and *ghi* to Brahman priests. A feast is then given to their caste-men.

At Kolhapur ancestors, holy men, and religious ascetics are worshipped by the rites known as the Puranic ritual, that is, no Vedic verses are repeated while performing these rites. It is a common belief in this province that the soul of the person who has committed a murder or has incurred debt and enmity is obliged to repay the debt by being born again as a servant of the debtor, or in some other subordinate capacity.

The soul is not said to have finally perished unless it merges into the divine self and attains salvation. The passions and desires of a dying man do not permit his soul ascending beyond a certain stage, where he or she remains as a ghost until the soul is purged of all his or her desires and sins by the performance of funeral ceremonies. For relieving ancestral spirits from the low order of *bhuts* and *pishachas*, *Shraddhas* are performed by their surviving relatives in such holy places as Prabhas, Gaya, and Pindtarak. These ceremonies are known as *Narayanbali*, *Nilotsarga*, and *Saptaha-parayan* (recitation of a sacred book for seven consecutive days).

Those persons who die with wicked thoughts still present and their desires not fulfilled enter the order of evil spirits, from which they are liberated after their desires have been satisfied and their wicked thoughts eliminated.

Bhuts and *pishachas*—ghosts, male and female—can be prevented from doing harm by recourse to certain processes. For instance, the wife of a Nagar of Gadhada in Gujara became a spirit after her death and began to torment the second wife of her husband by throwing her out of bed whenever she was asleep. To prevent this, the husband took a vow to perform a *Shraddha* at Sidhpur in the name of the deceased wife, after the performance of which the ghostly presence stopped harassing the new wife.

Bhuts and *pishachas* are believed by some people to be immortal, because they are supposed to belong to the order of demigods. In the well-known Sanskrit lexicon, *Amorkosha*, they are classed with divinities, such as *guhyaks* and *sidhas*. The *bhut* is defined as a deity that troubles infants and the *pishacha* as a deity that lives on flesh. *Bhuts* and *pishachas* are the attendants of Shiva. They are supposed to be demigods.

Preta is the spirit of a person who dies a sudden or unnatural death with many of his desires unfulfilled. His soul attains emancipation by a recitation of the *Bhagvat* on seven consecutive days. It is described in the *Bhagvat* how Dhundhumari, the brother of Gokarn, who had become a *preta*, was released from his *preta* existence by the performance of a *saptah* which his brother caused to be made. The *Garudpuran* mentions that King Babruvahan emancipated a *preta* by the performance of a *Shraddha*. The salvation (*mukti*) of a *preta* is in itself its death. This shows *pretas* to be of limited existence.

The span of life of the *bhuts* and *pretas* is very long, but those whose descendants offer them the usual oblations gain their emancipation sooner. There is a spring called Zilanand in the vicinity of Jhinjhuvada in Kathiawar, on the banks of which is a temple of Zilakeshwar Mahadev. The performance of the *Shraddha* by the side of this spring is believed to expedite the emancipation of the spirits of the deceased from ghostly life. Every year, on the new-moon day of the month *Bhadrapad* (August–September), a great fair is held on this spot, when people from long distances visit the place to get their relatives exorcised by the *Bhuvas* or exorcists.

It is believed, that though *bhuts*, *pretas*, and *pishachas* are immortal, they are scared away by the sound of a European band and of other musical instruments. It is said that all drums and other weird instruments, whether European or Indian, have the power of scaring away evil spirits.

An evil spirit called Babaro once entered the person of the uncle of Maldev, the king of Jhalavad, much to the king's annoyance. Maldev offered a stubborn fight to Babaro, who, unable to cope with Maldev, promised to extend his kingdom over those villages in which he would hang up bunting in one night. It is said that the present extent of the Jhalavad State territories was due to King Maldev's enterprise in hanging up bunting over these territories as asked by Babaro.

Though at the time of a man's death the faculties may hardly be sound, yet the *vasana*—the impressions—left on his mind by his past actions are in themselves good or bad enough to impress him so as to make his departing spirit assume a new form of life in keeping with them. For instance, a man following a particular profession becomes subject to dreams bearing on that profession. When the impression created by his actions in daily life is so deep as to induce dreams, his mind, even after death, leaves to his departing soul an inclination to be engaged in the subject of his mind's last activities. This is *vasana*.

It is a popular saying among Hindus that children inherit the nature of their parents. It is for this reason that high-caste Hindus do not utter the names of their eldest sons.

As the saying goes, *Pita putrena jayate*, that is, a father is born in the form of the son, so the *Pitriyas* are born as descendants of their children, or according to the *Bija vrikshanyaya*, as a tree springs from its seed, that is, its offspring, so parents take birth as children of the offspring.

The ancestors whose attachment to their children or family or wealth does not die with them reappear in the same family as descendants. It is also believed that persons dying with debts unpaid, with the consciousness that they must be paid, are reborn in this world for the discharge of their obligations.

It is not always that ancestral spirits reappear in the same family. It is said about the departed spirits that, after undergoing punishment for their sins and enjoying the fruits of their good actions, they come down to earth again as drops of rain, and forming part of the grain which grows on rain-water, make their way into the wombs of animals and are thus reborn.

On account of the community of their feelings, habits, and ideas in previous births, members of different families form different groups. The actions performed in this life keep them bound to one another either as recipients of the return of the obligations given in the past or as givers of fresh obligations. The members of a family stand thus to one another in the relation of debtors and creditors. It is for the discharge of these debts and recovery of dues that several individuals are united in a family. This naturally leads to the members of a family taking birth again in the same family for the proper discharge of debts.

A virtuous child is declared to have been born to return the debts contracted in its past lives, and a vicious one to recover the dues.

When a holy man or a recluse dies, his body is interred, and a platform rising waist high from the ground, or a small dome-shaped temple, is built over the spot. This is called a *samadh*. An image of Shiva is generally installed in the *samadh*; but sometimes the impressions on stone of the footsteps of the deceased (*padukas*) are installed instead. Instances of the latter are the *padukas* of Dattatraya, Gorakha, and Machchendra Nath.

Both the *samadh* and the image of the god Shiva, as well as the *padukas* installed therein, are worshipped by the people, who in course of time give currency to the belief that the *samadh* possesses certain miraculous powers, such as curing long-standing diseases, blessing barren women with children, &c. Offerings are made to the *samadh* by pious persons; and festivals or fairs are held in its honour by the inhabitants of the village in which the *samadh* is located.

Tombs raised over the graves of Muhammadan saints are held in equal reverence both by Muhammadans and Hindus. To these tombs offerings are made, and fairs are held in their honour.

Worship of Holy Men and Saints

Holy men receive personal worship during their lifetime. After they are dead, their relics—such as impressions of their footsteps, their photographs or busts—are worshipped with offerings of sandal paste, flowers, red powder, frankincense, lamps fed with *ghi*, and the swingings of lamps (*arati*).

Every sect of Hindus has a spiritual head, *Maharaja*, and it is considered meritorious to entertain and worship him on certain special occasions. The *Maharaja*, also known as the *Guru*, is received in great state. His followers form a procession and carry him in a palanquin or a carriage and pair accompanied with music. At the house of the person who invites him, the floor is covered with rich cloth, over which the *Maharaja* is led to a raised seat specially arranged for the purpose. He is then worshipped by the host with the same details as the image of a god. His feet are washed in a mixture of *ghi*, milk, honey, sugar, and water (*panchamrita*), which is sipped by the worshipper and distributed among the followers of the *Maharaja*. Very often the feet of the *Maharaja* are washed in water, which is considered as purifying as the *panchamrita*. Great festivity and rejoicings are observed on this day at the house of the *Maharaja's* host, where crowds of the *Maharaja's* followers assemble, eager for a sight of him. After spending about half an hour in the house, the *Maharaja* departs, first receiving valuable presents from the host.

Spiritual guides who claim the power of working miracles are held in high esteem by the people. Some of these guides are said to have control over spiritual beings or to possess their favour. These spirits are supposed to endow them with the power of preparing mystic threads, which, when worn round the waist, neck, or arm, cure various diseases.

Spiritual guides such as Shankaracharya, Vallabacharya, the *Maharajas* or spiritual heads of the sect called Swaminarayan, Lalo Bhagat, and Talo Bhagat are worshipped by their devotees with offerings of food, garments, and cash. In this age men who are really great are rare ; and even if there be some, they are invisible to the faulty vision of the present-day degraded mortals. A few come into contact with such holy men by virtue of the good deeds performed by them in their past lives. These are said to attain paradise by contact with the righteous.

In the Kadavasan woods, near the village of Daldi in Gujarat, there lives a *Bava* called Bhimputi, who is believed to possess miraculous powers. He surprises visitors by his wonderful feasts and commands vows from the afflicted by mitigating their sufferings. Every day, before breakfast, the *Bava* visits seven villages to collect sugar and flour, which he throws in handfuls over every ant-hill which he meets on his way. This act of charity has established him as a saint, and most of his prophecies are believed to be fulfilled.

A Musalman named Muhammad Chhail is held in great respect by the people on account of his great magical powers. He is believed to be in the good graces of a *Pir,* who has endowed him with the power of commanding material objects to come to him from long distances, and of breaking them and making them whole again.

Great men of antiquity often command worship as gods. A fast is observed by Hindus on the ninth day of the bright half of *Chaitra* (March–April), the birthday of Rama, whose anniversary is celebrated at noon on that day in his temple. On this occasion, all visitors to the temple offer a pice or two to his image and receive consecrated food, which consists of a mixture of curdled milk and sugar. The birth of Krishna is celebrated at midnight on the eighth day of the dark half of *Shravan* (July–August), when people keep awake for the whole of the night.

The Jains observe a fast for seven days from *Shravan Vad Baras,* that is, the twelfth day of the dark half of *Shravan* (July–August) to the fifth day of the bright half of *Bhadrapad* (August–September), in honour of Mahavir Swami, one of their spiritual teachers, who is believed to have been born on the second day of the bright half of *Bhadrapad* (August–September). This period is known as the *Pajusan,* during which the Jains cause the slaughter-houses and fish-markets to be closed and give alms to the poor.

A century ago there lived at Nalkantha a sage named Bhansab. He met a holy death by deep meditations, and a few days after rose up from his grave in his original form. This led him to be classed in the category of great men and to command divine worship.

Vithal, a sage of the Kathi tribe, is revered in Paliad. Savo, a devotee at Zanzarka, is worshipped by Dheds. Fehala, a Rajput, and Tolat, his wife, are enshrined at Anjar, a village in Cutch. Lalo, a Bania devotee of Sindhavar, received divine honours in his lifetime, and his image in Sayala is held in great reverence to this day. The tomb of Madhvagar, an Atit of Vastadi, situated in Unchadi, a village near Ahmedabad, is an object of worship. Harikrishna Maharaja, a Brahman saint of Chuda, received divine honours at Chuda and the Charotar.[1]

Spirits, how they arise

It is a common belief that the soul can leave the body temporarily.

When a man feels thirsty in sleep, his soul is supposed to leave the body to drink water, and if it finds the water-pots covered, not to return to the body, which is found dead the next morning. It is for this reason that most people either drink water or keep uncovered water-pots near them, at the time of going to bed.

In the Deccan and Konkan it is held that if while the spirit is absent during sleep the face of the sleeper is marked or coloured by some one, the spirit finds difficulty in re-entering the body of the sleeper.

Shankaracharya was a life-long celibate. Once in a discussion with the wife of Mandan Mishra, she put to him a question on the subject of the pleasures of married life. To answer the question it was necessary to have the experiences of a married life. To gain these experiences Shankaracharya's soul left his body and entered the corpse of a king just dead, and enjoyed

[1] For particulars of many other important shrines of saints, see *Folk-lore Notes of Gujarat*, pp. 94–97.

the pleasures of married life for six months in the company of the queen of the deceased king. It then returned to his body, which was preserved by his disciples according to his instructions, and answered the question put to him by the wife of Mandan Mishra.

It is related that the spirit of the daughter of a blacksmith in Luvaria returned to her body two hours after her death, after which she lived for a fortnight.

A similar story is told of a Nagar Brahman, who lived for some years after the return of his spirit to his body.

About forty years ago, the corpse of a Kanbi in Lilapur was carried to the burning ground for cremation, and there his spirit returned to his body. On being asked where he had been, the Kanbi replied that he had been to Dharmaraja, the lord of hell, who told him to go back to his body, saying that his life's thread had not yet ended. It is related that the Kanbi lived for some years after this incident.

Another instance of the soul departing and then returning to the body is that of a Kanbi woman in Lilapur, whose soul returned to the body after she had been carried to the burning ground. The woman lived for five years after this occurrence.

A Brahman in Limbdi named Vaijnath had, by the performance of *yoga*, obtained the power of sending his spirit out of his body and recalling it at pleasure.

A belief is current in the Sholapur District that a saint, Anand Murti of Brahmanal, who died at Sangli, resumed his body to save his disciples carrying it to Brahmanal, seven miles distant, and then left the body again.

The soul of a living being leaves its physical tabernacle during sleep and hovers about. It can go to and return from even the heavenly and infernal regions.

There are eighteen kinds of *siddhis* or accomplishments, one of which is the power of entering the body of another and returning to one's own body at will. The soul cannot exist separated from the body. When a person who revives after death is asked how he returned to life, he declares that he has been carried to the presence of the god of death by his messengers, being mistaken for another bearing the same name and living in the same locality. When such a mistake is detected, the god of death tells the soul of the man concerned that his life's span has not yet ended, and sends it back to the body, which appears to be dead.

Often the soul of a man ascends to his temples, when the man is supposed to be dead although he is alive. In such cases, when the soul descends, the man is supposed to come to life again.

It is believed by some people that if all the desires of a man are not satisfied at the time of his death, his soul leaves the body to satisfy them and subsequently returns to the corpse, whereupon the body revives.

A man dying with a keen desire for wealth keeps guard as a spirit over the possessions he leaves behind. A learned man proud of his great knowledge passes his time as a spirit in repeating what he has learnt.

A devotee in his meditative trance can send forth his soul whithersoever he pleases.

It is also believed that the soul of man leaves the body in sleep to enjoy those pleasures which it cannot enjoy in wakefulness.

The popular conceptions of the character and functions of the spirit known as a *bhut* or disembodied soul are as follows :

A spirit has no recognized form. It may assume the form of a human being, a goat, a blaze of fire, a whirlwind, a dog, an ass, a sheep, a man, a sound, or any other object it pleases. Some assume a terribly gigantic and fearfully uncouth frame, with big fang-like teeth, long matted hair, and a height that reaches the sky. At times they assume the form of a child and cry heart-breakingly at a concealed corner of a road. Should a passer-by, out of compassion, try to save it, the supposed infant begins to lengthen its legs to show its benefactor its real and supernatural dimensions. Sometimes it transforms itself into a gigantic and terrible being, taking possession of the man if he becomes afraid.

Some evil spirits manifest themselves as showers of burning charcoal, while some are so forward as to offer their services as guides to strangers from one village to another, or ask for tobacco, &c. Some assume the form of *Bhensasur*, a demon in the form of a buffalo, said to be a most malignant spirit.

The throat of a spirit is as narrow as the fine end of a needle, and yet it is believed to require a dozen potfuls of water to quench its thirst. It cannot get pure water, as such water is guarded by the god Varuna. It has, therefore, to quench its thirst with such dirty water as it can get. Similarly, it cannot get clean food, and has to satisfy its hunger on human excrement, the droppings of birds and other animals, urine, and the filth of houses.

It is generally believed that evil spirits do not cast shadows. All attempts to catch them prove futile, as they vanish in the form of a flame.

If it is sought to catch hold of a goat-shaped spirit, the ghost swells into such a monstrous size that the spectator gets terrified, whereupon the ghost finds an opportunity of disappearing in a flame.

It is believed that spirits prefer darkness to light and silence to noise. They live on the *Pipal* (*Ficus religiosa*) or *Shami* (*Prosopis spicigera*) trees.

A spirit presents itself to the vision of a man by blocking his way in the form of a goat or some other animal.

Spirits are believed to infest woods, unused wells, cellars, and old tanks. They are also found in ruins and cemeteries. As far as possible they keep themselves aloof from mortals; but at times they are visible to human beings, mostly to those destitute of religion and morals. They roam about and terrify people. Sometimes they enter the persons of human beings. Such men either gain in strength, fall sick, or become senseless. The spirits who possess them make them laugh or work, without being fatigued, with ten times the vigour they originally possessed.

Spirits keep their persons uncovered, feed upon flesh and blood, sleep during the day, and roam about at night.

Often a large concourse of spirits meet together and dance, sing, and make merry, uttering loud and fierce shrieks. A spirit has no back and has its feet reversed. It keeps away from man, but terrifies him by pelting him with stones from a distance.

On the fourteenth day of the dark half of *Ashvin* (September–October) all ghosts are believed to go about playing pranks with poor mortals and possessing them.

The *Navaratra* holidays are the season when spirits appear in many places.

Spirits enter corpses or possess human beings and speak through them as a medium. Sometimes they assume their original human form, and often torment people with disease. They present themselves as animals and pass away in a blaze. They hum in the air without being seen, wrestle with men, or carry unseen human beings from one place to another. Some women are believed to conceive by intercourse with male ghosts.

If a man happens to step into the circle made with water round the offering given to a spirit, he is possessed by the spirit. A house haunted by a spirit is the scene of great mischief.

Spirits are said to be most mischievous during the first part of the night. Their fury diminishes with the advance of night.

They are inimical to human beings, terrify them, and sometimes, assuming the form of a cobra, kill those whom they hated most during life.

They are pleased with offerings of blood.

To throw stones at houses and trees and to set them on fire are their usual pranks.

The spirit called *Jan* manifests itself as a giant, its height reaching the sky. If a man comes under its shadow, he is seized by it and dashed to pieces on the ground. On the contrary, if a man wins its favour, he becomes prosperous. Hence a proverb has been current of ' seizing another as by a *jan* ', meaning ' being attacked by a dire misfortune '.

There is a female spirit called *Chudel.* Its back is covered with flesh, its feet are reversed, its form is hollow, and its face handsome like that of a charming woman.

It is said that a woman dying in childbed becomes a *chudel.* Her form is a skeleton behind with the figure of a pretty woman in front. The left hand of the dead woman is sometimes cut off, as it is believed to be a potent charm for controlling a *chudel.*

It is believed that mastery over spirits can be obtained by dint of incantations. Those who subjugate spirits in this way have power to command them to do their behests. But the process by which such powers are procured is believed to be beset with dangers, and many lose their lives in so doing.

There is also a belief that a *bhut* or spirit can be brought under control by lopping off a lock of its hair or topknot and keeping it in one's custody.

It is said that this lock ought to be kept inside the right thigh by tearing a hole in the flesh. It is believed that the thigh can be cut open by a hair of the spirit without injury.

The spirit so subjugated should never be kept unemployed; otherwise it oppresses its master.

It is believed that the spirits of deceased persons become ghosts under the following conditions:

1. If scriptural ceremonies are not performed with the ceremonial offerings of rice-balls to the deceased.

2. If the deceased dies with a strong attachment to worldly objects.

3. If the death is unnatural, that is, caused by an accident.

All ghosts get absolution by the performance of propitiative ceremonies by their descendants as prescribed in the scriptures.

There are various beliefs current as to the state of the soul after death. The *Garudpuran* contains many passages illustrating its movements after it leaves the body. Says the book:

'When the soul leaves the body it assumes a form as small as a thumb. At this very moment it is caught by the servants of Yama while it is crying out "Ha! ha!" looking at its corporal receptacle.'

And again:

'Covering the body of the soul (which suffers intensely) and strangling it forcibly, the servants of the god Yama carry it away just as a culprit is carried by a king's soldiers.'

The verses that follow describe the miseries inflicted upon the poor thumb-sized soul for the sins committed by it during its lifetime. The sinful soul has to undergo similar miseries in hell. From hell it returns to this world guarded by the servants of Yama, to partake of the rice-balls and other articles of food offered by the sons or other relatives. It is then again taken to hell to suffer more miseries and penalties in expiation of past sins. Then it returns once more to receive the offerings of rice-balls made at *Shraddha* ceremonies. If, even after this, any desires remain unfulfilled, it has to continue a wretched existence in the other world.

In a chapter of the *Pretamanjari* of the *Garudpuran* it is stated that the souls of righteous men go to the next world unmolested.

Some people believe that the departing soul assumes a form like a thumb, and remains in that state until relieved by the performance of *Shraddha* by his heirs. It then enters the other world to enjoy the fruits of its good actions. The *Yamapuri*, or the city of the god of death, is 8,600 *yojans*—a *yojan* being equal to four miles—to the south of the earth. The lord of this place is Dharmaraja. Yama is his servant, whose duty is to carry the soul from one place to another.

Others maintain that two states await the soul after death according to whether it has performed righteous or sinful acts during life.

The righteous attain to heaven and enter the *Parshad Vaikunta* of Vishnu. The sinful go to hell or *Yamaloka*.

The sinful souls go to *Yamaloka* and are made to suffer the miseries of twenty-eight *naraks* or hells in proportion to the sins perpetrated by them, after which they return to the earth.

The following are some of the punishments meted out to wicked souls for their sins, in their next lives:

1. Those who murder Brahmans suffer from consumption.
2. Those who slaughter cows are born as tortoises.
3. Those guilty of female infanticide suffer from white leprosy.
4. One who kills his wife, as well as a woman guilty of causing abortion, becomes a beggar.
5. Those who commit adultery become impotent.
6. He who seats himself on the bed or seat of his preceptor is affected by skin diseases.
7. Flesh-eaters get a red body.
8. Those who indulge in drink get black teeth.
9. A Brahman partaking of prohibited food suffers from dropsy.
10. One who eats sweets without sharing them with the bystanders suffers from cancer in the throat.

11. One who offers polluted food to departed spirits suffers from black leprosy.

12. One who disobeys and despises his teacher suffers from wind (*apasmar*).

13. One who does not believe in the *Shastras* suffers from enlargement of the spleen or Bright's disease.

14. A perjurer is born dumb.

15. One who does not serve food equally to all the members at a dining-table loses one of his eyes.

16. Those who break off a marriage alliance are punished with thick (negro-like) lips.

17. Those who steal books lose their eyesight.

18. He who kicks a Brahman becomes lame.

19. A liar becomes a stammerer.

20. Those who listen to versions contradictory of what is generally believed to be true become deaf.

21. One who poisons another becomes a lunatic.

22. One who steals precious metals becomes indigent.

23. An incendiary is punished with a bald head.

24. Meat-sellers meet with misfortunes.

25. One who steals gold has his nails deformed.

26. He who steals food is born a mouse.

27. One stealing corn is born as a locust.

28. One stealing opium or other poisonous drugs is born a scorpion.

29. One who steals leaves or vegetables is born a peacock.

30. One who enjoys perfumes by stealing them is born a mole.

31. One who steals honey becomes a vulture.

32. One who steals flour, rice, &c., is born a monkey.

The state of the soul after death depends upon a man's good or bad actions in life.

The souls of the righteous leave the body without any trouble. The messengers of the god of death present themselves to these souls in the form of saints and carry them to that part of the heaven which is presided over by their favourite deity, by the eastern, northern or western gates. They are received there with great respect. Here they enjoy the fruits of their merit, after which they return to this world and are born either in the family of a wealthy virtuous man or in that of a poor

Brahman who has attained the knowledge of God. In this new life they accumulate further merit, in virtue of which they are endowed with a higher spiritual life in the following birth, and so on until they attain final emancipation.

After attaining salvation the soul becomes free from the wheel of birth and rebirth.

To the souls of the sinful, who leave their bodies with a great struggle, the messengers of the god of death present themselves in a terrible form. They are carried to hell by the southern gate, being constantly lashed on the way. There they are relegated to one of the twenty-eight pits of hell appropriate to their misdeeds, to suffer retribution for their sins.

The soul is carried to Dharmaraja after it leaves the body. Thence, with the permission of the god, it returns to this world and halts for thirteen days at the threshold of its house. On the thirteenth day an earthen jar filled with water is emptied on a *Pipal* tree (*Ficus religiosa*), after which its connexion with this world ceases. Then it returns to the heavenly judge of actions (Dharmaraja) and is again born in the species prescribed by him. The soul of a strictly spiritual being merges into the divine entity and becomes free from birth and rebirth.

Moksha or *Mukti*, that is final emancipation, is of two kinds: *sayujja* or merging into the divine form, and *samishya* or entering the divine order and living in this state so long as one's merits allow.

Dharmaraja keeps an account of the good and bad actions of all men in his book and dispenses justice according to it. A man guilty of adultery is sentenced to embrace a red-hot image of a woman; one who has slaughtered animals is devoured by those animals; while those who have committed the sin of murdering Brahmans are relegated to hell for ever.

There are seven rungs to the ladder which leads to the next world. The first is covered with a thick forest. The second bristles with pointed spears. The third is strewn with a species of thorns. The fourth has piercing blasts. On the fifth runs the river Vaitarna. The sixth is full of red-hot iron. The seventh is covered with deep streams.

After death, the soul has to cross the river Vaitarna (*vide* the fifth rung above) on its way to the next world. Those who have given cows in charity can cross this river without difficulty by holding the tails of the cows which present themselves to help them.

Those who have given shoes in charity can tread the third step with ease.

The sinful have to walk barefooted on ground studded with pointed spears, and to embrace red-hot iron pillars. It is with the object of avoiding these miseries that people distribute shoes and clothes in charity.

The sinful expiate their sins by passing through a cycle of 8,400,000 births. They have to be born 2,100,000 times in the class of creatures born of eggs, 2,100,000 times in the species of worms produced from sweat, 2,100,000 times from embryonic birth, and a similar number of times in the vegetable kingdom.

Those who lack virtue but commit no sins are born in the divine order of a low grade, such as the servants of Kuber, the attendants of the god Shiva, Gandharvas, Vaitals, Brahmarakshasas, Kushmands, and other demigods. Virtuous women are born as goddesses or *devis* or as *apsaras* or celestial songstresses. Those who have performed only a few acts of righteousness enter the ranks of Jakhinis, Kinnaris, Matrikas, and the maid-servants of the goddess Durga.

The souls of the righteous are carried by Yamadutas or the messengers of the god of death through five cities, by a route passing through beautiful gardens: while those of the sinful are led barefooted over brambles and pointed spears by roads running through dense forests hidden in pitchy darkness. The latter have also to cross large rivers and pass through streams filled with blood and pus. As they pass, eagles prey upon their bodies and they are bitten by venomous snakes.

The souls of those who have in life performed good actions pass through the sun and assume divine forms; while those of ordinary beings pass through the moon and return to this world.

In order that the departed soul may not find its way difficult, his heirs make a gift (*seraja*) to a Brahman of a bedstead, bedding, a lamp, corn, a pair of shoes and other articles, on the thirteenth day after death.

Those who meet a sudden or violent death, e.g. by being crushed under a falling house, by drowning in a well, by an accidental fall, by a snake-bite, &c., enter the order of *bhuts, pretas, pishachas*, &c., and are said to have gone to *durgati* or to a bad path.

In the Karnatak it is generally believed that those who are killed by tigers or other wild animals are reborn in such animals.

But those who die on a field of battle are believed to attain heaven.

According to another belief, persons dying a violent death have to pass through the same fate, that is, die violently, for the next seven lives.

Their souls are said to be liable to enter the *asurgati* or the order of devils. They are emancipated from this condition by the performance by their descendants of the ceremony called *Nil parnavavi* or of those ceremonies prescribed in the *Pal Shastra.*

It is also believed that such souls after entering the order of ghosts oppress and torment their descendants and relatives.

In the case of suicides, when the crime is proved before the god of death the culprit is hurled into a hell called *Maharaurava*, where he has to pass a thousand years. After the expiry of this period he is born again into this world, again commits suicide, and again meets the same fate after death. This is repeated seven times, after which he has to pass through 8,400,000 species of animals before again obtaining the human life.

If the suicide be caused by poisoning, the person in his next life becomes a serpent ; if by drowning or strangling, he becomes a ghost.

Some believe that the souls of persons meeting violent death enter the order of such ghosts as *Jinni, Mamo*, &c. For their emancipation, *Shraddhas* are performed by their descendants. At times these ghosts possess the persons of their nearest relatives, and through this medium declare their desires. If they express a desire to have a *palio* or pillar erected in their name, one is erected on the spot where they breathed their last. On this pillar is engraved a figure riding a horse, representing the deceased, which is besmeared with red lead or ochre. This representation is worshipped as a deity with offerings of frankincense, coco-nuts, and lamps fed with *ghi*.

The *palio* is called *surdhan* and is worshipped, especially on the death anniversary of the deceased.

In some castes the *surdhans* are installed in the house of the deceased.

There are various beliefs current as to the way in which spirits enter and leave the body.

According to one belief, when a person gets frightened by the apparition of a ghost, the ghost enters his body through one of the organs, and makes him senseless and violent.

According to another belief, a ghost, as stated above, takes an airy form and enters the body through any channel through which air can enter the body. It leaves the body by the same route.

There is also a belief that evil spirits enter the body of a man through any part of the body, and under their influence the person possessed dances, jumps, foams, or sits idle.

There is a further belief that a ghost enters the body through the thumb and gets out by the ears.

According to some, a ghost makes its way into the body through the anus and its exit by the same route.

Others maintain that it enters the body through the nostrils and gets out by the same passage.

Some say that it finds an entrance and outlet through the skull.

There are others who are of opinion that the immaterial form of a ghost can find admission into the body by the right side and egress the same way.

At Adivare it is believed that only Hindu saints and ascetics, after deep and devout meditation, are capable of removing the soul from the body. It is believed that their souls go to heaven during that period and return at pleasure. At present there are no such *Sadhus* in the district.

The people of Chaul in the Kolaba District do not consider it possible ordinarily for the soul to leave the body, but they state that the Swami of Alandi, who died in or about the year 1886, used to remove his soul from the body by means of *Yoga*.

At Bankavali in the Ratnagiri District, it is believed that

ghosts or evil spirits have the form of a human being, but their feet are turned backwards. They can assume any form they choose. Their character is ordinarily to trouble the people, but when satisfied they are said to prove friendly. The following story is narrated of a person who went to reside in one of the villages of the Konkan: His wife was first attacked by a ghost called *Girha*. The *Girha* troubled him much by making mischief in his house, viz. by taking away eatables or by mixing dirt in his food. At night he used to divest the couple of their clothes, and on one occasion an ornament was removed by the spirit from the person of the wife. Tired of these annoyances, the man left the village and went to reside at a distance, when, to the astonishment of the public, it happened that the ornament which was lost at the old village was restored to the man's wife while she was asleep in the new village, and nobody knew who brought it there. All this was believed to be the work of the *Girha*.

At Ubhadanda in the Ratnagiri District people believe that a *Bhut* is fierce in aspect and very troublesome, but when its wishes are complied with it becomes harmless. The *Bhuts* reside in jungles, burial, or cremation grounds, old trees, sacred groves, and deserted houses. They assume all sorts of shapes and forms. Sometimes they appear very tall, and they can instantly assume the shape of a dog, a cat, a tiger, or any other animal. Some ghosts are even seen fishing on the banks of rivers.

At Mitbav it is believed that the souls of those who die with their wishes unfulfilled take the form of a *Bhut*. They enter the bodies of people. Any woman who is attacked by the *Bhut* of a Pir becomes able to speak in the Pir's language, although it may not be her mother tongue. When a child or a person is suffering from the attacks of a spirit, incense is burnt, and it at once begins to tell the whereabouts of the spirit and the reason why the person has been attacked. He is then asked to state what he wants, and when the things which the spirit wants are offered, it goes away. Spirits are generally invisible.

The spirits that belong to the class of malignant *Bhuts* are of a ferocious appearance; but those that belong to the class of friendly *Bhuts* possess bodies like human beings.

At Naringre it is believed that spirits are cruel by nature and have no shadow, that they are capable of taking any form they like, and can perform miracles. At Pendur it is believed that *Bhuts* eat chillies, and that they do not speak with human beings. Spirits are said to remove and conceal their victims for a certain period of time. At Vijayadurg a *Bhut* is considered to be of mean character. People perform certain rites to bring it under subjection. Their actions are always contrary to nature. When a person begins to cry, dance, or eat forbidden things, &c., he is said to be attacked by a *Bhut*. When there is enmity between two persons, the one who dies first becomes a *Sambandh* and troubles his living enemy. At Basani there is a belief that there are two kinds of spirits. Some aim at the welfare of the people, and others are always troublesome. As they have no regular form they cannot easily be recognized. They can change their forms at any time.

The character of a *Bhut* is to trouble people and to take revenge on an old enemy. A person attacked by a spirit speaks incoherently and acts like a madman. In such cases the leaves of the Rue (*Ruta graveolens*) are used. The leaves are pounded and put under the patient's nose. In a few minutes the person who is possessed by the spirit begins to speak.

The people of Chauk in the Kolaba District believe that the main function of a *Bhut* is to frighten people, to beat them, and to make them perform unpleasant tasks and thereby to obtain food from them. At Poladpur it is believed that if a person is able to bring a *Bhut* under his control he can make it do every kind of work for himself. The people of Akshi believe that kindling fire without any reason and throwing stones at certain houses are the main functions of *Bhuts*. At Vavashi in the Kolaba District it is believed that *Bhuts*, while walking, never touch the earth, but always move through the air, and that they have no shadow. The old men of Shirgaum advise young children not to respond to the call of anybody at night unless the person calling is an acquaintance, for such calls are sometimes those of an evil spirit.

In the Kolhapur District it is believed that the character of a *Bhut* is like that of a human being. When a person is attacked by a spirit, a great change is observed in his language and actions. He begins to speak in the language of the *Bhut* by which he is attacked. If the ghost is of the female sex, the person speaks the language of females. It is believed that the souls of those who have been murdered or tormented assume the form of a spirit known as *Sambandh*, and trouble the murderer or the torturer by entering his body. It is said that in some cases the spirit does not leave the body of such a person till he dies, thus exacting revenge for his past misdeeds. In Khopoli in Ratnagiri it is said that the cow which is given to a Brahman while performing the funeral rites of a dead person helps him to reach heaven. He gets there by catching hold of her tail. There are three paths to the other world. They are *Bhaktimarga*, *Karmamarga*, and *Yogamarga*. The *Karmamarga* is believed to be superior to all. At Malad a belief prevails that the path to the other world is through the Himalayas. While going through the mountains of the Himalayas, souls find happiness or sorrow according to their acts during their lives. The people also believe that the soul returns every month on the date of the man's death to accept cooked food given to the *manes*, and reaches heaven at the end of one year. At Dahigaum it is customary among the Hindus to smear with cow-dung the place from which a dead body has been removed to the burning-ground. The place is then covered with rice flour, and is hidden under a basket, an oil-lamp being kept burning near by. The persons who accompany the corpse return home to look at the lamp, and it is believed that the soul of the deceased will pass to any creature or species of which footprints are seen on the rice flour.

At Kolhapur it is believed that the soul of a person after death attains that state to which he aspires at the last moment before his death. Virtuous persons who die without any desire reach heaven and remain there in the form of the stars, where they are believed to enjoy the happiness of heaven. Some of them are sent to this world when they wish to return. Sinners are said to reach hell in consequence of their misdeeds, but some remain in this world in the form of *Bhuts*.

The people of Achare in the Ratnagiri District believe that the souls of persons who die by accident return to the same caste, and have to remain there till the expiry of an appointed period.

The people of Chauk believe that persons dying a sudden

or violent death leave wishes unfulfilled, and are therefore compelled to remain in this world in the form of *Bhuts*.

At Rai in the Thana District it is believed that the souls of those dying a sudden or violent death attain salvation according to their deeds in their lifetime, but it is a current belief that those committing suicide take the form of a ghost, and those who die on battle-fields attain eternal salvation.

At Kolhapur it is believed that the souls of those who die violent deaths do not attain salvation, but are turned into ghosts.

The people of Ubhadanda in the Ratnagiri District believe that *Bhuts* do not possess visible human forms. They can assume any shapes they like, but there is a common belief that the hands and feet of *Bhuts* are always turned backwards.

The most favourable times for spirits to enter human bodies are midday, midnight, and twilight. Women in delivery as well as those in their menses are most liable to be attacked by spirits. It is generally believed that persons adorned with ornaments are attacked by spirits, especially in cases of women and children. Again, a common belief prevails in the Konkan that persons, and particularly ladies, decked with flowers and ornaments are more liable to be attacked by spirits than others. The people of Phonda are of opinion that spirits generally enter and leave human bodies through the organ of hearing, while the people of Naringre hold that the hair is the best way for spirits to enter. The residents of Ibhrampur state that the mouth and the nose are the favourite channels for spirits entering human bodies. At Mitbav it is believed that spirits attack people in the throat, and generally only those persons who are uncleanly in their habits are liable to be attacked. There are no special ways for entering human bodies. At Chaul a belief prevails that spirits enter the body when a person is suffering from any disease or when he is frightened.

It is said that when the body is unclean, a ghost can enter it through any of the organs.

The spirit of a woman dying in child-birth becomes a ghost and returns to the home, where it appears in the form of deceased, weeps, calls out, extinguishes lights, and otherwise frightens the inmates.

V

SPIRIT POSSESSION AND SCARING

Godlings, Mothers, and Demons

Besides the higher-grade deities, whose worship is enjoined and treated of in Hindu religious books, numerous minor deities, none of whom, however, find a place in the scriptures, are worshipped by the lower classes. The principle underlying the whole fabric of the worship of these minor deities, who for the most part are in origin supposed to have been the spirits of ancestors or heroes, has more in it of fear for their power of harming than of love for their divine nature. All untoward occurrences in domestic affairs, all bodily ailments and unusual natural phenomena, inexplicable to the simple mind of the villager, are attributed to the malignant action of these nameless and numerous spirits, hovering over and haunting the habitations of men. The latent dread of receiving injuries from these evil spirits results in the worship by the low-class people of a number of godlings (*devas*) and mothers (*matas*), as they are called. The poor villager, surrounded on all sides by hosts of hovering spirits, ready to take offence, or even to possess him, on the smallest pretext, requires some tangible protector to save him from such malign influences. He sets up and enshrines the spirit that he believes to have been beneficent to him, and so deserving of worship, or which he desires to propitiate, and makes vows in its honour, often becoming himself the officiating priest. Each such deity has its own particular locality. Thus there is hardly a village which has not a special minor deity of its own. But in addition to this deity, others in far-off villages are generally held in high esteem.

There are a number of ways in which these lower-class deities can be installed. Their images are made either of wood, stone, or metal. No temples or shrines are erected in their honour. An ordinary way of representing them is by drawing a trident (*trishul* , a weapon peculiar to Shiva, in red lead and oil on an upright slab of stone on a public road, on any dead wall, on the confines of a village, or a mountain-side, or a hill-top, in an underground cellar, or on the bank of a stream. Some people paint tridents in their own houses. The trident may also be made of wood, in which case its three points are plastered with red lead and oil and covered with a thin coating of tin. Sometimes carved wooden images in human shape, daubed over with red lead and oil, are placed in a small wooden chariot or in a recess about a foot square. In some shrines two brooms or whisks of peacock's feathers are placed on either side of the image. A slight difficulty overcome or a disease remedied by a vow in honour of any of these deities offers the occasion for an installation, and in all future emergencies of the same kind similar vows are observed. A mother (*mata* installed to protect a fortress or a street is called a fortress- or street-mother, whose priests are known as *Pothias*. At the time of installation, flags are hoisted near the dedicated places. A troop of dancers with jingling anklets recite verses, while the exorcist (*Bhuva*) performs the ceremonies. Generally installations are frequent during the *Navaratra* [1] holidays, when, if no human-shaped image is set up, a trident at least is drawn in red lead and oil. Some of these evil deities require, at the time of their installation, the oblation of a goat or a he-buffalo. Also, when a spirit is to be exorcized, the symbol of the familiar spirit of the exorcist is set up and invoked by him. After the installation, no systematic form of worship is followed in connexion with them. Regular forms are prescribed for the gods of the Hindu pantheon. But upon these gods the low-caste people are not authorized to attend.

In practice there are two forms of worship: ordinary and special. Ordinary worship is performed by bathing the deity—which can be done by sprinkling a few drops of water over it—burning a *ghi*- or an oil-lamp before it, and by offering a coconut and a pice or a half-anna piece. The last is taken away

[1] The *Navaratra* holidays, or *Pujas*, commence on the first day of the month of *Ashvin* (September–October).

by the priest, who returns generally half or three-quarters of the coco-nut as the sacred food (*prasad*) of the god.

There are no particular days prescribed for such worship, but Sundays and Tuesdays would seem to be the most favoured. On such days, offerings are made for the fulfilment of a vow recorded in order to avoid impending evil. In the observance of this vow the devotee abstains from certain things, such as *ghi*, butter, milk, rice, millet and betel-nut, till the period of the vow expires. When a vow is thus discharged, the devotee offers flowers, garlands, incense, food, or drink according to the terms of his vow. The burning of incense of Indian Bdellium is one of the commonest methods of worship.

The days for special worship are the *Navaratra* holidays, the second day of the bright half of *Ashadh* (June–July), *Divasa*, i.e. the fifteenth day of the dark half of *Ashadh* (June–July), and *Kali-Chaudas*, i.e. the fourteenth day of the dark half of *Ashvin* (September–October), the last month; besides other extraordinary occasions when a spirit has to be exorcized out of a sick person.

The *Navaratra* days are said to be the most auspicious days for worship of the mothers. People believing in the power of the mothers observe fast on these days. Most of them at least fast on the eighth day of the *Navaratra*, known as Mother's Eighth (*Mata-ashtami*), taking only a light meal which consists of roots as a rule, especially the plant known as Elephant-foot (*Amorphophallus campanulatus*), and of dates and milk. On the *Navaratra* days red lead and oil are applied to the images of the mothers, and a number of oblations are offered. The utmost ceremonial cleanliness is observed in the preparation of these viands. The corn is sifted, cleaned, ground or pounded, cooked, treated with frankincense, offered to the gods, and lastly partaken of before sunset, and all these operations must be performed on the same day; for the offerings must not see lamplight. Girls are not allowed to partake of these offerings. All ceremonies should be conducted with much earnestness and reverence; otherwise the offerings will fail to prove acceptable to the mothers.

On *Mata-ashtami* and *Kali-chaudas* devotees sometimes offer rams, goats, or buffaloes as victims to the mothers and godlings in addition to the usual offerings of food and *bakla.* The night of *Kali-chaudas* is believed to be so favourable for the efficacious recitation of certain mysterious incantations possessing sway over spirits, that exorcists leave the village and sit up performing certain rites in cemeteries, on burning-ghats, and in other equally suitable places where spirits are supposed to congregate.

On *Divasa*, the last day of *Ashadh* (June–July), low-caste people bathe their gods with water and milk, besmear them with red lead and oil, and make offerings of coco-nuts, wheat flour, or black gram. Particular offerings are believed to be favoured by particular deities; for instance, rice and pulse boiled together and oil, or flat unleavened loaves, are favoured by the goddess Meldi, boiled rice by Shikotar, and wheat and molasses by the goddess Gatrad, &c., &c.

On these holidays, as well as on the second day of the bright half of *Ashadh* (June–July), the devotees hoist flags in honour of the spirits, and play on certain musical instruments, producing discordant sounds. Meanwhile exorcists, believed to be interpreters of the wills of evil spirits, undergo self-torture, with the firm conviction that the spirits have entered their persons. Sometimes they lash themselves with iron chains or cotton-braided scourges. At times an exorcist places a panful of sweet oil over a fire till it boils. He then fries cakes in it, and takes them out with his unprotected hands, sprinkling the boiling oil over his hair. He further dips thick cotton wicks into the oil, lights them and puts them into his mouth, and throws red-hot bullets into his mouth, seemingly without any injury. This process secures the confidence of the followers, and is very often used by exorcists when exorcizing spirits from persons whose confidence they wish to gain.

The worship of mothers and godlings is a favourite method of exorcizing disease.[1]

In the cure of diseases by exorcizing the process known as *utar* is sometimes gone through. An *utar* is the making of a sacrificial offering of the nature of a scapegoat, and consists of a black earthen vessel, open and broad at the top, and

[1] *Vide* Chapter IX, *infra.*

containing offerings of food, a yard of dark-red silk fabric, one rupee and four annas in cash, pieces of charcoal, red lead, surmo-lead ore used as eye-powder, an iron nail, and three coco-nuts. Very often a trident is drawn in red lead and oil on the outer sides of the black earthen vessel. The exorcist carries the offering in his hands with a drawn sword in a procession, to the noise of the jingling of the anklets of his companions, the beating of drums, and the rattling of cymbals. After placing it in the cemetery, the procession returns with tumultuous shouts of joy and much jingling of anklets.

Sometimes exorcists are summoned for two or three nights preceding the day of the *utar* ceremony, and a ceremony known as *Danklan-beswan*, i. e. the installation of the *dankla*, is performed.[1]

Many sects have special deities of their own, attended upon by an exorcist of the same order. The exorcist holds a high position in the society of his caste-fellows. He believes himself to be possessed by the mother whose attendant he is, and declares, while possessed by her, the will of the mother, replying for her to such questions as may be put to him. The mothers are supposed to appear in specially favoured exorcists and to endow them with prophetic powers.

The following is a list of some of the inferior local deities of Gujarat and Kathiawar:

(1) *Suro-puro*. This is generally the spirit of some brave ancestor who died a heroic death, and is worshipped by his descendants as a family god at his birthplace as well as at the scene of his death, where a pillar (*palio*) is erected to his memory.

(2) *Vachhro*, otherwise known by the name of *Dada* (sire). This is said to have been a Rajput, killed in rescuing the cowherds of some Charans, who invoked his aid, from a party of freebooters. He is considered to be the family god of the Ahirs of Solanki descent, and is the sole village deity in Okha and Baradi Districts. He is represented by a stone horse, and Charans perform priestly duties in front of him. Submission

[1] 'A *dankla* is a special spirit instrument in the shape of a small kettle-drum, producing, when beaten by a stick, a most discordant and, by long association, a melancholy, gruesome, and ghastly sound.'—K. B. Fazlullah.

to and vows in honour of this god are believed to cure rabid dog-bites.

(3) *Sarmalio* commands worship in Gondal, Khokhari, and many other places. Newly-married couples of many castes loosen the knots tied in their marriage-scarves as a mark of respect for him. Persons bitten by a snake wear round their necks a piece of thread dedicated to this god.

(4) *Shitala* is a goddess known for the cure of small-pox. Persons attacked by this disease observe vows in her honour. Kalavad and Syadla are places dedicated to her.

(5) *Ganagor.* Virgins who are anxious to secure suitable husbands and comfortable establishments worship this goddess and observe vows in her honour.

(6) *Todalia.* She has neither an idol nor a temple set up in her honour, but is represented by a heap of stones lying on the village boundary. All marriage processions, before entering the village or passing by the heap, pay homage to this deity and offer a coco-nut, failure to do which is believed to arouse her wrath. She does not command daily adoration, but on occasions the attendant, who is a Chunvalia Koli, and who appropriates all the presents to this deity, burns frankincense of Indian Bdellium and lights a lamp before her.

(7) *Buttaya* also is represented by a heap of stones on a hillock. Her worshipper is a Talabdia Koli. A long season of drought leads to her propitiation by feasting Brahmans, for which purpose four pounds of corn are taken in her name from each threshing-floor in the village.

(8) *Surdhan.* This seems to have been some brave Kshatriya warrior who died on a battle-field. A temple is erected to his memory, containing an image of Shiva. The attending priest is an Atit.

(9) *Ghogho.* This is a cobra-god worshipped in the village of Bikhijada, having a Bajana (tumbler) for his attending priest.

(10) *Pir.* This is a Musalman saint, in whose honour no tomb is erected, the special site alone being worshipped by a devotee.

(11) *Raneki* is represented by a heap of stones, and is attended upon by Chamars. Her favourite resort is near the quarter inhabited by sweepers. A childless Girasia is said to

have observed a vow in her honour for a son, and a son being born to him, he dedicated certain lands to her; but they are no longer in the possession of the attendants.

(12) *Hanuman.* On a mound of earth there is an old worn-out image of this god. People sometimes light a lamp there, offer coco-nuts, and plaster the image with red lead and oil. A *Sadhu* of the Margi sect, a Koli by birth, acts as priest.

(13) *Shakta* (or *Shakti*). This is a Girasia goddess attended upon by a Chunvalia Koli. On the *Navaratra* days, as well as on the following day, Girasias worship this goddess, and if necessary observe vows in her name.

(14) *Harsidh.* Gandhavi in Barda and Ujjain are the places dedicated to this goddess. There is a tradition connected with her that her image stood in a place of worship facing the sea on Mount Koyalo in Gandhavi. She was believed to sink or swallow all the vessels that sailed by. A merchant named Jagadusa, knowing this, propitiated her by the performance of religious austerities. On being asked what boon he wanted from her, he requested her to descend from her mountain seat. She agreed on the merchant promising to offer a living victim for every footstep she took in descending. Thus he sacrificed one victim after another until the number of victims he had brought was exhausted. He next first offered his four or five children, then his wife, and lastly himself. In reward for his self-devotion the goddess faced Miani and no mishaps are believed to take place in the village.

(15) *Hinglaj.* This goddess has a place of worship a hundred and fifty miles from Karachi in Sind, to which her devotees make pilgrimage.[1]

(16) In the village of Jasdan, in Kathiawar, there is an ancient shrine of Kalu-Pir, in whose memory there are two sepulchres covered with costly fabrics, and a large flag floats over the building. Both Hindus and Musalmans believe in this saint, and offer coco-nuts, sweetmeats, and money to his soul. A part of the offering being passed through the smoke of frankincense, burning in a brazier near the saint's grave in the shrine, the rest is returned to the offerer. Every morning and evening a big kettle-drum is beaten in the Pir's honour.

[1] Hinglaj has been identified with the goddess Nanna of Babylon.

Other minor deities are Shikotar, believed by sailors to be able to protect them from the dangers of the deep ; Charmathvati, the goddess of the Rabaris ; Macho, the god of the Ahirs ; Meldi, in whom Vaghris believe ; Pithad, the favourite god of Dheds ; Dhavdi, who is worshipped by a barber ; Khodiar, Gela, Dadamo, Kshetrapal, Chavad, Mongal, Avad, Palan, Vir, Vaital, Jalio, Gadio, Paino, Parolio, Sevalio, Andhario, Fulio, Bheravo, Ragantio, Chod, Gatrad, Mammai, and Verai. There are frequent additions to the number, as any new disease or unusual and untoward incident may bring a new spirit into existence. The installation of such deities is not a costly concern, and thus there is no serious check on their recognition.

The worship of minor local deities in the Deccan and Konkan is connected with such castes as Guravas, Bhopis, Maratha Kunbis, Dhangars, Waghes, Murlis, Mahars, and Mangs. It is believed by the Brahmans that once an image is consecrated and worshipped, it should be worshipped uninterruptedly every day, and he who neglects to worship such an image daily incurs the sin of Brahman-murder. For this reason Brahmans generally do not worship minor local deities. In former times Brahmans who worshipped these deities were excommunicated by their caste-men. Such priests were compelled to wear a folded waist-cloth, and were forbidden to put on the sandal-paste mark in straight or cross lines. They were allowed to put on the circular mark of sandal paste. Another reason why Brahmans are not the priests or worshippers of such deities is that Brahmans cannot accept or partake of the offerings of cooked food, fowls, &c., made to them. Lower-class people can partake of such offerings, and are therefore generally the worshippers or ministrants of minor local deities.

At Palshet in the Ratnagiri District there are two village goddesses, viz. Jholai and Mharjai, and the priests of these deities are respectively a Gurav and a Mahar. The priests of goddesses are generally men of the lower castes. The guardian goddesses of the villages of Pule, Varavade, Nandivade, and Rila have Kunbis as their priests ; while the priests of the goddesses Mahalakshmi, Bhagvati, Mahakali, and Jogai are generally chosen from the Gurav caste. In the Konkan the

Rauls are the priests of the deities Vithoba, Ravalnath, and Bhavani; the Ghadis are the priests of the deities Sateri and Khavaneshwar; while the deities Mahadev and Maruti are worshipped by priests belonging to the Gurav caste. The goddesses Makhajan and Jakhmata at Sangameshwar in the Ratnagiri District are worshipped by priests who belong to the Gurav and Bhoi castes respectively. The god Ganpati at Makhnele has for his priest a Vani. The priests of the temple of Shiva at Lanje in the Ratnagiri District are Vanis. It is said that the priest of Pudnarik at Pandharpur is a fisherman by caste.

The priest of the goddess Narmata at Sidgad in the Thana District is a Koli; whilst the priests of Kanoba, Khandoba, and Vetal are of the lower castes. The goddesses Mahalakshmi of Kolwan and Vajreshvari of Nirmal have their priests chosen from the lower castes. The priests of Jari-Mari, Mhasoba, Bahiroba, Cheda, and other deities which are said to prevent contagious diseases, are always men of the lower castes.

The priests of the guardian goddesses of the villages Petsai, Dasgaum, and Nizampur are a Mahar, a Kumbhar or potter, and a Maratha, respectively. The priest of the guardian goddesses of Chaul in the Kolaba District belongs to the lower castes. The goddess Mangai has always a Mahar as her priest. Every day the god Shiva is required to be worshipped first by a priest of the Gurav caste. The priest of Bahiri, a corruption of the word Bhairav, one of the manifestations of Shiva, is a man belonging to the lower castes. Similarly the priests of Bhagavati, Bhavani, Ambika, Kalika, Jakhai, Jholai, Janni, Kolhai, Vadyajai, Shitaladevi, Chandika, &c., are persons belonging to lower castes.

The following list further exemplifies the custom of entrusting the worship of minor godlings to members of the lower castes in the Deccan:

LIST SHOWING NAME OF GODLING AND CASTE OF PRIEST

God.	Caste of Priest in Attendance.
1. Mariai . . .	Mang, Mahar, Lonari, Koli, Kunbi, Shimpi, Bhil.
2. Local Mahadev . .	Gurav.
3. Lakshmiai . .	Mahar, Mang, Bhil.

	God.	*Caste of Priest in Attendance.*
4.	Shrikeshav govind	Mali, Taru.
5.	Jakhai	Mang.
6.	Khandoba	Dhangar, Ramosi, Vaghe, Maratha, Gondhali, Gurav.
7.	Shitala	Mahar, Mang.
8.	Mahamari	Mang, Mahar, Bhil.
9.	Biroba	Dhangar.
10.	Satvai	Mahar, Mang, Chambhar.
11.	Muktabai	Mahar, Mang.
12.	Mhasoba	Kunbi.
13.	Rama of Lonikalbhar	Ramoshi.
14.	Tukai of Valha	Chambhar.
15.	Bhairavnath of Sirur	Nhavi, Gurav.
16.	Devi of Poona District	Maratha Kunbi.
	Devi of Khandesh	Bhil, Gurav, Bhutya.
17.	Mangoba	Mang.
18.	Mesai	Mahar.
19.	Malangi	Mahar.
20.	Kaknai	Mahar.
21.	Vir	Chambhar, Kunbi, Mali, Nhavi, Teli.
22.	Renuka devi	Kumbhar.
23.	Kalika devi	Gosavi.
24.	Bhairava of Vadner	Gurav.
25.	Saptashring devi	Maratha.
26.	Ananda-al	Gondhali.

The Heroic Godlings of the Konkan.

In the Konkan the minor deities are divided into the following five classes, viz.:

(1) Village deities,
(2) Local deities,
(3) Family deities,
(4) Chosen deities, and
(5) House deities.

The principal village deities are Hanuman or Maruti, Kalika, Amba, Vaghoba, Chedoba, Mhasoba, Bahiroba or Bhairav, Ganesh, Vira, Mhalsa or Mahalakshmi, Chamunda, Vetal, Khandoba or Malhari, Jogai, Bhawani, and Wagheshwar.

Local deities are generally found in special localities or sacred places known as *Kshetras* or *Punya sthanas*. Thus the god Rama is found at Nasik, Vithoba at Pandharpur, Krishna at Dwarka, Mahalakshmi at Kolwan, Vajreshvari at Nirmal in the Thana District, Mhasoba in the Ratnagiri District, Shitala at Kelwa Mahim, and Khandoba or Khanderai at Jejuri.

Khanderai is said to be an incarnation of Shiva. Khanderai killed the demon Mani-Malla who was devastating the earth, and he is therefore called Mallari or Malhari. Kunbis and lower-class Hindus in the Konkan as well as in the Deccan occasionally make a vow to the god Khandoba that if their desire is fulfilled they will offer their first-born male or female child to the service of the god. The male child thus dedicated to Khandoba is called Waghya and the female is called Murali. The Waghyas do not engage in any business, but maintain themselves by begging in the streets in the name of the god Khanderai. Muralis follow a life of prostitution. Waghyas and Muralis live as husband and wife, and their progeny are also called Waghyas and Muralis. They repeat the sacred cry *Jai Khanderayacha Elkot*, and give to people *bel-bhandar* of Khanderai consisting of the sacred *Bel* (*Aegle Marmelos*) leaves and turmeric powder. The god Khanderai is the family deity of some Deshasth Brahmans, who perform a family rite called *Tali bharane* on every *purnima* or full-moon day. The rite is as follows:

A plate (*tali*) is filled with coco-nuts, fruits, betel-nuts, saffron, turmeric, &c. Then a pot is filled with water, and on its mouth a coco-nut is placed. This coco-nut, with the pot, is then worshipped with flowers, sandal paste, &c., a lighted lamp filled with *ghi* is put in the same place, and the *tali* is waved thrice round the pot, which is supposed to contain the god Khandoba. Five persons then lift up the coco-nut with the *tali* and place it three times on the pot, repeating each time the word *Elkot* or *Khanderayacha Elkot*. The coco-nut is then broken into pieces, mixed with sugar, and is distributed among friends and relations as sacred food. On this occasion, as well as on the occasions of all days fixed for performing the special worship of the family goddess or family god of each family, the ceremony called the *Gondhal* dance is performed. On the same occasion another ceremony called *Bodan* is performed by the Deshasths and by the Chitpavans.[1] It is as follows:

[1] The two leading Brahman castes of the Deccan.

An image of the family deity is placed in a pot or plate, and it is then bathed in the five holy things, viz. milk, curds, *ghi*, honey, and sugar. Sandal paste is offered to it, as well as flowers, lighted lamps, and some sweets and incense. Five women whose husbands are alive (*suvasinis*) then prepare five lamps of wheat flour and wave them thrice round the face of the goddess or god, as the case may be. All the lamps are then placed in the plate in which the deity is kept, and the other materials of worship and food and sweet cakes are mixed together. Occasionally one of the five women becomes possessed with the spirit of the family deity, and confers blessings on the members of the family for their devotion. It is believed that those families which fail to perform periodically the *Bodan*, *Tali*, and *Gondhal* ceremonies in honour of their tutelary deity are sure to suffer from some misfortune or calamity during the year.

The local deities chiefly worshipped at Chaul, Kolaba District, are Hinglaj, Jakhmata, Bhagawati, Champawati, Mahikawati, and Golamba-devi. At the sowing and reaping times, people of the lower castes offer fowls and goats to these deities, and Brahmans offer coco-nuts. The local deity of the village Wavashi near Pen in the Kolaba District is said to possess the power of averting evil, and is accordingly held in great respect by the people of many villages in the District. Every third year a great fair is held, and a buffalo is sacrificed to the goddess on the full-moon day of the month of *Chaitra* (March–April). The priest of this goddess is a Gurav. Another celebrated local godling in the Kolaba District is Bahiri-Somajai of Khopoli. It is believed that a person suffering from snake-bite is cured without any medicine if he simply resides for one night in the temple of this goddess. Sacrifices of goats, fowls, and coco-nuts are made to this goddess at the time of sowing and reaping. The priests of this deity are known as Shingade Guravs. The worship of the local deity Bapdev is much in favour among the villages of Apta and the surrounding places. At the times of sowing and reaping, offerings of fowls, goats, and coco-nuts are made to Bapdev through the priest. The worship of the local deities Kolambai, Bhawani, and Giroba is prevalent in the Chauk villages. To the village mother of the village of Tale every third year a buffalo is sacrificed, and at an interval of two years goats are offered. The deities Shiva and Kalkai are worshipped with great reverence at Bakavali in the Ratnagiri District.

In many villages of the Ratnagiri District the goddess Pandhar is considered to be the chief goddess of the village. The priest is generally a Gurav or Maratha Kunbi. On every full-moon day coco-nuts are offered, and on the occasion of sowing and reaping goats and fowls are sacrificed to this deity. At Devgad there is a temple of the goddess Gajabai on the sea-shore. The priest of this goddess is a man of the Ghadi caste. On the first day of the bright half of the month of *Margashirsh* (November–December), special offerings of goats, fowls, and coco-nuts are made by the villagers. The deities Ravalnath, Mauli, Vetal, Rameshwar, and Hanuman are usually worshipped in most villages in Ratnagiri. The villagers in the Ratnagiri District have great faith in their local deities, and before undertaking any important business they obtain the consent or take the omen of the deity. This ceremony is known as *kaul ghalne*, and it is performed as follows:

Two betel-nuts or flowers are taken, and one of them is placed on the right side of the deity and the other on the left side. The worshipper then bows before the deity and requests her to let the nut on the right side fall first if the deity is pleased to consent; if not, to let the nut on the left side fall first. Naturally one of the two nuts falls first, and they interpret this as either consent or dissent, as the case may be. The villagers have so much faith in this omen that they make use of this method of divination to ascertain whether sick or diseased persons will recover or die. Special sacrifices are offered to these local deities whenever an epidemic like cholera occurs. In the Ratnagiri District, at many places, there are natural *lingas* of the god Shiva, and over these places temples are built. The priests of these temples are generally Jangams or Lingayat Guravs. No animal sacrifices are made at these shrines. At a short distance from the village of Makhamle there is a temple of the god Shiva under his title of Annayeshwar. The following legend is narrated in connexion with this temple: The place where the present temple stands once abounded with Mango (*Amana*) trees and formed a pasture for cattle. The cow of a certain man of the village daily used to go to graze at this place. The cow used to give milk twice a day, but one day she gave milk only once, and thereafter she continued to give it only once a day. The owner therefore asked the cowherd to ascertain the cause of this sudden change. One day the cowherd noticed that the cow allowed her milk to drop upon a stone. At this the cowherd was so enraged that he struck the stone with his scythe so hard that it was cloven in two and blood gushed forth. He hurriedly repaired to the village and related this wonderful phenomenon to the people. The villagers came to the spot, and decided to build a temple to the god Shiva over the stone. One part of the stone is in this temple and the other part was taken to the village of Kalamburi, where another temple was built over it.

In Sangameshwar village the Brahmans also worship the images of the local goddesses Chandukai, Jholai, and Sunkai. In the Konkan the deities Narayan, Rawalnath, Mauli, Datta, Vetal, and Shiva are worshipped everywhere. The following legend is told about the deity Vetal, the leader of the ghosts: In the Sawantwadi State there is a temple of Vetal in the village of Ajgaon. As part of his worship it is considered necessary to offer to this deity a pair of shoes every month. The people believe that after a few days the shoes become worn out. The inference drawn from this by the people is that at night the god Vetal goes out walking in the new shoes.

In the village of Khed in the Ratnagiri District a buffalo is offered to the goddess Redjai on the full-moon day of *Chaitra* (March–April) every third year. At Naringre offerings of coco-nuts, &c., are made to the deities Bhavakai, Chala, &c., on the first of the month of *Margashirsh* (November–December). It is said that one of the following deities is the village godling of every village in the Ratnagiri District, viz. Chandkai, Varadhan, Khem, Bahiri, Kedar, Vaggaya, Antaral, Manaya, Salbaya, and Vaghambari. A procession in their honour takes place in the months of *Chaitra* (March–April) and *Phalgun* (February–March). The priests are generally either Guravs or Maratha Kunbis. Fairs are held in their honour at seed-time and harvest. At these fairs fowls, coco-nuts, goats, fruits, &c., are offered to these deities. At Malwan on the no-moon day of *Shravan* (July–August) local deities and ghosts are propitiated by offering to them goats, fowls, &c.

At Anjarle there are two local goddesses, Sawanekarin and Bahiri. Offerings of goats and fowls are made to them in the months of *Margashirsh* (November–December) and *Phalgun* (February–March). Sometimes liquor and eggs are also offered. Offerings can be made on any day except Monday and *Ekadashi*, Tuesdays and Sundays being considered most suitable. At Ubhadanda in the Ratnagiri District Ravalnath and Bhutanath are held in great reverence. They are believed to be incarnations of Shiva. The priests are generally Guravs, Ghadis, Rauls, and Sutars. The following goddesses which are popular in the Ratnagiri District are believed to be incarnations of the goddess Durga, viz. Navala-devi, Vaghur-devi, Jakhadevi, and Kalkai. The chief local deity of the Dahanu subdivision of the Thana District is Mahalakshmi. She has seven sisters and one brother, two of the sisters being the goddess Pangala at Tarapur and the goddess Delavadi at Ghivali. Goats and fowls are offered to the Pangala-devi on the *Dasara* day. Her priest is a Gurav. It is said that the goddess Delavadi used to receive her garments from the sea, but now this is no longer the case, though it is still believed that the incense which is burnt before her comes floating from Dwarka. In the village of Edwan there is a goddess called Ashapuri, who used to supply her devotees with whatever they wanted. The devotee was required to besmear with cow-dung a plot of ground in the temple, and to pray for the things wanted by him. The next day, when he came to the temple, he found the desired things on the spot besmeared with cow-dung. At Mangaon the priest of the local goddess is either the headman or the *Gosavi* of the village. In the village of Dahigaon coconuts are offered annually to the village Maruti, and fowls and goats to the other local deities, in order that the village may be protected against danger and disease.[1]

[1] A curious belief is reported from this village to the effect that no Brahman may officiate as priest in the local temple of Shiva, contrary to the universal practice elsewhere.

In a few temples of goddesses like Jakhai, &c., the priest is of the Mahar caste. A great fair is held in honour of the goddess Vajra-bai or Vajreshwari near Nirmal in the month of *Kartik* (October–November). The priest of the goddess is a Gosavi of the Giri sect. Similarly in the Karnatak, low castes such as Holayas and Bedars are found to be the priests of the local godlings, Durgavva, Lakkavva, &c.

Kal-bhairav.

The god Kal-bhairav was brought into existence by the fury of the god Shiva, when he, being extremely angry with Brahma, cut off the fifth head of the latter. Kal-bhairav is the leader of all spirits and witches, and resides at Benares by the order of Shiva. His favourite haunt is a cemetery. His image is always represented as fierce and ugly.

It is said that this god once entered the mouth of Gorakhnath and performed religious austerities in that strange abode. Although Gorakhnath was nearly suffocated, he could only persuade Kal-bhairav to come out by extolling his glory, and by conferring on him the leadership of all spirits and the guardianship of the Kotvalu fortress at Benares.

Kal-bhairav does not command worship on any auspicious occasion. On the other hand, he is much revered by persons who practise the black art. On *Kali-Chaudas* day his devotees worship him in a cemetery, offer an oblation of food, and recite magic incantations till late at night.

The offerings favoured by Kal-bhairav are cakes of wheat flour, sugar, and fried cakes. The sacrifice of a live animal is also acceptable. The offerings after presentation to the god are given to black dogs.

Pregnant women in order to secure a safe delivery sometimes vow to abstain from *ghi* till they have offered an oblation to Kal-bhairav.

The following lines are often repeated in honour of this god:

'I worship Kal-bhairav, the giver of food and of salvation, of auspicious and comely appearance, who is kind to his devotees.'

There is a belief that if unmarried persons touch red lead, a cobra deity of the forest, Kshetrapal, takes them in marriage.

But the danger can be averted by vowing to dedicate a preparation of rice and pulse, red lead, a ball of molasses and sesamum seed, and some fruit to this god at the time of marriage.

The goddesses Bahucharaji (or Bechraji) and Ambaji are sometimes worshipped for the sake of safety during childbirth. The ceremony of *Nandi-Shraddha*, which was performed when Rama was born, is sometimes gone through at the birth of a child.

The Mothers

The mothers are sixteen in number, and are worshipped on such auspicious occasions as a sacrifice, a wedding, or a house-warming. Their installation consists in painting the following marks with red lac on the back walls of a house:

The marks are besmeared with molasses, and a little *ghi* and a piece of some precious metal are affixed to them. At the time of a marriage, fourteen are worshipped in the house, one outside the village limits, and one near the front door of the house where the wedding is celebrated.

The mothers are worshipped during the *Navaratra* holidays also. On this occasion small earthen bowls, with a hole in the centre of each, are plastered with red or green earth and wild nutmeg, and young girls carry them on their heads with burning lamps from door to door. At each house they receive oil for the lamp and a handful of corn. On the last day, i. e. on the ninth day, all the bowls are placed on the special site dedicated to the mothers. The songs, which are also accompanied by dancing, are called *garabi* or *garaba*.

The mothers are also supposed to be the planets which influence the life of a child in the womb, and their worship is believed to bring about an easy delivery.

There is also a family goddess who is referred to simply by the name of *Matrika* or Mother. In worshipping her, seven round spots are painted on a wall with red lac, and *ghi* is poured over them in such a manner as to form five small streams. A mixture of molasses and *ghi* is then applied to these spots with a piece of red cotton yarn. By this process the devotee secures the motherly regard of the goddess.

One of the deities which preside over child-birth is Randal Mata or Ranna Devi, who is said to be the wife of the sun. In order to secure an easy delivery, pregnant women take a vow that they will invite one or more bowls of this mother. The process of 'inviting the bowls' is as follows:

The tufts round the shell of a coco-nut are pulled out, the nut is besmeared with chalk, and marks representing two eyes and a nose are painted on it; or the nut is so placed that the two spots on its surface represent eyes, and the pointed tuft of fibres between them serves the purpose of a nose. A bowl is placed on a piece of cloth stretched on a wooden stool, and the coco-nut is placed over the bowl. It is then dressed in elegant female attire, and a *ghi*-lamp is kept constantly burning near it. This completes the installation of Randal Mata. Women bow down before this representation of the mother, and sing melodious tunes in its presence. On the morning of the following day, the image is carried to the temple of the village mother, the coco-nut is deposited there, and the garments are brought home. The coco-nut is subsequently taken by the Brahman attendant of the mother.

On the day of the installation it is customary to invite five married women whose husbands are living (*suvasinis*) to a feast of wheat and cakes. On the next day, when the mother is sent away, three virgins are entertained with rice, sugar, and milk.

In some communities a custom prevails of 'inviting the bowls of the mothers' on the occasion of the first pregnancy of a woman. On the day on which the bowls are to be invited, the pregnant woman takes a bath early in the morning, and calls upon thirteen married women whose husbands are living, whom she invites to dinner by marking their foreheads with red lac. A Brahman is called to set up the mothers, whose installation takes place in the same manner as that of Randal. The piece of cloth spread on the wooden stool is required to be green. When the unwidowed married women sit down to the dinner, the pregnant woman washes their right toes with milk and swallows that milk as *sharanamrit* (lit. the nectar of the feet). The married women are required to taste a morsel of some preparation of milk before they begin their meal. At night, a company of women dance in a circle round the mothers, singing songs. Next morning an exorcist is called, who declares the will of the mothers. On receiving a satisfactory reply from the exorcist, the party disperses.

Ganpati

Ganpati or Ganesh, about whose origin the traditional legends prevail, is represented with four hands, in one of which he holds a *kamandalu* (a gourd), in the second a *ladu* (a sweet-ball), in the third a *parashu* (an axe), and in the fourth a *jap-mal* (a rosary). He is sometimes called Dundalo (lit. big-bellied) because of his having a protuberant belly. He puts on a yellow garment and rides a mouse. His brother is Kartik-swami, who rides a peacock. His favourite dish consists of sweet-balls of wheat flour fried in *ghi* and sweetened with molasses. Siddhi and Buddhi are the two wives of Ganpati. Before their marriage their father Vishwarupa had made a promise that he would bestow the hands of both on whosoever circumambulated the whole earth within one day. Ganpati reasoned that a cow and a mother are equal in merit to the earth, and by passing round the former he got the hands of both. Ganpati is said to be the fastest writer of all, so that the sage Vyasa secured his services as a scribe, at the instance of Brahma, in writing the *Mahabharata*. When Ravan had conquered all the gods and made them serve in his household, Ganpati had to become a cowherd and to look after cows and goats.

On the fourth day of the bright half of *Vaishakh* (April–May) Ganpati is ceremoniously worshipped with red lead, red flowers, milk, curds, honey, &c. The image of the god is besmeared with red lead and *ghi*, and the remnant of this ointment is applied to the doors and windows of the house. Sweet-balls of wheat flour fried in *ghi* and sweetened with molasses are first dedicated to Ganpati, and are afterwards partaken of as the god's gift.

The people of Maharashtra observe the feast of Ganpati on the fourth day of the bright half of *Bhadrapad* (August–September), when an earthen image of Ganpati is made and worshipped with twenty kinds of leaves.

It is a custom among the Vaishnavas to draw an image of Ganpati in those vessels which are to be used for cooking food at the time of performing the obsequies of a deceased Vaishnava.

Hanuman or Maruti

In most villages in the Deccan the chief village god is Maruti or Hanuman, whose temple is situated at the entrance of the village. Maruti is considered to be an incarnation of Shiva, and is held in great reverence by all classes. A festival is held in his honour on the bright half of the month of *Chaitra* (March–April). On this occasion the temple is decorated with evergreens and flowers, the stone image of the god is newly painted or covered with red lead and oil, and garlands of the *Rui* (*Calotropis gigantea*) flowers are placed round the neck of the image; coco-nuts, plantains, betel-nuts, and leaves are offered to the god, camphor is lighted and waved round the image, incense is burnt, cooked food and sweets are offered, and money presents are made. Every worshipper brings with him some oil, red lead, a coconut, two betel-leaves, one betel-nut and a copper coin, and a garland of *Rui* flowers. These are given to the temple ministrant, who offers a part of the oil and red lead to the deity, places the garland round the deity's neck, and breaking the coco-nut into pieces, gives a piece or two to the devotee as the consecrated food of the deity. Saturday is the sacred day of the monkey-god Maruti. Every Saturday fresh oil and red lead are offered to the god by the devotees. The priests in most of the temples of Maruti are Guravs, Ghadis, Marathas, or Gosavis.

Every Saturday in the month of *Shravan* (July–August), called the wealth-giving Saturday, a special worship is performed in the temples of Maruti in Bombay as well as in the Konkan. On this day people fast the whole day and dine in the evening, after offering the god Maruti a preparation of rice and pulse, and cakes made of black gram (*Phaseolus radiatus*) flour.

There is no village in the Konkan which has not the honour of having a temple of the god Maruti. Maruti is supposed to guard the village against evils of all kinds. Care is therefore taken to build the temple of Maruti at the outskirts of the village. There is a tradition that at the time of leaving the Dandaka forest (the name given to Maharashtra in the *Mahabharata* epic), Rama asked Maruti to reside therein. It is for this reason, the people say, that every village in the Konkan and on the Ghats has a temple of Maruti. The god Maruti is worshipped in the village of Wasind on Tuesdays and Saturdays. In former days it was customary to establish an image of the god Maruti in a newly-built castle or fort. Hanuman, the son of Anjani and the wind or Marut, is known for his loyalty to his master and for his bravery.

In days gone by he utilized his strength for the protection of Saints, *Rishis*, Brahmans, and cows, and for this merit he was elevated to the rank of a Hindu god. He is a *Brahmachari*, i.e. bachelor, and is one of the seven heroes who are believed to be immortal, possessed of miraculous strength, and with an adamantine body (*vajramaya*). Maruti is supposed to be the originator of the *Mantra-Shastra*, by the study and repetition of which one obtains strength and superhuman power. Women desirous of bearing children go to the temple of Maruti, and there burn before his image lamps made of wheat flour and filled with *ghi*. The image of the god is represented in temples in two ways, that is (1) Vira Hanuman or warrior Hanuman, (2) Dasa-Hanuman or servant Hanuman. The former is found in a temple consecrated to the worship of the god Hanuman alone, whereas the latter is found in a temple dedicated to the worship of the god Rama.

Since Maruti is the god of strength, gymnasts tie an image of Maruti to their wrists, and they also consecrate an image of Maruti in their gymnasiums. The number eleven is said to be dear and sacred to him because he is believed to be an incarnation of the eleven Rudras. The birthday of the god Maruti, which falls on the fifteenth of the bright half of *Chaitra* (March–April), is celebrated in the Kolhapur District with great reverence. Those who wish to have a son draw the figure of Maruti on a wall in red lead, and worship it daily with sandal paste, flowers, and garlands of *Rui* (*Calotropis gigantea*). Others burn lamps made of wheat flour before the image of the god. Persons who are under the evil influence of the planets, and especially of the planet Saturn, worship the god Hanuman on Saturdays in order to propitiate the planets. On this day they make wreaths of the leaves and flowers of the *Rui* plant (*Calotropis gigantea*) and adorn his neck with them. They also offer him black gram and salt.

Hanuman is considered to be the master-deity of all good and bad spirits and those possessed by them, such as *bhuts*, *prets*, *pishachas*, *dakans*, *shakans*, *chudels*, *vantris*, the forty-nine *virs*, the fifty-two *vetals*, *yakshas*, and *yakshinis*, who are believed to obey his commands. Vows are observed in honour of Hanuman if a person is possessed by a spirit, or if he is scared by a sudden encounter with a devil, or if he happens to step inadvertently within spirit-possessed precincts. Persons who are possessed by evil spirits are exorcized by reciting verses in honour of Hanuman.

Kali-Chaudas, i.e. the fourteenth day of the dark half of *Ashvin* (September–October), is considered to be the most favourable day for practising the black art; and the god Hanuman is accordingly worshipped with much ceremony by exorcists on that day.

In the course of a *sadhana* (i.e. the process of procuring the fulfilment of certain desires through the favour and by the agency of spirits) the latter are conjured in the name of Hanuman, so that the *sadhana* may not prove inefficacious. For this purpose a special verse (*mantra*)[1] is repeated one hundred and eight times before the image of the god, the devotee

[1] The *mantra* runs as follows: '*Om namo Hanuman bala ghatapidam, panika rakhavala, lohaki kothadi, bajarka tala, deva-danava-kumar, nikal Hanuman asan, Mahadev basan, Hanuman hathela, bajarka khila.*' It is neither pure Sanskrit nor Gujarati nor Hindustani, but roughly it means: 'Bow to the young Hanuman, the tormentor of *ghata*, the guardian of water, the iron safe, the lock of *vajra*, the son of the gods and the demons. Take your seat, the receptacle of Mahadev, O stubborn god, O Nail of adamant.'

remaining standing all the time. A lamp of clarified butter is also lighted, and frankincense is burnt.

After the repetition of the verse, four nails are driven into the four corners of the seat of the votary, and it is believed that the *sadhana* is thus rendered sure of success.

The god Hanuman is sometimes worshipped when a serious epidemic is to be warded off. The usual mode of propitiating him in such cases, and also in exorcizing spirits, is to pour red lead and oil over his image, to make an offering of black gram (*Phaseolus radiatus*) and molasses, and to invest the image with a wreath of one hundred and eight flowers of *Ankdi* (*Gymnosporia emarginata*), or of as many leaves or berries of the same plant.

The influence of the god is believed to be so powerful in some places that it is said that an evil spirit is at once exorcized from the body of a person who observes certain ceremonies there. In some places the mere sight of the image of the god has the same effect, and it is believed that ghosts shriek and fly from the bodies of possessed persons, if these visit the images of Hanuman. In Kodolia, about half a mile to the west of Lilapur in Gujarat, there is a temple of Hanuman where persons suffering from fever go on a Saturday, and take a meal before 2 p.m., at which time the god goes out to graze his cows. This proceeding is believed to work a cure in cases of fever. A mere glance at the temple of Hanuman at Khandia and Saranghur, or of that image which is known as 'Bhidbhanjan', is sufficient to drive out evil spirits from the bodies of possessed persons. The same virtue is attributed to the images of Hanuman at Bhurakhia, near Lathi, and at Nariana, near Dhrangadhra in Kathiawar.

There are certain peculiar conjunctions of planets, which if they appear in a person's horoscope, always bring him misfortunes. In such circumstances the person is said to be under the influence of *panoti*. Such influence lasts for a period varying from one year to seven years and a half. When the planet Saturn enters the first, eleventh, or the twelfth constellation in relation to a person, the latter is said to be affected by *panoti* extending over seven years and a half. The *panoti* enters the life of such a person with feet either of gold, silver, copper, or iron: and in most cases the result is disastrous. If the *panoti* affects the head of a person, he loses his wits; if it affects the heart, it takes away his wealth; when it affects the feet, it brings bodily ailments. In order to counteract the evil effects of *panoti*, people worship Hanuman as the god who crushed the malignant goddess Panoti under his feet. On Saturdays red lead and oil, black gram, molasses are offered to the image of the god. Frankincense is burnt, a lamp is lighted, and a wreath of *Ankdi* flowers (*Gymnosporia emarginata*) is sometimes dedicated. A fast is observed on such days; and sometimes the services of a Brahman are engaged to recite verses in honour of the god.

There is a belief that Hanuman cries out once in twelve years, and those men who happen to hear him are transformed into eunuchs.

Oil which has been poured over the image of Hanuman and caught in a vessel is sometimes carried in a small metal cup and is burnt to produce soot used as collyrium. This is believed to improve the eyesight, and to protect a person from the influence of evil spirits. There is a saying in Gujarati that a person using it on *Kali-Chaudas* day cannot be foiled by any one.

Of the days of the week, Saturday is the most suitable for the worship of Hanuman. Of all offerings, that of red lead and oil is the most acceptable to him. When Hanuman was carrying the Drona mountain to the battle-field before Lanka, he was wounded in the leg by an arrow from Bharata, the brother of Rama. The wound was healed by the application of red lead and oil, and hence his predilection for these things. It is also said that after the death of Ravana and at the time of the coronation of Bibhishana, Rama distributed prizes to all his monkey followers, when nothing was left for Hanuman except red lead and oil.

Mostly *Ankdi* flowers (*Gymnosporia emarginata*) are used in worshipping Hanuman, but sometimes *Karan* flowers (*Pongamia glabra*) also are made to serve the purpose.

Evil Spirits and Demons

In Gujarat the following story is told to explain the origin of spirits known as *rakshasas*:

In mythological times Brahma, one of the gods of the Hindu Trinity, once left his body for a time. Some people began to molest the body, when he cried out, '*Rakho! Rakho!*' that is, 'Keep aloof! Keep aloof!' or 'Wait! Wait!' These people came to be called *Rakho*, which in course of time was corrupted into *rakshasas*. The beings who hold sway over *rakshasas* are called *Maharakshasas*. In the *Ramayana* and other Puranas, *rakshasas* are represented as feeding on human flesh.

A *rakshasa* is supposed to be sixteen miles in height and to roam about for his prey within a circle with a radius of sixteen miles. The *Maharakshasas* are supposed to have their abode in the seas. It is said that they burn or swallow ships sailing thereon. The *rakshasas* are supposed to number 60,000,000 and the *Maharakshasas* 20,000. Kubera, a *Maharakshasa*, is the lord of the *rakshasas*. It is said that the *rakshasas*, *Maharakshasas*, wizards and witches, were visible to the human eye in former times. With the commencement of the present era, they have become invisible.

It is a common belief that there is a bitter enmity between the gods and *rakshasas*. The former follow the path of virtue, while the latter lead immoral lives, devouring Brahmans and cows, feeding on flesh, and indulging in intoxicating drinks. The habitat of the *rakshasas* is the nether world, Rawan being their king.[1]

Maharakshasas are also known by the name of *Brahma rakshasas*. A Brahman dying without imparting all his learning to his disciples or with the guilt of the murder of a Brahman or a cow on him is believed to enter the order of *Brahma rakshasas* after his death. In this state he possesses a body without a head.

[1] The exploits of the *rakshasas* described in the Hindu epics such as the *Mahabharata* and *Ramayana* are well known and frequently related in the villages of the whole of the Presidency. It is unnecessary to reproduce such traditions in these notes.

There are numerous evil spirits known to exist in Gujarat, the names of which are as follows:

(1) Dakini, (2) Sakini, (3) Kushmand, (4) Zod, (5) Dholio, (6) Pale Marad, (7) Bhuchar, (8) Khechar, (9) Jalaj, (10) Jakharo, (11) Shikotrum, (12) Ashtabharo, (13) Chand Chani, (14) Chorosi Kantini, (15) Jogani, (16) Hathadi, (17) Miyali, (18) Ghanchini, (19) Mochini, (20) Baladi, (21) Molani, (22) Khuntini, (23) Suti, (24) Gavati, (25) Bethi, (26) Ubhi, (27) Avi, (28) Chaurar, (29) Madhu Pavanti, (30) Mansa Khavanti, (31) Bhasika, (32) Pratab, (33) Vira, (34) Vavanchara, (35) Chorasi Viru, (36) Nao Narasing, (37) Jaikha, (38) Jutaka, (39) Masida, (40) Gandharavi, (41) Jami, (42) Asmani, (43) Mamikula, (44) Zampadi, (45) Meladi, (46) Balla.

Of the above, the first forty-three, together with *Chudel* or *Vantri* and *Preta*, are believed by some to be the names of so many *Joganis* or female evil spirits or witches. The remaining are living *Dakans* or witches who are believed to cause illness or even death by their evil eye to those on whom they throw a glance.

Wizards live upon ordinary food, witches on air, while *Pretas* require nothing to eat for their maintenance. It is said that their backs and shoulders are covered with filth and emit an offensive odour.

It is generally believed that the spirits of such male members of low unclean castes as die a violent death become *Khavis*. Some believe that *Khavis* or *Khabith* is a Musalman ghost. Others hold that he is the lord of all ghosts. *Khavis* has no head. His eyes are located in his chest. He is as tall as a coco-palm or bamboo. He roams about holding in one hand a weapon and in the other a lump of flesh. Those over whom his shadow falls are said to fall ill. His appearance is so terrible that a person who sees him is frightened to death at the first glance. It is stated that he starts on his excursions after sunset.

The attendants of the god Shiva known as *Vaitalikas* are said to have no heads. They live in cremation grounds, as they have a burning desire to possess the bodies of deceased persons.

A belief runs that the trunk of the evil spirit called *Suropuro*, that is, the spirit of one who meets a heroic death, moves about like a *Khavis*.

It is a common belief that evil spirits haunt trees, groves, deserted tanks, and woods.

Vetal roams over burial and cremation grounds, as also *Bhuchar*, *Khechar*, *Kal Bhairav*, and a number of other spirits.

Jimp, *Babaro*, and some other ghosts reside in fortresses and unoccupied houses and roam about in the burning-grounds. *Chudel*, *Kotda*, and *Brahma rakshasa* make their abode on the Tamarind, *Shami* (*Prosopis spicigera*), *Babul* (*Acacia arabica*), and *Kerado* (*Capparis aphylla*) trees and in deep tanks and wells in deserted places. Their favourite haunts are river banks.

It is stated by some people that *Chudel*, *Vantri*, *Dakan*, *Jimp*, *Khavis*, and other spirits generally haunt cremation grounds, fields where battles have been fought, thresholds of houses, and latrines and cross-roads.

Some declare that spirits are also to be found in temples in which there are no images and in dry wells.

Preta is said to be as tall as a camel, the passage of its throat being as small as the bore of a needle. It is therefore believed to be always wandering about in quest of water.

The evil spirit *Jan* haunts mountains and forests and *Mamo* the centres of filth.

Khijadio Mamo lives in the *Khijada*, i. e. *Shami* tree (*Prosopis spicigera*), and *Amatho Mamo* in a grove of Mango trees. Spirits of high-caste people not emancipated from the trammels of birth and rebirth have their abode in the *Pipal* tree (*Ficus religiosa*).

It is related that once a number of boys, on their return from a tank to which they had gone on a swimming excursion, passed by a *Khijada* tree, when one of them suggested to the others to throw stones at the tree, saying that any one not doing so would fall under the displeasure of God. One of the boys threw a stone at a neighbouring *Babul* tree (*Acacia arabica*) with the result that on reaching home he fell ill in a fit of terror. He began to shake and said, 'Why did you strike me with a stone? I had resorted to the *Babul* tree from the *Khijada* and you struck me there. I shall not depart

N 2

until I take your life.' Evidently it was the *Khijadio Mamo* who had possessed the boy who spoke the above words; and an exorcist was called who drove him out by incantations; after which the boy recovered.

It is believed that a woman who dies an unnatural death becomes a *Chudel* and troubles her husband, her successor or co-wife, or her children.

There are three classes of *Chudels*, (1) *Poshi*, (2) *Soshi*, and (3) *Toshi*. Those women who have not enjoyed before death the pleasures of this world to their satisfaction enter the order of *Poshi Chudels*. They fondle children and render good service to their widowed husbands.

Those women who are persecuted beyond endurance by the members of their families become *Soshi Chudels* after death. They dry up the blood of men, and prove very troublesome to the members of the family.

Those women who bear a strong attachment to their husbands enter the order of *Toshi Chudels* and bring great pleasure and happiness to their husbands in this life.

Most high-caste people, on the death of their first wives, take an impression of their feet on gold leaves or leaf-like tablets of gold and cause their second wives to wear them round their necks. These impresses of feet are called mourning footprints. Among the lower castes, the hands or the feet of the second wives are tattooed in the belief that this prevents the deceased wife from causing injury to the second wife.

All female spirits called *Pishachas* or *Dakans* and male spirits called *Virs* or *Bhuts* oppress their descendants.

It is also believed that any male member of a family dying with certain of his desires unfulfilled becomes a *Surdhan* and oppresses the surviving relatives, while a female member troubles others as *Sikoturu* or *Mavali*.

The spirits of men who fall victims to tigers or other wild animals are believed to enter the ghostly order and wander about until they are relieved from this state by the performance of the prescribed *Shraddha* by some pious surviving relative. These evil spirits live in forests and eat nothing but flesh. If they do not get flesh to eat they eat the flesh of their own bodies. At times they put their relatives to great annoyance by entering their persons. To pacify them, stones known as *palios* are erected in their name, and their images are set up in the square cavities of walls. These images are besmeared with red lead and oil by their descendants on the fourteenth day of the dark half of *Ashvin* (September–October). The relief of such spirits is sought by the performance of a *Shraddha* either at Siddhapur or at Gaya.

It is believed that a woman dying in child-bed or during her sickness enters the order of ghosts variously known as *Chudels*, *Vantris*, or *Takshamis*. In order that she may not return from the cremation ground, mustard seeds are strewn along the road behind her bier, for a belief prevails that she can only succeed in returning if she can collect all the mustard seeds thus strewn on the way.

In some places, loose cotton-wool is thrown over the bier so as to be scattered all along the road to the cemetery. It is believed that the *Chudel* can only return to the house if she can collect all the cotton scattered behind her in one night. This is considered an impossible task, and no fear is therefore entertained of her return after the cotton has been scattered.

To prevent the return of the *Chudel*, some people pass underneath the bier the legs of the cot on which the woman lay in her confinement, while others drive in an iron nail at the end of the street immediately after the corpse has been carried beyond the village boundary. In some places the nail is driven into the threshold of the house. Even after the precautions mentioned above have been taken, to prevent the return of a *Chudel* or *Vantri*, *Shraddhas* are performed, and a number of Brahman women feasted on the twelfth and thirteenth day after death to propitiate her, as the fear of the mischief done by her is very strong.

A *Chudel* has no shoulders. Any passer-by coming across her is asked by her to take her to his home, and if he agrees, she accompanies him, passes the night in his company, and brings his life to a speedy end. In the village of Charadi, under the jurisdiction of Dhrangadhra State in Kathiawar, a Girasia named Halaji fell into the clutches of a *Chudel*, who was driven from his person by the enchantment of a *Jati* on condition that he should not go into the eastern part of the village.

It is believed that a woman can be relieved from the ghostly order of a *Chudel* by the performance of a *Shraddha* at Siddhapur.

Those persons that die while ousted from the houses built by them become ghosts, and residing in the houses, do not allow anybody to live therein, and leave the houses only when they are demolished.

Janchar, *Bhuchar*, *Jin*, and some other spirits are believed to haunt valleys. Some believe that those persons that meet their death in valleys become evil spirits and haunt the valleys.

Rakhevalio, *Andhario*, *Sevalio*, *Sulio*, and *Ragatio* are evil spirits that haunt the ruins of magnificent buildings and also valleys.

In the Deccan and Konkan *rakshasas* or malevolent spirits are believed to be very cruel. These evil spirits are held in great fear, and people try to avoid giving them offence. It is supposed that to cause displeasure to these demons may bring about death. With a view to propitiate them, offerings of cocks and goats are made to them every year regularly on fixed days. If a woman gives birth to a child which is extraordinary or horrible in size and appearance, it is believed to be a demon reborn. Such a child is supposed to bring bad luck to the family.

In the Karnatak evil spirits are believed to haunt burial-grounds, persons of fair complexion, pregnant women, &c.; they are said to be fond of food of red colour. Persons spirit-possessed can speak in the language used by the spirit before it was disembodied, e.g. a Brahman girl so possessed by the spirit of a Lamani girl is known to have spoken Lamani.

The Konkan people believe that in former days *rakshasas*, or malevolent demons, used to be tall, ugly, black, with long and loose hair, big teeth, and with their foreheads painted with red lead. They could assume any form they liked, were powerful, and could fly in the air. They were fond of human flesh. The people of Khopoli believe that *Khavis* is the ghost of an African *Sidhi*. This spirit is very malevolent, and exorcists find it very difficult to bring it under control. A strong belief prevails in the Konkan that those attacked by the spirits of non-Hindus are beyond cure.

In the Deccan, it is believed that the spirits of Thakars, Lamanis, Vaddars, Gavlis, and Phansepardhis reside in the jungles.

According to the belief of the people in the Kolhapur District, *Brahma rakshasa* is one of the most powerful spirits. It takes up its abode in the sacred *Pipal* tree (*Ficus religiosa*), and when it attacks a person, little hope is entertained of his delivery from its grasp.

The following are the principal malignant spirits of the Konkan and Deccan:

(1) *Vetal* is believed to be the king of spirits. Vetal is considered to be a deity and not an evil spirit. It enters into the body of an exorcist and helps him to drive away other evil spirits. Vetal moves in procession leading all the other ghosts to Maruti's temple.

(2) *Brahmagraha* is the ghost of a Brahman well versed in the Vedas, who is over-proud of his education.

(3) *Sambandh* is the spirit of a person who dies without an heir, and whose funeral rites have not been performed by any member of the family; but when invoked through an exorcist, it becomes harmless, and even favourable to the family. It is the spirit of a covetous person or a holy man who dies with his desires unfulfilled. It does not allow anybody to enjoy his wealth, and takes revenge on an enemy till death ensues. It haunts trees, especially the *Pipal*, *Umbar*, and Banyan, wells, and unoccupied houses.

(4) *Brahmasambandh* is the ghost of a Brahman who watches his buried treasure. It is harmless if the treasure is not disturbed.

(5) *Devachar* is the spirit of a Shudra who dies after his marriage. These (Devachar) spirits are said to reside on the four sides of a village. The spirits which reside in burial or cremation grounds, on river banks, and in old trees are said to be subordinate to these. Coco-nuts, plantains, sugar, cocks, and goats must be given annually to gain their favour.

(6) *Munja* is the spirit of a Brahman boy who dies immediately after his thread ceremony, but before the final ceremony is complete. It does not greatly affect its victim, but simply frightens. When it attacks, it is difficult to drive out.

It is cast out only when the patient makes a pilgrimage to a holy shrine. It resides in a *Pipal* tree (*Ficus religiosa*) or in a well. Munja wears small bells round the waist and is generally seen performing a *Sandhya*. Any member of the unclean classes touching the *Pipal* tree is believed to be promptly possessed by Munja.

(7) *Khavis* is the spirit of a Musalman or a non-Hindu. It is also the spirit of a Mahar, Vaddar, or Lamani, or a Mang. Also, it is held to be the ghost of a man who dies unmarried.

(8) *Girha* is the ghost of a person who dies by drowning, or of a murdered person. Girha is not very powerful and obeys the orders of the exorcists. It only frightens and troubles people. It lives by the water-side, and deceives persons at night by calling them by their names and leading them into false paths. It often troubles people while crossing rivers or creeks at night, and leads them to places where the water is very deep. It is said that the spirit Girha becomes the regular slave of a person who takes possession of the hair of its head, and gives him anything that he requires. It requests the person to return its hair, but this should not be given under any circumstances; for if Girha gets back its hair all sorts of misfortunes will befall the man. In Kolaba District it is believed that Girha is headless.

(9) *Chetak* is the ghost of a person of the Kunbi or Shudra caste. This spirit is also known as *Dav*.

(10) *Zoting* is the ghost of a man belonging to the Kharvi or Koli caste. It is also said to be the ghost of a Musalman. It stands with its legs apart, one on each of two trees, and is headless.

(11) *Vir* is the ghost of an unmarried person belonging to the Kshatriya caste. It is also said to be the ghost of a Rajput or a Pardeshi.

(12) *Cheda* is the ghost of an unmarried Mahar. It resides on mountains, in jungles, and the outskirts of the village. Cheda attacks domestic animals. It haunts fields and farms, and resides at public places where the *Holi* fires are annually kindled. To avoid being troubled by it, people offer annual sacrifices of fowls and goats.

(13) *Mhaṣoba* is the lord of the ghosts and is equal in might to Vetal.

(14) *Jakhin* or *Alwant.* Jakhin is the ghost of a woman who has a husband alive. Alwant is believed to be the spirit of a woman dying at child-birth or during her menses. It resides at burial or cremation grounds. Persons attacked by this spirit are taken to Narsinh wadi in Kolhapur State or Gangapur, which are celebrated as shrines for the removal of malignant spirits.

(15) *Lav* is the ghost of a woman dying during her sickness. Lav and *Vivashi* are the ghosts of rival wives.

(16) *Lavsat* is the ghost of a widow. It generally resides in burial and burning grounds, and attacks domestic animals and their calves. It is also said to tear clothes and eat corpses.

(17) *Hadal* or *Hedali* is the ghost of a woman who dies within ten days of child-birth or during her menses. It is supposed to be an evil spirit, but it can be kept in check by the use of a cane. It attacks all sorts of persons, but leaves them as soon as it is beaten. It dresses in green and lives in cremation grounds, or in the Tamarind tree.

(18) *Malavarid Jind* is the ghost of a miser, who takes the form either of a snake or a man. Like Brahmasambandh, he sits over the hoarded wealth and does no mischief unless some one tries to disturb the hoard.

(19) *Kabandh* is the spirit of a soldier sent to battle unwillingly. It haunts the battle-field, disturbing travellers who pass by the scene of the battle.

In the Deccan:

(20) *Pilar* is short of stature and moves in bands. He is both harmful and benevolent.

(21) *Vir* moves about dressed as a soldier with shield and sword.

(22) *Bir* is a very powerful attendant of Vetal.

(23) *Yadam Kadtai* is the spirit of a woman with many children. She troubles people to feed her children.

(24) *Mhaisasur*—a ghost that appears like a she-buffalo (Mhais). It then assumes a terrible form and so frightens any spectator that he passes blood and dies on the spot.

(25) *Karna-pishacha* is a spirit that whispers into the ear past and future events.

(26) *Ranoa* dwells in the jungle. It is said to unyoke bullocks at night. If the driver keeps to his cart till sunrise he gets off unscathed.[1]

Satvai is the ghost of a woman. It troubles women in child-birth, and kills their children on the fifth or sixth day after their birth. *Shakini* is the ghost of an unmarried girl. *Talkhamba* is the ghost of an unmarried person from the low castes. The people of Vijayadurg believe that one who hates and troubles the Brahmans and speaks ill of their religious duties becomes a *Brahmasambandh* after death. At Poladpur in the Kolaba District the ghost *Bapa* is represented by a stone painted with red lead and oil and placed at the boundary of a field. It is the guardian of the field, and protects the owner's interests. Offerings are made to it annually. If the annual offerings are neglected, it troubles the owner of the field. It also troubles others when disturbed.

The spirits known as *Kalkaiche Bhut* and *Bahirobache Bhut* are not troublesome. When they favour any person, he enjoys health and happiness for a period of twelve years; but after that period he is ruined. In addition to the varieties of malignant spirits already described, the following spirits are known at Shirgaon in the Thana District. They are—*Hirwa*, *Waghoba*, *Asaras*, *Gangud*, *Saitan*, and *Chaitannadya*. The spirit known as *Hirwa* requires the offerings of a bow and an arrow, *bhang*, bread, and garlic. *Waghoba* haunts jungles and troubles domestic animals. Coco-nuts and lamps of *ghi* are offered to it. *Asaras* are the deities that dwell in water. They infest the wells and ponds, and attack women and children at noon-time and in the evening. Red lead, coco-nuts, flowers, parched rice, and cakes are given to them.

At Shirgaon in the Thana District it is believed that the spirit *Hirwa* goes about headless. It troubles human beings and animals. The sea and the jungle are its places of abode. To avoid being troubled by it, *bhang*, coco-nuts, and fowls are given to it.

[1] See *S.B.B.C.*, pp. 200–3, for further notes.

The people of Dahigaon in the Thana District believe that the spirit known as *Pisa* goes about headless.

Some evil spirits haunt trees such as the *Pipal*, *Babul*, and *Adulsa* (*Adhatoda vasica*). Some have their haunts on a public road where three streets meet, or in a dirty place, some haunt old houses, and the rest prefer to reside in burial and burning grounds.

Many spirits are believed to dwell in burial or cremation grounds. Among them are *Vetal*, *Jakhin*, *Khavis*, *Khaprya*, *Zoting*, *Chetak*, *Girha*, *Alwant*, and *Lavsat*.

The spirits *Munja* and *Sambandh* are said to reside near houses and old trees that produce sweet-smelling flowers.

It is believed that all kinds of spirits assemble at night at the funeral ground when a body is burnt or buried.

In some places the evil spirits known as *Khavis*, *Zoting*, and *Kafri* are said to dwell on mountains and in jungles; while *Sambandh*, *Jakhin*, *Hadal*, and *Lavsat* are said to reside on trees.

In the Kolhapur District it is believed that the ghosts of persons dying on battle-fields infest mountains and jungles.

Generally in the Konkan, and especially in the Ratnagiri District, young mothers and their children are supposed to be liable to the attacks of the spirits *Satvai*, *Avagat*, *Alwant*, *Jakhin*, *Devachar*, and *Chalegat*. In the Deccan they are attacked similarly by *Ranubai-sanlubai* and *Shakini-Dakhinia*.

At Khopoli in the Kolaba District it is believed that a young mother and her child are generally attacked by the spirit of the dead wife of her husband, or by a *Hadal* or *Lavsat*. The spirit that attacks a woman during child-birth is difficult to drive out. The spirits are always afraid of cleanliness, and therefore, where there is cleanliness, there is very little fear of their attacks.

The people of Shirgaon believe that the fiend known as *Hedali* attacks a young mother and her child. They are generally attacked by these fiends on a public cross-road where three roads meet, or under a *Babul* tree, and also at wells. The *Bhutya*, or the sorcerer, makes use of his cane and of the dirty incense known as *Nurkya Uda*, and compels her to speak and to ask for what she wants. Sometimes she speaks and asks for the things required. Boiled rice and curds, and oil with red lead, are given to her. When she leaves the body, the person becomes insensible for a short time.

At Ubhadanda in the Ratnagiri District it is believed that those who are killed by tigers or other wild beasts are born as kings, or as members of a royal family, in the next generation. This belief is common to the greater part of the Deccan, Konkan, and Karnatak. On the other hand, the people of Bankavli are of opinion that those who suffer death at the hands of tigers and other wild beasts are turned into spirits. The spirit of a person killed by a tiger is called *Vaghvir.* In the Karnatak it is believed that those who fall victims to tigers, lions, wolves, bears, &c., are reborn in the form of such animals.

At Achare it is believed that persons killed by lions and tigers attain salvation, while those killed by inferior beasts go to hell.

The people of Ibhrampur believe that unmarried persons killed by tigers or other wild beasts take the form of a ghost. Males become *Girhas* and females become *Jakhins* and *Lavsats.*

At Pendur it is believed that persons killed by tigers and other wild beasts become *Brahma rakshasas.* The same form is assumed by those who die by accident. A murdered man becomes a *Devachar.*

For the purpose of preventing a woman dying in child-birth turning into a ghost, the following device is adopted: The corpse, instead of being burnt as usual, is buried underground, and four iron nails are fixed at the four corners of the spot on which the body is buried, and plants bearing red flowers are planted thereon.

It is generally believed that old unoccupied houses are haunted by evil spirits. Persons who wish to inhabit such houses first perform the *Vastu shanti* ceremony, and give a feast to Brahmans. In former times, in the districts that were ruled by the Portuguese, religious persecution prevailed. To escape from these persecutions, people were compelled to leave their houses unprotected. Before leaving their homes, they used to bury their treasure in the ground, and on that spot a human being or an animal was sacrificed in order that the spirit of the dead should hover about the place and prevent strangers from coming.

If there be any buried treasure in an old unoccupied house, the owner of the treasure is believed to haunt the house in the form of a ghost. If the treasure be near the temple of a deity, it is supposed to be under the guardianship of that deity.

At Vijayadurg it is believed that a person who builds a house in the days of his prosperity, and does not survive to enjoy it, becomes a *Sambandh*. He remains in that house in the form of a ghost, and troubles every one who comes to stay there, excepting the members of his family. A man who buries his treasure underground becomes a ghost after death, comes back to watch his treasure, and troubles those who try to remove it.

At certain forts in the Konkan where battles were fought, the souls of those slain in the battles are said to have assumed the forms of spirits, and to keep a watch over the forts.

In the Kolhapur District there is a village, Nigve, beyond the river Panch Ganga at a distance of three miles from Kolhapur, where the soul of a person named Appaji Kulkarni has assumed the form of a *Sambandh* and guards the buried treasures in his house. When anybody tries to dig up the buried money, the ghost enters the body of his daughter-in-law and begins to dance and cry out loudly, and does not allow any one to touch his treasure. It is also said that he strikes the ground with his stick at night. Another similar instance is cited in the case of the village of Latvade in the Shirol Petha, where Bapujipant Kulkarni continues to guard his house after death. He does not allow anybody to live in the house, and if any one is bold enough to sleep there at night, the spirit of Bapuji appears and throws him out of the house. The house is therefore uninhabited at present. His wife has adopted a son, but he has to live in another village, Vadange.

It is generally believed that *bhuts* or evil spirits prove beneficial to those who succeed in securing locks of their hair or subjugate them by incantations or magical rites.

Such spirits generally belong to the class of the *Bavan*, the *Vir*, the *Babro*, *Mamo*, *Vaital*, *Dadamo*, and *Yaksha*. Of these, *Mamo*, *Vir*, *Vaital*, and *Dadamo* prove beneficial through favour, while the rest become the slaves of those who subdue them.

It is believed that *Suro Puro* and *Dado* favour only their blood relations.

It is related that in building the numerous tanks and temples attributed to Siddhraj Jaysing, a former king of Gujarat, he was assisted by the spirit *Babario*, whom he had brought under his control.

A tradition is current that Tulsidas, the celebrated author of the *Ramayana* in Hindi and a great devotee of Ram, had secured personal visits from the god Hanuman through the favour of a spirit.

The king Vikrama is said to have received great services from the evil spirits *Vetal* and *Jal*.

At Kolhapur it is believed that the deities Etalai and Kalkai of the Konkan keep with them evil spirits as their servants. These servant spirits obey the orders of these deities. Some people in this district go to the temples of these deities and request them to lend them the services of these spirit servants. It is considered very lucky to secure the help of these spirits. The temple ministrant then requests the deity to give a *Kaul* or omen.[1] For this purpose the temple ministrant calls on the deity to enter his body, and when he is possessed by the spirit of the deity, he allows the applicant to take with him one of the deity's servants for a fixed period. The Gurav, or the ministrant, then explains to the person the period for which the spirit servant is given, and the amount of the annual tribute required to be given to the deity for the use of her servant. He also gives him a coco-nut and sacred ashes. The applicant then returns home, believing that the spirit servant will follow him, and from that time he prospers. This spirit servant is called *Chetak*, and it can be seen only by the person in whose charge it is given by the Gurav.

At Murbad in the Thana District the spirit known as *Vetal*, the king of evil spirits, is considered to be benevolent.

In the Karnatak districts, though the names of the evil spirits are mostly different, their characters and performances resemble those already described for the Konkan, Deccan,

[1] See p. 181, *supra*.

and Gujarat. Thus, the spirit of a woman dying in childbirth is called Addabanati, Hennachali, or Bantikoli instead of Hadal, while the spirit of a woman dying at the time of her sickness is called Kulakoli. The common spirits are known as:

(1) Brahmaraksha, (2) Yakshakimara, (3) Sakini-Dakini, (4) Kushmanda, (5) Birabetal, (6) Kollideva, (7) Malladchavdi, (8) Chamundi, Chavdi, or Chavandi, (9) Bavali, (10) Mahasati, (11) Hennagoli, (12) Gandagoli, (13) Vetal, (14) Kila, (15) Ranagoti, (16) Hulasu.

Chamundi is the spirit of a woman who dies in confinement. Brahmaraksha lives in trees, Yakshakimara in hills, and Sakini-Dakini in forests. Kollideva is a kind of will-o'-the-wisp, a wandering flame.

VI

TOTEMISM AND ANIMAL WORSHIP

Totems

AMONG the more primitive elements of the population in India generally, the worship of trees, animals, weapons, and implements of industry on the occasion of marriage, and in such fashion as tends to justify the inference that the object worshipped is regarded as an ancestor, is common and widespread. In the Bombay Presidency these objects are known as *devaks* in the Deccan and as *balis* in the Karnatak, and are a common feature of many tribes and castes in the Deccan, Konkan, and Karnatak. The significant points of this *devak* worship are :

(1) those who own the same *devak* may not intermarry ;

(2) the *devak* must in no circumstances be injured by those who acknowledge it. It and its products, i.e. the fruit if it is a tree, or the parts if it is an animal, e.g. the tusks of an elephant if the elephant is the *devak*, must be treated with respect, not used for food or ornament, or injured in any way.

The preparation of a complete list of the *devaks* and *balis* of the Bombay Presidency would necessitate a special inquiry. A large number, however, will be found in the pages of *Tribes and Castes of Bombay*, under the article on Marathas. It will be sufficient to give a few examples here.

Trees and plants.

(1) Mango.
(2) Babul (*Acacia arabica*).
(3) Bel (*Aegle Marmelos*).
(4) Bor (*Zizyphus Jujuba*).
(5) Chinch (*Tamarind*).
(6) Kadamb (*Anthocephalus Cadamba*).
(7) Rui (*Calotropis gigantea*).
(8) Shami (*Prosopis spicigera*).
(9) Nim (*Melia Azadirachta*).
(10) Banyan tree and others of the fig class.

Animals and birds.

(1) Horse.
(2) Mouse deer.
(3) Pig.
(4) Eagle.
(5) Tortoise.
(6) Crow pheasant.
(7) Buffalo.
(8) Peacock.
(9) Cobra.
(10) Goat.
(11) Elephant.
(12) Elk (*sambhar*).
(13) Monkey.
(14) Porcupine.
(15) Wolf.
(16) *Chital* (*Axis maculata*).

Implements of Industry.

(1) Spinning-whorl (*Chat*).
(2) Axe.
(3) Potter's patter.
(4) Oil-mill.
(5) Blowpipe } of the goldsmith.
(6) Pincers } of the goldsmith.
(7) Knife.
(8) Sword.

The following are instances illustrative of the abstention, on the part of those who worship such *devaks*, from using or injuring the same, as well as their products, in any way :

Those of the elephant *devak* will not injure an elephant or wear ornaments of ivory made from its tusks. Those of the elk *devak* will not injure the elk. Members of the tiger group are very averse to injuring a tiger, as for instance the Bhils, among whom the *Vaghs* or tiger section worship the tiger and grieve when they hear of a tiger being killed. They are said to prostrate themselves when they encounter a tiger. Among Kunbis, the Shelar or goat section will not eat the flesh of a goat, and those of the More or peacock section abstain from eating the flesh of a peacock. Among Bhandaris, the Padwals, or snake-gourd section, will not eat the snake-gourd. Those who respect the Banyan tree as a *devak* will not use the leaves of this tree for any purpose. Certain families among Kunbis, of the Banyan section, will not even take food from leaf-plates fashioned from Banyan leaves. Maratha traders of the Jack-fruit tree section will not eat the Jack-fruit. Similar instances can be multiplied indefinitely.[1]

It has been noted that the special occasion for the worship

[1] See for further details, *Tribes and Castes of Bombay*, particularly articles Gamvakkal and Halvakki Vakkal.

of the *devak* is marriage. It is, however, a common custom to worship it also

(1) on the occasion of occupying a new house for the first time;

(2) at the time of preparing the threshing-floor in the field when the harvest has been gathered;

(3) on the occasion of performing the thread-girding ceremony.

If the houses of the bride and bridegroom are in the same village or town, the installing, or setting-up for worship, of the *devak* takes place on the marriage day. Otherwise it takes place two or three days previously. In installing the *devak* the first step is to worship the household gods. The company then repair to Maruti's temple, the bride carrying a platter containing the *devak* or an image of it and an offering of food. Here the *devak* is formally worshipped, and then brought back to the bride's house, where it is either affixed to the marriage booth or placed with the household gods until after the completion of the marriage ceremony. Sometimes, after visiting Maruti's temple with the *devak,* the bridal party repair to the village potter's house, where the *devak* is again worshipped. This is an indication of the primitive nature of the rite.

Another method of *devak* worship is as follows: A small quantity of rice is put into a winnowing fan, and with it six small sticks of the *devak*, each covered with Mango leaves and cotton thread. These are worshipped as deities. Near the winnowing fan is kept an earthen or copper vessel filled with rice, turmeric, red powder, betel-nuts, sweet-balls made of wheat flour, *ghi*, and sugar; and on the top of the vessel is a small sprig of the *devak* and a coco-nut covered with cotton thread. This vessel is also worshipped as a deity, and offerings of sweet eatables are made to it. The winnowing fan is taken to the temple of Maruti. After the worship of this vessel, the regular ceremony of Holy-day blessing is performed. Twenty-seven mothers, or village and local deities, represented by betel-nuts, are consecrated in a new winnowing fan or a bamboo basket. Seven mothers are made of Mango leaves, six of which contain *Durva* (*Cynodon Dactylon*) grass, and the seventh *Darbha* (*Eragrostis cynosuroides*) grass. Each of them is bound with a raw cotton thread separately. They are worshipped along with a copper vessel as mentioned above. This copper vessel is filled with rice, betel-nuts, turmeric, &c., a sprig of Mango leaves is placed on the vessel and a coconut is put over it. The vessel is also bound with a cotton thread. Sandal paste, rice, flowers, and *Durva* (*Cynodon Dactylon*) grass are required for its worship. An oil-lamp is waved round the *devak*, the parents, and the boy or the girl whose thread or marriage ceremony is to be performed. An unwidowed woman (*suvasini*) is called and requested to wave this lamp, and the silver coin which is put into the lamp by the parents is taken by her. The father takes the winnowing fan and the mother takes the copper vessel, and they are carried from the marriage booth to the *devak* consecrated in the house. A lighted lamp is kept continually burning near this *devak* till the completion of the ceremony. After completion of the thread or marriage ceremony the *devak* is again worshipped, and the ceremony comes to an end. The deity in the *devak* is requested to depart on the second or the fourth day from the date of its consecration. No mourning is observed during the period the *devak* remains installed in the house.

In the Deccan, on the day before the marriage, the twig of the *devak* is brought home and worshipped. It is then carried first to Maruti's temple and then to a potter's. After worship at both places, it is brought to be tied to a post of the *Mandap*.

The system of surnames derived from trees, plants, and animals is prevalent in the Deccan, Konkan, and Karnatak. It seems to be connected with the totemistic custom described above. Thus we note in Marathi-speaking districts the names Landaga (wolf), Wagh (tiger), Dukre (pig), Mhas (buffalo), Popat (parrot), Salunkhe (cormorant), Padival (snake-gourd). It is reported from the Sholapur District that persons bearing such surnames as the above hold themselves to be descended from the wolf, tiger, pig, buffalo, &c., respectively.

An interesting practice in this connexion is that common in Gujarat, where a totem organization cannot be traced, of bestowing on children such names as Kagdo (crow), Kolo (jackal), Bilado (cat), Kutro (dog), &c., if one of these animals is heard to utter a cry at the time of the birth of the infant.

The instances of similar names derived from animals are:

(1) Hathibhai . . . *Hathi*—an elephant.
(2) Vaghajibhai . . *Vagh*—a tiger.
(3) Nagjibhai . . . *Nag*—a snake.
(4) Popatbhai . . . *Popat*—a parrot.
(5) Morbhai . . . *Mor*—a peacock.
(6) Chaklibhai . . . *Chakli*—a sparrow.
(7) Kido . . . *Kidi*—an ant.
(8) Mankodia . . . *Mankoda*—a black ant.
(9) Tido . . . . *Tid*—a locust.
(10) Hansraj . . . *Hansa*—a goose.
(11) Vinchi . . . *Vinchi*—a female scorpion.
(12) Olo . . . . *Olo*—an owl.
(13) Ajo . . . . *Aja*—a goat.
(14) Mena . . . *Mena*—a mina.

The following are instances of names derived from flowers, trees, and plants:

(1) Gulab . . . *Gulab*—the rose.
(2) Ambo . . . *Ambo*—the Mango.
(3) Tulsibai . . . *Tulsi*—the sweet Basil (*Ocymum sanctum*).
(4) Tulsidas . . . " " " "
(5) Kesharbai . . . *Keshar*—saffron.
(6) Gulalbai . . . *Gulal*—red powder.
(7) Bili . . . *Bel*—*Aegle Marmelos.*
(8) Dudhi . . . *Dudhi*—pumpkin.
(9) Lavengi . . . *Laveng*—clove.
(10) Mulo. . . . *Mulo*—radish.
(11) Limbdo . . . *Limbdo*—the *Nim* tree (*Melia Azadirachta*).
(12) Mako . . . *Maki*—maize.
(13) Champo . . . *Champa*—*Mesua ferrea.*
(14) Kakadia . . . *Kakadi*—a cucumber.

Instances of family or clan names derived from animals are as follows:

(1) Untia . . . *Unt*—a camel.
(2) Gadheda . . . *Gadheda*—an ass.
(3) Bedakia . . . *Bedako*—a frog.
(4) Balada . . . *Balad*—an ox.
(5) Godhani . . . *Godho*—a bull.
(6) Bhensdadia . . *Bhensa*—a buffalo.
(7) Ghetiya . . . *Gheta*—a sheep.

Animal Worship

The following animals are considered sacred and worshipped by the Hindus in Western India:

1. *The Cow.* Of all the animals the cow is considered to be the most sacred. The sanctity which attaches to the cow is due to the belief that in her body reside thirty-three crores of gods. She is generally worshipped daily in the morning for the whole year, or at least for the four months beginning from the eleventh day of the bright half of *Ashadh* (June–July) to the eleventh day of the bright half of the month of *Kartik* (October–November); and a special worship is offered to her in the evening of the twelfth day of the dark half of *Ashvin* (September–October).

The cow is believed to be the abode of all the deities and sages. She is compared with the earth in its sacredness, and it is considered that when she is pleased she is capable of giving everything required for the maintenance of mankind, and for this reason she is styled the *Kama Dhenu,* or the giver of desired objects. It is said that a person who walks round the cow at the time of her delivery obtains the merit of going round the whole earth. The cow is even worshipped by the god Vishnu.

The cow is considered next to a mother, as little children and the people in general are fed by the milk of a cow. Some women among high-class Hindus take a vow not to take their meals before worshipping the cow, and when the cow is not available for worship, they draw in turmeric, or white or red powder, the cow's footprints, and worship the same. At the completion of the vow the cow is worshipped, and then given as a gift to a Brahman. It is considered very meritorious to give a *Gopradan*—a gift of a cow along with her calf—to a Brahman. The sight of a cow in the morning is believed by all Hindus to be auspicious.

The milk, the urine, and the dung of a cow are used as medicines, and they are also given as offerings to the god in sacrifices. The greatest sanctity attaches to the cow. Her urine is sipped for the atonement of sins. The cow is also revered by the Parsis.

2 *The Horse.* The horse is believed by some people to be

the last incarnation of God. It is also believed to represent Vachhado, the deity who cures hydrophobia.

Some people believe the horse to be a celestial animal. It is said that in ancient times it had wings, traces of which are believed to be still visible in its knees.

Of the fourteen jewels obtained by the gods and demons by churning the ocean, one was a horse with seven mouths. Hence the horse is considered divine.

It is the vehicle of the deity Khandoba of Jejuri. It is worshipped on the *Dasara* holiday as in former days on the occasion of the horse sacrifice.

The horse draws the conveyance of the Sun. The horse is also associated with the planets Jupiter and Venus.

The mouth of the she-goat and the smell of the horse are considered sacred.

3. *The Elephant.* The elephant is considered divine because it is the vehicle of Indra, the lord of gods, and because its head was fixed on the trunk of Ganpati, the son of Parvati and Shiva. It is believed by some people that vows to offer coco-nuts to an elephant are efficacious in curing fever.

At the time of celebrating a coronation ceremony an elephant is worshipped. There is a tradition that in ancient times the coronation waters were poured over the king by a she-elephant.

The elephant, being the vehicle of the god Indra, is specially worshipped on the *Dasara* day. It is also believed that there are eight sacred elephants posted at the eight directions. These are called *Ashtadik-Palas,* i. e. the protectors of the eight different directions, and they are worshipped along with other deities on auspicious ceremonial occasions, like weddings, thread-girding, &c. The elephant is also connected with Mercury.

4. *The Lion.* The lion is considered sacred because it is believed to be the lord of the beasts of the forest and the vehicle of goddesses. It is believed to be the vehicle of Parvati, the consort of Shiva. The lion is also connected with the demon planet *Rahu.*

5. *The Tiger.* The tiger is worshipped with Vagheshvari Mata as it is believed to be her vehicle. The tiger is the conveyance of the goddess Ambaji.

6. *The She-buffalo.* Some sanctity attaches to the she-buffalo, as it is believed that a she-buffalo was given in dowry to a *Nag kanya* (snake girl) by her father.

To atone for a great sin a she-buffalo decked with a black wreath, iron, red lead, and marks made with the flour of black gram is presented to a Brahman.

In order to avoid calamities arising from the influence of inauspicious planets, Hindus worship the she-buffalo, and offer it as a gift to a Brahman. The she-buffalo is compared with the god of death, the reason being that Yama is believed to ride a buffalo. The Brahman who accepts this gift has to shave his moustaches and to undergo a certain penance. The cow-herds sometimes worship the she-buffalo. As it is the vehicle of Yama, the buffalo is specially worshipped by people when an epidemic occurs in a village. In certain villages in the Konkan districts the buffalo is worshipped and sacrificed on the same day.

7. *The Bull.* The bull is believed to be the vehicle of the god Shiva. In all temples of Shiva its image is installed, facing the image of Shiva in the centre of the temple.

The bull is respected as it is the favourite vehicle of the god Shiva, and is useful for agricultural purposes. The *Nandi* or bull is worshipped by Hindus. The bull is specially worshipped on the twelfth day of the bright half of *Kartik* (October–November). When performing the funeral rites of the dead, a bull is worshipped and set free. The bull thus set free is considered sacred by the people, and is never used again for agricultural or any other domestic purposes. It is connected with Mars and Saturn. In the Deccan the bull is worshipped in the bright half of *Shravan* (July–August), i. e. the *Pola*.

8. *The Donkey.* The donkey is believed to be the vehicle of the goddess of small-pox.

It is also believed that the god Brahma had formerly five mouths, one of which was like that of a donkey.

Among Marwari Agarvals, when a child has an attack of small-pox, a donkey is worshipped after first worshipping Devi. The donkey is generally considered as unholy by the Hindus, and its mere touch is held to cause pollution. But certain lower-class Hindus like the Lonaris consider it sacred, and worship it on the eighth day of the dark half of *Shravan* (July–August). In the Deccan the ass is worshipped by Kumbhars, Parits, Vadaris, and Ghisadis.

9. *The Dog.* The dog is believed to have divine vision and to be able to see the messengers of the god of death. Some believe that in its next life a dog becomes a man. The dog is also believed to be the vehicle of Kal Bhairav and is worshipped along with his image. Some people offer bread to dogs in the belief that they will bear witness to their merits before God. The dog is believed to be an incarnation of the deity Khandoba, and it is respected as the favourite animal of the god Dattatraya. But it is not touched by high-class Hindus. In the temple of Dattatraya dogs are worshipped by Hindus.

In the Deccan the dog is considered sacred and worshipped on the *Champashashti* day. The god Khandoba is believed to ride with his two wives, Mhalsa, a Lingayat, and Banai, a Dhangar. The latter is followed by her dog, and is therefore worshipped at the same time as Khandoba.

10. *The Goat* is worshipped by the Bharvads when they worship the goddess Machhu. The goat is believed to be holy for sacrificial purposes. It is worshipped at the time of its sacrifice, which is performed on numerous occasions to gain the favour of the gods or to propitiate evil spirits, not only those which cause disease.

11. *The Cat* is worshipped in the belief that by so doing a man can win over his opponents. It is considered a great sin to kill a cat.

In the Deccan the cat is jokingly called the maternal aunt of the tiger, and held to be an incarnation of the goddess Satvai. On *Panchavi* day it is held to be specially sacred and is allowed to stay by the side of the mother and child. A person killing a cat is required to do penance by going to Benares.

12. *The Deer.* The deer is supposed to be the conveyance of the moon as well as of Mars. It is considered to be holy by Hindus, and the skin is used by Brahmans and ascetics while performing their austerities. The deer's skin is also used on the occasion of thread-girding. A small piece of the deer's skin is tied to the neck of the boy with the new sacred thread.

13. *The Bear.* The bear is considered by some people to be a holy animal because the god Krishna married Jambuvanti, the daughter of Jambuvant, the heroic bear who assisted Rama.

14. *The Jackal.* It is held to be auspicious to hear the cry of a jackal when measuring grain at harvest time. It is therefore customary, in the Deccan, to invoke jackals at dusk, red powder and turmeric being offered them before commencing to measure the grain. The cultivators, after worshipping a jackal, cut off its head and keep it till the grain is ready to be measured, when they hide the head in the grain-heap. It is auspicious to see a jackal's mask, especially in the morning. In the Deccan, therefore, a jackal's mask is affixed to a wall in the house where it can be seen on rising. The *bhalu,* i. e. old female jackal, is considered to be unholy and inauspicious.

15. *The Tortoise.* It is generally believed that the earth is supported by a tortoise. So, whenever the goddess earth or Prithvi is worshipped, the tortoise is also worshipped.

16. *Fish.* Fish are considered sacred because they are supposed to carry the food (*pindas*) to the *manes* offered (in water) at the *Shraddha* ceremony.

17. *Alligators.* Alligators are worshipped in a pond at Magar Pir, near Karachi. They are worshipped as water deities by Hindus in many parts of the Presidency.

18. *The Owl.* An owl is considered to be a bird of such evil repute that, in all parts of the Konkan, it is considered necessary to perform expiatory rites when an owl perches on the roof. If these rites are not performed, it is firmly believed that some evil will befall the members of the family. Various omens are drawn from the cries of the spotted owl (*Pingla*), and these cries are known as Kilbil, Chilbil, and Khit Khit.

If an owl sits on the roof of a house, it is a sure sign of coming death to a member of the family.

A common belief about the owl is that none should throw a lump of earth at it, as the owl is believed to pick up the missile and throw it into a well or tank or any sheet of water, with the result that it gradually dissolves and disappears, and simultaneously the body of the person is said to be consumed.

If the screech of an owl perching on the top cross-beam of a house is heard on a Sunday or Tuesday night, the owner of the house should pass a dark woollen thread below the cross-beam, to which a nude person should add a knot at every screech of the owl. If such a thread be kept in an anklet, the wearer need have no fear of ghosts nor can he be seen by a witch.

If a person in sleep responds to the call of an owl, he is believed to expire within six months from that date.

If an owl screeches every night for six months on one's house or an adjacent tree, a terror seizes the members of the house that some sure and certain calamity not short of death is imminent.

An owl sitting on the house of a person and screeching is said to be uttering threats or forebodings of calamities and misfortunes, and is believed to foretell the death of some near relation.

Women who do not obey the commands of their husbands, who partake of their meals secretly before their husbands, or violate any of their duties towards their husbands, are believed to enter the order of bats or owls after their death.

According to another belief, men who have been incontinent become owls after death, while such women become bats.

Owls and bats are blind during the day, but they can see corpses and the spirits of the deceased and converse with them in their own tongue.

The spirits of the deceased are supposed to remain in their worldly tenement for twelve days, and owls and bats are supposed to be able to see them at night and talk to them.

At Devgad in the Ratnagiri District the cry or screech of a bat or an owl is considered inauspicious, and indicates the death of a sick person in the house.

At Chauk an owl is said to have some connexion with spirits. Its screech at night indicates the approaching death of a sick person in the house. The spotted owl is supposed to foretell future events by its movements and cries, while the bat is considered an inauspicious bird, and its appearance forebodes coming evil.

At Umbergaon people do not throw stones at an owl. For it is considered that the owl might sit and rub the stone, and that the person throwing it will become weak and wasted as the stone wears away.

The people of Kolhapur do not believe that there is any connexion between the bat or owl and the spirits of the dead, but they believe that, if an owl cries out in the evening or at night, it foretells the death of a sick person in the family. This applies also to the screech of a single spotted owl; but the screech of a pair of spotted owls is considered auspicious.

19. *The Eagle.* The eagle is the vehicle of the god Vishnu, and is a favourite devotee of that deity. It is therefore held sacred by Hindus.

20. *The Crow.* Crows are worshipped because they are supposed to represent sages.

Some people believe that crows were formerly sages. They are supposed to have divine vision, and food offered to them is believed to reach deceased ancestors.

A loaf is cut into three parts. One of them is designated *kal* (ordinary), the second *dukal* (famine), and the third *sukal* (plenty). Next, all three are offered to a crow. If the crow takes away the *kal*, it is believed that the crops in the following year will be normal; if it takes away the *dukal* a famine is apprehended in the following year, and if the *sukal*, it is believed that the crops will be plentiful.

The crow is generally held inauspicious by Hindus, but as the *manes* or *pitras* are said to assume the form of crows, these birds are respected in order that they may be able to partake of the food offered to the dead ancestors in the dark half of *Bhadrapad* (August–September) called *Pitrupaksha*.

It is necessary that the oblations given in performance of the funeral rites on the tenth day after the death of a person should be eaten by the crow. If the crow refuses to touch these oblations, it is believed that the soul of the dead has not obtained salvation; and hence it is conjectured that certain wishes of the dead have remained unfulfilled. The son or the relatives of the dead then take water in the cavity of their right hand, and solemnly promise to fulfil the wishes of the dead. When this is done, the crow begins to eat the food.

The harsh caw of a crow is taken as a sure sign of an impending mishap.

21. *The Cuckoo.* The cuckoo or *Kokil* is believed to be an incarnation of the goddess Parvati. This bird is specially

worshipped by high-caste Hindu women for the period of one month on the occasion of a special festival called the festival of the cuckoos, or *Kokila vrata*, which is held in the month of *Ashadh* (June–July) at intervals of twenty years.

22. *The Swan.* The swan is supposed to be the vehicle of the goddess Sarasvati. It is believed that its worship ensures success in any enterprise. If a swan is seen in a dream, it is considered to be a very good omen.

A swan is believed to be endowed with the power of separating milk from water. It is supposed to feed on rubies. It is found in Lake Man in the Himalayas.

23. *The Cock.* The cock is considered holy as it is believed to be the vehicle of the goddess Bahucharaji.

At Vankavli in the Ratnagiri District there is a custom among the low-class Hindus of a woman who has lost her second husband and wishes to marry for the third time, first marrying a cock, i. e. she takes the cock in her arms at the time of her marriage with the third husband.

24. *The Hen.* The hen is worshipped on the last Sunday of the month of *Jyeshth* (May–June).

25. *The Parrot.* The parrot is worshipped by singers desiring to improve their voice. It is also worshipped by dull persons desirous of improving their intellect.

26. *The Mouse.* The mouse, being the vehicle of the god Ganpati, is worshipped along with that deity on the *Ganesh Chaturthi* day, the fourth day of the bright half of *Bhadrapad* (August–September).

27. *The Peacock.* The peacock is the favourite vehicle of Sarasvati, the goddess of learning, and it is therefore respected by the people. It is also associated with Kartik Swami.

28. *The Monkey.* A male monkey is held holy, because it is supposed to represent the monkey-god Maruti.

The lizard, bat, kite, vulture, and ring-turtle (*titavi*) are considered as unholy and inauspicious by Hindus.

Hindus consider it meritorious to feed ants and fish, and to throw grain to the birds. Ants are fed by the people scattering sugar and flour on the ant-hills. It is believed that by feeding ants with sugar or flour a person obtains the merit of giving a feast to a thousand Brahmans.

In the Deccan black ants are held to be sacred, and red ants unholy. When the latter multiply and become troublesome, offerings of pulse, molasses, and dry coco-kernel are made to Marya.

All domestic animals are worshipped by the Hindus on the morning of the first day of *Margashirsh* (November–December).

On this day the horns of these animals are washed with warm water, painted with red colours, and a lighted lamp is passed round their faces. They are feasted on this day, as it is considered to be the gala day (*Divali* holiday) of the animals.

In the Konkan cattle are worshipped by the Hindus on the first day of *Kartik* (October–November), and they are made to pass over fire.

VII

THE EVIL EYE AND AVOIDANCE; WITCHCRAFT AND MAGIC

The Evil Eye

Campbell holds that the human eye became the chief home of evil influences for two reasons :

(1) Because his eye is the centre of power and influence in man.

(2) Because, with the increase of man's control over his surroundings, the belief in the countless host of souls or spirits, with which early experience peopled space and all things visible, narrowed and grew faint. The spread of man's control over beasts and plants as well as over certain of the powers of nature was accompanied by the spread of the doctrine that the subject races of stones, plants, and beasts were soulless ; that the dignity of housing a soul-guest belonged to no one except Man the Ruler.[1]

From this assumption Campbell draws a picture of power centring in the eye of man, and consequently the source of all sudden afflictions is traced by the credulity of the masses in many countries to a glance, usually of envy or covetousness, from the eye of a person who has the power to affect injuriously men, women, children, cattle, food, and all precious things.

Hindus throughout the Presidency generally believe in the injurious effects of the evil eye. If an accident befall anything of value, or it undergoes any sudden change, it is said to be due to the effects of an evil eye. Young children, domestic animals, and beautiful objects are specially liable to be affected by an evil eye.

The following are some of the methods of evading the effects of an evil eye:

1st. Dry chillies are waved round the body of the affected

[1] *S. B. B. C.*, p. 268.

person and thrown into the fire, and if they do not thereupon make a loud noise, it is said that the effects of an evil eye are averted.

2nd. Mustard-seed and salt are waved round the face of a child and then thrown into the fire.

3rd. Alum is waved round the child and then thrown into fire. The piece of alum thus thrown is sometimes believed to be changed into the form of a man or a woman. From this, conjectures are made as to the sex of the person by whose evil eye the patient is affected. The form or the figure is then broken by a toe of the left foot of the patient, and dry chillies, garlic, hair, rubbish from the house, and salt are mixed in the alum powder. The mixture is waved round the patient three times and then thrown into fire. Meanwhile the sorcerer repeats the names of all persons, things, and evil spirits suspected by him. After this performance has been repeated three times, the fire is deposited in a place where three roads meet.

4th. If the evil eye is believed to be that of a ghost, the sorcerer mutters some words to himself, waves ashes round the affected child, and blows them in the air.

5th. The evil eye of a tiger is removed from an affected animal in the following manner: An oil lamp is burnt in the eye of a dead tiger and the lamp is waved round the animal by a Mahar. The Mahar is given a loaf prepared from eight kinds of grain.

6th. Copper amulets and black-cotton strings charmed by a sorcerer are tied round the neck or arms of the patient.

7th. In the Karnatak an image is made from the wood of the *Pipal* (*Ficus religiosa*), waved in front of the person affected, and then burnt.

8th. Potsherds, old brooms, and old leather shoes are tied to fruit trees to protect them from the evil eye.

9th. When an invalid has recovered from an illness, it is the practice in the Karnatak to say that he is still suffering, to protect him from the evil eye.

10th. If food is affected by the evil eye, vomiting and fever are caused. To remedy this, similar food is placed outside the house, and red powder in water poured over it. It is believed that when this food has been seen by all the village, the influence of the evil eye will be removed.

11th. Flowers are waved round the patient and thrown into water.

12th. A red-hot earthen bowl is placed in an earthen dish, mouth downwards, and water mixed with buffalo dung poured over it. Both bowl and dish are then lifted, adhering together. When they separate, the effect of the evil eye has passed.

13th. An exorcist takes a broom and passes it over the sufferer from head to feet, uttering the name of the men suspected of the evil eye. A small piece of the broom is then cut off, spat upon, and trodden into the ground.

14th. A woman's robe is passed over the patient from head to foot.

15th. A cowrie with a black thread through it is tied to the sufferer's foot.

16th. In the Karnatak it is the custom to preserve water in which hands have been washed, to add the remains of food, and throw hot ashes into the mixture, to ward off the evil eye.

17th. The burning of a hair from the head of the owner of the evil eye, or one of his eyelashes, is held to ward off the evil influence.

18th. In the joined hands of the exorcist seven red chillies with stalks, hair, *Nim* (*Melia Azadirachta*) leaves, husks, a marking nut, salt, and mustard-seed are waved round the sufferer's face, the latter uttering the names of suspects. They are then taken out and burnt. If no unpleasant odour is given out, the evil effects are held to have passed.

19th. A buffalo's dung is stuck to the lintel post of the house, and a coarse black wick dipped in sweet oil affixed thereto. If this, when lit, gives a hissing sound, the effects of the evil eye are said to have passed.

20th. Charmed black-cotton strings moistened in salt water are tied round a stone and burnt.

21st. A wick steeped in oil is lit and waved round the person affected by the evil eye; then, on being held over water, if a drop falling into the water *hisses*, all is well.

When a child is to be removed from one village to another, rice is scattered at the boundary of the village, at the bridges, rivers, creeks, &c., that are crossed during the journey. Coco-nuts are waved round the child and thrown away at the boundary of the village and at places supposed to be haunted by ghosts. Before entering a house in a new village, a small quantity of boiled rice, bread, or grains of rice is waved round the child and thrown away. It is believed that when black ointment is applied to the eyes, cheeks, or forehead of a child, there is no fear of its being affected by an evil eye. This also depends on the position of the stars at the birth of a child. If anybody sees a beautiful thing and praises it, there is a chance of its being affected by an evil eye. It is believed that children, animals, trees, and even wood and stones, are apt to be affected by an evil eye. In order to avoid injury from an evil eye, coco-nut shells or a shoe are tied on a conspicuous part of a tree or a creeping plant, black beads known as *Drustamani* or *Vajrabuttu* are tied round the necks of children, and cowries and black beads are tied round the necks of animals. Even grown-up persons are affected by an evil eye. When a man is very ill or frequently becomes unconscious, coco-nuts, fowls, and boiled rice are waved round him and thrown away.

When the effects of an evil eye cannot be removed by ordinary methods, the evil influence is said to have entered through the bones. In order to remove it, people bring the bone of an animal in the evening, and after besmearing it with oil and turmeric powder, wash it in hot water. It is dressed in a yellow cloth, and black and red ointments are applied to it. It is then waved round the affected person, and thrown away in some place where three roads meet.

For evading the effects of an evil eye, salt, mustard-seed, hair, garlic, dry leaves of onions, dry chillies, and seven small stones from the road are put on the fire. The fire is then waved round the body of the affected person and thrown away. Charmed black-cotton strings are turned over burning incense and tied round the arm or the neck. Charmed ashes from the temples of certain deities are also applied to the forehead of the affected person.

At Ibhrampur in the Ratnagiri District it is believed that a person whose eyes have come under the influence of evil stars possesses the power of the evil eye. Ashes are taken on a Mango leaf and charmed with incantations for an evil eye, and then applied to the forehead of the affected person.

The people of Poladpur in the Kolaba District believe the effects of an evil eye to be as follows: A healthy child becomes sickly and cries, a man may suffer from indigestion or loss of appetite, a cow or a she-buffalo yielding plenty of milk suddenly ceases to give milk or gives blood in place of it, crops perish, a good image is disfigured or broken, and even stones are shattered to pieces.

The following devices are used to ward off such evil effects: A black mark is made on the forehead of children. Marking nuts and cowries tied with a black thread are fastened round the necks of animals. A little black spot is marked on an image. A worn-out shoe or a sandal is tied to fruit-yielding trees. Salt and mustard-seed are waved thrice round the face of a child while spells are uttered and thrown into the fire. Some people roll a cotton thread round a curry stone, wave it three times round the patient, and then put it into the fire; if the thread burns, the evil eye is held to have been removed. If the evil eye be on the food, three morsels of food are first raised to the mouth, and then thrown into the fire. Sacred ashes are applied to trees and creeping plants to remove the effects of an evil eye.

In the Deccan a house is protected by a black doll being suspended upside down, or figures of men are drawn in black on the wall, head downwards, or cowries or marking nuts on black thread are tied to the house front.

The people of Khopoli in the Kolaba District believe that the evil eye can be diverted from living creatures only, and not from inanimate things such as a stone or an earthen image. Sacred ashes are applied to the forehead of the suffering child in repeating the protecting praises of Rama, the seventh incarnation of Vishnu. Among Brahmans, rice grains are waved thrice round the face of a child and put into water. The water is then thrown away. Even flowers are waved round the faces of small children in the evening and thrown away.

At Chauk in the Kolaba District some people wave the left shoe thrice round the body of the affected person for the purpose of evading the effects of an evil eye. A red-hot iron bar is also cooled in water mixed with turmeric powder.

At Shirgaon in the Thana District water is drawn in a brass or a copper pot in the evening, and turmeric powder, rice, and any other edible articles on which the evil eye has fallen are put into it. Twenty-one date leaves, each of them with a knot, are then waved round the body of the affected person and thrown into the water-pot, burning coals being dropped into the mixture. The pot is next waved thrice round the body of the affected person, and kept in a corner of the bedroom for one night, with a basket, a broom, and a sandal or an old shoe placed on the top. It is then thrown away in the morning in some public place where three roads meet. If the water becomes red, it is supposed that the evil eye has been removed.

To cure the effects of the evil eye, in some places in the Konkan, a dough lamp is made with a black wick fed by oil. Chillies are then dropped into the lamp, which is waved round the person affected and thrown away.

The effects of an evil eye are sometimes visible on the face of a child in the form of small red pustules.

If a person is affected by an evil eye at the time of taking his meals, he loses his appetite. He also becomes weaker day by day. One of the modes of removing these evils is to wave fresh date leaves three times round the face of the affected person, and to throw them into water. Some people take water in a copper plate and extinguish in it burning sticks of the Tamarind tree, after waving them round the body of the affected person.

In the Deccan earth from where three roads meet, hair, salt, chillies, and thorns of the *Bor* tree (*Zizyphus Jujuba*) are passed round the patient and taken to three cross-roads.

At Kharbav in the Thana District five pieces of broken tiles are made red hot and put into water in which a small quantity of all the cooked food in the house has been mixed. Turmeric powder is also put into it. A penknife or some other iron instrument is then turned five times in the water. A winnowing basket and a broom are waved thrice round the face of the affected person, and placed over the water-pot.

In the Deccan and Konkan two big stones, of which one

has been waved round the face of a person affected by an evil eye, are struck one against the other. If the stone breaks, it is believed that the evil effect has been removed. Cow-dung is mixed with water in a brass or a copper plate, and dust from a public road, hair, and burning black-cotton cloth are put into another small vessel. This vessel is then waved round the person, and placed upside down over the mixture of cow-dung. If it sticks to the brass plate, this is supposed to be due to the evil eye.

In some cases a bone of a dead animal, chillies, salt, and sawdust are put on the fire and then buried at a cross-road, while in others the earth from three cross-roads, seven pieces of salt, seven chillies, and seven stalks from the thatch are passed over the person affected and burnt as a cure for the evil eye.

The people of Kolhapur believe in the effects of an evil eye. A child suffering from an evil eye turns pale and thin, and suffers from headache. To avoid these effects, elderly women make a mark with lamp-black on the face or brow of the child. Boiled rice and curds and bread and oil are also passed round the face of a child, and thrown into a public road.

There is a general belief in the Presidency, and especially in the Karnatak, that indecencies scare the evil eye. For this reason, the walls of temples, holy wells, and the chariots of the gods are decorated with indecent representations of gods and men.

In Gujarat the superstitious dread of an evil eye is to be seen mostly among ignorant people, especially among women. If a boy suddenly fall ill, they say, 'The boy was playing in the house wearing a fine dress and was prattling sweetly, when that wretch came to the house and her evil eye fell on him'; or, 'The boy was eating a dainty dish when that devilish woman came up and her evil eye influenced the boy'.

Persons born on a Sunday or Tuesday are generally believed to have an evil eye.

The evil eye causes its victim to vomit what he has eaten in its presence.

If a child weeps all day long, or a person finds his appetite very weak, the evil is attributed to an evil eye.

If milch cattle do not give milk, or if vermicelli, wafer

biscuits, pickles, rice cooked in milk and sweetened with sugar, or such other eatables are spoilt, it is believed that the evil eye is at the root of the trouble.

It is believed that the following objects are specially liable to be influenced by an evil eye:

(1) Persons having fine glossy hair, fiery eyes, exquisite form, refined gait, fine speech, or good handwriting; (2) good sportsmen; (3) pickles; (4) wafer biscuits; (5) vermicelli; (6) all attractive objects.

If a person falls ill after he is praised, he is said to have been a victim of an evil eye.

The precautions taken in Gujarat to evade the influence of the evil eye are as follows:

(1) When children are dressed and decked with ornaments, a spot is made on their cheeks or near their necks with a black pigment or collyrium, as it is believed that the dark colour is an antidote against the influence of the evil eye.

(2) Some efficacious inscription is engraved on a copper plate, which is suspended round the child's neck.

(3) A bead of the fever nut (*Caesalpinia Bonducella*) is also worn round the neck.

(4) A tiger's claw or tooth is worn round the neck.

(5) An iron ring is worn on the finger.

(6) A lime is worn in the turban or head-dress.

(7) An incantation in praise of Hanuman is written on a piece of paper and put in an anklet, which is worn.

(8) A piece of thread of five kinds of silk or cotton spun by a virgin is given seven knots on the fourteenth day of the dark half of *Ashvin* (July–August), and worn on the person.

(9) In order that sweetmeats and other eatables such as wafer biscuits, pickles, &c., may not be spoilt by an evil eye, a lime, an iron nail, or a knife is put into them.

(10) In order that a cot or cradle may not be broken by the influence of an evil eye, a black woollen thread is tied round it.

(11) To prevent rice cooked in milk and sweetened with sugar from being spoilt, a piece of charcoal is put into the pot in which it is prepared.

(12) While taking one's meal one should avoid the company of an evil-eyed person, but if perchance one happens to be

present, a morsel of the food should be thrown behind him or set aside on the ground as an offering to the evil eye.

If, in spite of the precautions mentioned above, the influence of the evil eye prevails, the following additional remedies are adopted to remove its effects :

(1) A red-hot charcoal is placed on a dinner-plate and covered with an earthen jar. A bowl filled with water is then passed round the head of the patient, emptied over the jar, and placed on it with its mouth touching the jar. Next, a scythe is placed over the bowl. The jar, which is heated with the heat of the burning charcoal placed under it, makes a hissing sound as soon as it is touched by the water in the bowl, and is said to speak. This process is performed after sunset.

In some places it is a belief that the plate to be used in this process must be of bell-metal, and that over the fire placed in it mustard seeds, chillies, and salt must be thrown before it is covered with the earthen jar.

(2) A sacrificial offering is taken to the village gate on a Sunday or Tuesday.

(3) Milk is passed three or seven times round the head of the ailing child, poured into a black earthen pot, and offered to a black bitch on a Sunday or Tuesday.

(4) The mother, or some other near relative of the child suffering from the effects of the evil eye, puts in a bell-metal cup mustard-seed, salt, chillies, and seven stones from the village gate, passes the cup thrice round the child's head, puts burning charcoal in the cup, and after it is heated, places it overturned in a bell-metal pot and pours over it water mixed with cow-dung, so that the cup adheres to the pot. By the adhering of the cup to the pot, the evil eye is held to have been fixed and the child is thus cured of its influence.

(5) An exorcist is engaged to wave a bowl filled with water round the head of the patient. He then drinks off the water, and the patient believes that the disease has been drunk with it.

(6) A handful of salt and chillies is passed thrice round the head of the patient and thrown into the fire. If the chillies burn without giving out fumes of an unpleasant odour, the evil eye is believed to be at the root of the illness.

(7) A little dust collected from a spot where two roads cross one another, or red lead and oil offered to Hanuman, a red chilli, an iron nail, and grains of black gram are packed into a piece of white cotton cloth with a black woollen thread, and tied to the cradle of the suffering child.

(8) A side of a loaf of millet flour is baked by being exposed to fire, clarified butter is applied to this side, and a fine cotton thread is passed round the loaf. Next, the loaf is waved round the head of the ailing child and thrown into fire. If the cotton thread is not burnt by the fire, an evil eye is believed to be the cause of the illness. Sometimes the loaf is offered to a black dog after it has been waved round the child's head.

(9) If the illness be due to the influence of the evil eye of a woman, she is called in and asked to pass her hand over the child's head.

(10) In order to avoid the effects of the evil eye, when a child returns home from an outside visit, a bowl filled with water is passed thrice round its head and emptied outside the house before it crosses the threshold.

(11) Grains of black gram, twigs of the shrub known as prickly pear (*Euphorbia neriifolia*), salt, and dust are passed seven times round the head of a person suffering from the effects of an evil eye, on the threshold of the house and thrown away.

(12) Grains of black gram, twigs of the prickly pear, salt, an iron nail, and charcoal are put into an unused earthen pot and taken to the village boundary with a bowl filled with water. The person carrying the pot and bowl should not look behind either on his way to, or on his return from, the village boundary. The pot is placed on the village boundary, and water is poured over it seven times from the bowl.

(13) A loaf baked on one side, with seven grains of black gram, seven grains of salt, and seven cotton seeds placed over it, is passed seven times round the patient's head and placed on a spot where two roads cross one another. The person carrying the bread should not look behind while carrying it.

In describing the objects that are in general repute, not only in the Bombay Presidency but elsewhere, as efficacious in warding off the effects of the evil eye, Campbell gives the following:[1]

1. Ass.
2. Bell.
3. Bird.
4. Camel.
5. Cameo.
6. Cima ruta or rue.
7. Crocodile.
8. Cross.
9. Eye.
10. Feathers.
11. Fire.
12. Flag.
13. Frog.
14. Glass.
15. Goat.
16. Grillo or mantis.
17. Hand.
18. Honey.
19. Horn.
20. Horse.
21. Horseshoe.
22. Hunchback.
23. Hyena.
24. Incense.
25. Iron.
26. Mask.
27. Milk.
28. Mirror.
29. Monkey.
30. Mouth.
31. Nail.
32. Numbers.
33. Onion.
34. Palm.
35. *Phallus* and indecencies.
36. Prayers.
37. Rites.
38. Salt.
39. Scapegoats.
40. Sea-horse.
41. Serpent.
42. Shell.
43. Siren.
44. Skeleton.
45. Skull.
46. Spitting.
47. Sulphur.
48. Sun-face.
49. Tongue.
50. Thread.
51. Tooth.
52. Water.
53. Wolfskin.
54. Words or incantations.
55. Writing.

To these may be added the following, which are in use in various parts of the Presidency:

1. Ashes.
2. Cowries.
3. Chillies.
4. *Swastik.*
5. Leaves of the *Nim* (*Melia Azadirachta*).
6. Hair.
7. *Mohor.*
8. Earth from three cross-roads.
9. Cooked food.
10. Mustard-seed.
11. Shoes.
12. Brooms.
13. Flowers.
14. Bear's hair.
15. Alum.

Opprobrious Names for Children

Those whose children do not live, or die in infancy, or who get children with difficulty, give them opprobrious names, as it is believed that objects so named, being considered of no value, are left unharmed both by men and by gods.

In the Deccan the child is sometimes placed in the lap of another woman, who has sons surviving, and she is allowed to give it an opprobrious name.

[1] *S. B. B. C.*, pp. 277 et seq.

Some people believe that children with opprobrious names are considered impure by Fate or Destiny, and consequently not molested by her.

It is believed by some that, as good names attract attention, giving opprobrious names averts the danger of the evil eye.

Some people throw a newly-born child on a dunghill and take it back, saying that they found it on the dunghill, with the belief that a child of such low origin cannot be snatched away from them by Fate. Such children are named 'Dunghill'. A portion of a dung-heap is occasionally brought into the lying-in room for this ceremony to be performed.

Some children in Gujarat are named Khoto, Amatho, or Jutho, all meaning 'false', with the belief that children so named are considered to belong to gods or Fate, and hence cannot be taken away from their parents by the god of death.

Some people exchange their children for sweets, or offer them to others and purchase them back at a nominal price. Others roll them in the dust and name them Dhulio or dust. Some put them in a cow-dung basket and name them Shanpadya. This is believed to ensure a long life to the children.

In the Deccan children are placed in the laps of low-caste women, such as Mangs, Bhils, Mahars, or Kolis. This is held to ensure them a long life. In such cases they are named Mangya, Bhilya, Maharya, &c.

Some make a vow of not cutting the hair of their children till they are taken to Ambaji, where their hair is cut for the first time.

Some treat their children as beggars until they attain the age of five years, that is, they are dressed till that age in clothes obtained by begging. Such children are given the name Bhikya, i. e. beggar. Some bore the nose of the child. In the Deccan the nose is pierced with a thorn of the *Bor* tree (*Zizyphus Jujuba*) growing on a grave. The navel cord is also cut with a stone, and the child given the name of *Dagadya* (stone) as a form of protection from the evil eye.

In some places a relative of the child's on the mother's side presents it with a necklace of gold beads shaped like large black ants. When the child attains the age of eight or ten years this necklace is offered to some god or goddess. The child is named Sankalio as it wears round its neck this chain (*sankal*).

Some weigh the child against corn and give the name of that corn to the child. The corn is then distributed among beggars, which is supposed to ensure a long life to the child.

Some make earthen figures of children, call them *Ila Ili* or *Pithad*, and carry them through the village on the full-moon day of *Phalgun* (February–March), in the belief that by so doing they ensure a long life to the children.

In the Deccan a stone named after the child is deposited with the village deity and recovered after the child grows up, thank-offerings being then made to the deity.

Generally, in the Konkan districts, opprobrious names are given to children when they are sickly, always crying, and weak, or when they are short-lived. It is believed that children improve in health when called by such opprobrious names.

Opprobrious names such as 'Stone', 'Pot', 'Rubbish', &c., are given to children in families in which the first children are short-lived. But their real names are different. The names of the well-known arithmetician Keru[1] Nana Chhatre, and his son Kondopant[2] Chhatre, are examples of opprobrious names.

Among high-class Hindus, the first son is not generally called by his real name, but by one of the opprobrious names given above.

Children are sometimes weighed against shoes or sandals, and also against cow-dung.

Hindus generally call their children by the names of their deities and ancestors, and they attribute the premature death of their children to their own misbehaviour towards such ancestors, or to their having abused them ; they fear that such abuse or misbehaviour has offended the ancestors. To avoid their displeasure and the consequent death of their children, the people give opprobrious names to their next born, such as 'Stone', 'Dung-heap', 'Pot', 'Dirt', &c. The custom of tattooing one side of the body of females also prevails in the Kolhapur District, especially in cases where the children in a family are short-lived.

[1] *Keru* = rubbish.

[2] *Kondu* = a pot.

In Gujarat it is related that a carpenter's children used to die in infancy, so he named one of his sons 'Pithad' and he lived. Since then, parents whose children do not live name them 'Pithad'. Some name their children 'Jivo', that is, 'Live', with the hope that they may live long.

The opprobrious and other special spirit-scaring names generally given to boys are as follows:

Useless, False, Refuse, Nose-bored, Black, Mad, Stupid, Eccentric, Sewed, Hill, Worthless, Bower, Creeper, Small, Lame, Fool, Dunghill, Parasite, Old, Lord (ironical), Recluse, Handsome (ironical), Peacock, Parrot, Fastened, Ragged, Not loved, The croaking of a frog, Fat, Bald-head, Womanish, Crying, Basket-hidden, Cow-dung-hidden, Manure, Beggar, Shameless, Coward, Noise, Poisonous, Stony, Beggar, Immortal, Negro-like, Hollow, Bitter, Deaf, Panther, Tiger, Meddlesome.

The contemptuous names given to girls are:

White, Small, Refuse, Black, Light as a flower, Nose-bored, False, Fat, Mad, Useless, Bitter.

The idea of giving such names to children is almost Asiatic in extent. Among Musalmans also such names are given; and even among the Persians and Arabs boys are given such names as the Stolen and the Black. Sometimes people arrange that their children be actually stolen; and some next of kin, generally the aunt, is made to commit the kindly felony. She afterwards returns the child for a certain amount in cash or clothes. The custom is as old as the scriptures, there being an allusion in the Koran to how the little Joseph was made to steal some garment of his aunt and was claimed as a forfeit by her. Speaking about Levi, the older brothers of Joseph say to the Egyptian soldiers, 'If he hath stolen (the king's goblet) verily the brother of his too did (formerly) steal'.

Witchcraft and Magic

Campbell draws attention to the fact that 'the roots of magic stretch down to the earliest struggles of human life, when sickness, death, and misfortune were held to be the work of evil spirits'.[1] There is no little support to be found in

[1] *S.B.B.C.*, p. 256.

present-day practice of all parts of the Bombay Presidency for his theory that 'the basis of magic is spirit possession; and spirit possession is the basis of the charm and talisman not less than the relation of the witch and her familiar spirit'.[1] Campbell quotes extracts from the *Atharvaveda* showing that magical spells were used in the earliest Hindu period,[2] and rightly shows by numerous examples that in Bombay 'witches, sorcerers, and enchanters practise both white, that is healing, and black, that is harming, magic'.[3] It is the lower castes, however, such as the Mahar, Dhed, Mang, Bhangi, and Madigar, who are generally believed to be specially skilled in witchcraft and exorcism. No doubt they, as the earlier inhabitants of the country-side, have always been regarded by the later immigrants as having a closer acquaintance with the local spirits, and, therefore, likely to be more skilled in the control of such dangerous influences.

This control is exercised by magic (*Chetak*), an art secretly learnt by women. It is a form of the black art. In the Deccan it is held that, in order to acquire the art, a woman must first sacrifice her son or her husband. A woman well versed in the spells of witchcraft is known as a *Chetakin*, i.e. witch, and can do any mischief she chooses. She can kill a child or turn any person into a dog or other animal by the power of her incantations. The *Chetakin* can remove the hair from the head of a woman, or scatter filth, &c., in a person's house, make marks of crosses with marking nuts on all the clothes or on the children, or play many other such tricks without betraying a trace of the author of the mischief. The following evils also are attributed to witchcraft: Failure of cattle to give milk, the vanishing of milk, curds, *ghi*, and sweetmeats from a sweet-seller's shop, the disappearance of property from a house, the loss of children. The *Chetakins* are able to mesmerize a man and compel him to do anything they want.

They follow revolting forms of ceremonies. All witches who have learnt the black art meet at night regularly, on the no-moon day of every month, at a burning-ground outside the village, or at Maruti's temple. On such occasions they go quite naked, and apply turmeric and red powders to the body

[1] *S. B. B. C.*, p. 256. [2] *Ibid.*, p. 257. [3] *Ibid.*, p. 257.

and forehead. While coming to the cremation ground, they carry on their heads burning coals in an earthen pot. At this meeting they repeat their incantations, taking care that none are forgotten. After completing the repetition of the incantations, they go round the village and return to their respective houses. They have no special haunts or seasons.

In the Deccan witches make bullocks of earth and make them move round their threshing-floor. This causes the transfer of grain from the adjacent threshing-floors to that of the witch. A similar process is performed with the object of getting milk from neighbours' cattle, i.e. earthen cattle are made and milked by the witch.

If, on a Saturday, a witch prepares a doll of black rags and asks it for the property of her neighbours, the articles asked for disappear from the neighbours' houses, and are received by the witch.

In the Kolhapur District a *Chetak* is said to carry out a witch's orders and is believed to bring corn and other things from houses or harvesting grounds. It is seen only by its mistress, the *Chetakin*. The *Chetakin* has to go once a year to the temple of the deity from whom the *Chetak* has been brought and to pay the annual tribute for the use of that *Chetak* or servant spirit.

It is said that there are witches at Kolwan in the Thana District. They are generally found among Thakars. Some of them visit the Ratnagiri District, but though no one can tell anything about their powers, ignorant people are very much afraid of them. It is believed that they can turn persons into animals by means of their incantations, and that they can themselves assume the forms of animals, i. e. a bull, a dog, a buffalo. The person once charmed by their spells is said to blindly abide by their orders.

In the Thana District a woman who can influence evil spirits to do harm to others is called a *Bhutali*. It is said that the *Bhutalis* assemble at the funeral grounds in a naked state on the full-moon day and on the no-moon day of every month, to refresh their knowledge of the black art.

A witch has dirty habits and observances. The chief sign for detecting a witch is a foam or froth that appears on the lips of her mouth when she is asleep. In the Deccan she is said to be known by insects issuing from her mouth when she sleeps. In the Deccan it is held that women who have no children or whose children do not live are likely to become witches. One way to guard against witchcraft is to remain on friendly terms with the witch, and not to hurt her feelings on any occasion. People generally keep a watch over the actions of a woman who is suspected to be a witch, and if she is found practising her black art, and is caught red-handed, they should pour into her mouth water brought from the shoemaker's earthen pot. It is believed that, when she is compelled to drink such water, her black art becomes ineffective. It is also a safeguard to cut off the ends of witches' hair and keep them in custody. Other witch-scaring devices are the piercing of marking nuts with needles, the strewing of ashes before the house, and driving a plough round the threshing-floor while in a state of nudity.

In the Deccan doll-images are made head downwards on the doors with marking nut, or shoes are hung with their soles turned upward. In places a charm is written on a piece of bark and affixed either to the house or to the cattle. This keeps witchcraft at a distance. Similarly, it is well to bathe on new-moon days or Saturdays, and to worship Maruti in the wet clothes worn.

In the Thana District it is believed that the skin round the eyes of a witch is always black, her eyes have an intoxicated appearance, her nails are generally parched and have a darkish colour, and the lower portions of her feet seem to be scraped. When any sorcerer gives out the name of such a witch (*Bhutali*), she is threatened by the people that, should she continue to give trouble in the village, her own black art or another spirit will be set against her; and she then ceases to give trouble.

There are some sorcerers in the Thana District who can move a small brass cup by the power of their magic. They can detect a witch by the movement of this vessel. When the brass vessel reaches the house of a witch, it at once settles upon the witch's head. She is then threatened by the people that she will be driven out of the village if found practising her black art.

In the Deccan and Konkan, when the people come to know of the existence of a witch in their village, they take special precautions at the time of harvest. They arrange to harvest a different kind of grain to the one selected for harvesting by the witch. After some time they go to the field of the witch, and discover whether there is a mixture of grain in her field. If they are convinced of the fact, they take further precautions. A squirrel is killed and its stomach filled with earth moistened by the witch's urine. The squirrel is then hung head downwards. This is said to cause the witch violent pains, and so to disable her. In places they keep a charmed copper amulet under the eaves at the main door of their houses, or make crosses with marking nut on both sides of a door. In the Deccan horse-shoes and nails taken from boots are affixed to front and back doors to keep away witches. At some places spots or circles are marked with lime on the front of a house, the object being to guard against the evil effects of the *Chetak's* tricks.

To protect cooked food from being spirited away by witches, people in the Deccan draw a circle round the cooking-place and put a grain measure bottom upwards in front of the food. There is also a custom in the Deccan of placing grains of rice dyed yellow and some insects upon an ant-hill under a *Hingani* (*Balanites Roxburghii*) tree on a Saturday. Next day a bough of this tree is cut and wooden pegs prepared therefrom. These pegs protect a cow-shed or milk-curds from the attacks of witches. In Khandesh it is believed that witches, during an epidemic, can cause the death of persons they desire to kill by boiling oil in special shaped vessels (*Kadhais*) and repeating, in the name of these persons, special incantations over the vessels.

By tying in a piece of cloth a bone, a lime smeared with red lead or red powder, &c., and placing it where four roads meet, witches are believed in the Deccan to bring under their spells any one who happens to walk over the bundle.

In the Deccan it is held that a witch can extract a man's liver by the power of her art. Their power of inflicting injury extends over a distance of 150 miles.

In the Deccan witches are said to keep dogs which they create by magic from the bones of women who die in child-birth. A witch is said to cast her spells while she is combing out her hair.

In Gujarat witches are known as *Dakans*. *Dakans* are of two kinds, human and of the order of ghosts.

Girls born in the *Ashlesha nakshatra* on the second day of a month, in the *Kritika nakshatra* on the seventh day of a month, and in the *Shatabhigha nakshatra* on the twelfth day of a month, are believed to be human *Dakans*. They cause the death of their husbands, and their evil eye injures all things and individuals that come under its influence.

Women who die in child-bed, meet an untimely death, or commit suicide, become *Dakans* or *Chudels* after death.

Some people believe that women of such low castes as Kolis, Vaghris, and Charans become *Dakans*. High-caste *Dakans* are rare.

A ghostly *Dakan* dresses in fine clothes and decks her person with ornaments. But she does not cover her back, which is horrible to look at. It is so frightful that any one happening to see it dies of horror.

Ghostly *Dakans* trouble only women. When possessed by them, the latter have convulsive fits, loose their hair, and cry out without any reason.

A ghostly *Dakan* lives with a man as his wife, brings him dainties, and turns the refuse of food into flesh and bones. The man gradually becomes emaciated and ultimately dies. It is believed that generally a *Dakan* kills a man within six months.

The *Dakans* do not allow calves to suck, cattle to give milk, or healthy persons to enjoy sound health. Sometimes they cause cattle to yield blood instead of milk.

A *Dakan*, by virtue of her powers, can ascend to the sky. She lives upon the flesh of corpses.

A *Dakan* can assume any form she likes. She appears as a cat, a buffalo, a goat, or any other animal. She can swell and shrink her body at will. Her feet are reversed.

Dakans haunt trees, cemeteries, deserted tanks, mines, or other desolate places. They also haunt ruins and places where four roads meet.

In the Konkan there are persons who practise black art of several kinds, such as *Chetak*, *Jaran*, *Maran*, and *Uchatan*.

Chetak is a kind of evil spirit brought from the temple of the goddess Italai of the Konkan. It is brought for a fixed or limited period, and an annual tribute is required to be paid to the goddess for its services.

Another kind of black art widely practised in the Konkan and the Deccan is known by the name of *Muth-marane.* In this art the sorcerer prepares an image of wheat flour, and worships it with flowers, incense, &c. A lime pierced with a number of pins is then placed before the image. The sorcerer begins to pour spoonfuls of water mixed with molasses on the face of the image, and repeats certain incantations. Meanwhile, the lime gradually disappears and goes to the person whose death it is intended to secure. The person aimed at receives a heavy blow in the chest, and at once falls to the ground, vomiting blood. Sometimes he is known to expire instantaneously. The charmed lime, after completing its task, returns to the sorcerer, who anxiously awaits its return, for it is believed that if the lime fails to return some calamity or misfortune is sure to occur to him. For this reason the beginner desiring to be initiated into the mystery of this black art has to make the first trial of his spells on a tree or a fowl.

Females are also initiated into the mysteries of *Jadu* or black art. Such women are required to go to the burning-ground at midnight in a naked state, holding in their hands hearths containing burning coals. While on their way they untie their hair, and then begin the recital of their incantations. There they dig out the bones of buried corpses, bring them home, and preserve them for practising black art.

Magic is used by the followers of the *Shakti* system of worship.

In the Kanarese districts a witch is known as a *Vammalati, Mayagi*, or *Matagarti.* She is believed to carry off women and children into tall trees and to set fire to houses. She takes the form of a cat or a dog.

Witches are believed to have holes in the palms of their hands so that any article placed in their hands falls to the ground. These tricks of witches can also be performed by men, found among the Madigars.[1]

[1] Vide *T. & C. B.*, ii, p. 442.

In the Kanarese districts the daughter of a certain Chanbasappa was believed to have been bewitched and turned into a tigress. By skill and charms Chanbasappa restored her to human form; but as she retained her tail and carnivorous habits, he allowed her to become a tigress again.

In the Karnatak witches are said to cause trouble by burying rice in a dunghill. It is believed that they can be recognized by the scared conduct of a cat.

VIII

DREAMS AND OMENS

Dreams

The beliefs current in all parts of the Presidency as to the cause of dreams are many. One of these is that the memory of known facts or incidents heard or seen causes dreams. Dreams are also supposed to be caused by disorders in the brain, by brooding constantly over a particular occurrence, by anxiety, or by the perpetration of sinful acts. Those who are indebted to the ancestral spirits are said to be troubled by dreams. A hearty meal at night just before going to bed is supposed to cause dreams.

There are three conditions of human existence: (1) *Jagriti*, that is, wakefulness; (2) *Swapna*, that is, dream; and (3) *Sushupti*, that is, sleep. The incidents which impress the mind strongly during wakefulness are reproduced in dreams. Very often thoughts that never occur to our minds strike us in dreams. These are ascribed to the impressions made on the soul during past lives.

It is said that the interpretation of dreams goes by contraries. But at times they are fully borne out. A good dream is an indication of future good, and a bad one of future evil. There are some persons whose dreams are always fulfilled. Dreams dreamt by persons pure of mind and heart seldom turn out false. Dreams occurring in the first quarter of the night are commonly believed to be fulfilled in a year, those in the second quarter of the night in six months, those in the third quarter in three months, and those in the last quarter in one month. A dream during an hour and a half before daybreak bears fruit in ten days, while that which comes just at daybreak is realized immediately.[1] In some places it is held that dreams which occur before midnight are never fulfilled.

[1] This superstition concerning the realization of dreams is common to the Deccan, Konkan, and Gujarat.

If a person has a bad dream, he should go to sleep at once, and not communicate it to any one. If he has a good dream, he should not sleep on that night after its occurrence. Early on the following morning he should communicate it to a preceptor or saint; but if neither be available, he should repeat it into the ears of a cow. A good dream should never be told to a bad or low-minded person.

If a man sleeps after a good dream and has a bad one; the former loses its force while the latter gains ascendancy and comes true.

It is a widespread tradition that Alauddin, King of Delhi, once entered the house of a blacksmith when the latter was asleep dreaming that he saw a treasure trove after having bathed in a stream and drunk a little water. At the same time Alauddin saw a small insect come out of the blacksmith's nostril, drink water from a neighbouring cistern, and return to the place from whence it first came. When the dream was over, the blacksmith woke and communicated it to Alauddin, which enabled the latter to spot the treasure, found by excavating the place where the insect was hidden.

To see or think or experience in dreams the following is considered to be auspicious:

(1) A cow, (2) a bullock, (3) an elephant, (4) a palace, (5) a mountain, (6) a high peak, (7) the droppings of a bird, (8) ointment, (9) weeping, (10) a king, (11) gold, (12) the crossing of the ocean, (13) a lamp, (14) flesh, (15) fruit, (16) a lotus, (17) a flag, (18) the image of one's favourite god, (19) a saint, (20) a Brahman, (21) an ancestral spirit, (22) a white snake biting the right side, (23) a flowering tree, (24) climbing a tree, (25) climbing the *Rayan* (*Mimusops hexandra*) tree, (26) a woman dressed in white, (27) walking over a layer of lead, (28) lifting a goblet filled with wine, (29) a lion, (30) the goddess of wealth, (31) a garland, (32) driving in a carriage to which an elephant, a lion, a horse, or a bullock is yoked, (33) swallowing the disk of the sun or the moon, (34) the hands or feet of a man, (35) worship of a deity, (36) barley, (37) rice, (38) sandal paste, (39) *Durva* grass (*Cynodon Dactylon*), (40) the moon, (41) the sun, (42) a goblet, (43) an ocean of milk, (44) jewels, (45) smokeless fire, (46) an image of the god Shiva, Brahma, or

Ganesh, or of the goddess Parvati, (47) a celestial vehicle, (48) the heaven, (49) the *Kalpavriksha*, i. e. the magic tree that satisfies all desires, (50) a river in flood, (51) fish, (52) curdled milk, (53) going on a pilgrimage, (54) ornaments, (55) crossing a river, (56) eating the flesh of a man's legs.

To see in a dream (1) a person leading a life of celibacy, (2) a virgin, (3) a green tree, or (4) students returning from school, is also believed to foretell good fortune.

A dream in which one of the following objects is seen is also supposed to be good:

(1) An assemblage of Brahmans, (2) a gardener, (3) milk, (4) a prostitute, (5) a shield and sword, (6) a musket, (7) a scimitar, (8) an antelope, (9) an unwidowed woman carrying on her head a jar filled with water, (10) a mongoose, (11) a peacock, (12) a woman carrying a child on her waist, (13) newly-washed dry clothes, (14) a costly fan, (15) a man dressed in white clothes, (16) a death.

The following objects seen, heard, or experienced in a dream are believed to forebode evil:

(1) Cotton, (2) ashes, (3) bones, (4) whey, (5) singing, (6) merriment, (7) laughing, (8) studying, (9) a woman dressed in red, (10) a red mark on the forehead, (11) a *gandharva* (heavenly bard), (12) a demon, (13) a wizard, (14) a witch, (15) a prickly shrub, (16) a cemetery, (17) a cat, (18) vomiting, (19) darkness, (20) a hide, (21) a public woman, (22) thirst, (23) a contest between two planets, (24) fall of a luminous body, (25) a whirlwind, (26) *vishotak* (a disease in which the skin is covered with ulcers), (27) one carrying away one's vehicle, wife, jewels, gold, silver, or bell-metal utensils, (28) the breaking into one's house, (29) the drinking of a poisonous liquid.

If in a dream one relishes a dish of sweetmeats, plays upon a musical instrument, or sees a widow dressed in the garment of an unwidowed woman, it is believed to prognosticate evil and bring misfortune.

Similarly, if in a dream the sleeper marries or hears the cawing of a crow or the bark of a dog, or an owl speak like a man, it portends misfortune.

Seeing an auspicious mark, or bathing in or being besmeared with oil, in a dream, is an indication of one's death in the near future. Going to the south riding a he-buffalo, or seeing a widow, brings misfortune.

If a man in health comes across a corpse in a dream, he apprehends illness. If a patient does the same, he fears death.

In the Deccan and the Konkan the following dreams are believed to be lucky and propitious: To swim through a river or the sea, to rise to the sky, to see the sun, the moon, and the planets, to climb to the top of a house, temple, or palace, to drink liquor, to bathe in blood, to be smeared with dung or covered with lice, and to eat rice and curds. It is also believed that the sight of white objects in dreams foretells success in any work or undertaking that may be in view. A deity, a Brahman, a king, a married woman decked with ornaments, a bullock, a mountain, trees full of fruits, climbing the *Umbar* tree (*Ficus glomerata*), a mirror, meat and flowers, if seen in dreams, are good omens. Climbing the *Palas* tree (*Butea frondosa*), an ant-heap, the bitter lime tree (*Melia Azadirachta*), to marry, to wear red clothes or red flower garlands, to eat cooked meat, to receive oil, cotton, or iron, to bathe after rubbing the body with oil, to lose hair or teeth, to be drowned in mud, to lose the nose or ears, to take poison, to embrace a corpse, to see the sun and the moon without lustre, and to see shooting stars during dreams, are said to be bad omens.

At Mitbav in Ratnagiri District dreams are believed to be caused by indigestion and restlessness. To embrace a dead body in a dream, to see troubled waters, to dine heartily, are said to be bad omens. Feasting friends and receiving gifts from them are said to be good omens.

At Phonda in the Ratnagiri District dreams are said to indicate things that have happened, or are about to happen in the near future. All white substances other than cotton, salt, and bones, are considered auspicious, and all black substances excepting a lotus, a horse, an elephant, and a deity, are considered inauspicious.

At Ibhrampur in the same district horrible dreams are good omens, while pleasing dreams indicate approaching calamities.

At Pendur in the Ratnagiri District it is believed that dreams foretell future events. It is believed that a dream will prove correct and effective if the person dreaming has asked three questions and received three answers in his dream. Those dreams which are caused through cold are called *Jalap*. They are generally false dreams, and no good omens are derived therefrom.

In the Konkan it is believed that ancestors who take interest in the welfare of their descendants and guardian spirits appear in dreams and foretell future events, so that the dreaming person may take the needful precautions to avoid the coming calamities.

At Kalse in the Ratnagiri District it is believed that dreams in the last part of the night, i. e. just before daybreak, and in which great men are seen, generally prove effective. If anybody sees himself married in a dream if is supposed that he will hear of the death of some relative.

The people of Poladpur in the Kolaba District believe in dreams; and when some of their deities appear in dreams and give them advice or directions, they are careful to follow them. Sometimes even evil spirits appear in dreams, and advise the people to do certain things to avert calamities. People who have faith in such spirits act according to their wishes, and if they fail to do so, trouble is sure to follow.

The people of Khopoli in the Kolaba District believe that if a person sees in a dream the dead body of a near relative, it indicates that the person whose corpse was seen in the dream will live long.

At Birwadi in the Kolaba District it is believed that if a person sees a snake in a dream, a son will be born to him; if he sees hell, he is sure to obtain wealth. If he sees gold, it is a sure sign of losing wealth. Again, if a person sees himself taking his meals in a dream, it indicates that his death is nigh at hand.

At Malad in the Thana District omens are derived from dreams. In case of bad dreams the god Vishnu is remembered, and the gods Shiva and Maruti are also worshipped.

At Belapur wood, cow-dung cakes, and turbid water, if seen in dreams, foretell calamities. White clothes, beautiful flowers, and food containing sweetmeats are considered auspicious,

At Murbad in the Thana District it is believed that all black things, and white things such as ashes, are inauspicious when seen in dreams, but a black cow, white flowers, and pearls are auspicious.

At Kolhapur dreams are believed to be caused through some mental derangement or bodily disorder. It is customary to derive omens from dreams, but their nature greatly depends upon the different times at which these dreams occur.

At Varud in West Khandesh it is believed that to see gold in a dream is an indication of the approaching death of the dreamer, and to see food is unlucky. It is lucky to see cow-dung and refuse. There is a widespread belief in the Deccan that dreams foretelling future events are caused by sleeping under the cross-beam of the roof. Dreams are said to be caused by sleeping with a hand on the chest. The following are held to be auspicious articles to dream of:

A god, a horse, a king, an ancestor, a cobra, one 's own death, a bird flying, an elephant, muddy water, fire, a railway train, a cart, *ghi*, *juvari*, a funeral procession.

The following are held to be inauspicious:

Food and water, a black snake, a bare-headed man, a woman dressed in black, an earthen jar, a lemon, milk, a white object, clear water, a she-buffalo, a river in flood, new clothes, a woman in confinement.

To dream of a death in one 's own family is an indication that news will be received of a death in another family. In the Ahmednagar District it is held that to dream of a dog, a woman dressed in green, a *sanyasi*, or of an ancestor tendering advice, forebodes interruption in the performance of the daily worship of the gods. In the same district it is believed that a man will die soon if he dreams of embracing his own corpse, of riding on a donkey, of taking poison, or of a bridegroom anointed with oil about to bathe. It is inauspicious to drop a lighted lamp, or see a friend stouter than he actually is, in a dream. In East Khandesh it is thought lucky to dream of weeping or crossing water or of being drowned, but to see a man laughing is inauspicious.[1]

[1] In a book, *Harit-sanhita*, the subject of the influence of dreams on human happiness or misery is fully treated.

The book says: If the sun, the moon, the congregation of the stars, a lake

Good and Bad Omens

The following are generally held to be auspicious omens:

While going on any business, to come across the throbbing of the right eyelid and of the right arm of a man, and of the left eyelid and left arm of a woman;[1] a Brahman coming in front with a cup and a spoon in his hand after taking his bath; the appearance of a peacock, the crow-pheasant, the *Chatak* (*Cuculus melano-lucus*), and the mongoose, especially when they pass on the left side of a person going on business.

The following are considered to be auspicious when seen within a hundred paces by a person starting out on business:

Brahmans, unwidowed women, boiled food, meat, fish, milk, any kind of corn, the bird *Chash* (*Coracias indica*) passing by the left side, the appearance of the moon in front, a person coming across one's path with vessels filled with water, and a married couple, a cow with its calf, images of the gods, coconuts and other fruit, a mother with five children, white clothes, an umbrella, meat, a weapon, a mirror, the sound of a musical instrument, a horse, an elephant, deer, crow, a corpse being taken to burial or burning, a Musalman first customer, spilling of medicine, oil, ink, music, a monkey, and the *pingala* (spotted owl) on a tree, a man with a basketful of fruit, a swan, a bee with honey, a representation of the figure *Swastik*, a person carrying bread, red or turmeric powder, a maiden, white articles, a fisherman carrying fish, jewels, curds, flowers, a lighted lamp, a jackal, a spiritual preceptor, a public woman,

filled with clusters of expanded lotuses, or crossing the sea or a river full of water be seen or experienced in a dream by a man, he attains wealth, happiness and prosperity and relief from diseases. If a cow, a horse, an elephant, a king, or a flower called *prashasta* is seen in a dream by a sickly person, his illness disappears; if by one laid in sick bed, he is cured; if by one confined in a jail, he is released. If a child grinds its teeth and weeps in a dream, it indicates liquidation of pecuniary liabilities. One who sees a man die in a dream is blessed with longevity. A bite by a white snake in a dream is an omen of increase of wealth. All black objects except a cow, a horse, a king, an elephant, and fish, seen in a dream, are the precursors of disease and calamity. One who sees in a dream his body devoured by crows, foxes, dogs, wolves, asses, buffaloes, birds moving in the sky, tigers, fishes, alligators or monkeys, experiences in the immediate future a heavy loss or a terrible disease.

[1] It is to be noted that if, on the contrary, the left eye and arm of the man or the right eye and arm of a woman throb, the omen is inauspicious.

a Mahar or a Mang, a washerman coming with a bundle of washed clothes, and a marriage procession.

In the Karnatak a *Maina* and a couple of Brahmans who have just fed are lucky omens when met on the left hand.

The following objects, acts, and persons are generally believed to be inauspicious:

Oil, buttermilk, a couple of snakes, a monkey, pig, and an ass, firewood, ashes and cotton, a person with a disfigured nose, a man dressing his hair in the shape of a crown, red garlands, wet clothes, a woman wearing red cloth, an empty earthen vessel, a Brahman student and an unmarried Brahman, a widow, a bare-headed Brahman, a cat going across the path, a dog flapping his ears, meeting a barber with his bag, a beggar, sneezing, or the asking of a question at the time of departure, waiting, meeting a person with an empty vessel, howling of dogs and jackals, a pair of crows playing on the ground, and a lighted lamp extinguished by its fall on the ground, a cat from left to right, a *Manbhav* in the morning, a bare-footed person at a physician's house, a frightened man, a carpenter's customer with the wooden peg of a grinding wheel, an owl, a widow, a bare-headed man, a man carrying firewood or cow-dung cakes, a goldsmith, an empty-handed Mahar, a he-buffalo, a Ringed turtle-dove, passing through the house, a party returning from the burning ground.

While plans or proposals are being made, it is considered inauspicious if any one sneezes or the sound of a lizard is heard. Meeting a person of the depressed classes whose touch is pollution, or a Brahman who accepts funeral gifts, is also considered unlucky. Meeting a woman who is in her menses, a mourner, a buffalo, a snake are held to be inauspicious. An iron vessel or an iron bar, cow-dung cakes, salt, grass, a broom, a vulture, and a washerman bringing with him dirty clothes are also considered to be unlucky omens. A dead snake, an oil-seller, a Brahman or woman not brow-marked, a king not chewing betel, black articles, a lizard falling on one's body, are inauspicious.

There are various beliefs entertained by people regarding the meaning of omens.

1. If when leaving the house on a visit or with some definite

object in view, a deer crosses one's path from right to left, it is considered a bad omen, while crossing from left to right is considered good. On returning home, this omen is read in the reverse way to that just stated.

2. When starting on a journey, the braying of an ass on the right is a good omen, and on the left, evil.

3. If on leaving the house a man meets an unwidowed woman or a virgin with a jar filled with water on her head, it is an indication that the object of the expedition will be accomplished.

4. While starting on a good errand, if one breathes through the left nostril or comes across a person carrying a basket of eggs, it is a good omen.

5. If at the time of leaving for a visit to another town or village, the position of the moon in the circle explaining the position of stars with reference to one's birthday stars be in the rear or on the left of that position, it is a bad omen, but if it be in the front or on the right it is a good omen.

The moon in front means fulfilment of the intended purpose, on the right it confers happiness and prosperity, at the back it causes death, and on the left, loss of wealth.

6. The note of the falcon on the right while going out and on the left while returning is a good omen, but the opposite is bad.

7. A cat or a serpent crossing one's path is ominous of evil; but if either passes on the right, it foretells good.

8. A jackal howling in the evening prognosticates damage by fire to the town or village; its howling at midnight predicts robbery; while in the last part of the night it foretells good.

9. *Kag-rashias* (expounders of the utterances of crows) know the good and bad indications of the cawing of crows.

10. The wailing notes of the bird *Favadi* forebode evil.

11. If the Ringed turtle-dove sweeps the roof of one's house continuously for a number of days, a calamity is supposed to be imminent for the inmates of the house.

12. If a dog barks in front of a man it is considered to be a bad omen.

In the Karnatak a parrot, conch shell, elephant, horse, dog, tambourine, an ox, a cow, two jars full of water, cymbals, singing, a dancing lesson, prostitutes, mongoose, tender shoots of plants, flowers, fruit, two Brahmans, a mirror, unwidowed women, meat, a pot of palm-juice liquor, and live fire are good omens. Also :

The noise of a bell, a sleeping dog on rising flapping its ears, a horse neighing, are auspicious.

The sight of a king, an armed man, a Dhed, a Bhangi, or a Darji is also considered to be an auspicious omen.

The sight of boys going to or returning from school is a good omen.

A labourer carrying a load of fuel on his head, a corpse in front, a potter carrying earth on his head or on his donkey, a woman carrying her son, a man carrying molasses, are all auspicious omens.

A male monkey or a donkey crying on the right while going out, and on the left while returning home, is considered to be a good omen.

Wine and good speech are also considered good omens.

The sight of a herdswoman, a dog scratching its right side, a cuckoo singing on a tree, or a black sparrow is a good omen.

Fuel, hides, grass, vegetables, a smoking fire, sesamum oil, molasses, a barren woman, an enemy, a disorderly mob, a man besmeared with oil, a eunuch, mud, wet clothes, an ascetic, a beggar, are all considered to be bad omens, if one sees them while going on business.

The sight of dry cow-dung cakes is supposed to be a bad omen.

The sight of a widow or of a corpse is unlucky.

Weasels crossing the road, dogs flapping their ears, a man carrying a black earthen vessel, a woman with loose hair, a person carrying clarified butter, a man with grey moustaches, a man having no hair on his chest, a cat-eyed man, a person carrying flour, are all bad omens.

The sight of the husk of corn, a man with a medicinal application, or a lunatic, is a bad omen.

In Gujarat the question, 'Where are you going ?' is held to be highly inauspicious, and should not be put unless with the object of bringing misfortune on the person so questioned.

The mixture of whey, mud, and cow-dung, a recluse with

matted hair, a man spitting, a cough, and a man with the whole of his head shaved are bad omens.

Similarly, the sight of a drunkard, black gram, or cotton-seed is a bad omen.

A bride stumbling on her entry into the bridegroom's house is said to be a bad omen.

A dog scratching its left side with its paw, a man riding a he-buffalo or a donkey, two Banias, one Musalman, one male goat, one ox, five she-buffaloes, six dogs, three cows, or seven horses, confronting a man on starting from the house are ominous of evil.

Lucky and Unlucky Days and Numbers

It is a general belief among all classes of Hindus in the Bombay Presidency that Saturday is an unlucky day, and in some places Friday and Tuesday are also considered inauspicious.

Sunday is considered as an ordinary day, neither lucky nor unlucky, but sowing seed and watering trees is strictly forbidden on Sunday. It is believed that trees do not bear well if watered on Sundays.

Monday, Wednesday, and Thursday are believed to be auspicious or lucky days. It is said that a thing suggested or thought of on Friday cannot be carried out successfully.

Tuesday and Friday are considered unlucky days for beginning a new task. Wednesday and Saturday are said to be inauspicious for visiting another village.

It is a common belief that one should not go in certain directions on certain days; for doing so results in what is called *disha-shul,* i. e. pain caused by directions.

Going to the north on Sunday, to the west on Tuesday, to the north-west on Monday, to the south-west on Wednesday, to the south on Thursday, to the south-east on Friday, and to the east on Saturday is considered ominous of evil.

According to another belief, Sunday and Thursday are inauspicious for going to the south-east; Monday and Friday, to the south-west; Saturday and Tuesday, to the north-west; and Wednesday, to the north-east.

Some people believe that by going to the west on Monday or Saturday one secures the fulfilment of the desired object.

Many hold that the favourableness or otherwise of the days for going in particular directions varies according to the occasion.

In the Karnatak Sunday and Thursday are auspicious days for travelling towards the west, Saturday and Wednesday to the south, Monday and Friday to the north, and Tuesday to the east.

Wednesday and Friday are auspicious days to be shaved.

The auspicious days for sending a girl to her husband's house are believed to be Monday, Thursday, and Friday. Sunday and Tuesday are also considered auspicious for a girl to go to her home, but they are considered very unlucky for her to return to her parents.

It is forbidden to eat baked split gram on Sunday, but it is favoured on Friday.

Wednesday is considered to be a lucky day for sowing corn and making purchases of new articles. Thursday is believed to be auspicious for sending a boy to school for the first time.

Wednesday is considered unfavourable for the separation of brothers and sisters, but it is considered a suitable day for their meeting.

It is believed that if a man wears new clothes on Sunday they will be burnt; if on Tuesday, they will be lost; if on Wednesday or Saturday, a quarrel with some one is the result.

It is considered auspicious to go to a Chamar on Sunday, to a prostitute on Monday, to a Kachhia on Tuesday, to a washerman on Wednesday, to a Brahman on Thursday, to a Bania on Friday, and to a barber on Saturday.[1]

The beliefs regarding the lucky and unlucky days of a month are similar to those of the lucky and unlucky days of the week.

According to some, all the days of the bright half of a month are auspicious for performing any good act, while the days of the dark half are considered favourable for perpetrating black deeds.

[1] A Chamar is a tanner, a Kachhia is a seller of vegetables, and a Bania or Vani is a grain merchant; see *T. & C. B.*, ii, pp. 121, 190; iii, p. 412.

Some believe that the 1st, 3rd, 5th, 6th, 8th, 10th, 11th, 13th, and the full-moon day of a month are auspicious, while the 2nd, 4th, 7th, 9th, and 14th, whether of the bright or dark half, as well as the new-moon day, are inauspicious.

According to another belief, the 1st, 6th, and 11th days of a month are good; the 3rd and 8th are dates of success (that is, acts commenced on these days are crowned with success); the 5th, 10th, and 15th are *purna tithis*, that is, complete days (meaning that the moon on these days appears full one-third, full two-thirds, and completely full); while the 2nd, 7th, and 12th are auspicious days.

The 4th, 9th, and 14th days of a month are inauspicious.

Some hold that if the 1st, 4th, 12th, 14th, and 30th day of a month fall on a Saturday they are good; otherwise bad.

The 1st, 13th, or 14th day of either the bright or dark half of a month, as well as the full-moon and new-moon day, are considered unfavourable to patients.

The 2nd, 14th, and the last day of a month are considered unlucky. Those days on which there is a *panchak*—a grouping of constellations lasting for five consecutive days—are very inauspicious for commencing auspicious acts.

A belief prevails that any one dying in a *panchak* draws five companions to heaven, that is, his death is followed by the death of four others of the same village.

A son born on the full-moon day is believed to turn out brave, but is supposed to forebode evil to the parents.

Some numbers are believed to be auspicious and some inauspicious. There is a book on this subject in which some good or evil is attributed to each number. One who wants to know the result of the undertaking in hand puts his finger on any number in the book, and the expounder of the science, reading the passage bearing on the number, explains how the undertaking will end.

The following are instances of the beliefs prevailing regarding the lucky and unlucky numbers, which vary in different parts of the Presidency:

An odd number is generally believed to be inauspicious. It is for this reason that newly-married girls are not sent to their husbands' houses for the first time in any of the odd years of their age. They are also not sent back to their parents' houses in an odd year of their age for the same reason.

The numbers 2, 6, 11, and zero are believed to be lucky, 4, 5, 8, and 10 are unlucky, and 1, 3, 7, and 9 are considered as middling or moderate.

The numbers 5, 7, 9 are said by some to be auspicious, and 1, 3, 11, and 13 inauspicious.

Odd numbers are auspicious, and even numbers are said to be inauspicious.

The numbers 5, 7, 9, 10, 11, 13, 15, and 21, are believed by some to be lucky, while 3, 4, 8, and 12 are considered unlucky.

The numbers 12, 18, 56, and 58 are considered inauspicious.

Some people believe that the numbers 1¼, 5, 7, 21, 108, and 1,008 are lucky, while 12 is unlucky.

In the Deccan 2, 3, 5, 7, 9, 11, are lucky numbers; again, all odd numbers are there said to be lucky. In places 1 to 5 are lucky only. Also 4, 8, and 1, 3, or again 3, 9, 13, 18, are reported to be inauspicious. In the Karnatak similar beliefs obtain, 1, 4, and 8 being held to be unlucky numbers.

A belief exists that if a company of three start on a mission, the mission is sure to fail. This has given rise to the proverb, 'Three persons going on an errand meet with great danger'.

A zero is believed to be inauspicious. In monetary transactions or bargains, therefore, all numbers ending in a zero are avoided. If such numbers are unavoidable, the sign of ¼ is placed after them. The number 12 is considered unlucky, to avoid which 11½ is used in its place.

It is a belief that if in the sales of cattle and certain other things the price is raised by 1¼, it results in good both to the seller and buyer.

It is for this reason that in subscribing to charitable funds people write 401 instead of 400 and so on. But 1¼ is preferred to 1 in valuing things. So in all purchases and sales 1¼ is added to the actual price of a thing.

The numbers 5 and 7 are believed to be auspicious, because on starting on a journey from the house one is given five betel-nuts as a sign of good omen, while in all auspicious ceremonies seven betel-nuts are used.

IX

DISEASE DEITIES, AND CURING OF DISEASE IN HUMAN BEINGS

Disease Deities

'The unwilled is the spirit-caused' according to Sir James Campbell. It is clear from the following practices collected from all parts of the Presidency that diseases are held to be spirit-caused, and the remedy to lie in exorcizing the spirit, in order to transfer it from the victim to some other recipient, which is then driven away or destroyed.

In some villages in Gujarat, when there is an outbreak of a serious epidemic, it is customary to drive a goat, a ram, or a buffalo beyond the village boundary, with the disease on its back. The back of the animal which is chosen for this purpose is marked with a trident in red lead and covered with a piece of black cloth, on which are laid a few grains of black gram and an iron nail. Thus decorated, it is driven beyond the limits of the village. It is believed that an animal driven in this way carries the disease wherever it goes.

Very often the animal used in this ceremony is kept tied to a post all its life, in the belief that by so doing the disease remains enchained. Jain teachers confine a disease in a bottle and bury it underground. Sometimes a disease is passed on to a crow, and its legs tied to a pillar, thus making it a life-long prisoner.

Once upon a time, when there was an outbreak of cholera in a certain village, a holy man happened to arrive on the scene. He caught two rams, made them move in a circle, and left them in the burning-ground, where they died, the epidemic disappearing with their death. Hence a belief gained ground that an epidemic of cholera can be expelled by passing it on to two rams or goats.

It is related that, at Gondal in Kathiawar, a case of cholera was cured by a Bhangi by waving a cock round the patient's head.

Such diseases as cholera and small-pox are believed to be brought on by the wrath of the mother goddesses known as *Matas, Matrikas,* or *Devis* and to be caused by neglecting to offer the usual oblations. In order to propitiate them, Brahmans are engaged to recite the *Chandipath* [1] and to make sacrificial offerings. Very often a special ceremony is observed, in which all the villagers go outside the village to take their meals, and return home in the evening after witnessing the offering of coco-nuts to the sacrificial fire.[2]

A widespread belief personifies diseases as evil spirits who are fond of human prey. To ward them off, a stream of milk is poured out in the village or a magic thread is passed round it.

There is a popular tradition that in ancient times cholera was subjugated by King Vikrama, and was buried underground. Once upon a time the British excavated the place of burial in the belief that treasure was concealed there, and thus cholera was released. After many soldiers had fallen victims, the disease deity was at last propitiated by an oblation, and was handed over to the Bhangis.[3]

This association of low castes, such as Bhangis, Dheds, or Mahars, with cholera is present in most of the beliefs current about the disease. There is a story that formerly a number of students had put up in a house by which a Bhangi was in the habit of passing frequently. He daily used to hear the students reciting the sacred texts, and this produced in his mind the desire to become a Sanskrit scholar. For this purpose, having concealed his low birth, he went to Benares, and by diligent study soon became a learned man. He even married a girl of high caste. But his imposture being at last discovered, he burnt himself to death, and his ashes gave rise to the disease known as cholera.

At the present day, if the epidemic breaks out, the Bhangis

[1] The *Chandipath* is a poem in honour of Chandi, the wife of Shiva, i.e. Kali or Parvati.

[2] This ceremony is known as *Ujjani*.

[3] A similar tradition exists in Bijapur, where one of the Adil Shahi kings is said to have shut up disease spirits in a house. When the English troops took possession of Bijapur, they broke into the house in search of treasure, and released the disease spirits (vide *S. B. B. C.*, p. 244).

are often suspected in some way or other of having brought it about. It is said that they make images of the flour of black gram, and after piercing them with needles and pins, either throw them into the wells which are daily used by the villagers, or bury them in a spot over which the people frequently pass. Sometimes, it is said, the images are smeared with red lead and bathed in dirty water before being cast into the village well. The whole affair is managed very secretly and at the dead of night. The slightest rumour of such proceedings causes a tumult in the village, and the Bhangis are then in danger of being severely handled by the enraged villagers.

Another method by which the Bhangis are supposed to bring about cholera is to sprinkle the blood of a black cow on the image of Hanuman. The god is deeply offended at the insult, and in consequence spreads cholera in the neighbourhood. For this reason, offerings are burnt before Hanuman in order to stop an epidemic of cholera.

Bhangis are also accused of causing an epidemic by means of boiling the ear of a buffalo and the flesh of an ox together in one vessel, it being believed that the virulence of the disease varies in proportion to the extent to which the boiling proceeds. This process is supposed to cause a disease among cattle also.

Another belief is that Bhangis charm seeds of black gram and cloves by repeating magic incantations over them, and afterwards strew them on a highway in order that those who step on them may be attacked by cholera or some similar disease. One motive suggested for such action is that they are thereby likely to receive their garments, which would be used for covering the bodies. Also, at the outbreak of such an epidemic, clothes, coco-nuts, *ghi*, molasses, wheat flour, &c., are offered by the people to the Bhangis, who in return give a piece of thread of black wool, to be worn by the afflicted persons.

But apart from such beliefs, the appearance of an epidemic is also attributed to other causes. There is the usual belief that it is caused by the diminution of virtue and the increase of sin among people, and the consequent wrath of the gods, who are only propitiated by the people again reverting to righteous ways and by the performance of sacrifices in their honour.

There is also a belief that the sixty-four female spirits known as *Joganis*, when they are desirous of victims, cause baneful epidemics among mankind, the remedies in such a case being such as offering a goat or a he-buffalo to them, or the observation of an *Ujjani* in their honour.[1]

The following tale is related regarding an occurrence said to have taken place not long ago in the village of Verad in Kathiawar. The headman of the village, who was a Rajput by birth, but who had lost his caste owing to irregular conduct with a woman, died of fever, and as he was an outcaste his body was buried instead of being cremated. Soon after a number of persons in the same village happened to die of the same fever, and the people conjectured that the late headman's corpse must be lying in its grave with its face downwards, chewing the cloth in which a corpse is wrapped. Many thought that the health of the village would not be restored until the corpse was replaced in the correct position with its face upwards and unless the cloth was taken out of its mouth. None ventured to do so, being dissuaded by the fear of meeting with a worse fate. But although they did not open the grave, yet they arranged for certain vows to be taken in honour of the dead man, and that put a stop to the disease.

Another story from the same place is that when small-pox once raged furiously in that village, the people of the place celebrated a magnificent feast of dainties prepared of wheat flour, *ghi*, molasses, rice, and pulse, and afterwards the Dheds of the village lopped off the head of a dead he-buffalo, burying it at the spot where the feast was held.

The following remedy is resorted to throughout the Presidency for checking the disease of cholera:

A small cart of Mango wood is made and worshipped. Five jars, filled with *ghi*, milk, liquor, cow's urine, and water, and a small goat are placed in the cart. The cart is moved from the village temple of Maruti and taken out of the village through the main gate, and thence round the village from left

[1] See p. 258, *supra*.

to right. As it moves, five-twisted raw cotton thread is passed along and the contents of the five jars in the cart are poured out in a small stream on to the ground. When the cart completes the round, that is, comes back to the village gate from which it started, the goat in the cart is buried alive. The cart is then taken beyond the village boundary and there left, it being thought that the disease is left with the cart. After the cart has been taken to the neighbouring village, a charmed peg is sometimes driven into the ground near the village boundary to prevent the epidemic from crossing back again. On the day on which this ceremony is performed nobody from the village is allowed to leave the village, neither are outsiders admitted to it.

Bhangis are supposed by some to accomplish the same result by the help of evil deities who are first gratified by the offering of victims. One of such deities is Ramdepir, to whom the offering of a victim is made by the people, through the medium of Bhangis, for the prevention of cholera.

An outbreak of cholera offers a good opportunity to the Bhangis, who extort dainties and small sums of money from the people. Persons attacked by cholera often seek the services of a Bhangi, and promise him liberal gifts if they are cured.

It is said that the Bhangis have to present an offering to their evil goddess every third year, and that in so doing they kill a black animal before the goddess. They then place an iron pan full of sesamum oil on the fire, and suspend the body of the animal above it. It is believed that as many human beings will fall victims to cholera as the number of the drops of blood that fall from the body of the animal into the iron pan.[1]

Another deity whose wrath is supposed to be responsible for the breaking out of cholera is Mahamari Devi, i.e. the Cholera Mother. The worshippers of this goddess are Bhangis. She is believed to send forth cholera when her oblations are stopped, and her favour is regained by renewing the offer of these oblations. Sometimes a sacrifice to Kali in her incarnation as Chandi is performed at the principal village gates,

[1] A similar belief was prevalent in Bombay in 1896 when the bubonic plague broke out; those who died of plague being alleged to have been victims of this practice.

and the *Chandipath*[1] is recited at the other gates. A number of Brahmans and virgins are also feasted, and presented with garments. Exorcists go round the village playing upon the harsh unpleasant drum known as a *danklan*. A goat is then taken to the temple of the Mata, and the exorcists, after cutting out its tongue, dip their hands in its blood and strike them against the doors of the temple. The goat is killed and similar blood-marks are made upon every door in the village, as well as on the village gates, where an iron nail is driven into the ground with an incantation. A lime is then cut, and an oblation is offered to the Mata. This process is believed to stop the progress of the epidemic.

In the Deccan an exorcist, stripped naked and covered with leaves of the *Nim* (*Melia Azadirachta*), moves round the streets carrying an egg and pouring out a stream of liquor. He lights camphor and burns incense.

Other deities connected in popular belief with cholera are the goddesses Visuchika and Chandika. Visuchika is conciliated by burnt offerings: the recitation of the *Chandipath* wins the favour of Chandika. There is also a giantess named Karkata who is supposed to be responsible for cholera. She is said to have sprung from the sweat on the forehead of Brahma and to reside in the lunar sphere. In the Karnatak the outbreak is generally the occasion for propitiating the goddesses Durga (i.e. Kali) and Dyamava.

One of the remedies adopted to stop an epidemic of cholera is to propitiate Shiva by the performance of sacrifices, and by bestowing gifts on Brahmans and other holy men. Sometimes vows are observed with the same object in honour of a minor local deity.

Small-pox is believed to be the act of the goddess known as Mother Shitala, i.e. Shitala Mata, who spreads the disease whenever she is desirous of having victims. Thus, in cases of small-pox, the patient very often receives no medical treatment, the only remedies adopted being directed towards the propitiation of the Mata. The patient is made over to the Mata and then repurchased for a rupee and a quarter. A number of vows are taken in the Mata's name, to be fulfilled

[1] *Vide* p. 258, *supra*.

after the patient has recovered. Many people accomplish their vows before Shitala at Kalavad in Jamnagar. A vow to visit this place after the patient's recovery, and to abstain from certain things till the day of the visit, is taken by the mother of the affected person in case of a severe attack. But almost every village contains a temple of Shitala, and those who cannot go to Kalavad vow in the name of the local Mata. One of such vows is to go to the temple of the Mata with a burning hearth on the head. Such a vow is generally undertaken by the patient's mother.

In the Deccan the goddess Kakasat, who takes the form of a rough perforated stone, is installed at the temple of Maruti. During the epidemic the household dirty water is poured over this image daily, while the holy water and ashes of the goddess are applied to the patient.

Ordinarily in a case of small-pox, the patient is not allowed to bathe till he is completely free from all traces of the disease. A bath is then given on a Sunday, a Tuesday, or a Thursday, with water which has been heated by being placed in the sun. An image of Shitala is set up in the house near the water room, and the patient worships the image after the bath. The image is drawn in cow-dung with two cotton seeds to represent the eyes. An offering of grain, *ghi*, molasses, and curds is made to the goddess. Five virgins are invited to dinner, and are served with cold food. All the members of the household also partake of cold food. On the 7th or the 13th day of the bright half of a month the patient is taken to the temple of Shitala, when a coco-nut is broken in the presence of the goddess. Half of the coco-nut is brought home, the other half being carried away by the Mata's attendant. Some people place a new earthen vessel filled with water near the goddess. Silver eyes, which may be worth anything between half an anna and half a rupee, are dedicated to the Mata.

The first visit to the Mata should take place on a Sunday or a Tuesday. The things vowed to the goddess are dedicated on this occasion. It is also necessary to go to the goddess again on the next Tuesday or Thursday after the first visit. This time only water and red lac are offered.

During the course of the disease no low-caste person and

no woman in her monthly courses are allowed to cast his or her shadow on the patient. The women in the house are prohibited from combing their hair, or churning curdled milk, or indulging in sexual intercourse. Such acts are believed to cause extreme displeasure to the Mata, who then causes some limb of the patient to be affected. Branches of *Nim* (*Melia Azadirachta*) leaves are suspended over the doors of the house, and also round the patient's bed. The same leaves are used to fan the patient.

When a child suffers from the disease, it is often weighed against dates, which are first dedicated to the goddess, and then distributed amongst the poor. The child is taken to bow down before the goddess after nine or ten days from the date of attack, and the mother of the child offers several things to the Mata, among which are grapes, sugar, a pinch of flour, a small earthen bowl full of water, and a blank sheet of paper.

Different things are dedicated to the goddess according as the disease affects one part of the body or another. For instance, flour of millet is offered in case of bronchitis; silver models of the human eye when the disease affects the eyes; a black earthen vessel full of curds in case of morbid heat; a piece of black paper in high fever, and salt if there is an itching sensation. The Mata is said to live on cold food and to be very fond of things which have a cooling effect, such as fruit, sugar, &c. The same things are given to the patient as food.

To secure the protection of Shitala for their children, women annually observe the vow of *Shili-satem* on the seventh day of the dark half of *Shravan* (July–August).[1]

Women whose relatives have recovered from a dangerous attack of small-pox observe a vow on every seventh day of the dark half of every month. They first bathe with cold water and, after offering an oblation of grain, *ghi*, and molasses, take their meals only once during the day. This food has to be prepared on the previous day.

The small-pox deity, Shitala Mata, is described as riding an ass in a nude state with the half of a winnowing fan for an

[1] *Vide* Chapter X, p. 283, *infra*.

umbrella and with a swing in one hand, and a broom in the other. But more usually the Mata is represented by a mere trunkless head in stone, besmeared with red lead. This is said to be the head of Babhrivahan, the son of Bhima, the second of the Pandavas by a Nag mother. At the time of the great war between the Pandavas and Kauravas, he was sent by his mother from his residence in the regions below this world to assist his father, and as he did not know the Pandavas, he was asked to join the weaker side. On coming to the earth he first met with Krishna, who exacted a promise from him to lop his own head off. In return, Krishna promised him that he would be immortal, invisible, and worshipped by all, and the head was set up on the flag of the Pandavas. This head began to trouble the Pandavas after their victory, and could only be quieted by the promise of Krishna to have him recognized as a deity with unlimited powers. This head afterwards came to be known as the controller of small-pox. How the head of the male Babhrivahan came to be identified with Shitala is not explained.

There is a tradition that a cultivator once recovered his eyesight, lost in an attack of small-pox, by worshipping Shitala Mata, and by vowing not to tie his lock of hair till his blindness was cured.

It is said that the powder-like substance which falls from the scabs of small-pox cures cataract if applied to the eyes.

Some persons attribute fever to the wrath of Vishnu, and declare that it can be avoided by the recitation of the names of Vishnu. Others believe it to be due to the anger of Shiva, and say that it can be cured by pouring a stream of water over the image of Shiva, by offering *Bel* leaves (*Aegle Marmelos*) to him, and by reciting the verses in his honour. Others, again, ascribe it to the displeasure of the gods Vishnu and Shiva, saying that the heat is caused by the wrath of Shiva.

The following are some of the remedies adopted in cases of fever:

(i) The recitation of sacred hymns in honour of the gods.

(ii) The worship of Narsinh.

(iii) Pouring a stream of water on the image of Shiva, with the recitation of verses in his honour.

(iv) Drawing the spell (*jantra*) of Mrityunjaya (lit. Death-conquering, an epithet of Shiva) as shown below.

(v) Tying a magic thread round the arm. On a Sunday or a Tuesday a woollen thread or a piece of five-coloured silken thread is taken to a holy man, who mutters a few mystic words, and makes seven knots in the thread. The thread is treated with frankincense, and then tied round the arm.

Periodical fevers are similarly believed to be under the control of spirits. There is a story connected with almost every sort of fever, and it is believed that a person who listens to such a story is cured of the fever. The following legend is connected with intermittent fever occurring on alternate

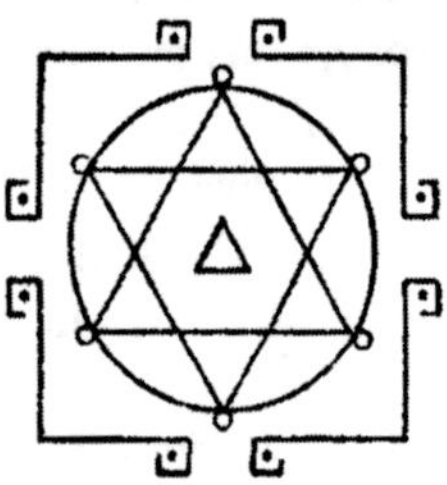

days: Once a grain dealer, on his way to a village, came across a Banyan tree, where he unyoked his bullocks and went to a distance to seek for water. Ekanterio (the spirit controlling intermittent fever) resided on this tree, and when the merchant had gone sufficiently far he stole from behind the tree and carried away the merchant's carriage together with his family. The merchant was much surprised to miss them on his return, but he soon found out the author of the trick, and pursued Ekanterio. The spirit, however, would not listen to the merchant's entreaties to return his carriage, and the matter was at last referred for arbitration to Bochki Bai. The latter decided in favour of the merchant, and confined Ekanterio in a bamboo tube. He was released on the condition that he would never attack those persons who listen to this story.

There is a flower garden to the west of Jodia in Kathiawar, where there is a tree called the mad tree. Vows in honour of this tree are believed to be efficacious in curing fever.

In the Konkan, Deccan, and Karnatak, when epidemic diseases prevail, the people of the village assemble and prepare a basket known as *Paradi*, in which are placed cooked rice, coco-nuts, limes, liquor, betel-nuts, a burning wick, red flowers, and black gram. The basket is then carried out of the village, along with a cock or a goat having a red garland round its neck, and deposited outside the village boundary. To carry this basket, a person belonging to the Mahar caste is generally selected. The people of the next village similarly carry the basket round their village limits; and it is finally thrown into the sea. It is believed that if the basket of offerings to the disease deities is carried from one village to another, it is sure to bring the disease with it. Great care is therefore taken to throw the offerings into the sea. In cases of small-pox, a feast is given to women whose husbands are alive. In some cases boiled rice is mixed with the blood of a cock, and on the rice is placed a burning black cotton wick in a coco-nut shell with a little oil in it. The whole is then carried beyond the village boundary and thrown away. In the Ratnagiri District epidemic diseases like cholera, small-pox, plague, &c., are supposed to come from disease deities, and in order to avoid the danger of such diseases the people of the village go to the temple of the village deity and pray for protection. The special form of worship on such occasions is the seeking of a *Kaul* or omen from the deity. Even Musalmans seek for an omen. The omen is sought in the morning on Sunday, Tuesday, Thursday, and Friday, by placing a flower on the image of the god and noting to which side it falls. When an epidemic of plague broke out for the first time at Sangemeshwar, the people of the village at once proceeded to worship the village deity; but a few cases of plague occurred, even after worshipping the village goddess. When the people went to the temple and asked the reason why the plague continued, it was announced by the deity through the temple ministrant that she was helpless in the case of plague, and desired the people to worship Shiva, thereby signifying that the village deity has limited powers, and that the power of averting great evils lies with Shiva, the god of destruction. In cases of small-pox, married women whose husbands are alive (*suvasinis*) are worshipped with turmeric powder, coco-nuts, flowers, &c., and incense is kept burning in the house. The deity of small-pox is also specially worshipped for a number of days. It is represented by a brass or copper pot, with a coco-nut placed over it. This process is called *mand bharane*, i.e. arranging the materials of worship. The girls in the house sing songs in praise of the small-pox deity. It is believed that in this way the severity of the disease is reduced.

At Achare in the Ratnagiri District it is believed that epidemic diseases such as cholera, small-pox, &c., are caused by the anger of the spirits *Jari* and *Mari*; and in order to satisfy those deities animal sacrifices are offered at the time of their worship. There are no other deities who cause such diseases.

At Kochare in the Ratnagiri District a woman whose husband is alive is made to represent *Jari* and *Mari*, and is worshipped with flowers, red powder, and black ointment. She is given a feast of sweet things; and rice and coco-nuts are put into her lap by another woman whose husband is alive (*suvasini*). She is then carried in procession through the village with beating of drums and the singing of songs.

At Vijayadurg in the same district, in cases of small-pox, the child suffering from the disease is made to sleep on a silk garment. Flowers are thrown upon the patient's body, and are given to him to smell. Incense is burnt in the house. On the seventh day from the beginning of the disease, the child is first bathed in milk and then in water. Black scented powder (*Abir*) is thrown on the body. After two or three days an image representing the deity is made of flour, which is worshipped, and a feast is given to Brahmans and unwidowed women.

At Navare in the Ratnagiri District, in cases of small-pox, the diseased child and the person into whose body the small-pox deities called *Bayas* enter are worshipped with black scented powder (*Abir*), flower garlands, &c.

At Pendur in the Ratnagiri District the wrath of the female deities or *Matas* is supposed to be the cause of epidemic diseases, and these deities are accordingly worshipped for their pacification.

At Chaul in the Kolaba District Shiva is worshipped by Brahmans when epidemic diseases prevail in a village. The worship consists in repeating *Vedic* hymns. The nine planets are also propitiated by sacrifices of boiled rice, &c. There is a famous temple of the goddess Shitala at Chaul where the deity is worshipped by Brahmans, who recite *Vedic* hymns whenever small-pox prevails in the village. The incantations of the goddess and invocations to Shitala are also repeated in the *Pauranic* style. The women walk round the temple every day as long as the signs of the disease are visible on their children. The goddess is worshipped with turmeric and red powders, and clothes and fruits are given to her. There is another temple at Chaul, of the goddess Shri Golaba *Devi*. This goddess is also worshipped when other epidemic diseases prevail in the village. *Saptaha*, i. e. continuous worship for seven days, is also performed in honour of the deity. The gardeners of the village worship this deity every Tuesday morning with coco-nuts gathered from every house in the village. This temple is being repaired at present.

When epidemic diseases prevail in the village of Poladpur in the Kolaba District, Shiva is worshipped by continuously pouring water over the deity's head or phallus. Sacrifices of fruits and animals are also offered to the village deity. Where there is a temple of the deity Mari or Mahamari, the deity is worshipped through a Brahman, and sacrifices of cocks and goats are offered to her.

At Medhe in the Kolaba District Shiva is worshipped in order to avert an epidemic, and Hanuman is worshipped to avert fevers.

At Malad in the Thana District, when an epidemic prevails in a village, the goddess Chandi, i. e. Kali, wife of Shiva, is worshipped and the sacrificial fire is kindled in her honour. On the last day of worship a goat is set free as a sacrifice to the deity. The offering of boiled rice (*bali*) and the goat are taken beyond the boundary of the village, and handed over to the people of the neighbouring village, who follow the same procedure, and at last both the sacrifices are thrown into the sea. The goat generally dies, as it does not get water and food till it reaches the sea.

In the village of Anjur in the Thana District, in cases of long-standing fevers, the Brahmans observe the ceremony of propitiation by water (*Udak Shanti*). It is as follows: An earthen pot filled with water is placed on the ground. On the top of the pot is placed a round plate in which the image of the son of Vishnu is consecrated. Four Brahmans sit on the four sides of the pot and repeat their *Vedic* hymns. These four Brahmans are supposed to be the four mouths of the god.

It is believed by the people that by performing this ceremony the fever is made to disappear.

At Rai in the Thana District some people believe that malarial fevers are averted by placing secretly a small stone on the head of the god Hanuman.

In the Kolhapur District the nine planets are worshipped in the house to ward off diseases such as cholera, small-pox, fevers, &c. The goddess Lakshmi is worshipped in order to avert small-pox, the worship being generally performed in a garden or a grove of Mango trees, when parched rice, coco-nuts, and lemons are offered to her. The people assembled at the spot partake of the food. To avert fever, the people perform a certain ceremony ordained in the Shastras. If the sick person is supposed to be under the evil influence of the planet Saturn, the planet is invoked by repeating verses, and worshipped with the usual offerings. Garments such as a robe and bodice are offered to the goddesses Mari and Kalubai. When an epidemic disease such as cholera prevails in a village, the people of the village install the cholera deity at a place where four roads meet, and worship her for seven or eight days with much ceremony. Every one brings offerings of coco-nuts, limes, flour, cooked rice, and curds, &c., with the beating of drums, to offer to the deity. After worshipping the goddess in this manner for eight successive days they sacrifice a he-buffalo before her. The deity is then put upon a bullock cart and carried through the village with the beating of drums and much ceremony, to be thrown away beyond the village boundary along with the offerings.

In many parts of the Konkan, epidemic diseases are attributed to witchcraft by low-caste people. The power of averting such diseases lies in the hands of the village deities. They are therefore propitiated by the sacrifices of cocks, goats, and coco-nuts. Persons well versed in the incantations of evil spirits are called *Bhagats* or exorcists. Some of them keep evil spirits at their command. The poor people believe that what these exorcists foretell is sure to occur. It is believed that the spirit dwells on the tongue of these exorcists. When these spirits are hungry, they are let loose in the village by the sorcerers for the destruction of the people, thus causing an epidemic. When a spirit is to be destroyed, the people of the village assemble in a mob and attack the sorcerer; a small quantity of blood is taken from his tongue and water from the earthen pot of a potter (Kumbhar) is poured upon it. It is believed that by so doing the spirit is permanently destroyed and the sorcerer either forgets all his incantations or they become ineffective. The spirit is called the mouth-spirit (*Tond bhut*), and it sometimes troubles even animals.

At Chauk in the Kolaba District the people believe that the devotees of the goddess Mari bring on epidemic diseases by the use of their incantations, and in order to satisfy them offerings are made to Mari which are taken by the devotees (*Bhagats*). At Vade in the Thana District epidemic diseases are attributed to witchcraft. There are some women who are supposed to bring on, or at least foster, the growth of such diseases by their evil incantations. Such women are threatened or punished by the people, and sometimes they are even driven out of the village. In the village of Anjur of the Thana District, if a man vomits blood accidentally and falls ill, or dies, it is believed to be due to the act of sending a bewitched lime or throwing a handful of rice over which incantations have been repeated.[1] If there be any sorcerer in the village who has learnt the same incantations, he alone is able to return the spell to the sorcerer who first used it. At Shirgaum in the Thana District, when epidemic diseases prevail in the village, the people of the village take a turn round the village in a body and kill a buffalo.

In the Ratnagiri District, in cases of malarial fevers, pieces of certain kinds of herbs or peacock's feathers are fastened together with black cotton strings, and tied round the arm or neck of the person suffering from the disease. Sacred ashes are put in a copper amulet and applied in the same way. Certain secret spells are repeated at the time. It is believed that the power of the spells is lost if they are disclosed to the public. At Murud in the Ratnagiri District the spells of the god Narsinh, the fourth incarnation of Vishnu, are repeated for the exorcism of diseases. Some verses are repeated in cases of pain in the right or left side of the body. Besides the

[1] See p. 241, *supra*. This is known as *Muth-marane*.

verses, some signs and figures are drawn on birch leaves, and tied round the arm or the neck of the patient. At Vavashi in the Kolaba District spells are in vogue for the exorcism of diseases such as liver and spleen affections. For exorcizing eye diseases black cotton thread is tied to the ear. At Chauk in the Kolaba District ashes are applied to the body of the sick person after repeating certain spells over them. At Malad in the Thana District, for exorcizing diseases caused by evil spirits, certain letters of a verse in praise of Narsinh are written on a birch leaf, and the leaf is tied round the arm of the sick man with a copper amulet. In order to drive out the evil spirit permanently, the god Narsinh is worshipped, and sacred fire is kindled to propitiate the deity. For the worship of Narsinh the ministrant required must be a regular devotee of Narsinh, and he must also be a *Panchakshari*, i. e. one who knows the incantations for evil spirits. In the village of Shirgaon in the Thana District, in addition to copper amulets and black threads of cotton, spells of Musalman saints are in vogue for exorcizing disease. At Kolhapur the higher classes perform the religious ceremony (*Anushthan*) to propitiate Shiva, the god of destruction, in order to avert disease, and also make vows to the same deity. The lower classes offer coco-nuts, fowls, or a goat. They sometimes go to the exorcist for ashes in the name of the god, and apply them to the forehead of the diseased person.

At Adivare in the Ratnagiri District the following practices are adopted for driving out evil spirits that cause disease: Incense is burnt before the exorcist, drums are beaten, and then the exorcist takes a burning wick in his hand and frightens the diseased person by striking the ground with a cane or a broom of peacock's feathers. He also cries out loudly. He then draws out the evil spirit from the body of the diseased person, and puts it in a bottle, which is either carried out of the village and buried underground near a big tree or is thrown into the sea. The process of exorcizing is sometimes accompanied by dancing and loud cries. The person who suffers from evil spirits is taken to Narsinhwadi in the Kolhapur State, where patients are believed to find a cure. Occasionally the exorcist, when possessed, does not dance as at other places, but freely uses abusive epithets to drive out the evil spirits; and on such occasions the threats are repeated loudly by the scarer. While dancing, the exorcist makes a show of different kinds of fits. They are similar to those made by a person suffering from hysteria. He also stands and sways his body to and fro for some time, then assumes a serene and quiet attitude, and begins to cry out loudly. There are some sorcerers at Dasgaon in the Kolaba District who dance and cry out loudly in order to drive out the evil spirits from the body of the diseased. At Malad in the Thana District dancing is used in exorcism. The following is a description of one of these dances: Songs of the deity which is to be summoned on the occasion are sung along with the music of a kind of cymbal and the beating of a leather drum. The man in whose body the deity is to make its appearance takes his bath and sits by the side of a small prayer carpet. A small quantity of rice is put in front of the carpet, and a copper pot filled with water is placed on the rice. The musicians slowly strike their instruments with a loud clash, and the exorcist's body begins to shake. The shaking of the body is a sure indication of his being spirit-possessed. He then sits upon the carpet and begins to throw grains of rice into the copper pot containing water, gives out the name of the particular spirit with which he is possessed, and the cause for which it has attacked the patient. He finally explains the measures and rites by which the spirit can be driven out. The people abide by his directions, and the patient is thus cured.[1]

At Padghe in the Thana District, when an evil spirit is to be driven out from the body of the patient, the latter is asked to hold in his mouth a betel-nut or a lemon. After some time, the betel-nut or the lemon is put into a bottle; the bottle is then tightly corked and buried underground. A copper pot is filled with water; and the diseased person is asked to hold the pot upside down. If the water runs out it is believed that the spirit has disappeared.

In the Thana District dancing is practised in cases of spirit possession, but it is resorted to among the lower castes only.

[1] The carpet is known as an *asana* or seat of the gods; cf. *Swastik, Ashtadal* and *Padmasana*, p. 41, *supra*.

While dancing, the sorcerer cries out loudly, and throws grains of black gram on the body of the diseased person after repeating certain spells. This rite is styled *Bharani* or the process of charming.

At Kolhapur dancing is not used in exorcism, but the people suffering from evil spirits sometimes dance and cry out loudly. Some of them loose their hair while dancing, and even strike their heads. Some quarrel like combatants, and some of them try to make speeches like orators. There is a temple of the god Shri Datta at Narsinhwadi in the Kolhapur State, to which people suffering from evil spirits are brought for a cure. These people cry out loudly when the palanquin of the spiritual head is carried through the village, and spirits usually quit the bodies of their victims at this time, for it is said that they cannot bear the proximity of the holy person. Patients are also cured by residing in the village for a certain period. On this account the village of Narsinhwadi is considered very holy. A big festival is celebrated in this village annually on the twelfth day of the dark half of *Ashvin* (September–October). Feasts are given to the Brahmans, the expenses being borne by the Kolhapur State.

In all parts of the Konkan, and in the Kolhapur State, the exorcist is respected by low-caste people. His duties are to ask an omen from the deity on behalf of the people and to alleviate their sufferings. His appointment is occasionally, though not always, hereditary, the clever member of the family generally following the profession of his father. Low-class people are afraid of sorcerers because they might injure them if they are offended. They therefore are careful not to cause them displeasure. Any one who learns the wicked spells after attending regularly the burial and burning grounds for some days becomes an expert, and many follow the profession. In the Ratnagiri District the chief function of the village sorcerer is to worship the village deity. All kinds of gifts and presents intended for the deity are made through him.

At Chidhran in the Kolaba District Bhutes, a caste of beggars, are the devotees of a goddess. Some of them are known as *Bhagats*. *Devrishis* are very rare.[1]

[1] The difference between a *Devrishi* and a *Bhagat* is as follows: A *Devrishi*

At Chaul in the Kolaba District Bhutes go begging in the morning every day for the first nine days of the month of *Ashvin* (September–October). On the tenth day the Bhute is given a pice from every house. There Bhutes are devotees of the goddess Shakti. At Sasawane in the Kolaba District the village sorcerer comes to beg every day and is given rice, &c., but during the first nine days of the bright half of *Ashvin* (September–October) he is given copper coins.

In the Ratnagiri District it is believed that evil spirits are fond of things like a cock, coco-nuts, boiled rice, &c., and when a person considers himself attacked by evil spirits, these things are waved round his body and thrown away at some distance from his residence, either where four roads meet or beneath a tree haunted by spirits. This is generally done in the evening, but if necessary it can be done at any time. The person who goes to throw these things away is prohibited from looking behind. The articles required for an offering on such occasions are boiled rice, red powder, and an oil lamp made of black cotton wick. For these rites a man from the Ghadi, Gurav, Raval, or Mahar caste is invited at night, and he is paid in cash for his services.

At Ibhrampur in the Ratnagiri District the cocks and goats used for driving out evil spirits from the body of the patient are not thrown away, but are eaten by the exorcist.

At Dasgaon in the Kolaba District a basket (*Paradi*) containing black glass beads, bangles, turmeric and red powders, sweetmeats of five sorts, flowers, a coco-nut, a burning scented stick, and rice, is waved three times round the body of the patient, and thrown away outside the village.

At Kolhapur the use of fowls, goats, limes, coco-nuts, copper coins, dry chillies, and salt is in vogue, not only in cases of driving out spirits from sick persons, but also as a protection against spirits, when a person performs a feat such as bending an iron bar, or doubling with his hands a silver coin, or winning a victory in wrestling. The articles are then waved round him and thrown away in order that he may not suffer from an evil eye.

removes the evil spirits by simply repeating incantations, while the *Bhagat* removes them by bringing the evil spirit into his own body and by dancing, &c.

A curious rite prevails in the Deccan. A lamp is prepared from a female buffalo's dung and four black wicks are inserted and fed with oil. Four red chillies, stem downwards, are inserted in the lamp and it is then waved round the patient. It is then carried away to a certain place by a man holding a pot full of water. This must be done without uttering a sound. He empties the pot where the lamp is left and returns home.

In the Karnatak, in cases of illness, the name of the disease with some words of abuse is written on a piece of paper and pinned to a neighbour's house with a thorn, during the night. The neighbour, by reading the words on this paper, is said to contract the disease in place of the patient.

Transfer of Disease

In the Konkan it is believed that men who are well versed in the incantations of witchcraft and sorcery sometimes transfer diseases from one person to another. Vaccination is believed to be a method of transferring disease to other persons.

In the Thana District a method of transferring disease from one person to another is in practice among the common people. It is as follows: A woman without a child cuts secretly a little piece from the garment of a woman who has children. She next burns the piece, puts the ashes into water, and the mixture is then drunk by the barren woman. It is believed that, by so doing, the evil spirit of the disease that is troubling the barren woman is transferred to the other who has children. The barrenness of the first woman then disappears and she bears children. It is said that if the second woman comes to know of the mischief before using that garment, she discontinues the use of the same and no harm is done to her.

In the Deccan it is believed that if a coco-nut is waved round a sick person and given to another to eat, the illness is transferred from the sufferer to the latter. An animal, such as a goat or a fowl, may be used in place of the coco-nut.

Similarly, in the Karnatak the practice exists of transferring rickets from children by tying their clothes to a *Pipal* tree (*Ficus religiosa*).

In the Thana District the methods of transferring disease are called *Muth-marane*, i. e. a bewitched lime or a handful of rice, is sent to the person to whom the disease is to be transferred. Various incantations are also secretly repeated with the object of transferring the disease to an enemy.

At Kolhapur the following ceremony is practised in the case of persons suffering from swollen glands. Rice, black gram, &c., are tied in a yellow cloth, and three knots are made in it. This is then kept for one night under the pillow of the diseased person. It is taken out the next morning and thrown away at a place where three roads meet. It is then supposed that the person who steps on the bundle first is attacked by the disease, and the one for whom the rite is performed is cured. A similar rite prevails in the Deccan for the cure of boils, seven knots being made in the cloth, and millet being used in place of rice.

In the Deccan eggs, flour, bread prepared from three kinds of grain, oil, &c., are waved round a patient and taken to four cross-roads; any one stepping on the place of deposit takes the sickness from the sufferer.

Belief in the practices adopted for transferring disease from one person to another obtains mostly among women, who have recourse to such practices for curing their children.

One of such practices is to lay a suffering child in the cradle of a healthy child. This act is believed to result in transferring the disease of the ailing child to the healthy child. Another practice is that the mother of the sickly child should touch the mother of a healthy child with the object of transferring the disease of her child to the child of the latter. Some believe that the mere contact of an ailing child with a healthy child is sufficient to transfer the malady of the former to the person of the latter. Others maintain that this can be brought about by a mother either by touching the cradle of another child or by touching the person of another woman. There are others who hold that the disease of a sickly child can be transferred to another child by feeding the latter with the leavings of the former. There is a further belief that a mother can transfer the disease of her suffering child to the child of another woman by applying the end of her robe to the end of the robe of the latter. In some places, when a child begins to weaken, its mother makes an idol of cow- or buffalo-dung, and keeps it fixed to a wall of the house, in the belief that the child will be cured slowly as the idol dries. It is stated that instances are actually known of the recovery of children by this process. As a rule superstitious women practise rites on Sundays or Tuesdays, as it is believed that to be efficacious they must be practised on these days.

In the Deccan women are reported to make a practice of transferring disease from a sick to a healthy child by marking the latter's body with marking nut, giving it the sick child's water to drink, and by cutting its hair.

In the Deccan it is held that if a scorpion bite two persons at one time, the poison can be transferred to one of the two by exorcism.

If the leavings of a sick person are given to a healthy person to eat, the sickness is transferred.

Mhasoba, Vetal, Devi, &c., are offered sacrifices to transfer sickness.

Some diseases are attributed to *vir* possession. *Virs* are male spirits fifty-two in number. The exorcists are believed to have control over them, and are supposed to be able to detect an illness caused by possession by a *vir*. In such cases they drive away the evil spirits from the patients by magic incantations, or transfer them to others by waving a certain number of grain seeds round the head of the patient. By another process they can confine the evil spirit in a glass bottle, which is buried underground.

In order to eradicate a dangerous disease, an offering is frequently made to a dog, in the belief that by eating it the disease is transferred to the dog.

If a woman whose daughter is ill speaks to a woman with a son the disease passes to the son, and vice versa.

In some places diseases of long standing due to spirit possession are cured by employing an exorcist, who, accompanied by others of his order, goes to the patient's house, makes a bamboo bier, waves an offering round the patient's head, and lays himself on the bier with the offering by his side. The bier is carried to the burning-ground by four persons, to the accompaniment of the beating of drums, followed by the exorcists, who throw round flat cakes of flour into the air as the procession moves on. When the party reach the burning-ground, the bier is put down, and the exorcist, shaking violently, gives the offering to a spirit of the place. He then prostrates himself four times with his face turned towards the four directions and drives a nail into the ground at each turn. Next, he lets loose a goat or a ram, to which the *vir* in the body of the patient is supposed to be transferred.

When a man is suffering from a sore or swelling on the eye-lid, he goes to another person's house and strikes earthen vessels against his door, saying, 'I have shaken the vessels. May the sickness be with me to-day and with you to-morrow.' It is also stated that such a patient goes to the house of a man who has two wives while the latter is asleep, and taps his door uttering the words, 'May my sickness, the breaker of the house, be to-day with me and to-morrow with thee'. This process is believed to transfer the disease from the person of the patient to that of the husband of the two wives.

A common method for transferring disease is to wave water round a sick person and give it to another to drink. Similarly, a goblet filled with water is passed round a patient's head and offered to an exorcist, who drinks off the contents.

A belief prevails all over Gujarat that a disease can be passed from one species of animals to another, and various practices are adopted to effect this. Generally an exorcist arranges the transfer. Accompanied by a troupe of dancers and drummers, he visits the house of the sick person and, after examining corn seeds which have been waved round the patient's head on a night preceding a Sunday or Tuesday, declares that the evil spirit possessing the patient requires a living victim. A cock, goat, or a male buffalo is then brought as a substitute for the patient, is waved round him, the tip of its right ear is cut off, and it is offered to the goddess (*mata*), that is, it is released to stray as it pleases. These goats, &c., are called *mata's* goats, *mata's* cocks, or *mata's* male buffaloes, and are seen wandering about in many villages. Sometimes the goat, &c., is killed before the image of the *mata*, and the exorcist, dipping the palms of his hands into its blood, presses them against the doors of every house in the village. It is believed by some people that the animal to which a disease is conveyed in the above manner dies of its effects.

In some places the patient is supposed to be possessed by a goddess instead of by an evil spirit. A goat, cock, or a male buffalo is offered to the goddess in the same way as to an evil spirit.

It is a common tradition in Khakhi Jalia, a village in the vicinity of Kolki in Kathiawar, that a holy man named Narandas, when laid up with fever, was in the habit of passing on the disease to his blanket, and after a time drew it back to his own person.

X

WOMEN'S RITES

Women's Vows and Ceremonies

In the changing circumstances of life, women more readily have recourse to religious vows in order to secure fulfilment of their wishes than men. These wishes are usually for a long and happy married life, for the birth of a son, and for domestic peace. This fondness of women for vows has brought into vogue a number of religious observances which are practised by women only. Instances of such vows and ceremonies are:

1. Eva- or Jiva-vrat.
2. Gautrat-vrat or Bolchoth.
3. Rishi-panchami.
4. Vat-Savitri.
5. Mangala-Gauri.
6. Pithori.
7. Shila-satem.
8. Haritalik.
9. Shiva-mutha.
10. Govatsa or Vasu-dvadashi.[1]

The object of the Eva-vrat (or Jiva-vrat) is to secure eternal exemption from widowhood (*janma suvasini*), the day for this vow being the last day of *Ashadh* (June–July). It is then necessary to observe a fast till the evening; and the only food allowed is a preparation of wheat, taken at nightfall.

On the fourth day of the dark half of *Shravan* (July–August) women observe a vow known as the *Gautrat-vrat* or *Bolchoth* with the object of securing male progeny or long life for their husbands. In the morning the woman worships a cow and her calf (which must both be of the same colour), applies a little cotton to the horns of the cow, and makes an auspicious mark on the foreheads of both with red lac. She then places an

[1] Some interesting information regarding these vows and ceremonies will be found in *Hindu Holidays*, by B. A. Gupte.

offering of betel and rice before the cow, takes four turns round the pair, and whispers in the ears of the cow the words, 'Your truth and my devotion'. A Brahman then recites the appropriate legend.[1]

After narrating this story, the Brahman takes the betel and other things placed before the cow. The woman then returns home and takes food for the first time during that day, the meal consisting of loaves of Italian millet flour and a preparation of *mag* (*Phaseolus Mungo*). Some women take *ghi* and rice cooked in milk and sugar; but any preparation of cow's milk is strictly forbidden. Similarly, there is a prohibition against using things which have been cut by a knife or scissors.[2]

The rite of *Rishi-panchami* is performed on the fifth day of the bright half of *Bhadrapad* (August–September) to make amends for sins committed without knowledge. On this day women go to a river, a well, or some other sacred place, cleanse their teeth with the leaves of the *Aghada* plant (*Achyranthes aspera*), and bathe with something on the head. They then take some stones from that place and worship them as *Rishis*. On the conclusion of the worship, they partake of fruits and of rice grown without ploughing (*niar*). On the *Vat-Savitri* day women worship a Banyan tree or its boughs in order to avert the danger of widowhood. The ceremony falls on the fifteenth day of the bright half of *Jyeshth* (May–June). On this day women put on a necklace made of fifteen leaves of this tree, and prepare a dish from nine handfuls of wheat. They also wear a piece of string (*dora*) on their persons to ward off the evil of widowhood. The *Pithori* is a vow taken to worship the goddess *Pithori* on the last day of *Shravan* (July–August).

[1] The story tells how a woman and her daughter-in-law, intending to observe this vow, killed and cooked a calf by mistake; covered with shame, they locked themselves up in their house, and refused admission to the neighbours, to whom they confessed their crime. On searching for the remains of the calf, the neighbours discovered that it had been miraculously restored to life.

[2] From very ancient times there has been a prejudice in India against things cut by a knife or scissors. Thus, the wearing of garments made of pieces sewn together is a comparatively modern habit. The woman's robe (*sari*) is worn as it comes from the loom, and articles of costume which have in any way been cut or sewn must not be worn on certain special occasions. (*Vide* my work on *The Cotton Fabrics of Bombay*, Bombay Government Press, 1896.)

This ceremony is believed to secure the blessing of a son to a married woman who has no male issue.

Shila-satem is a vow observed by women on the seventh day of the dark half of *Shravan* (July–August) to secure the protection of the small-pox goddess, *Shitala*, for their children. On this day the goddess is said to visit every house and to roll herself on the hearth. No fire is, therefore, lighted in the hearth on this day; for if the goddess comes and is scorched by the fire, she is sure to bring misfortune on that household. For this reason, a number of dainties and all the food necessary for the day are prepared on the previous day. On the day of *Shila-satem*, seeds of millet are spread on the hearth, and after being sprinkled with red lac, a cow-dung bowl containing a plant is placed upon them. The women of the house bathe with cold water and take only one meal during the day. They further abstain from sewing and embroidering during that day. Sometimes a Brahman is engaged to recite the *Shitala* legend from *Rudrayamal*.[1]

On the *Haritalik* day, i. e. the third day of the bright half of *Bhadrapad* (August–September), women make images of earth of Parvati and her two friends and worship them and fast the whole day. They may, however, partake of leaves of the *Rui* tree (*Calotropis gigantea*) on this occasion. The observance of this rite contributes to their good fortune. Even girls of tender years observe this fast. The worship of *Mangala-Gauri* is a ceremony performed by married girls for five successive years on every Tuesday of the month of *Shravan* (July–August). Similarly, the goddess Mahalakshmi is worshipped on the eighth day of the bright half of *Ashvin* (September–October). On the *Makar-Sankrant* day women worship two earthen pots tied together, containing grain and red and yellow powder, and present them to a Brahman. The *Shiva-mutha* consists of a handful of corn offered to the god Shiva by married girls on every Monday in the month of *Shravan* (July–August).

The women of the Thana District fast the whole day on *Vasu-dvadashi*, that is, the twelfth day of the dark half of

[1] This tale relates how the goddess *Shitala* scorched herself on a certain woman's hearth. Owing to her curse, the woman's son died, but was restored to life by the goddess on being propitiated by the mother.

Ashvin (September–October). At night they worship a cow, give a calf in charity, and then take their meal. It is to be noted that this ceremony is performed by women who have children.

The worship of the goddess Randal is a favourite with Gujarati women. A bower is erected for the installation of the goddess, and a wooden stool is placed therein. A piece of fine cloth is spread on the stool, and a figure is drawn in seeds of corn. A bowl with a coco-nut on it is placed over the figure. The coco-nut has two eyes painted on it in black collyrium and a nose in red lac, and is decorated with rich clothes and ornaments to represent the goddess Randal. *Ghi* lamps are kept constantly burning before the goddess for three consecutive days and nights. An invitation is sent to the neighbouring women, who bring offerings of *ghi* to the goddess, and dance in a group at night to the accompaniment of melodious songs. Sometimes, if a child is ill, or some misfortune is apprehended, a certain number of unmarried girls and unwidowed women are invited to a feast in honour of Randal.

On the *Nagpanchami* day, i.e. the fifth day of the bright half of *Shravan* (July–August), women draw an image of a cobra, and worship it with sprouts of Italian millet. In some places it is the custom to avoid all food but rice and fish on this day.

Besides the observance of these vows and ceremonies, there are other ceremonies, auspicious as well as inauspicious, in which women alone can take part. Only women are concerned with all those ceremonies which are gone through on the birth of a child. On the twelfth day after birth, a name is given to the child by its aunt. The ceremony of making an auspicious mark on the throne of a king is performed by an unwidowed or an unmarried girl.

At the time of a marriage, women make the auspicious mark on the forehead of the bridegroom and carry an iron lamp to fetch earth from the village boundary for the sacrificial altar. They take a prominent part in all marriage ceremonies. For nine days preceding the date of marriage the bride and the bridegroom are besmeared with yellow turmeric powder, when auspicious songs are recited by a party of women invited to witness the ceremony. When the bridegroom reaches the entrance of the marriage bower, he is welcomed there by his mother-in-law, who carries him on her hip to his seat in the marriage booth.

It is necessary to make certain marks on the corpse of a woman, and these marks are made by women only. Similarly, women alone take part in the ceremony of getting a widow's hair shaved on the ninth day after her husband's death.

The Shastras have enjoined the worship of certain high-grade deities, and have prescribed certain ceremonials for the purpose. But women are not authorized to make use of these ceremonies. The reason is that the Shastras regard women as inferior to men, and do not grant them the privileges given to the latter. They are not allowed to learn the Vedas, nor may the Hymn to the Sun (*Gayatri*) be taught to them. It follows that women are not capable of performing the ceremonial worship of the higher-grade deities, Vishnu, Shiva, Ganpati, &c.; it is men only who may worship the *Shami* tree (*Prosopis spicigera*) on the *Dasara* day, or light the fire at the Holi festival. From all these rites women are debarred. They may not perform funeral ceremonies. The god Kartakiya may not be worshipped by women, for he is said to have pronounced a curse on all women who visit his temples. Women are similarly debarred from taking part in the worship of Hanuman on the occasion of his birthday (*Hanuman Jayanti*) at the full moon of *Chaitra* (March-April).[1]

Cure of Barrenness

There are various rural methods in vogue in Gujarat for the cure of barrenness.

One of these is for the barren woman to swallow the navel-string of a new-born child. Another is to partake of a preparation made from seven pieces of dry ginger, or from a mixture of dill seed, dry ginger, gum arabic, molasses, &c. In order to secure the desired effect, the mixture must be eaten seven times every Sunday or Tuesday, seated on the cot of a woman in child-bed.

[1] See *Hindu Holidays*, B. A. Gupte, p. 84.

In the Deccan the wearing of a charmed string (*bhaldori*) round the waist is said to be a cure for barrenness.

The longing for a child is also believed to be satisfied by partaking of the food served to a woman in confinement, sitting on her bed, either on a Sunday or Tuesday.

There is also another preparation which is believed to cause conception. It consists of a mixture of *Pitpapdo* (*Justicia diffusa*), sugar-cane, and butter. In order to be efficacious, it must be taken on seven consecutive days commencing from the fourth day of the monthly period.

Conception is also believed to be favoured by administering the gum of the *Babul* tree (*Acacia arabica*) dissolved in milk for three days commencing from the third day of the monthly periods. Some believe that, in order to be effective, this mixture must be taken standing. In some places, seeds of a vegetable called *shivalangi* (*Amorphophallus commutatus*) are also administered.

To secure conception, a bit of coral is also eaten, with the face turned towards the sun.

Other preparations taken in the belief that they cause conception are:

(1) Myrobalans put in a preparation of wheat-flour cooked in water and sweetened with molasses; (2) extract of the fruit *Sarangdha*; (3) *Parascha Pipala* (*Thespesia populnea*) mixed with clarified butter; (4) gum mixed with plantains; (5) juice of the cooked leaves of the *Arani* (*Premna integrifolia*); (6) powder of *Nagchampa* (*Mesua ferrea*) put into milk; and (7) the roots of *Bhong ringdi* (a poisonous plant) mixed with the milk of a cow; (8) a *Bel* fruit (*Aegle Marmelos*) taken in milk.

In the Kanarese country women swallow a scorpion cooked in butter, and a lock of a child's hair similarly cooked, to cure barrenness.

It is also believed that if a barren woman succeeds in carrying away grains of rice from the folds of the upper garment of a pregnant woman and eats them cooked in milk, her desire for a child will be satisfied.

In celebrating the first pregnancy ceremony of a woman (*Simant*), the pregnant woman is taken for a bath to a dunghill or to a distance of about thirty yards behind the house. After the bath is over, she returns home, walking over sheets of cloth spread on her way. On this occasion her company is coveted by barren women for the purpose of tearing off unseen a piece of her upper garment, as this is believed to bring about conception. It is said that if a woman succeeds in doing this, she conceives, while the victim has a miscarriage.

Some believe that a slight pressure by a childless woman on the upper garment of a pregnant woman is sufficient to bring about the result mentioned above. Others hold that a slight blow on the shoulder of a pregnant woman by a childless woman satisfies the desire of the latter for a child. Conception is also said to be effected by marking children with marking nut. The child so marked is said to waste away. Children are also branded while at play. It is believed that branding, to have efficacy, must be inflicted on a Sunday or Tuesday. The operation is generally performed in the evening with a red-hot needle. It is said that the branded child dies, while the branding barren woman conceives a child.

In the Deccan it is held that a barren woman touching another woman suckling her offspring will become pregnant, but that the other woman's offspring will die.

Offering bread to black dogs is also supposed to be a cure for barrenness.

Conception is also favoured by passing under the bier or palanquin holding the corpse of an ascetic or holy man while it is being carried to the cemetery. Some believe that such an ascetic or saint must be a follower of the Jain faith. Others maintain that the desired end can be secured only by wearing round the elbows the grains of rice or coins offered to the bier of a saint on its way to the cemetery.

Other methods practised for the cure of barrenness are as follows:

Some women collect in an earthen pot the dust trodden on by a child-bearing woman, and eat a little every day till it is exhausted.

In the Deccan the threshold of the house of a child-bearing woman is worshipped, secretly, and in a nude state.

Some throw grains of black gram over the bed of a woman in confinement.

In Kanarese districts a woman will throw her shadow on a small child on the fourth day of her monthly illness, to cure barrenness.

Others daub their foreheads with the blood emitted by a woman in her sickness.

There are some who pour water in a circle at the village gate on a Sunday or Tuesday, and when in their periods partake of the powder of *mindhal* (*Randia dhumetorum*) mixed with coarse wheat flour fried in *ghi* and sweetened with molasses or sugar, seated on the threshold of the house.

Many wear round their necks leaves (*bhojapatras*) on which the mystical figure given opposite is drawn by an exorcist.

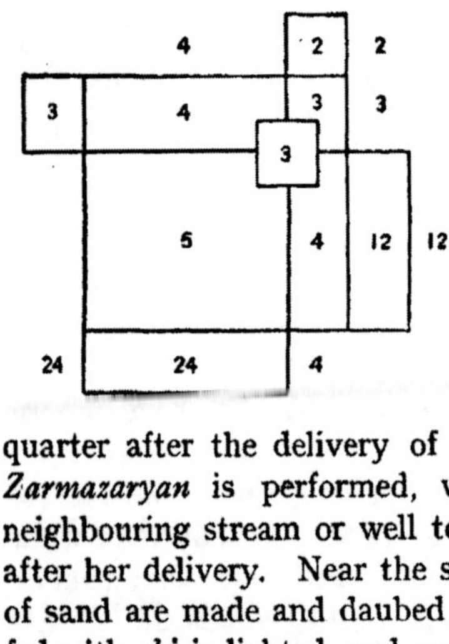

Pieces of paper on which the following spell is written by an ascetic, woven in a string made of five kinds of silk, are also worn round the elbows:

Swaha aum rhin kling swaha.

About a month and a quarter after the delivery of a woman, a ceremony called *Zarmazaryan* is performed, when the woman goes to a neighbouring stream or well to fetch water for the first time after her delivery. Near the stream or well five small heaps of sand are made and daubed with red lead. Next, a lamp fed with *ghi* is lighted, and seven small betel-nuts are offered to the stream or well. A coco-nut is then broken, and a part of it is thrown into the water as an offering. Next, the woman fills a jar with the water of the stream or well and returns home, taking with her six out of the seven betel-nuts offered to the stream or well. On her way home she is approached by barren women, who request to be favoured with one of the betel-nuts, as it is believed that swallowing such a betel-nut causes conception. Some believe that only the smallest of the seven betel-nuts has the power of producing this result. Others hold that this betel-nut must be swallowed on the threshold of a house.

Eating coco-kernel and molasses sitting on the threshold of the house on the fourth day of the monthly period, is also believed to be a remedy for the cure of barrenness.

Placing a box containing a small silver coin or burning a straw hut on a spot where three roads cross one another is also said to favour conception.

In some places a black earthen pot containing charcoal and grains of black gram is placed on a spot where two roads cross one another, on a Sunday or Tuesday. On this day the barren woman has to take her meals without salt.

Cutting off a lock of a child's hair and keeping it in custody is also believed to satisfy the longing of a barren woman for a child. This result can also be obtained by securing a piece of a garment of a suckling child.

Some worship daily a coco-nut and a betel-nut consecrated with incantations. In the Deccan women worship eleven idols of Maruti on eleven Saturdays, or Shiva on twelve successive Mondays.

Some take a bath on the third day of their periods, and stand on the threshold of the house with their hair sprinkled over with red powder. Next, a *ghi*-fed lamp is offered to the deities, and the devotee prostrates herself before the lamp.

It is also believed that barrenness can be cured by religious vows, by offering alms in propitiation of malignant planets such as Mars, and by reciting the incantation called *Gopal Santan* to please the deity Gopal (Krishna).

One of the religious vows of this nature is to observe fasts on twelve consecutive Sundays or Tuesdays. On these days the devotee fixes her gaze on the sun and offers him worship, after which she takes a meal prepared in milk without salt or sugar.

Some hold a recitation of the *Chandipat* a hundred times through Brahmans with sacrificial oblations of clarified butter, sesamum seed, a kind of rice, Indian Bdellium, sandalwood, and sugar-candy. Others have the story of the *Harivansha* recited on seventeen consecutive days, during which period the devotee (i. e. the barren woman) abstains from sexual enjoyment. This ceremony is believed to exorcize the fiend of barrenness.

Some keep a vow of standing on their legs for the whole day on the fourteenth of the month of *Phalgun* (February–March) and of breaking their fast after worshipping the sacred pyre.

There is another vow called the full-moon day vow, the observance of which is believed to favour the birth of a son.

Pouring water at the root of, or circumambulating, a *Pipal* (*Ficus religiosa*) or *Babul* (*Acacia arabica*) tree after a bath on Mondays or Saturdays, without removing the wet clothes, is also believed to cause conception.

Some observe the vow of entertaining thirteen Brahmans and thirteen virgins to a feast, and of setting up an image of the goddess Randal.

Others, again, wander about under the full moon, carrying on their heads a pitcher containing a lighted rag in oil.

The following rites are in vogue for the cure of barrenness in the village of Dabhol in the Ratnagiri District:

(1) Walking round the *Pipal* tree (*Ficus religiosa*) daily; (2) Observing a fast for sixteen successive Mondays; (3) Performing the worship of Shiva after observing the aforesaid feast.

At Kalshe in the Ratnagiri District a barren woman is required to walk round a *Pipal* (*Ficus religiosa*) tree every day in the morning, and if the barrenness be attributed to the disfavour of any deity or the attack of an evil spirit, the same deity or the evil spirit is invoked and worshipped by the woman herself, or through a medium who knows the appropriate mode of worship.

To steal an earthen image of the god Ganpati, to make a cross or a *Swastik* [1] with marking nut on the bodies of children, and the worship of the god Maruti or some other powerful deity at midnight in the no-moon by a barren woman, after divesting herself of her clothes, are rural methods for the cure of barrenness observed in the Konkan.

At Bandivade in the Ratnagiri District copper amulets and black cotton strings are used to cure barrenness.

To walk round *Pipal* (*Ficus religiosa*), *Shami* (*Prosopis spicigera*) and *Umbar* (*Ficus glomerata*) trees, to circumambulate the temple of a particular deity, and to make vows to that

[1] See Chapter I, p. 40, *supra*.

deity, are methods in practice for cure of barrenness in the Konkan.

At Vijayadurg in the Ratnagiri District it is believed that beating a woman at the time of an eclipse is one of the surest methods of curing barrenness. Some people give charity, observe fasts, worship certain deities, and make vows to them to obtain children.

At Ubhadanda in the Ratnagiri District stealing the idol of Krishna when it is being worshipped on the eighth day of the dark half of *Shravan* (July–August), the birthday of the god Krishna, and putting a coco-nut or a betel-nut in its place, is believed to be the best method of curing barrenness.

At Chauk in the Kolaba District the same plan of stealing the idol of the god Krishna is observed as a cure for barrenness. But here the idol is returned with great pomp, and replaced in its original place after the birth of a child. The godlings *Hanuman* and *Bawan Vir* are also worshipped for the cure of barrenness.

At Poladpur in the Kolaba District the favourite method of curing barrenness is to obtain copper amulets and black or red cotton strings from a holy man.

The following are the methods in vogue for the cure of barrenness at Khopoli in the Kolaba District:

(1) To inquire from a sorcerer the cause of barrenness, and then to perform the rites mentioned by him.

(2) To use copper amulets and cotton strings taken from an exorcist.

(3) To walk round the *Tulsi* (holy Basil) plant, the *Pipal* (*Ficus religiosa*), or the Banyan tree daily in the morning after worshipping it.

(4) To feed another woman's child or to give milk to a child.

At Nala in the Kolaba District a woman wishing to have a child is required to strike with a knife the Jack-fruit tree (*Artocarpus integrifolia*), the Tamarind, and the *Nagchampa* tree (*Mesua ferrea*) during an eclipse. It is believed that by so doing the woman will bear a child, and the trees will also bear flowers and fruits.

At Medhe in the Kolaba District the following methods are in vogue for the cure of barrenness:

(1) To worship the god Shiva and to observe fasts on Mondays.

(2) To worship the god Ganpati and to observe fasts on the fourth day of the dark half of every month.

(3) To walk round the temple of Maruti and *Pipal* (*Ficus religiosa*) and *Umbar* (*Ficus glomcrata*) trees every day, in the morning.

At Padaghe in the Thana District images of Rama and Krishna are put into the lap of a barren woman on their respective birthdays, i. e. the ninth day of the bright half of *Chaitra* (March–April) and the eighth day of the dark half of *Shravan* (July–August). Coco-nuts are also placed in her lap with these images.

At Manikpur in the Thana District the goddess *Shitala* is worshipped by women to cure barrenness. They observe fasts, and go to the temple of the goddess bare-footed, with their hair loose and throwing milk on their path. They offer to the goddess wooden cradles and children's toys in fulfilment of their vows.

At Shirgaon in the Thana District it is said that the repetition of the spell *Santan Gopal jay* is resorted to as a cure for barrenness.

At Wade in the Thana District women make vows even to minor deities such as Chedoba to get rid of barrenness. They also use copper amulets and cotton strings procured from a sorcerer well versed in the use of spells.

At Dahigaon in the Thana District the worship of the god Shri Satya Narayan is held to cure barrenness. Some women also distribute to the poor molasses equal to the weight of a child.

In the Deccan Biroba, Munja, Salvai, and Mhasoba are worshipped during the monthly periods to cure barrenness.

At Borkhed in East Khandesh District a visit to the local tomb of a Musalman saint, and compliance with the instructions of a holy man who resides there, coupled with the drinking of the juice of *Shami* leaves (*Prosopis spicigera*), are said to cure barrenness.

At Dehari in the Thana District the village goddess Dehari is invoked and worshipped by women for the cure of barrenness. In the Kolhapur District the help of the family deities and of the household deities is invoked. Women take turns round the Banyan, *Pipal* (*Ficus religiosa*), and *Umbar* (*Ficus glomerata*) trees. Some make vows to the gods, and perform certain propitiatory rites as well as the *Narayan Nagabali.* A snake is made from the flour of Panic seed and another made of gold is put into it. It is then burnt like a dead body. All the ordinary funeral rites are performed. After performing the eleventh day rites, sacred fire is kindled at night-time, and after keeping vigil for the whole night milk and a money offering are given to Brahmans. A feast is given to eleven Brahmans on that day. On the twelfth day sixteen Brahmans are fed, and on the thirteenth five Brahmans are given a feast, after performing the *Shraddha* rites. On the fourteenth day, again, a feast is given to about 100–500 Brahmans according to the means of the host. It is believed that, after the performance of these rites, there is an end to the troubles and misfortunes of the family.

In the Deccan women bathe on new- and full-moon days at the junctions of two rivers to cure barrenness, offering to the rivers betel-nuts, dry dates, and pomegranates. They are sometimes bathed in cow's urine. In places the husband takes the bath on behalf of the woman, or again both husband and wife bathe together at the river junction, always a specially holy place.

In Kanarese districts a woman will take an oil bath on the fourth day of her sickness. The oil dripping is collected and poured down the throat of an infant. The latter falls sick and the woman is said to conceive.

In Nasirabad, East Khandesh, the cure of barrenness is described as follows:

(1) At midnight on a new-moon day, the woman is taken to a river and given an old robe to put on. Wearing this robe and with hair loose down her back, she enters the water waist-deep, and immerses herself to the recitation of incantations by an exorcist, who throws water over her with his hands. She then comes to the bank, naked, after throwing the old robe into the river. She worships the river, waving lighted camphor placed on a betel leaf given her by the exorcist. She then takes a second plunge into the river and resumes her clothes.

(2) On a new-moon night the woman is bathed in water brought from seven wells at the meeting of three roads. While naked, she goes to Maruti's temple, which she circumambulates twenty-one times, from left to right, before resuming her garments. If she meets any one or is spoken to during the performance of this ceremony, it is believed to lose its efficacy.

In the Deccan, to facilitate delivery an image of Shiva is placed under water and kept submerged till after the event. Similarly, water is poured over the image of Maruti and then given to the woman in labour to drink. In some places the root of the *Rui* (*Calotropis gigantea*) is tied to the waist of a woman in labour to facilitate delivery. In others she is made to drink water squeezed out of the end of the waist-cloth of a life celibate (*Brahmachari*). It is occasionally the practice to make a married couple, taking the name of the woman in labour and her husband, to stand next to a jar full of water; a number of persons place themselves in line between the wife and the woman in labour. Water is then passed from hand to hand till it reaches the woman; who drinks it.

In West Khandesh a ring is made from the root of the *Aghada* (*Achyranthes aspera*) plant and put into the hair of the woman in labour, to hasten delivery. Water in which a coin of Akbar has been washed is also said to be highly efficacious for the same purpose.

CIRCUMAMBULATIONS

Circumambulations (*pradakshina*) round images and other holy objects are considered meritorious and to cause the destruction of sin. The subject has been dwelt on at length in the Shastras. It has been seen above that such circumambulations are frequently practised for the cure of barrenness.

The object round which turns are taken is either the image of a god, such as of Vishnu, Shiva, or Ganpati, the portrait of a spiritual guide, his footmarks engraved or impressed upon some substance, the fire-pit, the holy cow, some sacred tree or plant, such as the Banyan tree, the *Pipal* (*Ficus religiosa*), the *Shami* (*Prosopis spicigera*), the *Amba* (Mango tree), the *Asopalava* or *Asoka* tree (*Polyalthia longifolia*), or the *Tulsi* (holy Basil) plant.

It is said to have been a custom of the Brahmans in ancient times to complete their daily rites before sunrise every morning, and then to take turns round temples and holy objects. The practice is much less common now than formerly. Still, visitors of both sexes to a temple or an idol usually are careful to go round it a few times at least (generally five or seven). The usual procedure at such a time is to strike gongs or ring bells after the turns, to cast a glance at the pinnacle of the temple, and then to return.

Women observing the monsoon vow, lasting from the eleventh day of the bright half of *Ashadh* (June–July) to the eleventh day of the bright half of *Kartik* (October–November), first worship the object, round which they wish to take turns, with a mixture of milk, curds, sugar, *ghi*, and honey. The number of turns may be either 5, 7, 21, or 108. At each turn they keep entwining a fine cotton thread and place a milk and sugar ball, or a sugar cake, or a betel leaf, or an almond, a coco-nut, a fig, or some other fruit before the image or the object walked round. These offerings are claimed by the priest who superintends the ceremony. When a sacred tree is circumambulated, water is poured out at the foot of the tree at each turn.

During the month of *Shravan* (July–August) and during the intercalatory month, men and women observe a number of vows, in respect of which, every morning and evening, they take turns round holy images and objects.

People observing the monsoon vow, known as the marriage of *Tulsi*, worship that plant and take turns round it on every eleventh day of both the bright and the dark halves of each of the monsoon months. The *Gautrat-vrat* necessitates perambulations round a cow and the *Vat-Savitri-vrat* round the Banyan tree.[1] The Banyan tree is also circumambulated on the *Kapilashashthi* day (the sixth day of the bright half of *Margashirsha* (November–December) and on the no-moon day of *Bhadrapad* (August–September).

Women who are anxious to prolong the lives of their husbands take turns round the *Tulsi* (holy Basil) plant or the Banyan tree. At each turn they wind a fine cotton thread. At the end of the last turn, they throw red lac and rice over the

[1] *Vide* p. 282, *supra*.

tree and place a betel-nut and a pice or a half-anna piece before it.

The Shastras authorize four circumambulations for Vishnu, three for the goddesses, and a half (or one and a half) for Shiva. But the usual number is either 5, 7, 21, or 108. In taking turns round the image of Vishnu, one must take care to keep one's right side towards the image, while in the case of Shiva, one must not cross the small passage for conducting water poured over the *phallus* of Shiva.

Sometimes in circumambulations the votary repeats the name of the deity round which the turns are taken, while the priest recites the names of the gods in *Shlokas*. Sometimes the following verse is repeated:

'I am sinful, the doer of sin, a sinful soul, and am born of sin. O Lotus-eyed One! protect me and take away all sins from me. Whatever sins I may have committed now, as well as in my former births, may every one of them perish at each footstep of my circumambulation!'

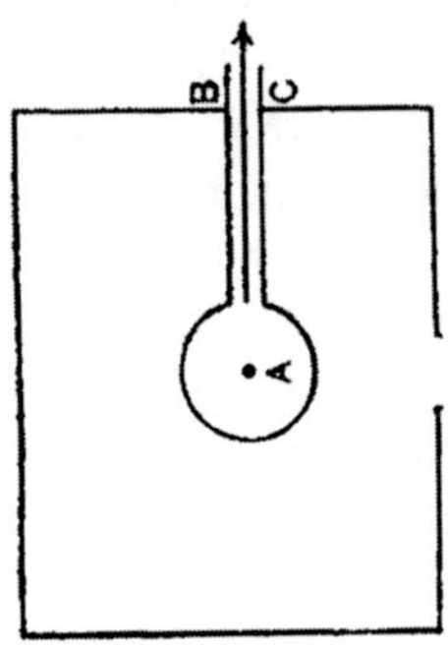

A. Phallus.
B–C. Water-passage.

The recitation and the turns are supposed to free the soul from the reincarnation. Alms are given many times to the poor after circumambulations.

The reason why such turns are taken during the day is that they should be taken in the presence of the sun, the great everlasting witness of all human actions.

The custom of moving round such sacred objects as the Banyan, the *Pipal* (*Ficus religiosa*), the *Tulsi* (holy Basil) plant, the *Umbar* (*Ficus glomerata*), the *Avali* (*Phyllanthus emblica*), &c., is prevalent in the State of Kolhapur.

The women of the Konkan walk round *Pipal* (*Ficus religiosa*), *Tulsi* (holy Basil), and *Umbar* (*Ficus glomerata*) trees every Saturday, and on the fifteenth day of the dark half of a month when it falls on Monday. Sometimes, however, women make a vow to walk round a temple or a sacred tree one hundred thousand times; and for the fulfilment of this vow they walk round the temple or tree for about seven or eight hours every day. If they find it difficult to make up the number of rounds themselves, they ask their near relatives to assist them in their undertaking.

Puberty Ceremonies

Among Gujarat Hindus no special ceremonies are performed when a girl attains puberty, except that on the third or fifth day she is bathed by an unwidowed woman and dressed in green or saffron-coloured robes. She is given rice in milk, sweetened with sugar, and is presented with a piece of green satin.

In some places the girl is bathed on the fourth day and given coarse wheat flour sweetened with molasses to eat. She then bows to her mother-in-law and makes her a present of half a rupee. The mother-in-law blesses her and presents her with a bodice cloth. After the bath, a mark with red powder is made on her forehead and she is taken to the temple of the family deity. Occasionally, the red powder mark is made under the girl's right arm in the belief that this ensures to her the birth of many children.

In some localities the girl is bathed on the third day, dainty dishes are served her, and she is presented with a coco-nut by each of her kinsfolk. In some castes, when a girl attains puberty, a feast of cooked rice and molasses is given to the caste people. In others, pieces of coco-nut kernel are distributed among children, and the girl is presented with a robe and bodice by her parents-in-law. In the case of many castes, a girl is not allowed to cook before she attains puberty.

Among high-class Hindus in the Konkan, when a girl attains puberty, sugar is distributed among the friends and relatives of her husband. She is then seated in a gaily dressed frame. Dishes of sweets, which are brought by the girl's parents and the relatives of her husband, are given to her for the first three days. She takes her bath on the fourth day, accompanied by the playing of music and the beating of drums. Sweetmeats in dishes are brought by the relatives till the day of *Rutushanti* (the bridal night). The *Rutushanti* ceremony is one of the sixteen ceremonies that are required to be performed during the life of every Hindu. This ceremony is performed within the first sixteen days from the girl's attaining her puberty, the fourth, seventh, ninth, eleventh, and the thirteenth being considered inauspicious for this purpose. While performing this ceremony the following three rites are required to be observed. They are:

The worship of the god Ganpati, the special ceremony for invoking divine blessings, and the ceremony for propitiating the nine planets. The ritual is as follows:

The husband and the wife are seated side by side on wooden boards to perform the above three rites. The plantain tree worship is performed by the pair. The sacred fire is required to be kindled. The juice of the *Durva* grass (*Cynodon Dactylon*) is then poured into the right nostril of the bride by her husband. This is intended to expel all diseases from the body of the girl and to secure safe conception. They are then seated in a frame, and presents of clothes, ornaments, &c., are made by the parents of the girl and other relatives. After this the husband fills the lap of the girl with rice, a coco-nut, five betel-nuts, five dry dates, five almonds, five plantains, and five pieces of turmeric. The girl is then carried to a temple accompanied by the playing of music. A grand feast is given to the friends and relatives at the close of this ceremony.

Temple Women

The practice of dedicating girls to a life of prostitution after marriage to the gods is common throughout the Deccan, Konkan, and Karnatak. Thus, in the Deccan, persons who have no children make a vow to Khandoba at Jejuri, in Poona District, that the first-born, male or female, shall be offered to him. The females offered in fulfilment of such vows are called *Muralis*. They are married to the god Khandoba, and earn their livelihood by begging in villages. A male child thus offered to the god is called a *Vaghya*.[1]

In the Karnatak there is a custom of offering children to the deities Yellamma and Khandoba in fulfilment of vows made in order to get a child. The child is taken to the temple of these deities to the strains of music. The temple ministrant

[1] *Vide* Murli, *T. & C. B.*, iii. 70.

asks the child to stand on a wooden board on a heap of rice in front of the deity, and puts into its hands a flat basket of bamboo, tying to its neck the image of the deity. A female child is married to the dagger of the deity. When once this ceremony has been performed, parents abandon their rights to such children. When these children come of age, the male can marry but the female cannot. The latter earns her livelihood begging in the name of the goddess Amba with a basket in her hand. A male child offered to the goddess Yellamma or to Mayaka is called *Jogati*, and a female, *Jogatin*.[1] Children offered to *Firangai* and *Ambabai* are called *Bhutya* (male) and *Bhutin* (female).[2] Similarly, a girl married to the god Basavana is known as a *Basavi*.[3]

In the Konkan districts there is a class of women known as Bhavins who are married to a dagger belonging to the god. They are also called *deva yoshita*, i.e. prostitutes offered to the god. They have no caste of their own. They retain the name of the caste to which they originally belonged, such as Marathi, Bhandari, Sutar, &c., before the caste name of Bhavin.[4] The following is the usual procedure for a woman who wishes to become a Bhavin: She must repair to the temple of a village deity at night, and in presence of the people assembled in that temple she takes oil from the lamp burning in the temple and pours it upon her head. This process is called *Deval righane*, i. e. to enter the service of the temple. After she has poured sweet oil from the lamp upon her head, if she be a married woman, she has no further connexion with her husband. She becomes the handmaid of the temple, and is free to behave as she likes. Daughters of such Bhavins who do not wish to marry undergo the process of sword marriage and follow the occupation of their mothers. The sons of the Bhavins have an equal right to the property of their mother, but any daughter who marries a lawful husband loses her share in the property of her mother. A Devali follows the occupation of blowing the horn or playing the cornet, and is entitled to hold the torches in the marriage ceremonies of the people in the village. Many

[1] *Vide* Jogtin, *T. & C. B.*, ii. 104.
[2] *Vide* Bhute, *T. & C. B.*, i. 194.
[3] *Vide* Lingayat, *T. & C. B.*, ii. 373.
[4] *Vide* Bhavin, *T. & C. B.*, i. 145.

of them learn the art of playing upon the tabor (*mrudunga*) and are useful to those who recite legends of the gods with music and singing. Some of them become farmers, while others are unoccupied.

Bhavins follow the occupation of a maid-servant in the temple, but their real occupation is that of public women. They are not scorned by the public. On the contrary, they are required to be present at the time of a marriage to tie the marriage-string of a bride, for they are supposed to enjoy perpetual unwidowhood (*janma suvasini*). Some of the houses of Bhavins become the favourite resorts of gamblers and vagabonds. In the absence of a daughter, a Bhavin purchases a girl from a harlot, and adopts her as her daughter to carry on her profession.

In the Karnatak Talwars, a division of the great Berad tribe, who desire to follow a life of prostitution must first be wedded to the image of Hanuman. Similarly Kasbis, Dasas, Holeyas, and Kabbers marry their daughters either to Hanuman or Basava, after which they may follow a life of prostitution, as they consider that the god is their husband. Before the marriage ceremony at the temple, the girls are stamped by a religious teacher with the name or image of the god to whom they are to be married.[1] Other gods to whom such women are married with this object are Parashram, Virbhadra, Kanakappa, and Raghunath.

After the death of her husband, in the Karnatak districts, a woman may undergo a certain ceremony known as making the pearl solid, after which she is free to marry one of the local gods with the object of leading an immoral life for the rest of her days.

[1] *Vide T. & C. B.*, i. 82.

XI

VILLAGE, FIELD, AND OTHER RITES

RITES FOR SELECTING A VILLAGE SITE

THE foundation of a new settlement in Gujarat is carried out in various ways. A series of unusual accidents befalling the residents of a village makes them doubtful of the security of their residence, and produces a desire to move to a safer home. Very often on such occasions exorcists are possessed by the mothers, and declare the will of the gods regarding a new settlement. Sometimes a change of home is recommended to the villagers in a dream; sometimes a heavenly voice is said to direct the change, in addressing one of the villagers.

An astrologer has first to be consulted as to the auspicious date on which the boundaries of the new settlement should be marked out. Three or four days before the delimitation, learned Brahmans are sent to purify the chosen site by the recitation of sacred incantations. On the appointed day the headman of the village leads a procession to the site, and performs the ceremony of installing the village gods. It is said that, at the time of founding a new settlement, it is necessary to install and worship the five deities, namely, Hanuman, Ganpati, Mahadev, Vishnu, and Devi. Hanuman is installed at the village gates, and is propitiated with an offering of balls of wheat flour and fried cakes. The images of Ganpati and Vishnu are set up in a central place in the village, temples being built for them in due course. Mahadev is generally installed on the village boundary, and has a temple built for him afterwards. Devi may be set up anywhere: her installation is not permanent, nor does she receive systematic worship. But more generally only Ganpati, Hanuman, and Devi are installed on this occasion. Occasionally other deities, such as the Earth, Shesh Nag, the nine planets, the pole-star, and Kshetrapal, are also worshipped.

The village gates are fixed after the ceremony of installation, and a string of *Asopalav* leaves (*Polyalthia longifolia*), with a coco-nut in the centre, is fastened across them near the top. Here the ceremony of *khat-muhurt*, i. e. the worship of Mother Earth, is performed, and afterwards the headman, accompanied by a Brahman, who recites incantations, either winds a cotton thread besmeared with red lac round the village or pours a stream of milk along the village boundaries. The headman has further to perform a sacrifice (*homa*) at the gates of the village, when a company of Brahmans recite holy passages in honour of Hanuman and Devi. At the time of the completion of the sacrifice, when an oblation of *ghi* is thrown on the fire, all persons present offer coco-nuts to the sacrificial fire.

In some places it is usual to worship the newly chosen site itself, and then to drive into the ground a wooden peg besmeared with red lac, called the peg of Shesh Nag, which is first ceremoniously worshipped with red lac, sandal ointment, and rice.

After these ceremonies, the villagers are at liberty to build their own houses within the new settlement. When the houses are complete and ready for habitation, it is necessary to perform the ceremony known as *vastun* (or *graha-shanti*) for the propitiation of the nine planets. Both the day of installing the gods and the day of the *vastun* ceremony are observed as festivals, at which Brahmans are feasted and wheat flour and wheat balls are offered to the gods.

The new settlement may be named after the deity whose advice brought about the move or after the headman. It is sometimes named after the particular incident which drove people to seek their new home.

Wherever a village is founded in the Konkan or Deccan, it is customary to establish a village deity as the guardian of the village. The deities chosen are Maruti, Kali, Chandkai, Varadani, &c. In the Konkan goddesses are preferred, while above the Ghats generally Maruti is preferred. Certain ceremonies are performed for consecrating the place to the deity, and sometimes the deity is called after the village, as Marleshwar, &c. By many lower-class people the goddess Pondhar is often selected as the guardian of a new village. At Shahpur, if the newly founded village is to be inhabited by high-class Hindus, the deities Maruti and Durga are selected as village gods, but if it is to be inhabited by lower-class people, then such deities as Mhasoba, Chedoba, Jakhai, &c., are chosen. In the Thana District the following deities, viz. Maruti, Cheda, Chandkai, and Shiva, are chosen as village deities. Cheda is represented by a long piece of wood or stone besmeared with red powder, and is placed on the outskirts of the village. No Brahman is necessary for establishing a Cheda. The priest is generally a Kunbi or Mali, and he establishes the deity by offering it a goat or fowls and coco-nuts. Sometimes the guardian deity of a new settlement is decided upon by taking an omen (*Kaul*). Two or three names of deities are selected, betel-nuts or flowers are placed on the sides of the guardian deity of the neighbouring village, and that deity in whose name the betel-nut falls first is chosen as the deity of the new village. At Chaul the deity Bapdev is very popular among the lower classes. It is represented by a big stone fixed on mortar and besmeared with red powder. When it is established for the first time in a village, a Brahman is required to offer the first worship, but after this it is worshipped by a priest of a lower caste. The Mahars in the Kolaba District select the deity Jhaloba as the guardian of a new settlement. In many cases the deity of their former village or of the neighbouring village is named by a Bhagat or exorcist, who becomes possessed.

In the Karnatak the rites followed are similar to those in vogue in the Deccan, with the exception that the gods usually installed are Basava, Dyamava, Kareva, and Vastava Hanuman.

Cultivation Rites

Various ceremonies are performed by cultivators at the time of ploughing the soil, sowing, reaping, and harvesting. These ceremonies differ in details in different localities.

In all places an auspicious day for ploughing and sowing is fixed in consultation with an astrologer. On the day when ploughing is to be commenced, the front court-yard of the house is cow-dunged and a *Swastik* is drawn on it with grain (*Sorghum vulgare*).

In the Deccan the forehead of the sower is marked with sandal-wood paste, grains of corn and rice are stuck to it, and all say, 'Let there be plenty'.

A dish of coarse wheat flour is prepared, and served to all members of the cultivator's family at the morning meal. Their foreheads are marked with red powder, and a pice and betel-nut are offered to the household gods. Hand-spun cotton threads, marked at intervals with red powder, are then tied round the plough and to the horns of the bullocks, which are to be yoked to the plough. The yoke is also worshipped.

Next, the farmer stands waiting at the front door of his house for good omens,[1] and when a few are seen, sets out for his field.

In the Deccan, at the time of sowing, five stones are white-washed and worshipped. A new earthen jar filled with water is placed near them, food is offered, and a feast given to the village servants.

In some places the foreheads of the bullocks are daubed with red lead, clarified butter is applied to their horns, and they are fed with molasses. In others, a betel-nut is placed over the *Swastik* and given to the person who first meets the farmer on leaving his house. In some localities, again, the farmer holds the plough over the *Swastik,* touching it with the end, eats a morsel of molasses, and bows to the *Swastik* before starting.

As a rule, seed is not sown on Saturdays or Tuesdays. Wednesday is believed to be the most favourable day for this purpose.

Sowing is commenced from that corner of the field which has been pronounced by the astrologer to be the best for the operation.

In the Deccan Mhasoba is worshipped with red lead at the time of ploughing and sowing. The agricultural implements, which are washed and marked with red lead, are also worshipped.

Sunday is believed to be the most auspicious day for reaping. While reaping, a part of the crop is offered to the image of Kshetrapal and to other village deities. In order to secure

[1] *Vide* Chapter VIII, *supra*.

a good harvest, sweets are offered to the village gods on the eighth or tenth day of the bright half of *Ashvin* (September–October) or on the second day of the bright half of *Kartik* (October–November).

In the Deccan, at reaping time, the baskets are worshipped with offerings of incense, camphor, coco-nuts, turmeric, and red powder. Burning incense is waved round the corn measure. A goat is offered to the grain heap.

In the Deccan, before threshing begins, the mark of a hand is made with red powder on the stake to which the bullock is tied, and rice is offered to it. Cooked food and goats are offered to the minor godlings. This ceremony is known as *dohota*.

No crop is brought into the house before a part of it has been offered to the local deities.

When juice is to be extracted from sugar-canes, the mill is first worshipped. In the shed erected for storing the jars of molasses, an image of Ganpati is installed and worshipped before placing the jars in the shed. A Brahman and an un-widowed woman are then worshipped.

The first jar of molasses and two bits of sugar-cane are offered to the local deities.

Before reaping cotton offerings are made to the village gods.

In the Karnatak, at the time of ploughing, the earth and the plough are worshipped. At the time of sowing, the seed drill is dressed up in woman's clothes and the lap is filled with offerings. At the time of reaping, Brahmans and Jangams are fed, sheep and fowls are slain and eaten after being offered to the spirits. Milk and *ghi* are poured on the crop before reaping.

In the Hasta constellation during the monsoon, when there is a thunderstorm, a rice-pounder is struck seven times against the main cross-beam of the house in the belief that the sound thus produced destroys insects.

To scare the insects called *itidio*, vows are observed in honour of a saint known as Itidio Pir.

In order that insects and worms may not spoil the corn stored in a granary or in earthen jars, the ashes of the fire of the *Holi* festival or leaves of the *Nim* tree (*Melia Azadirachta*) are mixed with it.

To prevent insects from spoiling wheat, millet, &c., mercury and ashes are put into them, while it is believed that grain cannot be eaten by insects if it is mixed with dust from a place where three roads meet.

In Gujarat, in order to drive away insects, a ceremony called *Adagho Badagho* or *Mariyun* is performed on the *Divali* holiday. It is as follows:

One man holds a lighted torch in his hand, and another an earthen jar, which he beats with a small stick. The two men pass through every nook and corner of the house and the cattle-shed crying, '*Adagho* may go, *Badagho* may go', that is, 'May troubles and diseases disappear; may bugs, serpents, mice, scorpions, mosquitoes, and other insects die out.' Next they proceed, repeating the same words, through the streets to the village boundary, where the torch, the earthen jar, and the stick are thrown away, thus ending the ceremony.

For the protection of crops of gram, wheat, and sugar-cane against injury by rats, a ceremony is performed in which a thread over which incantations have been repeated by an exorcist is passed round the crop, and an image of Ganpati is installed and worshipped with offerings of sweet balls of wheat flour.

In some places the ceremony is performed somewhat differently. Instead of passing a thread round the field, the exorcist walks round the field repeating incantations, holding in his hand a pot containing fire, over which is placed a pan containing *Balsamodendron*. This ceremony is generally performed for the protection of sugar-cane crops against the attacks of jackals. It is believed that an animal entering the field after the performance of this ceremony has its gums stiffened.

In the Karnatak, for the protection of a field, ashes are brought from the potter and scattered over the field before sowing.

In all parts of the Presidency offerings of coco-nuts, fowls, or goats are annually made to the spirits that guard the fields. They are generally made at the time of the sowing or the harvesting of a crop. When making these offerings, the farmers pray to the god to give prosperous crops every year.

They prepare their cooked food in the field on the first harvesting day and offer it first to the gods with the above-mentioned offerings.

At Bandivade in the Ratnagiri District, while commencing the sowing of crops the farmers worship a certain number of bullocks made of rice flour and then throw them into the pond or river adjoining the fields. Some people give a feast to Brahmans at the end of the harvesting season.

Ceremonies in connexion with ploughing, &c., are not observed for all lands. But fields which are supposed to be haunted by evil spirits are worshipped at the time of ploughing, and the evil spirits are propitiated. There is a custom of worshipping in the fields the heaps of new corn at the time of harvest, and this custom generally prevails in almost all the Konkan districts.

At Phonda in the Ratnagiri District a mixture for sprinkling on the crops (*Shivar*), generally composed of boiled rice mixed with curds, is kept at the corner of a field at the time of reaping. This ritual is known by the name *Chorawa*.

In the Deccan, at the time of threshing, five stones are placed in a grass bag (*mudha*) and a twig of the *devak*[1] is stuck therein.

At Dasgav in the Kolaba District there is a custom of carrying one onion in the corn taken to the fields for sowing and placing five handfuls of corn on a piece of cloth before beginning to sow the corn. In many places in the Konkan, in *Bhadrapad* (August–September), at the time of sowing crops, a fair called *Palejatra* is held by the people, and every farmer breaks a coco-nut in the field in order to secure a good harvest and protection for the cattle against wild beasts or disease. At the time of harvesting it is customary with many of the cultivators in the Konkan to place a coco-nut in the field and to thresh it with the first sheaf several times before the regular operation of threshing is begun.

At Vada in the Thana District ploughs are worshipped by the farmers on Saturday and then carried to the fields for ploughing. At the time of harvesting the wooden post to which the bullocks are tied is worshipped by them, and at the

[1] *Vide* Chapter VI, *supra*, p. 210.

close of the harvest the heap of new corn is worshipped and coco-nuts are broken over it.

In the Deccan the bullocks and drivers of the carts bringing the harvest are worshipped by waving lighted lamps round them, before the grain is stored.

In the Karnatak the farmers worship the plough before beginning to plough the land. At the time of sowing the corn they worship the drill. At the time of transplanting the crops they split a coco-nut, and worship the stone consecrated by the side of the field after besmearing it with red powders, making at the same time a vow to sacrifice a goat for the prosperity of their crops. At the time of harvesting they also worship the heap of new corn, and after giving to the deity offerings of coco-nuts, fowls, or goats they carry the corn to their houses.

In the Konkan districts the village deity is invoked to protect the cattle. People offer fowls and coco-nuts at the annual fair of a village deity, and request her to protect their cattle and crops. They have to offer a goat or buffalo to the deity every third year, and to hold annual fairs in her honour. The procession known as *bali* is one of the measures adopted for averting cattle diseases.

In order to protect the crops from wild pig the people of Umbergaon in the Thana District plant in their fields twigs of the *Ain* tree (*Terminalia tomentosa*) on the fourth day of the bright half of *Bhadrapad* (August–September) every year.

In order to scare noxious animals or insects from the fields, the owners of the fields throw charmed rice round the boundaries of their fields. In the Deccan and Konkan the figure of a tiger made of dry leaves of sugar-cane is posted at a conspicuous place in the fields for protecting the crops of sugar-cane. Then, one of the party is held to represent the tiger, and is asked to run, beating his mouth with the palm of his hand as he runs. The rest of the party pursue him and beat him with pieces of the cane.

In the Deccan, in order to protect fruit and vegetable gardens from insect pests, water is brought by the cultivator, in a nude state, from a sacred well.

In the Konkan every village farm is supposed to be under

the guardianship of the minor godlings, the majority of which are called ghostly godlings (*Bhuta-Devatas*). In some cases the field guardians are also the Brahmanic godlings Maruti and Shiva. To the Brahmanic guardians of the field coco-nuts and flowers are offered at the sowing and reaping seasons, and to the rest fowls, coco-nuts, and sometimes goats or sheep. The higher classes feed one or two Brahmans in order to propitiate the deities of the fields; and for the propitiation of the minor deities of the field the lower classes perform a rite called *Dalap*. This rite is performed by a man of the Gurav, Ghadi, or Raul caste by sacrificing to the field deity a goat or fowls and coco-nuts. The priest repeats prayers for a good harvest, and then distributes portions of the offerings among the people assembled there for witnessing the rite. In the Ratnagiri District, on the no-moon day of *Jyeshth* (May–June), people assemble in the temple of the village deity and perform a rite (*Garhane*) in order that they should have a good crop, that their village may be free from diseases, and that their cattle may be protected. A similar rite is performed on the first day of the bright half of the month of *Margashirsh* (November–December), and on this occasion sometimes a goat or sheep is sacrificed at the boundary of the village. In order that there should be a good harvest, the villagers of Kankaoli worship, on certain days from the month of *Kartik* (October–November) to the month of March, the minor deities of the field by offering them fowls, coco-nuts, &c. At Achare some people worship the god of the clouds on the day on which the *Margashirsh* constellation begins, and they believe that thereby plenty of rain is ensured for the season. For good harvests and for the protection of their cattle, the villagers of Achare pray to the village godling in the month of *Jyeshth* (May–June), and then go in procession from the temple of the village deity to the boundary of the village, where they sacrifice a cock and offer some cooked rice with a burning wick upon it to the deity that presides over the fields and harvests. In the village of Palset in the Ratnagiri District the goddess Khema is worshipped by the villagers to obtain good crops, and for the protection of their cattle. The special worship takes place on the full-moon day of *Margashirsh* (November–December), and on this occasion the sacred

Gondhal dance is also performed. In certain villages of the Ratnagiri District, to secure a good harvest, people worship the godling Mahapurush at the beginning of the sowing and reaping operations, and offer the deity fowls, coco-nuts, and cooked rice. In the village of Malwan, at the sowing and reaping seasons, the villagers usually make offerings of fowls and coco-nuts and goats to the guardians of the fields, but Brahmans and such Kunbi farmers as do not eat flesh make offerings of cooked rice mixed with curds. At Ubhadanda village, in order to secure a good harvest and for the protection of the cattle, the villagers worship the spirits *Sambandh* and *Devachar.* At Kochare annual prayers are offered to the godling Gavatdev for the protection of the village cattle. People believe that some deity resides in every farm or in every collection of fields, and that good or bad harvests are due to the deity being pleased or displeased. In order that there should be plenty of rain and that the cattle should be protected, the villagers of Malgund assemble in the temple of the village deity and offer prayers on the full-moon day of *Phalgun* (February–March) and on the first day of the bright half of *Margashirsh* (November–December). In the Kolaba District, for the protection of cattle and for good crops, prayers are offered to the god Bahiri and the spirits *Khavis* and *Sambandh.*

At Chauk in the Kolaba District the villagers perform a special worship of Krishna in order that the village cattle may be protected. At Akol, on the fifth day of the bright half of *Bhadrapad* (August–September), people throw parched rice over their fields and houses so that the rats may not run over them. At Malad in the Thana District, for the protection of cattle, the tiger-god Waghoba is worshipped at night on the twelfth of *Ashvin* (September–October), which is called the Tiger-twelfth (*Waghbaras*). In some villages of the Thana District the deity Waghoba or Waghya is worshipped on the twelfth day of the dark half of *Kartik* (October–November). On that day the cowherds collect a quantity of milk and prepare a mixture of rice and molasses, by mixing molasses and cooked rice. They then proceed to the stone image of the deity in the jungle, and besmear it with new red lead. They pour a portion of the sweet milk over the stone, offer prayers for the protection of their cattle, and partake of the remaining milk. At Agashi and neighbouring villages, before the fields are ploughed, the villagers assemble and collect a certain sum of money, with which they buy goats, fowls, red powder, coco-nuts, and parched grain. A goat and some cocks are then sacrificed to the spirits residing in the cemeteries and at the boundary of the village. Coco-nuts besmeared with red powder are also offered to these godlings. A goat decorated with garlands and red powder is then made to walk round the village three times at night, accompanied by the villagers, who throw parched rice while passing. This rite is called 'binding the boundary', and is supposed to protect the village crops and cattle. No farmer dares to sow his seed unless this rite has been performed. After having taken this precaution, every farmer appeases his family deity, i. e. Khandoba, Bahiroba, Kankoba, &c., by performing a ceremony at home called *Deopan* or *Devaski*, which relates to the worship of ancestors. Most of the farmers regard one of their dead ancestors as their chief deity, and represent him in their house by a coco-nut. They do not enter on any new business without first offering prayers to this coco-nut, and they also believe that they can bring evil upon their enemies by simply cursing them before the deified coco-nut. The only materials generally required for the worship of this coco-nut are red powder, incense, and flowers. On rare occasions, goats and fowls are sacrificed. It is believed that the ancestor in the coco-nut likes to be worshipped by the wife or husband (as the case may be) of the person represented by the coco-nut. Some farmers, in addition to the coco-nut, worship a stick or cap of their ancestor along with the coco-nut, and offer prayers for the protection of their cattle, for good rain and harvest, and also for the destruction of their enemies.

To prevent a tiger from attacking cattle, a circle of the flour is drawn round them by an exorcist reciting incantations. If a tiger tries to enter this protected area its mouth at once becomes swollen.

In some places salt heated over the fire of the *Holi* is put into the food given to the cattle in the belief that this protects them from disease. Instead of salt, some people give cattle leaves of castor-oil plants roasted over the fire of the *Holi*.

In some places, on the *Divali* holiday, a torch and a rice-pounder are placed in the cattle-shed, and the cattle are made to cross over them one by one. This process is believed to protect them from disease.

Vows in the honour of Ashpal or Nagdev are observed for the protection of cattle.

Protection of Harvest and Cattle

When a cow or she-buffalo is about to calve, a packet containing a few pebbles or cowries, the red lead from the image of Hanuman, dust collected from a place where four roads meet, and grains of black gram is tied to its horns by an indigo-coloured thread, in the belief that this protects the animal from the effects of the evil eye.

To guard cattle against an attack of cow-pox, women observe a vow called *Shila-satem* on the seventh day of the bright half of *Shravan* (July–August).

Diseases among cattle are believed to be brought on by the wrath of minor deities, such as Shitala, Mahakali, or the sixty-four Joganis. The exorcists (*bhuvas*), when they are possessed, declare to the people which particular deity is exasperated, whereupon that deity is conciliated either by offering dainties or a goat or a ram, or by the observance of an *Ujjani*. A stream of milk (*dharavadi*) is poured on to the ground adjoining the village site, and garlands of *Asopala* or *Ashoka* leaves (*Polyalthia longifolia*) are fastened on the doors of the offended deity's temple. It is also customary to place offerings at a spot where three roads meet in order to propitiate the evil spirits who frequent such places.

The disease known as *Kharava* affects the hoofs of cattle, in which it produces irritation; it is generally due to worms in the hoofs. In the case of this and other cattle diseases occurring, a mystical arrangement of words of the twelve names of Arjuna is written on a piece of paper and tied round the neck of the diseased animal in a piece of indigo-coloured cloth, fastened over the gates through which the cattle pass, or suspended over the street by which the cattle go out to graze. This charm is called a *jantra*, and is as follows:

Shrisakha	Dhanurdhari	Gajidhana	Krishnasakha
Dhananjaya	Lalanlarkha	Kapidhwaj	Jayahari
Gudakesh	Pitabhava	Narsinh	Parth

Sometimes the paper on which the charm is written is placed in a hollow bamboo stick which is then fastened over the gates. The charm is believed to have power to cure the disease.

Muva-keshibi causes saliva to flow continuously from the mouths of animals. A piece of leather thong or a piece of black wood on which magic spells have been cast is suspended over the village gates or is tied to the neck of the animal in the case of this disease occurring. But if this is not successful in checking the course of the disease, it is usual to swallow the offerings (*chelans*) of Mungi Mata (the Dumb Mother). For this purpose the *bhuvas* of the Mata, who are Bharvads, are invited to the stalls of the affected cattle, where they recite magic incantations amidst tumultuous shouts and yells. After this they are fed with rice, *ghi*, and sugar, this latter process being called 'swallowing the offerings of the *Mata*'. In the event of this process being of no avail in restraining the disease, the headman of the village, in the company of his wife, performs a *homa* sacrifice in the places dedicated to the *Matas*, and offers a sacrificial oblation, when all the villagers dedicate coco-nuts to the sacrificial fire.

In the Deccan the cattle are bathed in water in which fish have been washed.

Sometimes the wrath of the god Gorakhdev is supposed to be responsible for cattle diseases. A bunch of the leaves of a poisonous medicinal plant, *Ankdi* (*Gymnosporia emarginata*), is passed seven times over the body of the ailing animal with the prayer 'May Gorakhdev be pleased', and a coco-nut is dedicated to the god.

Another method of checking cattle-disease is to bury the corpse of an animal which has died thereof near the village gates. It is believed that this puts a stop to any further deaths among cattle from the same disease.

When disease prevails largely among cattle, a belief gains ground that the Dheds (who flay the dead cattle and sell their hides) have poisoned the drinking water of the cattle in order to increase their earnings.

Mention has already been made of the deities which protect the cattle and to whose displeasure diseases among cattle are attributed. It is said that such diseases are very common during the *vishi* of Shiva. A cycle of twenty years is called a *vishi*, three such cycles making a complete *samvatsar* of sixty years. Each of such *vishis* is presided over and named after one of the three gods of the trinity, Brahma, Vishnu, and Shiva. The *vishi* of Brahma is characterized by protection and creation, that of Vishnu by growth, and that of Shiva by destruction, the last often bringing on such calamities as plague, famine, and diseases among cattle.

The following remedies are practised by the village people in the case of certain cattle diseases:

In the case of hoof disease or the like, there is a practice of burying a plough near one's gates, which is afterwards covered with dust gathered from three streets and is worshipped with a branch of a tree, a plate of iron, and red lead. This ceremony has to be performed either on a Sunday or a Tuesday, and the man who performs it has to remain naked at the time.

For the cure of *valo* (a disease in which the throat is inflamed), pieces of the stalk of *Kukad-vel* (*Luffa echinata*) are tied round the neck or the horns of the diseased animal, and no other food except *ghi* and molasses is allowed to it for two or three days. A handful of salt is sometimes thrown on the back of the animal. Sesamum oil is also said to work as a good remedy in the case of the same disease.

Another cure for the same disease is to pass a knotted bamboo stick with seven knots seven times over the back of the ailing animal.

Ghi is sometimes used as a medicine in the case of cow-pox among cattle. To animals suffering from a stye in the eye an ointment prepared from the horn of a deer is applied, while a mixture of whey and salt is said to be useful in most eye maladies. The treatment for the swelling of the belly is a mixture of molasses, *ajamo* (*Carum Roxburghianum*), and *sanchal*, i.e. salt mixed with myrabolans.[1] To cure an animal of *khapari* (a disease which affects milch cattle), the milk of the affected animal is poured on a *Bor* tree (*Zizyphus Jujuba*). If after delivery some part of the embryo remains inside an animal, milk and molasses are given to expedite its removal.

Sometimes, in cases of hoof disease, the ailing animal is made to move about in hot sand and is treated with salt, which is first fried on the fire of *Holi*.

In Chalisgaon tiger flesh is washed and the cattle passed through the smoke to cure disease. In the Deccan generally a plough is buried edge upwards beyond the village boundary; pieces of black cloth are tied to the village gate and the cattle passed underneath; a shoe is passed over their backs, wooden images of the diseased cattle are offered to Saloba, lime is put on their horns, and rice and curds passed over their back and round their feet.

A disease called *Okarinu* (i. e. vomiting) sometimes breaks out among sheep. In this case the shepherds separate all the affected animals from the herd and remove them to a distance. All the sheep which die of the disease are buried deep in a pit, which is guarded for several days, lest some other animals dig it up and let loose the buried epidemic by exposing the carcasses. It is believed that the contagion of this disease lies in the ears; and the ears of all the sheep in the herd are carefully watched if they bleed.

The twin gods Ashivini Kumar are sometimes propitiated by means of the performance of religious austerities in their honour in order that they may put a stop to a disease among cattle.

When cattle-disease breaks out in a village the people of the Ratnagiri District generally prevent the healthy cattle from mixing with the diseased, and the people of the neighbouring villages take precautions against using the milk, &c., of the diseased cattle. At such times the cattle of the village in which the disease breaks out are prohibited from entering the neighbouring villages. At Ubhadanda in the Ratnagiri District the deity named Maha Girha is worshipped in connexion with cattle diseases. At some places a feast is given to Brahmans, and in certain villages of this district a man is

[1] Also known as *padelon*.

painted like a tiger, carried out of the village, and bathed in a river. It is believed that this is one of the remedies for averting cattle diseases. At Phonda in the Ratnagiri District, when cattle-disease breaks out, a goat or a cock is sacrificed at the temples of the village deity. At Basani in the Ratnagiri District the gods of the Mahars, as also the village deity, are worshipped in connexion with cattle diseases. In Hubli and the Karnatak a practice prevails of killing a wild boar and burying it feet upwards beyond the village boundary. At Vavashi in the Kolaba District, when cattle-disease prevails in a village, a pig is killed and buried on the border of the village. A sweet-oil lamp in the shell of a crab or a lobster is kept burning in the cowshed. The owner also cleans the cowshed and burns sulphur, camphor, dammar, and other disinfectants. At Varsai in the Kolaba District an omen is sought from the village deity to prevent cattle diseases, that is, the village deity is consulted through the temple ministrant, who acts as the spokesman of the oracle. At Medhe in the Kolaba District the village deity, Bahiroba, is worshipped in connexion with cattle diseases. The diseased animals are minutely examined, and the affected part of their bodies is branded with a red-hot iron. In the village of Umela in the Thana District the village deity is worshipped and sacrifices are offered to her. Milk from the affected villages is prohibited, and vegetables are not fried in oil during the prevalence of the disease in the village. At Kolhapur the people make vows to the god, and ashes from the temples are brought and applied to the forehead of the cattle. Cotton strings are tied to the feet or the necks of the cattle in the name of the god. They also make vows to the deities Tamjai and Waghjai, and offer to them eyes made of silver, a new cloth, a fowl, or a goat, when their animals are cured of the disease.

Kshetrapal is believed to be the guardian spirit of fields, and *Suropuro* and *Mamado* are believed to protect harvest and cattle. It is also believed that the spirit *Jakhara* protects crops and cattle.

The spirits *Devachar* and *Chalegat* are considered to be the special protectors of crops and cattle. Offerings of fowls and coco-nuts are made to them annually.

At Kochare in the Ratnagiri District the spirit known as *Viswati* is believed to be the special protector of crops and cattle.

The people of the Kolaba District consider that the spirits known as *Mhashya*, *Khavis*, and *Bandav* are the protectors of crops and cattle. At Dahanu in the Thana District the spirit *Cheda* is believed to be the guardian of crops and cattle.

The people of Kolhapur believe that the deities of the fields protect the crops and cattle. Those who are in possession of a *Chetak* [1] are sure to find their crops and cattle protected by this servant spirit. A belief runs that if a cousin (father's brother's son) becomes a spirit after death, he proves beneficial to the cattle of his relatives.

Rites for causing or stopping Rainfall

When there was scarcity of rain the Hindus formerly invoked Indra, the god of rain, by means of sacrifices, but such sacrifices are now rarely performed, as they are very costly. The general method of ensuring rainfall in these days is to drown the *phallus* of Shiva in water and to offer prayers to that deity.

The following rural rites are intended to ensure sunshine and to check excessive rain. A man born in the month of *Phalgun* (February–March) is requested to collect rain-water in the leaf of the yam, and the leaf is then tied to a stick and kept on the roof of a house. Burning coals are also thrown into rain-water after passing them between the legs of a person born in the month of *Phalgun* (February–March).

In order to secure sunshine and favourable weather, oblations are offered to the local deities, sacrificial offerings are made, and flags are suspended from the doors of temples.

Similarly, to ensure a favourable rainfall, a grand festival is observed on an auspicious day. On this day all agricultural work is stopped and sweet balls called 'clouds' (*megh*) are eaten by the people.

The potters and the Chudbudki Joshis observe the following ceremony for causing rainfall: A *phallus* of Shiva made of mud is consecrated on a wooden board, and a naked boy is asked

[1] *Vide* p. 236, *supra*.

to hold it on his head. The boy carries it from house to house and the inmates of the houses pour water over the *phallus*. Brahmans and high-class Hindus pour water on the *phallus* at the temple of the god Shiva continuously for several days. This is called *Rudrabhisheka*, i.e. the worship of Shiva (Rudra). It is a religious rite in which eleven Brahmans are seated in a temple to repeat prayers to Shiva.

The *Swayambhu*, i.e. natural *phallus*, of Shiva is supposed to have influence over the fall of rain.

The people of the Thana District believe that the following ceremony causes a fall of rain: Stones are taken out of a pool and worshipped. They are then carried to every house in the village, and water is poured upon them by the inmates. There is a temple of the god of clouds at Viranath in the Thana District.

In Gujarat, for the most part, the people seem to be unacquainted with the belief that certain stones possess the virtue of influencing the rain. Some persons, however, attribute this quality to the stones on such sacred mounts as Girnar, Abu, and Pavagadh. There is a point called Tonk, on Mount Girnar, of which it is said that rain is certain to fall whenever any one succeeds in climbing it. There is also a common belief that marble, if heated, has influence over rain.

It is a common practice to submerge the image of Shiva in water with the object of bringing rain. Similarly, the image of the goddess Harshadh is sometimes bathed when rain is desired. The male and the female attendants of the goddess are at the same time given a bath, and an offering of rice cooked in milk sweetened with sugar is made to the goddess.

The changes in the seasons are attributed by some to Brahma, Vishnu, and Shiva. Brahma sends down the rain and produces corn, grass, &c., Vishnu protects and nourishes the harvests in winter, and Shiva causes the heat of the summer. There is also a belief that these three gods go down in turns to nether regions, and stay there for four months. Vishnu descends on the eleventh day of the bright half of *Ashadh* (June–July), and on that day the rainy season begins. When Vishnu comes up and Shiva takes his place, people experience the cold of winter: but as this god always keeps a smoke fire burning near him, the waters under the surface of the earth, such as those in the wells, remain hot during this period. Such waters are cooled when Shiva returns and Brahma goes down to the nether regions: but the return of Shiva causes summer on the earth.

According to another belief, the sequence of the seasons is controlled by the sun-god. There are six seasons; and the changes in the seasons depend upon the position of the sun in the twelve signs of the zodiac. Each season lasts for a period of two months, during which time the sun travels through two signs of the zodiac.[1]

The belief is as old as the Vedas that demons sometimes obstruct the fall of rain, and confine the waters of the clouds. It is Indra who fights with them and breaks through their castles by means of his thunderbolt, sending down showers of rain for the benefit of his worshippers. So, whenever there is an unusual drought, people still invoke the aid of this god, and celebrate a festival in his honour (*Ujjani* or *Indramahotsava*). Sacrifices are performed to propitiate the god, and Brahmans are entertained at a feast. Sometimes the festival is celebrated outside the village, where people go in large parties to dine together.

Another favourite ceremony supposed to cause rain to fall is the submersion of the image Shiva in water, by blocking up the passage round the phallic image of Shiva, by which water poured over the image usually runs off. This ceremony is known as *Jala-jatra*.

Sometimes the assistance of the saint Shringhi is invoked to bring about a fall of rain. The image of the saint is installed in water, incantations are recited, and prayers are offered before a sacrificial fire. This ceremony of rain-soothing (*Parjanya-shanti*) is said to have been performed within recent years in Bombay, and to have been successful in bringing rain. It is also said that rainfall can be caused by singing a song or

[1] *Vasant* is the period which the sun takes to pass through *Min* (Pisces) and *Mesha* (Aries). *Grishma* corresponds to the time during which the sun passes through *Vrishabha* (Taurus) and *Mithun* (Gemini). During *Varsha* the sun moves through the signs *Karka* (Cancer) and *Sinha* (Leo), and during *Sharad* through *Kanya* (Virgo) and *Tula* (Libra). *Hemant* is the time which the sun takes to travel through *Vrishchika* (Scorpio) and *Dhanu* (Sagittarius). *Shishir* occurs when the sun stands in *Makar* (Capricornus) and *Kumbha* (Aquarius).

a sacred hymn to a certain tune. There is a tradition that the well-known saint Narsinha Mehta once sang this tune on the occasion of the celebration of the first pregnancy of his daughter, and the performance was immediately followed by a shower of rain. Rain which is brought down in this manner can be put a stop to by singing to a different tune.

Low-caste women have recourse to the following expedient to bring rain: Five or six of them place a quantity of muddy earth on a wooden stool, which is carried by one of them. The lump of mud is covered with leaves of a creeper,[1] and is called *mehulo* or *meghalo.* The whole party then sing songs, and visit every house in the village. A bowl of water is poured over the *mehulo* and the women receive some corn for their trouble.

Some believe that when the worship of the village gods is neglected and when the people grow corrupt, ill-treat the saints, and are given to the killing of cows and Brahmans, Yama, the god of death, directs his colleagues, Indra and Varuna, to threaten the world with a drought. The rainfall returns only when the people revert to righteous ways, and after Indra and Varuna have been conciliated by offerings.

The lower classes of the people believe a prolonged cessation of rain to be due to the wrath of local minor deities, aroused by the neglect of their worship. In such a contingency, therefore, they prepare cakes of black gram, wheat flour, balls of gram fried in oil, and other dishes, and offer them to the local gods for their propitiation.

To stop an incessant fall of rain, people often observe the *Aladra* vow. The headman issues a proclamation that on a particular day none should cook, churn whey, fetch water, wash clothes, or attend to any of the multifarious household duties; but that all should pass the day in prayer. A complete cessation from toil in favour of earnest devotion to divine powers is the peculiar feature of this vow. People do not abstain from food; but food must be prepared on the previous day. If the rains do not cease in spite of this vow, but threaten the village with inundation, the headman leads a procession to the confines of the village and makes an offering to the waters.

[1] *Gidotan* or *Tindotan.* I have not been able to find the botanical equivalent.

In some places a spinning-wheel, sometimes specially constructed of human bones, is turned by a naked person in the reverse direction to the usual one, with the object of causing the cessation of immoderate rainfall.

In the Karnatak, to check a storm of hail, Dhangars catch a black sheep from their herds by the hind legs, and drag it from left to right, then throw it in the direction they wish the hail to go.

Baris, Kunbis, and Dhangars in Khandesh cut their little fingers and mutter incantations over the blood that flows. This sends away rain and hail. Similarly, they protect betel-leaf gardens from excessive rain by sprinkling blood from their little finger along the boundary line.

A cessation of rain is also believed to be brought about by offering an oblation to the god Kasatia, and by the observance of the vow called 'Tying the knot of Kasatia'. The vow lasts for three weeks, and those who observe it do not partake of anything except rice (or, according to others, *jiran*, a kind of spice).

Some persons attribute a heavy fall of rain to the wrath of Indra, and offer ceremonious prayers to appease that god. In some places people engage the services of magicians to restrain the fall of rain. Farmers sometimes brand the rain by casting burning sparks upon it, in order to stop an incessant fall. Vows in honour of the ocean are also observed with the same object.

In order that there should be a fall of rain, some people besmear the *phallus* of Shiva with cooked rice and curds. In the Ratnagiri District, whenever there is a scarcity of rain, people go to the field of the god Parashram, and there pray to Parashram to send rain. Sacrifices are also offered to Indra, the god of rain, in order that there should be plenty of rain. Some believe that there are certain enchanters who by the power of their charms are able to prevent the fall of rain.

In the Ratnagiri District the following ceremony is performed by the cultivating castes to avert drought: All the male villagers assemble together at an appointed place, and there they select one of them to impersonate the god-protector of cattle, *Gowala-deva*. All of them then go about in the village from house to house. The owner of every house sprinkles water over the assembly, and curds and butter-milk over the body of the *Gowala-deva*. They are also given rice, pulse, vegetables, &c. After visiting most of the houses in the village, the assembly, headed by the *Gowala-deva*, go to the bank of a river. Here they cook the food, offer it first to the *Gowala-deva*, and then partake of the remainder as sacred food from the *Gowala-deva*. Others make an image of the stone-god *Dhondal-deva* in order that there should be plenty of rain. Sometimes people repeat incantations addressed to the rain so that rain should fall. The goddess Navachandika is worshipped in order that there should be rain. The Kunbis perform a peculiar rite for checking the fall of rain. They ask a person born in the month of *Jyeshth* (May–June), or in one of the three following months, to fetch some rain-water in a yam leaf, and this is fastened to the eaves of thatched houses by means of a string. Note that, if this rite is to be performed in the month of *Jyeshth* (May–June), a person born in that month only is required and no other; and so forth. In order to check an excessive fall of rain the villagers sometimes ask a boy to take off his clothes and then to catch rain-water in the leaves of the yam. The leaves containing the water are then tied to the eaves of the house. The people say that during the rule of the Peshwas there was a class of enchanters who had the power of causing a failure of rain. To check the fall of rain, some people ask naked boys to throw burning coals into the rain-water. A rain-hood made of leaves is kept in the rain upside down, the goddess Holika is worshipped, boughs of the *Avali* tree (*Phyllanthus Emblica*) are conveyed to a place where four roads meet and stones are heaped over them, and eaves of thatched houses are beaten by boys who do not wear clothes, all these acts being done by the villagers with a view to preventing an excessive fall of rain.

The people of the Thana District believe that different deities preside over the season, e. g. Mars presides over the spring, Venus over summer, the moon over autumn, and Saturn over winter. When the people are in need of rain they say to the god of rain, 'Let us have plenty of rain to-morrow and we will give thee, O God of rain, rice mixed with curd'. The same offer is made to the god of rain even when they do not want it. The following practice is said to cause rain: The villagers go from house to house with boughs of the *Nim* tree (*Melia Azadirachta*) on their heads, and water is then poured upon them by the inmates. The fall of rain is supposed to cease if a person born in the month of *Phalgun* (February–March) extinguishes burning coals in rain-water when his garments have been removed.

In the Deccan boys cover their heads with twigs and leaves of the *Nim* (*Melia Azadirachta*) and go round naked. Water is poured over their heads and thus rain is brought.

Some stones are supposed to have influence over rainfall. There is a big stone at Varasai in the Kolaba District on which are drawn certain images. The people believe that it rains hard if this stone is held straight and then swung to and fro. Some people perform the following rite, known as the *Dhondil-jagya*: They ask a person of the Kaikadi or Od caste to remain naked and break the string round his waist. A small image of black earth is made and placed upon his head. The boy then conveys the image from house to house in the village. A woman in each house sprinkles water over the image, while the boy dances, saying, '*Dhondil jagya, Paus jagya*'. It is believed that it rains in the direction in which the water sprinkled falls. A person who accompanies the boy gathers corn at every house. A dinner is then prepared, and the people of the caste to which the boy belongs partake of it heartily. It is also said that making water in a standing posture causes the fall of rain. The god Rameshwar at Chaul in the Kolaba District is said to have control over rain. In the temple of this god there is a reservoir known as the rain pond, which is opened after performing a sacred rite, if there be a scarcity of rain. There are also other reservoirs in the temple, but no occasion has yet arisen to open them. Some people believe that the god Agni regulates the seasons.

Eaves of thatched houses are cleansed with a brush made from the leaves of coco-nut trees in order that a fall of rain should be prevented.

When the rainfall is irregular, people sometimes seek the protection of the gods Annadeva, Annapurna, and Kriya

Bhaudai. Six small coins are collected from every house in the village to make what is called a *chhakadi,* and the whole amount is then bestowed in charity in the name of the above-named deities.

Rain during the Ashlesha and Magha constellations is destructive to the crops, and is a sign of the wrath of Indra, who should be appeased with sacrificial offerings.

A curious practice is reported from Ranebennur in the Dharwar District. To cause rain, a market is held round the temple of Dyamava and Durgava for five weeks, when it is believed that the goddesses, disgusted with the filth thrown near their temple, send rain. It is also held that by disinterring the corpse of one who has died of white leprosy and throwing it into the river, rain is brought. To stop rain, burning brands must be thrown at the rain, when the rainfall will at once cease.

XII

MISCELLANEOUS BELIEFS AND PRACTICES

Worship of Implements and Tools

Hindus of the Presidency consider as sacred all objects that are the means of their livelihood, and for this reason the Brahmans hold in veneration religious books, the goldsmiths make offerings to their fire-pots, blowpipe, and pincers, oilmen worship their oil-mill, and do not touch them with their feet. Similarly, the broom, the measure of capacity, the corn-sieve, the sweet-oil lamp, fire, the levigating slab, are reverenced by those who use them, and must not be touched with the foot. In case any one accidentally happens to touch such sacred objects with his foot, he apologizes and bows to them.

Hindus of the Presidency worship annually on the *Dasara* day the arms and all the instruments or implements by which they earn their livelihood. The corn-sieve, the winnowing basket, the rice-pounder, the plough, the wood-bill, and other such implements are worshipped on this day, as well as the objects already mentioned.

In the Kolhapur District all instruments and implements are worshipped by the people one day previous to the *Dasara* holiday. This worship is called *Khandepujan*, i.e. sword worship. People also worship all agricultural instruments, and tie to them leaves of *Pipal* (*Ficus religiosa*) and Mango trees.

A new winnowing fan is considered to be holy. It is filled with rice, fruits, coco-nuts, and betel-nuts, and a piece of bodice cloth is spread over it. It is then worshipped and given to a Brahman lady in fulfilment of certain vows, or on the occasion of the worship of a Brahman married pair.

At Rewadanda in the Kolaba District some people worship a wood-bill on the sixth day from the birth of a child. It has already been shown how the rice-pounder (*Musal*) is worshipped as a marriage guardian by Maratha Kunbis, at the time of thread and marriage ceremonies.[1]

Sieves are considered sacred for the following reasons:

1. Because articles of food such as flour, grain, &c., are sifted through them.

2. Because, on auspicious occasions, when women go to worship the potter's wheel, the materials of worship are carried in a sieve.

3. Because the fire used for igniting the sacrificial fuel is taken in a sieve, or is covered with a sieve while it is being carried to the sacrificial altar.

4. Because at the time of performing the ceremony when commencing to prepare sweets for a marriage a sieve is worshipped.

5. Because, in some communities such as the Bhatias, the bride's mother, when receiving the bridegroom in the marriage booth, carries in a dish a lamp covered with a sieve.

The flour collected by Brahmans by begging from door to door is supposed to be polluted. But it is considered purified when it is passed through a sieve.

The corn-pounder is considered so sacred that it is not touched with the foot. If a woman lie down during day-time, she will not touch it either with her head or with her foot.

One of the reasons why it is considered sacred is that it was used as a weapon by Baldev, the brother of Krishna.

It is one of the articles required for performing the reception ceremony on a bridegroom entering the marriage booth.

It is believed that a fall of rain is expedited by placing a corn-pounder erect in a dish when there is a drought.

Among Shrigaud Brahmans, on the marriage day, one of the men of the bridegroom's party wears a wreath made of a corn-pounder, a broom, and other articles. Some special marks are also made on his forehead. Thus adorned, he goes with the bridegroom's procession and jokes with the parents of both the bride and bridegroom. His doing so is supposed to bless the bridal pair with a long life and a large family.

On the marriage day, after the ceremony of propitiating the nine planets has been performed in the bride's house, in some

[1] Vide *supra*, Chapter VI, p. 210.

castes one and in others three corn-pounders are kept near the spot where the planets are worshipped. Next, five unwidowed women (*suvasinis*) of the family hold the corn-pounder or corn-pounders and beat it or them five or seven times on the floor, repeating the words ' On the chest of the ill-wisher of the host '. The corn-pounders are bound together by a thread.

If a woman has to take part in an auspicious ceremony on the fourth day of her monthly periods, she is made to thresh one maund of rice with a corn-pounder. Her fourth day is then considered as the fifth, and she becomes eligible for taking part in the ceremony.

The plough is considered sacred because it is the chief implement for cultivating the soil. It is worshipped on the full-moon day of *Shravan* (July–August), which is known as a *Balev* holiday, the worship being known as ' planet worship ' (*Grahan-pujan*).

Some people consider the plough sacred because Sita, the consort of Ram, was born of the earth by the touch of a plough. Others hold it sacred as it was used as a weapon by Baldev, the brother of Krishna.

On account of the sanctity which attaches to the plough it forms part of the articles with which a bridegroom is received in the marriage booth by the bride's mother.

In some places, on the *Balev* day, a number of persons gather together near a pond, and each of them fills an earthen jar with the water of the pond. Next, one of the party is made to stand at a long distance from the others with a small plough in his hands. The others then run a race towards the latter. He who wins the race is presented with molasses and a coco-nut.

It is customary among Brahmans to perform the worship known as the *Balev* ceremony after the performance of a thread ceremony. In Native States the prime minister and other State officials and clerks join the ceremony, the principal function of the ceremony being performed by the prime minister. In villages this function is performed by the head-man of the village. The party go in procession to a neighbouring village or a pond, where an earthen image of Ganpati besmeared with red lead is installed on a red cloth two feet square. Near this image are installed the nine planets, represented by nine heaps of corn, on each of which is placed a betel-nut. This is called the installation of *Balevian.* A plough about two feet in length is kept standing near the *Balevian* with its end buried in the ground. The prime minister or the village headman worships the plough, after which four potters (Kumbhars) wash themselves, and holding four jars on their heads, run a race. Each of the potters is named after one of the four months of the rainy season. He who wins the race is presented with the plough. The expenses of the ceremony are paid from the State treasury or the village fund.

According to a popular saying, a broom should not be kept erect or trampled underfoot. This suggests that brooms are held sacred.

When a newly born infant does not cry, the leaves of a broom are thrown into the fire and their smoke is passed over the child. It is said that this makes the child cry.

Some people consider brooms sacred because they are used in sweeping the ground (that is, the earth, which is a goddess). In some places children suffering from cough are fanned with a broom. In some castes a broom is worshipped on the marriage day.

A belief is common that if a man sees a broom the first thing after getting up in the morning, he will not pass the day happily. Some believe that if a broom be kept erect in the house, a quarrel between the husband and wife is sure to follow. There is also a belief that if a person thrashes another with a broom, the former is liable to suffer from a gland under the arm.

Beliefs about the Godling Kshetrapal

A belief prevails that an insane maiden is cured of her insanity if married to the field god Kshetrapal. It is generally believed that if a betrothed girl touches red lead, she is carried away by Kshetrapal. The belief that Kshetrapal carries away the bride from the marriage altar is so common that a stone representing the god is placed on the marriage altar and touched by the bridal pair at every turn round the sacrificial fire. If this is not done, disastrous consequences follow, to avert which that portion of the marriage ceremony in which Kshetrapal is propitiated has to be performed a second time.

Disagreement between husband and wife soon after marriage is attributed to the wrath of Kshetrapal. To bring about a reconcilation between them, they are taken to a triangular field and married there to propitiate the god.

Scaring Children

There are various ways of frightening crying children to silence, one of which is to invoke evil spirits. Occasionally the names of goblins such as Bagulbawa, Buwaji, Gosavi, &c., are mentioned to scare them.

When a child continues to cry for a long time, the mother says, 'Keep quiet, *Baghada* has come.' 'O *Bau*, come and take away this child.' '*Babara*, come here. Don't come, my child is now silent.' 'May *Baghada* carry you away.' These exclamations are uttered in such a tone and with such gestures, that generally the child is at once frightened into silence.

In addition to the spirits mentioned above, *Bhokadi*, *Chuda*, *Dakana*, *Satarsingo*, and other spirits are also invoked to frighten a weeping child to silence.

A *Bava* or *Bairagi*, a *Fakir*, a tiger, a dog, a cat, or a rat are all presented to the child as objects of terror, and are called one after another to silence it.

Nudity Rites

People who practise the art of attaining mastery over spirits and fiends usually remain naked while they are engaged in the performance of their mysterious rites. There are many branches of this black art, and although not held in respect by high-class Hindus, it is popular among the lower classes. There is a belief that knowledge of this art dooms a person to hell; but it secures to those who master it a position of much importance, and therefore finds many followers. The art consists in the knowledge of certain mysterious incantations which enable a person to influence the spirits and to bring about certain results through their agency. Not only has every person, when learning this art, to remain naked, but all those who make experiments in it afterwards must observe the same precaution. The night of the fourteenth day of the dark half of *Ashvin* (September–October) is considered to be the most favourable time for the practice of this art of remaining naked. On this day, it is the custom to go stripped to a cemetery in the dead of night, and to cook food in a human skull as an offering to the spirits residing in the neighbourhood. On the same night, some sorcerers, after stripping themselves, are said to ride round the village on some mysterious conveyance.

From Pachora in East Khandesh it is reported that persons who desire to gain the favour of Maruti must fetch a skull or a heart of a corpse, going naked for the purpose to a burial-ground on a Saturday, on a new-moon day, at an eclipse, or at *Makar Sankrant.*

A practice is noted among low-class people of performing a rite before the goddess Jhampadi for the sake of progeny. The man who performs the rite has first to go naked to a cemetery on a Sunday night, and to fetch therefrom the ashes of a corpse. At the time of the rite the man takes his seat on a corpse, fills a hollow bracelet with the ashes brought from the cemetery, and puts it on his arm above the elbow.

Dhobis, Malis, Valands, and other low-caste people remain naked while worshipping Bhairav. In the performance of the propitiation of such deities at Kal-bhairav, Batuk, Mani, Griha, &c., the devotees remain unclad. The worshippers of the goddess Jakshani also remain naked when they attend upon her.

Persons who practise the art of curing men from the effects of snake-bite by means of incantations have to sit naked under water in order to gain efficacy for their incantations.

Followers of certain religious sects, such as *Devi-panth, Shakti-panth,* and *Aghori-panth,* remain naked while worshipping or offering victims to their gods.

The hook-shaped instrument which is used by thieves in boring a hole through the walls of a house is sometimes prepared by a blacksmith and his wife on the night of the fourteenth day of the dark half of *Ashvin* (September–October), both being naked at the time. Instruments prepared in this fashion are believed to secure success for the thief, who scrupulously sets aside the first booty acquired by the help of this implement for the blacksmith as a reward for his services. He does not grudge the reward, however large the booty may be.

In making dice, according to the directions of certain well-known treatises, the workers should remain naked.

There is a belief that granulations in the eyes of a child are cured if the maternal uncle fetches naked the beads of the *Arani* tree (*Premna integrifolia*), and puts a circlet of them round the neck of the child.

If a person disrobes himself on hearing the screech of an owl, and then ties and unties seven knots in a piece of string, repeating the process twenty-one times, the piece of string is believed to possess the virtue of curing periodical fever. Another remedy for the same ailment is to go to a distance of three miles from the village and there to eat food which has been cooked in a state of nudity.

In the preparation of certain medicines, such as those known as *Nargudikalpa* or *Gujakalpa*, some drugs have to be procured by a naked person.

A Brahman boy must be naked at the time of the performance of his thread investiture ceremony. After the ceremony the maternal uncle of the boy presents garments to him, which he thereupon puts on.

The god Kalbhairav is worshipped by a naked person on the fourteenth day of the dark half of *Ashvin* (September–October). Those learning to practise the spell known as *Muth-marane* [1] are also required to remain naked while studying it. They learn this lore on an eclipse day on the bank of a river. The rite called *Somaya* is performed by the host when his clothes are off his body. On a certain Monday in the month of *Shravan* (July–August) a lamp of wheat flour is prepared and burned by adding *ghi*. This lamp is regarded as a deity, and is worshipped solemnly. During the performance of this ceremony, as well as the preparation of the requisite food, the host and the hostess are required to remain naked.

On the *Somavati-Amavasya* day women worship a *Pipal* tree (*Ficus religiosa*), and offer it a hundred and eight things of one

[1] See Chapter X, p. 241, *supra*.

kind. Women desirous of having a son perform a certain rite at midnight, without clothing. If one wishes to have a son, one has to go through a ceremony called the *Hanuman* in a naked state.

Sneezing and Yawning

Campbell remarks that the convulsion of sneezing is generally held to be caused by a spirit.[1]

There are various superstitious beliefs entertained by people of the Presidency regarding sneezing.

According to one belief, if a person sneezes face to face with another who is about to begin an auspicious act, such as starting on a journey, decking his person with ornaments, performing a marriage ceremony, and the like, it portends misfortune to the latter; but a sneeze on his right or at his back foretells good. A sneeze in front of a person starting to perform an auspicious act is supposed to mean that a blow has been struck on his forehead, suggesting that the act should be stopped. If, in spite of this warning, the act is commenced, evil consequences are sure to follow.

A sneeze at a man's back confirms the unobstructed fulfilment of the act taken in hand, as it is believed to have patted the man on his back or shoulders in token of approval.

In the Deccan it is held that if a man sneezes while talking he is telling the truth.

A woman sneezing behind a man who is talking is held to be very inauspicious.

Sneezes on either side, right or left, portend neither good nor evil.

As a rule, sneezes are believed to forebode evil, and it is considered highly unmannerly to sneeze while one is about to begin an auspicious act or start with a good purpose.[2] If, in spite of this etiquette, one sneezes, he excuses himself by saying that he is suffering from cold.

Some people believe that a sneeze in front is an indication of a broil on the road, a sneeze on the left side portends loss of money, one from above is a harbinger of success, one from below foretells danger, while the sneeze of the man who is

[1] *S. B. B. C.*, p. 232.

[2] Cf. Dubois, vol. i, p. 249.

engaged in, or is starting on, the act contemplated is believed to be very injurious. A sneeze on the right is considered neither good nor bad.

The sneeze of a sick man is held to be an indication of his recovery. To sneeze in the presence of a sick man, however, has a bad effect on his condition.

Persons possessed by spirits cannot sneeze.

A sneeze in the east causes anxiety, in the south-east foretells happiness, in the south speaks of coming loss, and in the south-west is an indication of good. A sneeze from the west or north-west is considered good, from the north injurious, and from the east auspicious.

If a man sneezes while passing through a door, water is thrown on the threshold and lintel to ward off the evil influence.

Some lines from the sayings of Gorakhraj run to the effect that a sneeze in the east causes anxiety, one in the south-east inflicts a sound beating, one in the south brings a visitor or guest, one in the south-west subjects the person concerned to a taunt, one in the west bestows a throne, one in the north-west promises sweets or dainties, one in the north foretells good, one in the north-east brings disappointment, while one's own sneeze is so ominous that one should never start out on any business after sneezing.

If a man sneezes while lying on his back it is believed that sweet dishes will be offered to him.

The beliefs enumerated above relate to sneezes which occur on certain week-days. The sneezes which occur on Sundays have the following consequences :

A sneeze from the east is good, one from the south-east points to delay in the fulfilment of one's intended object, one from the south brings in profit, one from the south-west results in death, one from the west in happiness, one from the north-west throws one into the society of good men, one from the north is productive of pecuniary gain, and one from the north-east of general well-being.

It is a common belief that if, while one is about to commence some act, somebody sneezes once, the act is doomed to fail, and to avoid failure it must be postponed. But if the sneeze is repeated, no harm ensues.

A sneeze by an ailing person is believed to be a sign of his recovery, and more sneezes by the same person are supposed to indicate his complete recovery, even though the symptoms be not favourable.

A sneeze by a cow at the commencement of an auspicious act is supposed to be the worst possible omen, and a sneeze by a cat is proverbially a portent of failure in any act taken in hand at the time.

A yawn is generally believed to be harmless, as it does not foretell either good or evil. Still as sometimes it results in accidental instantaneous death, the elders of a person when he yawns exclaim, 'Be long-lived! Patience! Live long!' and the spiritually disposed repeat the name of the god of their devotion.

Lest spirits may make their way into the body of a person through his mouth when he is yawning, or lest his soul may pass out of it, some people pinch him to stop the yawn, while others utter the words 'Ram, Ram' to divert his attention.

In the Karnatak it is held that sneezing and yawning is due to possession by a spirit known as *Naga-vayu*. A single sneeze is unlucky, two sneezes are auspicious. If a man yawns while his future is being told to him by a fortune-teller, the result is held to be highly inauspicious.

Sneezes are held in the Karnatak to have varying significance according to the status or occupation of the person sneezing. Thus when a baby in a cradle, a potter, cultivator, washerman, prostitute, a Jangam, or a Holaya sneeze, good results are sure to follow. The sneeze of a barber, carpenter, or tailor indicates some coming evil. If a shepherd or Teli's wife sneeze, death is indicated. To sneeze while catching a hen or while bringing fire is a sign of approaching quarrels and loss of material description.

In certain parts of the Karnatak and the Konkan it is believed to be inauspicious to sneeze facing towards the north, east, south-east, or south, whereas it is lucky to sneeze when facing west or south-west.

In the Konkan people find good or bad omens in sneezing. It depends upon the time and the position or standing of the person who sneezes. If a sick person sneezes it is presumed that he will recover from his illness within a very short period. Sneezing at the time of conversation or when contemplating any particular task or business is held to be inauspicious. Hence, if anybody sneezes at the beginning of a task, or at the time of starting out on any such task, the occasion is unfavourable. Yawning is said to be caused by a relative or friend remembering the person who yawns. In ancient times happiness and calamities were foretold by a voice from the sky, and in modern days they are indicated by sneezing. People are much concerned by the acts of sneezing, and often inquire whether it is a good or bad omen to sneeze at the beginning of any work or undertaking.

If a man sneezes while contemplating any task or business, the sneezing is considered inauspicious. Sneezing at the time of taking food, i. e. while at meals, while sleeping, and while sitting on a praying carpet, is considered auspicious.

In the case of exorcists yawning, this is considered to indicate that the disease they are attempting to cure will disappear.

In Kolhapur and the Konkan it is believed that sneezing and yawning indicate the call of death, and therefore it is customary among the Hindus to snap the thumb and the middle finger at the time of yawning, and to repeat the words 'Live for hundred years' at the time of sneezing, while some add the name of Rama, meanwhile snapping the thumb and finger.

If a woman sneezes while a man speaks, it is lucky, and if a man sneezes, it is unlucky. The reverse is the case in respect of females.

According to Campbell, the general belief about yawning is that a spirit jumps down the yawner's throat.[1]

Silence Rites

Silence and secrecy are considered essential in working mystic lore, for it is a belief that if learnt openly such lore loses its power.

The ceremony for obtaining command over Kal-bhairav is performed in perfect silence at midnight on the fourteenth day of the dark half of *Ashvin* (September–October).

[1] *S. B. B. C.*, p. 233.

Silence and secrecy are also essential in the ceremonies which are performed for subjugating such evil spirits as Meldi and Shikotar and the Mothers (*Matas*).

The Jain Shravaks have to observe perfect silence at the time of performing the *Shamag Padakamanu* (a form of devotion to their god).

Some people observe a vow of keeping silent while taking their meals either for life or during the monsoon.

Great secrecy is required to be observed on the occasion of the special worship of Shiva which is performed on the first day of the bright half of the month of *Bhadrapad* (August–September). This rite is known as the Silence Vow, and should be performed only by the male members of the family. On this day all the members of the family have to remain silent while taking their meals. Women do not speak while cooking, as the food which is to be offered to the god must be cooked in silence.

Newly married girls have to perform the worship of Mangala-Gauri successively for the first five years on every Tuesday in the month of *Shravan* (July–August), and it is enjoined that they should not speak while taking their meals on that day. Some people do not speak while taking their meals on every Monday of *Shravan* (July–August), and others make a vow of observing silence and secrecy at their meals every day. All Brahmans have to remain silent when discharging the functions of nature.

Certain persons observe silence at their meals during the period of four months commencing from the eleventh day of the bright half of *Ashvin* (June–July) to the eleventh day of the bright half of *Kartik* (October–November). Certain classes of Hindus observe the penance of secrecy in the additional month that occurs at the lapse of every third year.

Silence is essential at the time of performing certain austeri ties such as sun-worship, worshipping the gods, and the repetition of the *Gayatri* and other such verses. Secrecy is specially observed when a disciple is initiated by his spiritual guide into the sacred incantations.

Secrecy and silence are essential when learning the incantations for curing snake-bite, the evil eye, and the evil spirit of

Vetal. All followers of the Shakta sect must worship the goddess (Durga) very secretly. Silence is also observed by people in welcoming to their homes and worshipping the goddess Parvati in the bright half of *Bhadrapad* (August–September) every year.

At Vade in the Thana District, one day previous to the planting of rice crops, the farmer goes to his field before daybreak with five balls of boiled rice, coco-nuts, and other things. There he worships the guardian deity of the field and buries the balls of rice underground. He must do this secretly and remain silent during the whole period. He is also forbidden to look behind while going to the field for the purpose.

Secrecy and silence are observed when performing the rites for the control of evil spirits. Widow remarriages among the lower classes are performed secretly. The pair wishing to be remarried are accompanied by a Brahman priest and the marriage is performed at a distance from the house. The priest applies red lead to the forehead of the bride and throws grains of rice over their heads, and a stone mortar is brought in contact with the backbone of the bride. The priest then turns his face and walks away silently.[1]

Vows

Hindus make various kinds of vows in order to procure male offspring, to regain their health when suffering from illness, or for other desirable objects. In fulfilment of such vows they make offerings of goats, fowls, sugar, sweetmeats, plantains and other fruit, costly dresses, ornaments, &c., to deities and give food to Brahmans.

Special ceremonies called *Laghurudra* and *Maharudra* in honour of Shiva, the god of destruction, are also performed. Some people make vows to observe fasts, to feed Brahmans, to build paths or footsteps leading to temples, and to distribute coins and clothes to the poor; while others promise to hang wreaths of flowers and Mango leaves on the entrance of the temple, and hoist flags over it. Rich people erect new temples

[1] For widow remarriage rites, see *T. & C. B.* articles dealing with the lower castes of the Presidency.

to various Hindu deities or dig wells. Some observe fasts to propitiate the goddess Chandika, i. e. the wife of Shiva, and worship her during the first nine days of the bright half of *Ashvin* (September–October). Women make a vow to walk round the *Audumbar* (*Ficus glomerata*) or *Pipal* (*Ficus religiosa*) tree, and to distribute coco-nuts, sugar, molasses, copper, or silver equal to the weight of their children.

Vows are made by people with the object of securing health, wealth, and children, and other desired objects such as education, &c.

Vows are also made to obtain freedom from disease or such other calamities. When any person in the family becomes ill, or when a sudden calamity befalls a family, an elderly member of the family goes to the temple of a deity and makes certain vows according to his means, fulfilling them as soon as the calamity or disease has disappeared.

At Khopoli in the Kolaba District people who have no children, or whose children die shortly after birth, make a vow to the Satvai whose temple is at a short distance from Khopoli. The vow is generally to bring the child into the presence of the deity and to feed five or more married Brahman couples. Such vows are fulfilled after the birth of a child. Some worship the god Satya Narayan on a grand scale, and others propitiate the god Shiva by the ceremony of sprinkling water over his image (*Abhisheka*). Some offer nails made of gold or silver to the goddess Shitala after the recovery of a child suffering from small-pox. Eyes and other parts of the body made of gold and silver are also occasionally offered in fulfilment of vows. People abstain from eating certain things till the vows are fulfilled.

There is a shrine of the god Shankar at Kanakeshwar, a village by the sea-side two miles from Mitbav in the Ratnagiri District. Many years ago it happened that a rich Musalman merchant was carrying his merchandise in a ship. The ship was in a sinking condition in a storm at a distance two or three miles from Kanakeshwar. The merchant, despairing of his life and goods, made a vow to erect a fine temple for the shrine of Kanakeshwar if he, his vessel, and its cargo were saved. By the grace of God the vessel weathered the storm and he arrived safely in his country with the merchandise. In fulfilment of this vow he erected a fine temple over the shrine of Shri Shankar at Kanakeshwar. This temple is in good condition to the present day. Many such vows are made to special deities. When the people obtain the objects of their desire, they attribute the success to the favour of the deity invoked; but when their expectations are not fulfilled, they put the blame on their fate and not on the deity.

Change of Sex

In the Puranas there are instances of males being transformed into females, and females into males. For example, the female Amba was transformed into a male, and we also learn that the male Narad was transformed into a female. Arjuna, the third brother of the Pandavas, is said to have changed his sex, and turned into Bruhannada.

It is related that in ancient times the son of a certain sage once disguised himself as a girl, with the result that he was actually changed into a girl. He was thereafter called Mudralopi and married to the sage Agastya.

The warrior Shikhandi, who assisted the Pandavas in killing Bhishma (who had vowed not to raise his arms against a woman), was at first a girl, and was subsequently transformed into a boy by the boon of the gods.

There is supposed to be a forest of Parvati in a continent called Ilavrit. Any man visiting it is at once turned into a woman. A king named Sudyaman visited this forest and was transformed into a woman. It was only after appeasing Parvati by a sacrifice that he was restored to his original form.

It is believed that, in the land of fairies, children are transformed into the opposite sex by the spell of the inhabitants.

Tradition relates that all the children of a certain Solanki king died in infancy, except the last child, a girl. She was dressed in male attire and passed for a boy. When the pretended boy attained marriageable age, he was betrothed to a princess. When the day fixed for the marriage drew near, the king became anxious and went on an hunting expedition to pass the time. On his way back from the hunt he became very thirsty, and quenched his thirst with the water of a pond near which a temple of Bahucharaji stands to this day. His bitch, which was with him, leapt into the pond, and on coming out of the water was found to be transformed into a dog. On seeing this, the king brought his daughter and bathed her in the pond, with the result that she was transformed into a boy. The king then built a big tank on the spot, which is known by the name of *Man*.

At Kolhapur there are no instances known of a change of sex. The goddess Yellamma has a high reputation in this district for making a change in the habits and deportments of men and women, especially among low-caste people. It is believed that the curse of this goddess has the power of destroying the virility of males, whereupon they behave like females. Many instances of this type can be seen at the fair of the goddess Yellamma, which is held in *Margashirsh* (November–December); men dressed in women's clothes, and vice versa, are often seen at this fair.

A belief is current that change of sex can be effected by the performance of the *Shatachandi* or by the spells of Rudra, Bahucharaji, Ashapuri, and Mahakali.

It is also believed that change of sex can be effected by the spells of magic.

There is a further belief that *Yogis* by their incantations, and *Mahatmas* by their blessings or curses, can effect a change of sex.

Human Sacrifices

In ancient times human sacrifices were offered on certain occasions. Nowadays, in place of a human being, a coco-nut or a pumpkin (*Cucurbita maxima*) is offered. At the time of making the offering, the coco-nut is plastered with red lead and other holy applications and covered with a silk cloth. The pumpkin is offered by cutting it into two pieces with a stroke of a knife or sword.

Sometimes an image made of the flour of black gram is sacrificed in place of a human being. This sacrifice is generally made on the eighth or tenth day of the bright half of *Ashvin* (September–October).

In place of human blood, milk mixed with red powder and molasses is offered.

In ancient times, when a well was dug or a fort built, a human sacrifice was made to it in the belief that this would ensure a supply of water in the well, and render the fort impregnable. To-day, when a well is commenced, blood from the fourth finger of a man is sprinkled over the spot.

It is also related that in ancient times, when a king was crowned, a human sacrifice was offered. Nowadays, instead of this sacrifice, the king's forehead is marked with the blood from the fourth finger of a low-caste Hindu at the time of the coronation ceremony.

There are many practices and customs which appear to be the survivals of human sacrifices. These survivals are visible in the offerings of fowls, goats, buffaloes, and fruits like coconuts, *brinjals*, the pumpkin gourd, and others.

Human sacrifices are not practised in these days, but among the Karhada Brahmans there is a practice of giving poison to animals in order to satisfy their family deity. It is said that they used to kill a Brahman by giving him poisoned food.

It is believed that the people belonging to the caste of Karhada Brahmans used to offer human sacrifices to their deity, and therefore nobody relies on a Karhada Brahman in these days. There is a proverb in Marathi which means that a man can trust even a butcher (*Kasai*), but not a Karhada.

As they cannot offer human sacrifices in these days, it is said that during the first nine days of the bright half of *Ashvin* (September–October) they offer poisoned food to crows, dogs, and other animals.

At Kalshe in the Ratnagiri District the servants of gods, i. e. the ministrants or the Bhopis of the temple, prick their breasts with a knife on the *Dasara* day, and cry out loudly the words 'Cut, cut'. No blood comes from the breast as the wound is slight. This appears to be a survival of human sacrifice.

Precautions at Birth of a Child

The special precautions that a father has to take at the birth of a child are:

To arrange for a suitable place or a room provided with the materials required for the occasion, and to ensure the correct moment for the birth of the child. No person other than a midwife is allowed to enter the room for the first ten days. A pot is kept filled with water and a twig of the *Nim* tree (*Melia Azadirachta*) in the entrance of the house, and all persons entering the house have to wash their feet with this water.

A knife or some other sharp weapon is kept under the bed of the woman in order that the mother and her child may not be attacked by a spirit.

The chief reason for ensuring the correct moment for the birth is that, if the birth takes place at an unlucky hour, special rites are necessary for averting the evil effects. These rites consist in the recitation of certain holy verses, and in giving presents of money, sesamum, molasses, clarified butter, &c., to Brahmans and alms to the poor.

At Modhe in the Kulaba District it is customary for the father to throw a stone in a well, a pond, or a river, at the birth of his son, and then to look at the face of the child.

In some places there is no belief that the father has to take special precautions at the birth of his child, except that care is taken to note the exact time of the child's birth for the purpose of casting its horoscope correctly. An inkstand and pen are also placed in the lying-in room, as it is believed that the Creator writes the destiny of a child as soon as it makes its appearance in the world. In some places in the Deccan, however, the father bathes and makes special offerings at the time of birth of an offspring.

All children born in *Jyeshth nakshatra*, *Mula nakshatra*, or *Yamaghanta* are said to cause the death of their male parent. Such children were left to starve uncared for in forests in olden times; but nowadays they are kept alive, as certain performances are believed to avert the evil. One such performance is to see the child only after clarified butter has been given in donation. Another is to see its face after it has been bathed with the water collected from eighteen wells in a pot with a thousand holes. In a third, the parents of the child hold in their hands goblets filled with clarified butter, and see their faces reflected in them before the child is presented to the sight of the father.

Such children are named Mulubhai, Mulchand, Muli, or Mulo.

A child born in the month of *Jyeshth* (May–June) prognosticates poverty.

If the birth-time of a child happens to fall within the ecliptic period, that is, the period of nine hours before an eclipse takes place, as well as in the duration of the eclipse, the father does not see the child before performing certain rites. To do so is supposed to bring misfortune.

If a man has a child in his twentieth year he does not see the child before he completes it. If a child is born at a wrong juncture or conjunction of the stars, the father does not see it for twenty-seven days. A child born on the fourth, fourteenth, or fifteenth day of a month is supposed to become a burden to its father.

It is a common belief that a woman in child-bed should not see the face of her husband nor he of her.

APPENDIX

QUESTIONS ON FOLK-LORE

By W. CROOKE

Author of *The Popular Religion and Folk-lore of Northern India*

I. NATURE POWERS

1. Give any indications of the connexion of the worship of the Deota or minor local deities with the lower races, as, for instance, where the village deity is served by a priest drawn from the lower castes.

2. Give any current beliefs about sun-worship. How and at what periodical feasts is the worship conducted and what form of ritual is adopted ?

3. Give any customs of moving round temples or sacred objects in the course of the sun in the heavens : cases in which women after child-birth are exposed to the sun : conception believed to be caused by exposure to the rays of the sun : the use of the Swastik as an emblem.

4. Give any legends or customs connected with moon-worship : the spots on the surface of the moon : the moon as a healer of disease : the custom of drinking the moon's rays : any ceremonies at new or full moon.

5. Give any legends and rites connected with eclipses.

6. Similarly for star-worship ; superstitions connected with the rainbow ; the Milky Way.

7. Rites connected with worship of the earth mother : sacred things not to fall on earth : occasions when people sleep on the earth.

8. Superstitions connected with thunder and lightning.

9. Popular belief regarding earthquakes.

10. Collect instances of and ritual for worship of sacred rivers ; springs, waterfalls, water spirits and goblins, prejudice against saving drowning people, ceremonies at digging and dedication of wells, well water as a cure for disease, instances of sacred lakes, palaces under the water.

11. Instances of sacred mountains and legends connected with them; dread of climbing mountains.

12. Name any deities supposed to control the weather, and describe the modes of causing or averting rain, of checking storms and hail.

13. Give instances of any rites in which women alone take part or from which they are excluded, any rites in which the worshipper must be nude.

14. Are there any sacred stones which are believed to influence the rain?

15. Note any superstitions in connexion with aerolites and meteors.

II. THE HEROIC GODLINGS

16. Describe the ritual and any legends or superstitions connected with the worship of Hanuman, Bhimsen, Bhishma.

17. Name and describe the local deities most generally worshipped in your neighbourhood. What legends are connected with them? Who are their priests? What offerings and on what occasions are offerings made to them?

18. How is the local deity of a new settlement selected and installed?

19. What local deity is considered responsible for crops and cattle? When and how is he worshipped?

20. Describe the worship of Bhairon or Bhairava, Ganesa, the Matris or Mothers, the deities of the jungle, those who assist parturition.

III. DISEASE DEITIES

21. Describe the worship of any deities who are believed to have the power of averting or causing disease, such as cholera, small-pox, fever, &c.

22. Is epidemic disease attributed to witchcraft, and, if so, what precautions are taken? Give particulars of observances in connexion with cattle-disease.

23. What methods are in vogue for the exorcism of disease? Give examples of any rural charms used for this purpose.

24. Is dancing used in exorcism? If so, give instances of religious dances.

25. What are the position and functions of the village sorcerer, and how is he appointed?

26. Give examples of the offering of rags, coins, &c., at sacred trees, wells, &c.

27. Give any methods of transferring disease to another person.

28. Give instances of the use of scapegoats.

IV. THE WORSHIP OF ANCESTORS AND SAINTS

29. Give instances of worship of ancestors, the belief that spirits are mortal, and that the spirits of the dead are reborn in children.

30. Give instances of miracle-working tombs, and of saints who have been deified in modern times.

31. Give instances of Mohammedan saints whose worship has been adopted by Hindus.

32. Give the rural methods in vogue for the cure of barrenness.

V. THE WORSHIP OF THE MALEVOLENT DEAD

33. What are the current beliefs as to the cause of dreams and the omens derived from them ?

34. Is it considered possible for the soul to leave the body temporarily ? If so, give instances.

35. What is the popular conception of the character and functions of the Bhut or disembodied soul ?

36. What beliefs are current as to the state of the soul after death ; the path to the other world, the condition of souls in the other world, the possibility of the soul returning thence ?

37. What belief is current as to the souls of those dying by a sudden or violent death ?

38. What are believed to be the appearance and habits of the Bhut ?

39. In what way do spirits enter or leave the body ?

40. What is the current theory regarding sneezing and yawning ?

41. What is known of the Rakshasa or malevolent demon ?

42. Name and describe any other varieties of malignant spirits.

43. Do any evil spirits go about headless ?

44. What special evil spirits infest burial or cremation grounds, and what are the other haunts of such spirits ?

45. Does any special class of evil spirit infest mountains, jungles, trees ?

46. What fiends attack the young mother and her child ?

47. What belief prevails as to the spirits of those killed by tigers or other wild beasts ?

48. What form does the ghost of a woman dying at child-birth or during her menses assume ?

49. Is there any belief that the father has to take special precautions at the birth of his child ?

50. Is there any belief in a connexion of the bat or owl with spirits of the dead ?

51. Describe the evil spirits which haunt ruins and guard buried treasure, or occupy caves and mines.

VI. THE EVIL EYE AND THE SCARING OF GHOSTS

52. Describe the belief in the evil eye and the modes of evading it.

53. Does the belief in giving opprobrious names to children prevail, and, if so, how is it accounted for ?

54. Can you give instances of change of sex ?

55. Illustrate the value of the following protection against evil spirits : iron and other metals, coral and shells, precious stones, blood, incense, spittle, salt, water, grain, colours, grasses, tattooing, leather, garlic, glass.

56. Describe the amulets generally used.

57. Illustrate the sacred circle as a protective.

58. Illustrate the belief in omens, numbers, lucky and unlucky days.

59. What means are adopted to help the spirit to the other world, to prevent it from returning and to secure its goodwill to the survivors ?

60. Illustrate the prevalence of earth burial and cremation, the customs of shaving the hair, placing food or other articles for the use of the dead.

61. Does the spirit reappear in the form of insects and animals ?

62. Are the earthen vessels of the household broken at death ? If so, why ? Describe rites connected with mourning.

63. What spirits are benevolent ?

64. Illustrate the belief in tree spirits.

65. What spirits are special protectors of crops and cattle ?

66. What spirits are invoked to frighten children ?

VII. TREE AND SERPENT WORSHIP

67. Name any sacred groves in your neighbourhood and describe any prejudice against cutting trees.

68. Are any trees specially connected with any local deity or saint ?

69. Name any trees which receive particular respect or devotion and note any legends or superstitions in connexion with them.

70. Does the custom of marrying a bride or bridegroom to a tree prevail? Any instances of marriage to a god, religious prostitution?

71. Give instances of snake worship and shrines of serpent deities, of deified snake heroes.

72. Does the belief prevail that snakes guard treasure? Give details.

73. What snake festivals are observed? Describe the ritual.

74. What is the village treatment of snake-bite?

75. The snake has a jewel in his head, he is connected with the rainbow, he has a palace under the water, he weds mortal girls, he protects the household—illustrate these beliefs.

VIII. TOTEMISM AND FETISHISM

76. Can you quote any beliefs which are suggestive of Totemism? Are any clans named after or do they claim descent from animals or plants? What animals are treated with special respect by particular tribes? Do special castes refuse to eat any special food?

77. Are any local deities specially associated with animal worship?

78. Illustrate the worship of stocks and stones. Is any respect shown to perforated stones?

79. Are there any modern survivals of human sacrifice?

80. Are fetish stones supposed to cure disease or to be the abode of spirits?

81. Are any fetishes peculiar to particular families or castes?

82. Is special respect shown to the corn-sieve, the winnowing basket, the broom, the rice-pounder, the plough?

83. Give instances of fire-worship. Is the sacred fire maintained in any shrine? Is fire made by friction for special rites.

IX. ANIMAL WORSHIP

84. Illustrate from local examples the worship or respect paid to the horse, ass, lion, tiger, dog, goat, cow, buffalo, antelope, elephant, cat, rat and mouse, squirrel, bear, jackal, hare, crow, fowl, dove and pigeon, swan, and other birds, alligators, fish and insects, and give any legend or superstition in connexion with them.

X. WITCHCRAFT

85. How far does the belief in witches and their powers prevail? Do they appear as animals and have they special haunts and seasons?

86. What ordeals are used to test a witch and what means to guard against her witchcraft?

XI. GENERAL

87. Describe the rural ceremonies in connexion with ploughing, sowing the various crops, reaping and harvesting.

88. Rites intended for the protection of cattle, to ensure sunshine and favourable weather, to scare noxious animals or insects, to protect special crops—illustrate these from local custom.

89. Are there any rites in which secrecy and silence are essential?

90. Describe the observances at the Holi.

91. Give details of any rites performed when boys or girls attain puberty.

INDEX